HOW TO GIVE YOUR MGB V8 POWER

Also from Veloce Publishing

SpeedPro Series

4-Cylinder Engine – How to Blueprint & Build a Short Block for High Performance by Des Hammill
Alfa Romeo DOHC High-performance Manual (SpeedPro) by Jim Kartalamakis
Alfa Romeo V6 Engine High-perfomance Manual (SpeedPro) by Jim Kartalamakis
BMC 998cc A-Series Engine – How to Power Tune by Des Hammill
The 1275cc A-Series High performance Manual (SpeedPro) by Des Hammill
Camshafts – How to Choose & Time them for Maximum Power by Des Hammill
Cylinder Heads – How to Build, Modify & Power Tune Updated & Revised Edition by Peter Burgess
Distributor-type Ignition Systems – How to Build & Power Tune by Des Hammill
Fast Road Car – How to Plan and Build New Edition by Daniel Stapleton
Ford SOHC 'Pinto' & Sierra Cosworth DOHC Engines – How to Power Tune Updated & Enlarged Edition by Des Hammill
Ford V8 – How to Power Tune Small Block Engines by Des Hammill
Harley-Davidson Evolution Engines – How to Build & Power Tune by Des Hammill
Holley Carburettors – How to Build & Power Tune New Edition by Des Hammill
Jaguar XK Engines – How to Power Tune New Edition by Des Hammill
MG Midget & Austin-Healey Sprite – How to Power Tune Updated Edition by Daniel Stapleton
MGB 4-Cylinder Engine – How to Power Tune by Peter Burgess
MGB V8 Power – Third Edition by Roger Williams
MGB, MGC & MGB V8 – How to Improve by Roger Williams
Mini Engines – How to Power Tune on a Small Budget 2nd Edition by Des Hammill
Motorsport – Getting Started in by SS Collins
Nitrous Oxide High-perfromance Manual by Trevor Langfield
Rover V8 Engines – How to Power Tune by Des Hammill
Sportscar/Kitcar Suspension & Brakes – How to Build & Modify Enlarged & Updated 2nd Edition by Des Hammill
SU Carburettors – How to Build & Modify for High Performance by Des Hammill
Suzuki 4WD by John Richardson
Tiger Avon Sportscar – How to Build Your Own Updated & Revised 2nd Edition by Jim Dudley
TR2, 3 & TR4 – How to Improve by Roger Williams
TR5, 250 & TR6 – How to Improve by Roger Williams
V8 Engine – How to Build a Short Block for High Performance by Des Hammill
Volkswagen Beetle Suspension, Brakes & Chassis – How to Modify for High Performance by James Hale
Volkswagen Bus Suspension, Brakes & Chassis – How to Modify for High Performance by James Hale
Weber DCOE & Dellorto DHLA Carburettors – How to Build & Power Tune 3rd Edition by Des Hammill

Those were the days ... Series

Alpine Rallies by Martin Pfundner
Austerity Motoring by Malcolm Bobbitt
Brighton National Speed Trials by Tony Gardiner
British Police Cars by Nick Walker
Crystal Palace by SS Collins
Dune Buggy Phenomenon by James Hale
Dune Buggy Phenomenon Volume 2 by James Hale
Motor Racing at Brands Hatch in the Seventies by Chas Parker
Motor Racing at Goodwood in the Sixties by Tony Gardiner
Three Wheelers by Malcolm Bobbitt

Enthusiast's Restoration Manual Series

Building a Dune Buggy – The Essential Manual by Paul Shakespeare
Citroën 2CV, How to Restore by Lindsay Porter
Classic Car Body Work, How to Restore by Martin Thaddeus
Classic Cars, How to Paint by Martin Thaddeus
Reliant Regal, How to Restore by Elvis Payne
Triumph TR2/3/3A, How to Restore by Roger Williams
Triumph TR4/4A, How to Restore by Roger Williams
Triumph TR5/250 & 6, How to Restore by Roger Williams
Triumph TR7/8, How to Restore by Roger Williams
Volkswagen Beetle, How to Restore by Jim Tyler
Yamaha FS1-E, How to Restore by John Watts

Essential Buyer's Guide Series

Alfa GT Buyer's Guide by Keith Booker
Alfa Romeo Spider by Keith Booker & Jim Talbott
Jaguar E-Type Essential Buyer's Guide by Peter Crespin
MGB Essential Buyer's Guide by Roger Williams
Porsche 928 Buyer's Guide by David Hemmings
Triumph TR6 Essential Buyer's Guide by Roger Williams
VW Beetle Buyer's Guide by Ken Cservenka & Richard Copping
VW Bus Buyer's Guide by Richard Copping and Ken Cservenka

Auto-Graphics Series

Fiat & Abarth by Andrea & David Sparrow
Jaguar MkII by Andrea & David Sparrow
Lambretta LI by Andrea & David Sparrow

General

1 1/2-litre GP Racing 1961-1965 by MJP Whitelock
AC Two-litre Saloons & Buckland Sportscars by Leo Archibald
Alfa Romeo Giulia Coupé GT & GTA by John Tipler
Alfa Tipo 33 by Ed McDonough & Peter Collins
American Ford in Miniature by Randall Olson
Anatomy of the Works Minis by Brian Moylan
Armstrong-Siddeley by Bill Smith
Autodrome by SS Collins & Gavin Ireland
Automotive A-Z, Lane's Dictionary of Automotive Terms by Keith Lane
Automotive Mascots by David Kay & Lynda Springate
Bahamas Speed Weeks, The by Terry O'Neil
Bentley Continental, Corniche and Azure by Martin Bennett
BMCs Competitions Department Secrets by Stuart Turner, Marcus Chambers & Peter Browning
BMW 5-Series by Marc Cranswick
BMW Z-Cars by James Taylor
British 250cc Racing Motorcycles by Chris Pereira
British Cars, The Complete Catalogue of, 1895-1975 by David Culshaw & Peter Horrobin

Bugatti Type 40 by Barrie Price
Bugatti 46/50 Updated Edition by Barrie Price
Bugatti 57 2nd Edition by Barrie Price
Caravans, The Illustrated History 1919-1959 by Andrew Jenkinson
Caravans, The Illustrated History from 1960 by Andrew Jenkinson
Chrysler 300 – America's Most Powerful Car 2nd Edition by Robert Ackerson
Citroën DS by Malcolm Bobbitt
Cobra – The Real Thing! by Trevor Legate
Cortina – Ford's Bestseller by Graham Robson
Coventry Climax Racing Engines by Des Hammill
Daimler SP250 'Dart' by Brian Long
Datsun Fairlady Roadster to 280ZX – The Z-car Story by Brian Long
Ducati 750 Bible, The by Ian Falloon
Dune Buggy Files by James Hale
Dune Buggy Handbook by James Hale
Ferrari Dino – The V6 Ferrari by Brian Long
Fiat & Abarth 124 Spider & Coupé by John Tipler
Fiat & Abarth 500 & 600 2nd edition by Malcolm Bobbitt
Ford F100/F150 Pick-up 1948-1996 by Robert Ackerson
Ford F150 1997-2005 by Robert Ackerson
Ford GT40 by Trevor Legate
Ford Model Y by Sam Roberts
Ford Thunderbird by Brian Long
Funky Mopeds by Richard Skelton
Honda NSX by Brian Long
Jaguar, The Rise of by Barrie Price
Jaguar XJ-S by Brian Long
Jeep CJ by Robert Ackerson
Jeep Wrangler by Robert Ackerson
Karmann-Ghia Coupé & Convertible by Malcolm Bobbitt
Land Rover, The Half-Ton Military by Mark Cook
Lea-Francis Story, The by Barrie Price
Lexus Story, The by Brian Long
Lola – The Illustrated History (1957-1977) by John Starkey
Lola – All The Sports Racing & Single-Seater Racing Cars 1978-1997 by John Starkey
Lola T70 – The Racing History & Individual Chassis Record 3rd Edition by John Starkey
Lotus 49 by Michael Oliver
MarketingMobiles, The Wonderful Wacky World of, by James Hale
Mazda MX-5/Miata 1.6 Enthusiast's Workshop Manual by Rod Grainger & Pete Shoemark
Mazda MX-5/Miata 1.8 Enthusiast's Workshop Manual by Rod Grainger & Pete Shoemark
Mazda MX-5 (& Eunos Roadster) – The World's Favourite Sportscar by Brian Long
Mazda MX-5 Miata Roadster by Brian Long
MGA by John Price Williams
MGB & MGB GT – Expert Guide (Auto-Doc Series) by Roger Williams
Mini Cooper – The Real Thing! by John Tipler
Mitsubishi Lancer Evo by Brian Long
Motor Racing Reflections by Anthony Carter
Motorhomes, The Illustrated History by Andrew Jenkinson
Motorsport in colour, 1950s by Martyn Wainwright
MR2 – Toyota's Mid-engined Sports Car by Brian Long
Nissan 300ZX & 350Z – The Z-Car Story by Brian Long
Pass Your Theory and Practical Driving Tests by Clive Gibson & Gavin Hoole
Pontiac Firebird by Marc Cranswick
Porsche Boxster by Brian Long
Porsche 356 by Brian Long
Porsche 911 Carrera – The Last of the Evolution by Tony Corlett
Porsche 911R, RS & RSR, 4th Edition by John Starkey
Porsche 911 – The Definitive History 1963-1971 by Brian Long
Porsche 911 – The Definitive History 1971-1977 by Brian Long
Porsche 911 – The Definitive History 1977-1987 by Brian Long
Porsche 911 – The Definitive History 1987-1997 by Brian Long
Porsche 911 – The Definitive History 1997-2004 by Brian Long
Porsche 911SC Super Carrera, The Essential Companion by Adrian Streather
Porsche 914 The Definitive History Of The Road & Competition Cars by Brian Long
Porsche 924 by Brian Long
Porsche 944 by Brian Long
Porsche 993 'King of Porsche' – The Essential Companion by Adrian Streather
RAC Rally Action by Tony Gardiner
Rolls-Royce Silver Shadow/Bentley T Series Corniche & Camargue Revised & Enlarged Edition by Malcolm Bobbitt
Rolls-Royce Silver Spirit, Silver Spur & Bentley Mulsanne 2nd Edition by Malcolm Bobbitt
Rolls-Royce Silver Wraith, Dawn & Cloud/Bentley MkVI, R & S Series by Martyn Nutland
RX-7 – Mazda's Rotary Engine Sportscar (updated & revised new edition) by Brian Long
Singer Story: Cars, Commercial Vehicles, Bicycles & Motorcycles by Kevin Atkinson
SM – Citroën's Maserati-engined Supercar by Brian Long
Subaru Impreza 2nd edition by Brian Long
Taxi! The Story of the 'London' Taxicab by Malcolm Bobbitt
Triumph Motorcycles & the Meriden Factory by Hughie Hancox
Triumph Speed Twin & Thunderbird Bible by Harry Woolridge
Triumph Tiger Cub Bible by Mike Estall
Triumph Trophy Bible by Harry Woolridge
Triumph TR6 by William Kimberley
Turner's Triumphs, Edward Turner & his Triumph Motorcycles by Jeff Clew
Velocette Motorcycles – MSS to Thruxton Updated & Revised Edition by Rod Burris
Volkswagen Bus or Van to Camper, How to Convert by Lindsay Porter
Volkswagens of the World by Simon Glen
VW Beetle Cabriolet by Malcolm Bobbitt
VW Beetle – The Car of the 20th Century by Richard Copping
VW Bus – 40 years of Splities, Bays & Wedges by Richard Copping
VW Bus, Camper, Van, Pickup by Malcolm Bobbitt
VW Golf by Richard Copping & Ken Cservenka
VW – The air-cooled era by Richard Copping
Works Rally Mechanic by Brian Moylan

First published in February 2006 by Veloce Publishing Limited, 33 Trinity Street, Dorchester DT1 1TT, England. Fax 01305 268864/e-mail info@veloce.co.uk/web www.veloce.co.uk or www.velocebooks.com
ISBN 1-904788-93-9/ISBN 13 978-1-904788-93-5/UPC 6-36847-00393-7
Readers with ideas for automotive books, or books on other transport or related hobby subjects, are invited to write to the editorial director of Veloce Publishing at the above address.
British Library Cataloguing in Publication Data – A catalogue record for this book is available from the British Library. Typesetting, design and page make-up all by Veloce Publishing Ltd on Apple Mac.
Printed in the UK by HSW (Hackman & SW Printers).

TOTALLY NEW EDITION!

HOW TO GIVE YOUR

MGB V8 POWER

Roger Williams

VELOCE PUBLISHING
THE PUBLISHER OF FINE AUTOMOTIVE BOOKS

Veloce SpeedPro books -

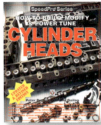

ISBN 1 903706 76 9

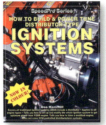

ISBN 1 903706 91 2

ISBN 1 903706 77 7

ISBN 1 903706 78 5

ISBN 1 901295 73 7

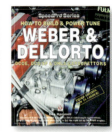

ISBN 1 903706 75 0

ISBN 1 904788 93 9

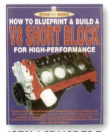

ISBN 1 874105 70 7

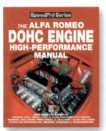

ISBN 1 84584 019 4

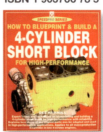

ISBN 1 903706 92 0

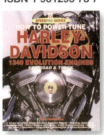

ISBN 1 903706 94 7

ISBN 1 901295 26 5

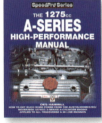

ISBN 1 84584 023 2

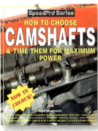

ISBN 1 903706 59 9

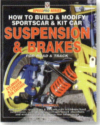

ISBN 1 903706 73 4

ISBN 1 904788 78 5

ISBN 1 901295 76 1

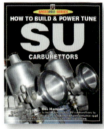

ISBN 1 903706 98 X

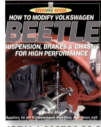

ISBN 1 903706 99 8

ISBN 1 84584 005 4

ISBN 1 904788 84 X

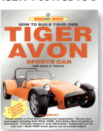

ISBN 1 904788 22 X

ISBN 1 903706 17 3

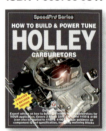

ISBN 1 84584 006 2

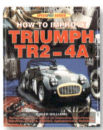

ISBN 1 903706 80 7

ISBN 1 903706 68 8

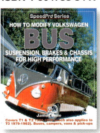

ISBN 1 903706 14 9

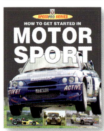

ISBN 1 903706 70 X

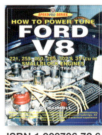

ISBN 1 903706 72 6

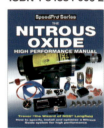

ISBN 1 904788 89-0

ISBN 1 904788 91 2

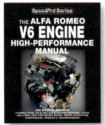

ISBN 1 84584 021 6

- more on the way!

Contents

Acknowledgements & about the author

ACKNOWLEDGEMENTS

This book would never have been written without the encouragement and assistance of a great number of people. While I appreciate every contribution, the full list is too extensive to mention everyone but I hope all will accept my grateful thanks. I do, however, wish to single out a few contributors, without whom there really would have been no book, starting with Dan Masters, founder of *Advance Auto-Wire* and also editor of the *British V8 Newsletter*. Dan has been a wonderful source of US information for a number of years but he really surpassed himself for this book. Without his unstinting time, patience, and technical, photographic and electrical input, the book would definitely have been a shadow of what you see here. However, Dan was not alone in that – Tom Hoagland, Dan Lagrou, Pete Mantell, Kurt Schley and Larry Shimp also provided a huge amount of information and invaluable photographic support on the US scene. Chris Crane and the team at RPI Engineering were equally supportive with the latest UK/Rover information and

pictorial backing. Dan & Kurt also read the manuscript while Roger Parker of the MG Owners Club reviewed the finished book. All made many absolutely invaluable suggestions.

Thanks guys – this book is only here as the result of your collective help.

ABOUT THE AUTHOR

Roger Williams was born in 1940 in Cardiff, brought up in Guildford and attended Guildford Royal Grammar School.

Aircraft became Roger's first love and he joined the de Havilland Aircraft Company in 1957 as a production engineering apprentice, and very quickly added motor cars to his list of prime interests. During the ensuing six years he not only completed his apprenticeship and studies, but built two Ford-based "specials" and started on a career in the manufacturing engineering industry as production engineer. Works managerial and directorial posts followed, and these responsibilities, together with his family commitments, reduced his time for

motoring interests to exiting the company car park at the fastest possible speed!

Roger's business interest moved on to company doctoring, which he enjoyed for some ten years, specialising in turning round ailing engineering businesses. In 1986 he started his own consultancy business and renewed his motoring interests. His company specialised in helping improve client profitability by interim management or consulting assignments, whilst his spare time was – and continues to be – devoted to motor cars or writing.

Roger has owned numerous MGBs, all of which he rebuilt over a period of some seven years. He still has two of his all-time favourites – the V8 powered variants – and has two MGB books in print. More recently Roger has become involved with the Triumph marque and has restored a TR6 and, currently, a Stag.

Roger is married and lives in France. He has two married daughters and is a Fellow of the Institution of Mechanical Engineers and a Fellow of the Institution of Production (now Manufacturing) Engineers.

Foreword

Having known Roger Williams for too many years to mention, I am delighted to have been asked to write the foreword to this third edition of *How to Give Your MGB V8 Power*. He had the foresight during years of research to compile the first edition of this book. During this time we worked closely together and I can say with confidence that the new edition will be the mine of the information that an individual needs to carry out a successful and well-balanced MGB V8 conversion.

There is no doubt that Roger's first book has already helped many enthusiasts realise their dream, as the number of conversions registered with the MG Car Club's V8 Register alone confirms. This new edition is timely in the sense that, with commercial production of the Rover V8 engine at Solihull finally coming to an end as I write this, one might be forgiven for thinking that the future of MGB V8 conversions is less than bright. The truth, however, is vastly different as any enthusiast contemplating such a conversion is better served now than at any time in the past. In this third edition Roger has covered more engine options than in earlier editions and takes into account the numerous developments that have become available from the growing and dedicated network of specialists.

Roger's style is easy to read yet informative; he writes from a practical 'hands-on' point of view, encapsulating the experience of many converters, professional and amateur in the UK and USA.

Looking back it seems we've come a long way since the early 1970s when Ken Costello had the vision to transplant the Rover V8 engine into an MGB. His success did not go unnoticed by British Leyland which was spurred-on to develop its own GT V8, a car which ultimately never quite realised the success it really deserved. When production ended in 1976, a mere 2591 cars had been produced. In 1993 a V8-powered MG returned briefly to the scene with Rover's limited-production MG RV8. However, as good as the RV8 is, many enthusiasts still seek the satisfaction of building their own car to their own specifications. Having served countless V8 conversion enthusiasts over the years, this is a desire I can well understand, and, at the end of the day, helping such enthusiasts realise their dream is what this book is all about.

Enjoy and happy V8 motoring.

Clive Wheatley

Introduction

The MGB and MGB GT are probably two of the most beautiful and affordable classic cars but subsequent automotive developments make them seem noisy and they are out-performed by all but the most modest of today's family hatchbacks. Ken Costello recognised this and began installing the Rover 3500cc V8 in customers' MGBs. BL, as it was then, MG Rover now, asked to see a Costello conversion, liked it and gave Ken a car and engine to convert. Ken cannot recall BL paying for the conversion but does remember Lord Stokes asking what he would do if BL marketed a V8 MGB itself. He replied "carry on". BL did and he did, although only 2591 such GTs were manufactured.

However, there are far more than the original number of V8 powered MGBs about today! Furthermore, it is extraordinary to think that design and development work on the MGB and MGB GT continues today – 30+ years after the last car rolled off the production line. True, the work is outside the MG Rover Group portals – although it has made its contribution in recent years by launching the MGR V8 and by providing body-shells specifically for retro-fitting Rover V8 engines. Both developments capitalised on the growing interest in putting large engines in little cars, and V8 engines in MGBs in particular.

While Rover/Heritage was working away to satisfy the appetite of MG enthusiasts, Land Rover was developing larger capacity engines to counter the need for more power from engines increasingly strangled by emissions constraints. Thus, since writing my initial book, 3900, 4200 and 4600cc Rover V8 engines have been born too – offering the prospect of quite startling performance when mounted within an MGB! Speaking of large engines in little cars, there has been a growing practice in the USA of fitting Ford and Chevy V8 engines into the MGB. These provide even greater cubic capacity and power – which may account for growth in demand and in the number of enthusiasts wanting to go MGB V8 motoring on both sides of the Atlantic.

Furthermore, the development of numerous other performance enhancing gearboxes, suspensions, wheels and brakes has also continued outside the Rover Group, bringing with them an amazing growth of options. In fact, I have been amazed at the interest the earlier editions of this book generated, particularly in the USA. However, expectations are changing. While 12 or 15 years ago (when I wrote the first edition) 200bhp/200 lb-ft engines seemed to provide an adequate balance of power with the braking and suspension systems available, today the trend is for 300+bhp power-plants – clearly I needed to provide information showing that the MGB's gearbox, suspension and braking systems need to be radically changed if they are to safely transmit this sort of power to the road. This third edition sets out to do just that.

Conversely, the book does not set out to act as a guide to restoring an MGB, nor does it purport to be the definitive guide to rebuilding or modifying your engine (although some relevant information is included) or indeed any major component you may use in your V8 conversion. These topics are well covered elsewhere.

The MGB Roadster and MGB GT cars are, for the purposes of planning a V8 conversion, virtually identical and have been treated as such. Thus ,when you see the term 'MGB' this applies to both models. On the odd occasion when there are differences between the two variants, I have made reference to the respective car in the form 'Roadster' and 'GT'.

Roger Williams, Limousin, France

Using this book and essential information

USING THIS BOOK

Throughout this book the text assumes that you, or your contractor, will have a workshop manual specific to your vehicle to follow for complete detail on dismantling, reassembly, adjustment procedure, clearances, torque figures, etc. This book's default is the standard manufacturer's specification for your vehicle type so, if a procedure is not described, a measurement not given, a torque figure ignored, you can assume that the standard manufacturer's procedure or specification for your engine should be used.

It is essential to read the whole book before you start work or give instructions to your contractor. This is because a modification or change in specification in one area can cause the need for changes in other areas. Get the whole picture so that you can finalise specification and component requirements as far as possible *before* any work begins.

ESSENTIAL INFORMATION

This book contains information on practical procedures; however, this information is intended only for those with the qualifications, experience, tools and facilities to carry out the work in safety and with appropriately high levels of skill. Whenever working on a car or component, remember that your personal safety must **ALWAYS** be your **FIRST** consideration. The publisher, author, editors and retailer of this book cannot accept any responsibility for personal injury or mechanical damage which results from using this book, even if caused by errors or omissions therein. If this disclaimer is unacceptable to you, please return the pristine book to your retailer who will refund the purchase price.

In the text of this book "**Warning!**" means that a procedure could cause personal injury and "**Caution!**" that there is danger of mechanical damage if appropriate care is not taken. However, be aware that we cannot foresee every possibility of danger in every circumstance.

Please note that changing component specification by modification is likely to void warranties and also to absolve manufacturers from any responsibility in the event of component failure and the consequences of such failure.

Increasing the engine's power will place additional stress on engine components and on the car's complete driveline: this may reduce service life and increase the frequency of breakdown. An increase in engine power, and therefore the vehicle's performance, will mean that your vehicle's braking and suspension systems will need to be kept in perfect condition and uprated as appropriate. It is also usually necessary to inform the vehicle's insurers of any changes to the vehicle's specification.

The importance of cleaning a component thoroughly before working on it cannot be overstressed. Always keep your working area and tools as clean as possible. Whatever specialist cleaning fluid or other chemicals you use, be sure to follow – completely – manufacturer's instructions, and if you are using petrol (gasoline) or paraffin (kerosene) to clean parts, take every precaution necessary to protect your body and to avoid all risk of fire.

Chapter 1
What car, engine & gearbox?

PLANNING THE CONVERSION

It really is worthwhile spending time planning the conversion. Part of the planning and preparation process should involve visiting suppliers, talking to owners of converted cars at your local MG group/club and exploring some relevant exhibitions. Explore the various options and the effect each has on your budget. Prepare yourself for the fact that the larger the engine you choose, the greater the number, and extent, of the changes you'll be required to make – collectively generating **big** expense if you choose the most powerful engine options.

For the car to be both safe and a pleasure to drive, the conversion **must** be a balanced one – i.e. **all** the constituent components must fit together and be suited to each other. If you go for an engine with modest power, e.g. a 3500cc/215in^3 unit producing 190/200bhp, you will be able to use a correspondingly modest gearbox (an ex-SD1, 5-speed, for example) and standard SD1 clutch. While the rear axle location will be less than ideal, you will be able to think about retaining the original front and rear suspension arrangements, requiring relatively few low-cost upgrades. The front brakes will benefit from slight improvement, again at minimal cost. However, if you decide to fit

Engine power band		Gearbox	Clutch	Front suspension	Rear axle	Rear suspension	Front brakes	Wheels & tyres
Moderate	Up to 200bhp	Rover SD1 SD1/Lt77	Std 9.5in Rover SD1	Standard + tel dampers	3.07 MGB	Standard + tel dampers	Standard MGB GT V8	185x70 H 14in dia x 6J
Medium	200 to about 250bhp	Rover R380 or T5	10in	Coil-over modification	3.08 SD1 possible LSD*	Anti-tramp + tel dampers	22mm x 280 dia vent + 4 pots	195x65 V 15in dia x 6J*
High	Over 250bhp	T5 or T5Z or Tremec 3550	10.5in	Coil-over & spl design*	Live axle with LSD or IRS**	Trailing link + coil springs	22mm x 290 dia vent + 4 pots	205 x 65 ZR 16in x 7J**

* All possibly fitted with 5-stud hubs and wheels
** Fitted with 5-stud hubs and wheels

a 400bhp engine, not only must the clutch and gearbox be upgraded, so should the car's structure and suspension. The rear suspension, in particular, will need significant and costly upgrading. Further, with the added power, the car will still need to stop safely, requiring much better brakes than MG provided for its slightly ponderous 1800cc model. The size of the brakes is limited by the space available within the 14in wheels; you are going to need to plan for enlarged brakes **and wheels** that will do the stopping and roadholding jobs. Then there are the tyres. All these components (and many others) must be selected and installed in harmony with each other – and that takes thought and planning. To help, I've devised a small table (left) summarising the **minimum** major component upgrades that would be involved as you move from modest, through medium, to a high-powered conversion. Please remember that the numerous additional components involved (induction, ignition, cooling, starter, etc.) will also need upgrading and consequently incur exponential cost increases as you move up the power bands. You have to plan for a balance that fits your budget.

MGBs were in production for many years and, not surprisingly, numerous changes evolved with the end result that there are now several models to choose from if you are seeking an MGB to convert to V8 power. If that is your plan, be advised that the amount of work involved in the conversion can vary considerably depending upon the model you buy and the engine (and to a lesser extent the gearbox) you plan to fit. It is possible to buy one particular model, a particular engine and its mating gearbox and more or less drop the engine straight into the car. On the other hand, that same model MGB might require a modest amount of sheet-metal changes to the engine bay should you elect to fit a different engine and gearbox combination. Consequently, choosing the model, its

potential engine and the most suitable gearbox requires thought and planning.

As you plan your conversion, remember that the car was designed for a 100bhp power plant. 200bhp has proved to be within the car's structural capability but 300bhp can, without the essential upgrades, severely and dangerously damage the bodyshell. Therefore, do not lose sight of the objective – to build a safe, balanced, fun car; it is very easy to end up with a monster. It is my opinion that a 4.0/4.2-litre engine gives the right balance of safety and performance. While there are still challenges to building and driving such a car, the planning and organising can be part of the enjoyment.

Your plan may also be influenced by costs, the time you can devote to the project, the skills and equipment available, or by the car, engine or gearbox you have in the garage. You need to assess your priorities and plan accordingly so that the project is completed within your parameters. We will start by exploring each model in a little detail, but we also need to explore the consequences of your engine and gearbox choices.

WHAT MODEL?

There are other considerations that we will explore a little later, but bodyshell changes must be high on the list of concerns for many readers – so we'll start there. All converted MGBs, regardless of the model and the proposed engine will (I suggest) need a reinforced hole cut in each inner wing/fender to allow for the passage of the exhaust manifolds/headers. As a rule of thumb, the last model off the production line will be the easiest to convert, particularly if you choose to fit a Buick/Rover engine and Rover gearbox, as the engine bay was designed to accept this engine. Conversely, the earlier the car/model you select, the greater the amount

1-1-1 The rubber-bumper MGBs were produced from 1974 – albeit in two slightly differing versions. This one has had a Buick 215 V8 dropped straight into the car with only minor changes to the engine's front pulleys. Note the 'Special Tuning' front spoiler/valance fitted to this and ...

1-1-2 … my Rover V8 engined chrome-bumper MGB. The chrome-bumpered MGBs were produced from 1962 to 1974. The front spoiler is non-standard but helps cool the engine and increase front-end stability. Note the completely standard bonnet/hood.

of work involved in a V8 conversion, even if you use the Buick/Rover engine and gearbox. For any given model, the conversion work increases if you choose to fit a Ford or Chevy engine.

Bodyshell alterations

No particular MGB holds bodyshell alteration advantages for those wishing to fit the Chevy engine. The engine requires bulkhead, engine mounting and, possibly, radiator bracket alterations regardless of the model involved. This is not so if you are thinking of a Buick/Rover or the Ford 302 engine.

Starting with the cars that require the fewest changes – rubber-bumper (pictured at 1-1-1) 1800cc cars were produced with the necessary bulkhead shapes to accept either the 1800cc 4-cylinder or the Buick/Rover P6 V8 engine. The SD1 Rover engine needs a few minor changes to the front-end pulleys but will otherwise drop straight into a post-1976 MGB without further changes. Thus, if you were to go shopping for an MGB to convert to V8 power and were happy with using the Rover engine (or its US predecessor), the easiest option would be to purchase an MGB rubber-bumper model made after September 1976 with a VIN number post-410001. The Ford 302 will also fit this engine bay, although the car's engine-mounting brackets will require repositioning.

The previous generation of rubber-bumper cars (made between October 1974 and September 1976, with VIN numbers GHN5 360301 to 410000 or GHD5 361001 to 410000) only requires two fairly minor engine bay alterations to allow the fitting of Buick/Rover V8 and Ford 302 engines. In order to make space for the larger V8 engine, the position and design of the radiator-mounting frame needs to be changed. The second alteration is recommended but is not absolutely essential for Buick/Rover engines: a change to the later, single-stud design of engine-mounting bracket will make your subsequent engine-fitting task easier and also allows the (longer/later) steering column to pass through the mounting bracket. This model MGB had, what is to my mind, the ideal dashboard/fascia. As mentioned in the previous paragraph, you will definitely need to replace the engine-mounting brackets to allow the Ford to fit. Obviously any of the MGB dashboard/fascias can be used but the ones fitted in this short production period replicate those used in the original MGB V8s.

If, like many, you prefer the aesthetics of the chrome-bumpered cars seen at 1-1-2, you can buy rubber-to-chrome-bumper conversion kits. However, these still leave the rubber-bumper models standing an inch or so (approximately 25mm) higher off the ground than the earlier chrome-bumper variant. This detracts from the car's roadholding but can be countered with a suspension lowering kit. So Buick/Rover and Ford engine enthusiasts may still find the minimal bodywork changes offered by these cars attractive.

1-1-3 Here is a close-up of the RV8 rear spring and anti-tramp locationing. Again, the original MGB front spring mounting has a bolt through it. Two additional mounting holes are provided beneath the original: the higher one for the spring, the lower for the RV8's anti-tramp bars. Note the extra material thickness with which Rover supplements the mounting holes – for good reason!

There is another option for Buick/Rover engined cars – buy any car you like and a new V8 chrome-bumper Heritage bodyshell – but for the moment we will assume you are not planning the purchase of a new bodyshell. All chrome-bumpered cars will require the common radiator and engine mounting alterations already outlined and will also require alterations to the bulkhead/firewall to provide clearance for the V8 engine's cylinder heads. If you plan to use the Rover or Ford engine, these bulkhead/firewall changes are fairly small but, if fitting the Chevy engine, you may find these alterations more onerous and complicated. The extent of these changes are detailed within the respective engine chapters, but the changes to chrome-bumpered cars does not always stop at the firewall/bulkhead.

There are two basic models of chrome-bumpered car. Cars made between November 1967 and November 1974 were fitted with a four-synchromesh gearbox and a wide, flat-topped gearbox/transmission tunnel. However, cars made from the start of MGB production and up to October 1967, the Mk1 model, were fitted with a three-synchromesh gearbox and had a narrower transmission tunnel with a pronounced hump in the area of the gear lever. These Mk1 cars require all the preceding bodyshell modifications and very extensive transmission-tunnel changes too regardless of the engine or gearbox you select. Consequently, my advice would be to not try a V8 conversion on this Mk1 MGB variant unless you have some experience of automotive sheet-metal working.

New bodyshells

You now have a comparative outline of the various bodyshell changes required by each MGB model and appreciate that the working with an early model and/or selecting an engine other than a Buick/Rover can add to the complexity of the conversion. However, if you see a need to restore your car or a prospective purchase simultaneously with its conversion, some time spent reflecting on the work involved may be worthwhile. First and foremost, in light of any V8's power, the structural parts of the MGB **must** be in A1 condition.

The restoration, structural integrity and V8 (Buick/Rover engine and gearbox) conversion changes are already taken care of if you buy a new Heritage bodyshell – and we will look at this solution in detail later in the book. A new Heritage bodyshell gives you complete freedom (subject to local registration authorities approval) to start with one model MGB but finish with another. For example you could start with a rubber-bumpered car (even a GT if you wanted) and finish with a chrome-bumpered V8 Roadster. The new shells are available with all the Buick/Rover radiator, engine-mountings, bulkhead/firewall and exhaust exit modifications pre-fitted for even the largest Rover engine – and this is my recommended course of action. Rover has seen fit, with the RV8, to strengthen even a new shell as shown in photo 1-1-3. This modification is already incorporated into the Heritage shells.

With the Ford engine you will need to adjust both the engine-mounting bracket and form the exhaust exit holes in the inner wings/fenders seen in photograph 1-1-4. With the Chevy power plant you will have to effect the same changes and some significant firewall/bulkhead and footwell alterations also.

When buying an MGB for conversion using a new bodyshell, you need not be concerned about the condition of the original bodyshell, paint, engine, gearbox, radiator etc. While it adds to the volume of work involved, your (hopefully low-cost) purchase can differ from your ultimate target. A GT will provide a great many of the parts you need, even if you ultimately have a V8 Roadster in mind. You will need a number of additional conversion parts, however, the wheels (and therefore the hubs) should fit your ultimate concept, and it is desireable to have the trim, suspension, steering,

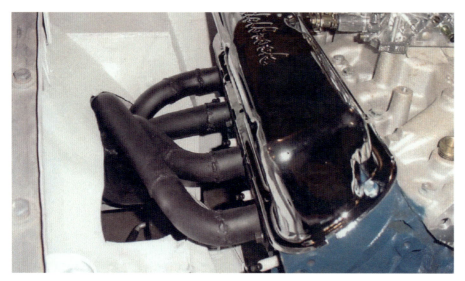

1-1-4 These Ford exhaust manifold/headers had to be formed at home, as did the exit holes in the inner wing/fender. These additional exits are essential for Ford & Chevy engines and I think highly advisable for Buick/Rover-engined cars. The manifold/headers for Buick/Rover engines are readily available pre-manufactured.

bumpers, dashboard/fascia/instruments, lights, etc., in the best shape possible.

Other purchasing considerations

If you are planning a V8 conversion with a modest engine, you may choose a donor car that fits in with your preferred road wheel style – wire wheels or bolt-ons. However, wire-wheels are not a good idea for anything above the most modest of V8 conversions, so, if a medium- or high-power conversion is your objective, only buy a car with bolt-on disc wheels. The hubs may then be of use to you.

In the UK it's possible to purchase a rusty, rotten, damaged but original MGB GT V8 and refit the components into a new MGB Roadster bodyshell. Naturally, this has its attractions, although I deplore this practice. There were only 2591 original V8s built and, no doubt, many of these have succumbed to the ravages of time – so this route depletes an already rare species. Added to which, you miss out on the opportunity to improve the breed. Buy an original GT V8 by all means, but do please restore it to its former original GT glory. If you are serious about a V8 Roadster, start from scratch and you'll finish with a better car as the result of your efforts.

If you live in a wet or otherwise hostile climate you could save the cost of purchasing a new bodyshell if you start your conversion on a repatriated, ex-warm-climate 1800 Roadster. Californian cars are not as plentiful as they once were but South Africa is now providing some superb examples and in rhd configuration. Most warm-climate repatriations are available complete for less cost than a new Heritage bodyshell and, provided they are from a genuine warm/dry climate, you'll be able to use the bodyshell without any significant structural refurbishment. Treat cars offered as ex-warm-climate with caution: ensure your prospective purchase is corrosion-free and has spent its entire life in a dry climate.

1-2-1 A beautiful conversion using one of the Buick/Rover family of 215in^3/3500cc engines – in this case an Oldsmobile 215. The radiator is a standard/stock MGB GT V8 unit, the rocker-covers are Offenhauser as is, I suspect, the central inlet manifold. The air-filter is a 14in diameter x 2in high 'Low Rider' unit.

It is a matter of personal preference but, if the law of supply and demand is anything to go by, then a chrome-bumper Roadster MGB V8 is generally considered the most desirable of MGB models. In my view this car is most likely to ensure you recoup your costs should you ever wish to sell your converted car.

During the course of the conversion you are likely to end up with some surplus parts like engine, gearbox, radiator, exhaust and carburettors, even a spare bodyshell. The black rubber-bumpers may be surplus if you are intent on chrome versions. You are unlikely to want these spare parts hanging around your garage. A part-exchange deal with a supplier/painter/restorers is one possible means of selling these surplus parts but you will get a better price if you advertise them for a modest charge on the internet or via the various MG clubs' 'spares for sale' columns. Members of both the MGCC and the MGOC advertise spares on a free-of-charge basis and the NAMGBR also offers a 'spares for sale' column.

If you buy a car with an aluminium bonnet/hood, retain and use it regardless of the engine you plan. If you are thinking of a Ford or Chevy engine, go searching the spares columns for a good aluminium

1-2-2 Another beautifully converted MGB – a chrome-bumpered model with a Ford 302 snugly in place. The radiator is a Griffin aluminium unit, the cylinder heads are also aluminium supplied by Edelbrock, and the prominent distributor is the stock Ford diameter. If you were to fit a 'Low Rider' air filter to this engine you would need to fit a smaller diameter distributor also.

1-2-3 This is a Chevrolet 302 V8. Few were made and it is the same size as all the small-block Chevys but, in spite of its generic name, it is not small enough to fit into the MGB's engine bay without removing the heater and its mounting platform completely, and relocating the brake and clutch reservoirs.

bonnet/hood to take a few pounds off the front end and sell the steel one that will likely come with your purchase.

However, we still have to decide what engine and gearbox to fit – so let's start by exploring some engine options.

WHAT ENGINE?

There are pros and cons associated with the wide variety of options you may consider for your MGB engine transplant. Some superb cars have been constructed using a wide variety of alternative engines: the Chevy 350, Buick 231 V6, GM60° V6 and the Mercedes-Benz all-aluminium V8s or V6s. I have focused on three of the most popular V8 engines that are available on both sides of the Atlantic.

I carried out a survey of UK and US MGB V8 conversions and the result, coupled with the information that follows, should help you decide what engine to use in your own conversion. In the UK about 90 per cent of converters used one variation or another of the Rover aluminium engine, while in the USA 80 per cent of finished conversions use the Buick/Oldsmobile/Pontiac/Rover (BOPR) generation of engines. Ford 302 engines currently account for 10 per cent of the total. They were the second most popular engine but are undoubtedly growing in popularity. Nevertheless, they are far behind the Buick/Rover completed conversions. Chevrolet 350 small blocks and 'others' more or less divided the remaining 10 per cent between them.

There is no right-way of carrying out an MGB V8 conversion. Certainly there is no right combination of car, engine or gearbox. Largely because they are proven, have lots of grunt from low-down in the rev-range and result in a predictable fun sports car, this book focuses on the ever-popular practice of shoehorning the Buick/Rover aluminium V8 (pictured at 1-2-1), the Ford 302 (1-2-2) or the Chevy (1-2-3) into the MGB. Whichever engine you choose, there will be areas of commonality.

However, in view of its popularity, this book leans towards the use of one of the many Buick/Rover engines. Not only will it be the easiest engine to fit but its weight allows the car's front/rear balance and predictable roadholding characteristics to be to be retained – subject to prudence – when driving enthusiastically on wet roads. The engine's aluminium construction is the key to this feature but its size, sump, range of capacity/power options, tuning

equipment and ready availability (at least in the UK) all help convince me it's the engine of choice. Not everyone agrees with me these days, so lets explore the attributes of the short-listed engines.

Availability

Your selection of the engine that is to power your conversion may depend upon your geographical location. In the UK the Rover V8, in one of its many guises, is readily available at reasonable cost, particularly if you are comfortable with the 3500cc and 3900cc versions.

The Rover V8 engine is to be found in the USA in various capacities. The 4.2-litre engine is surprisingly common and, to my mind, makes for an almost ideal MGB engine, second only to a late 4.0-litre Rover unit. The BOPR earlier 3500cc/215in³ engines are still around and offer the same light weight as the later Rover units and, consequently, should be on any US enthusiast's shortlist of power-plants. Also available on both sides of the Atlantic are the later Rover engines (seen at 1-2-4) with their 4600cc/282in³ capacity. US modifiers are spoilt for choice as they also have a plentiful supply of Ford 302, seen fully

1-2-5 Possibly more powerful than some Ford 302 crate motors, this one (destined for a TR6) came equipped with GT40 aluminium heads, roller cam, Edelbrock inlet manifold and dual Edelbrock 1404 (500cfm) carburettors. You might have difficulty closing the MGB's bonnet/hood with those air filters but they will not take long to change for something slimmer.

dressed at 1-2-5, and Chevy small-block engines to choose from. These engines are heavier but offer even larger capacity, the opportunity of very high power/torque outputs and have a huge array of aftermaket tuning equipment available, including aluminium cylinder heads on view at 1-2-6, which do reduce the incremental weight to more manageable proportions. I will identify sources for Ford and Chevy engines in the UK in due course.

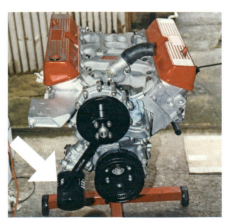

1-2-4 This is a late 4600cc Rover engine but all Buick/Rover engines require the oil-filter (arrowed) be repositioned and all Rover engines of the SD1, and post-SD1, era need their large front pulleys changing.

1-2-6 Aluminium cylinder heads are essential to both Ford and Chevy engines destined for an MGB's engine bay. They are available as the aftermarket fitment seen here, but also with either brand of engine when purchased as a new/complete crate unit.

Weight

A heavy engine can adversely affect the original car's 50:50 weight distribution and detract from the car's predictable roadholding. The MGC suffered from too much weight at the front, the consequential handling problems and the bad publicity effectively brought the car's life to a premature end. The standard by which we should judge all transplants is shown in photograph 1-2-7

Furthermore, perhaps with one exception, weight rarely works for you. A gearbox with a torque rating of 200lb-ft in a car weighing 3500lb will handle the output of an engine with over 200lb-ft provided the weight of the car is nearer 2500lb, as should be the case with a small sports car like the MGB. However, the Ford and Chevy engines are both significantly heavier than the BOPR aluminium engines. This will require you to further upgrade the brakes (to counter the additional inertia of the heavier car) and the front suspension to counter the additional weight at the front end. The table below outlines the comparative sizes and weights of our shortlist of engines.

Although this table only compares engine weights, do not forget that the MGB gearbox is a weighty unit, particularly with overdrive fitted. As will be discussed, modern 5-speed gearboxes can easily be obtained in aluminium cases, going a long way to redressing the balance.

1-2-7 This MGB engine and gearbox weigh in at 465lb (but that excludes a 30lb overdrive unit), meaning a straight engine substitution needs to tip the scales at about 360/375lb.

1-2-8 The front portion of the SD1 and post-SD1 Rover sumps seen here might have been made to fit the MGB, for it provides the perfect shape and clearance over the MG's crossmember without any alterations to engine or crossmember.

Power

As far as power is concerned, you can roughly work this out from an engine's cubic inch capacity. In standard tune, as a rule of thumb, 1in^3 capacity generates 0.9bhp. However, most engines can easily and safely be tuned to generate 1bhp per in^3 – when comparing engines this is the power output you should be measuring them against.

The power to weight ratios of the respective engines is also an important consideration. Interestingly, the Toyota twin overhead cam, 32-valve SC400 ex-Soarer 1UZFE EFI engine offered the best power/weight ratio of all the engines I studied, however, the difficulty of squeezing this engine into the MGB engine bay kept it off the short-list and so the Rover 4600cc came top. The Ford 302 came next and the Chevy third – but you can view each of the short-listed engines' power/weight ratios in the table above. Nevertheless, expect the aluminium Toyota engine to eventually replace the popularity of Rover engine.

Sump shapes compared

We have talked about the various engine bay changes that each model and each engine requires, but there is one more important detail to weigh-up. The MGB

Engine	Width inches	Length inches	Height inches	Weight approx lb	Weight per BHP/key points
MGB 110ci/1800cc all cast-iron	17	23	24	397	3.6/original four cyl engine
Buick-Rover 215/3500 alloy V8	26	28	27	350	1.63/lightest alternatives
Rover to 282ci/4600cc alloy V8	26	28	27	355	1.26
Ford 302 Iron V8 – 4900 to 5600cc	24	29	27.5	485	1.58/more cubes but more weight
Ford 302 with alloy heads	24	29	27.5	435	1.42/shortlist but watch sump
All iron Chevy 350ci/5700cc V8	26	28	27	575	1.64/much too heavy
Chevrolet 350 with alloy heads	26	28	27	525	1.50/possible, but only just

front suspension crossmember poses complications for some engines and we need to discuss minimising sump/oil-pan/front crossmember interference. As far as the MGB's crossmembers are concerned, those from rubber-bumper MGBs provide an extra 1in clearance from the engine sump/oil-pan compared to a chrome-bumpered crossmember.

The crossmember is only one half of the sump/oil-pan clearance issue. The Rover SD1 sump/oil-pan shape (seen at picture 1-2-8) is ideal for fitting this engine into an MGB as the first 8in are very shallow and the full depth of the sump does not come into effect until the back ⅔ of the engine. Thus engines fitted with SD1 sump/oil-pan fit over standard/stock MGB front crossmembers without difficulty. The early Rover engines (as fitted to P5B and P6 cars, and the even earlier Buick/Pontiac/Olds engines) all had slightly deeper (front) sumps and if your engine is from this early production period, just find and fit an SD1 or later sump to provide clearance over the MGB's front crossmember. There is no need to change the oil pick-up point.

The majority of Chevy sumps are similar in shape to the Rover sump. If you are unlucky enough to have an engine that has a deep front section to its sump, find an alternative – there are plenty of suitable Chevy sumps/oil-pans.

Conversely most Ford sumps and oil pick-up arrangements are not initially suited to the MGB as they generally have a front oil pick-up point and the full-depth front sump pictured at 1-2-9. There are solutions and we will explore them in chapter 3 but they add to the complexity of choosing a Ford.

Whatever the engine, if you have sump/oil-pan clearance difficulties there are several less than ideal fall-back options:
● modify your own sump/oil-pan.
● have a special oil-pan/sump made up, not forgetting, in the case of the Ford engine, that you will need a compatible oil pick-up arrangement. Canton Racing Products in the USA can make any bespoke oil-pan/sump if you have a major problem.
● fit a new front suspension assembly with a low crossmember construction.

Distributors

The Chevy distributor rarely causes a space problem in an MGB. It is mounted on top and to the rear of the engine, at the point of maximum headroom within the engine bay. The Rover and the Ford engines both have front mounted distributors. The Rover is canted at about 20° (seen at 1-2-10), and, provided the engine has been properly dropped into the engine bay, this too will

1-2-9 This Ford sump might seem designed to maximise the difficulties, however, the Rover sump starts from below the crankshaft centreline whereas the Ford starts on the crank centreline. So the Ford is not as difficult as it seems and we'll explore solutions in chapter 3.

1-2-10 Distributor – what distributor? It's hiding behind the top hose in this Buick conversion.

rarely cause any grief. However, the Ford distributor seen at 1-2-11 may cause bonnet/hood clearance problems and may necessitate the use of an MGC bonnet or a shorter Crane distributor.

Cost rankings

The most variable but probably the most important consideration of all is cost. Your geographical location will have a huge bearing on what you will have to pay for each engine as will the state of tune, how many ancillaries are included and how sharp your bargaining skills are. There are many ways you can reduce the costs. If you buy well, you may be able to fit a used engine as purchased. If it needs some refurbishment, you may choose to assemble the engine yourself. However, I have tried to rank the respective costs of a complete new or fully reconditioned ready-to-run engine. In the UK this might be described as an out-of-the-box or complete engine, known as a 'crate' engine in the US.

My estimates in ascending order of cost are:

Buick/Rover 3500cc/215in^3
Ford 302 with alloy heads
Rover 3.9-litre
Chevy 350 with alloy heads
Rover 4600cc/282in^3
Rover 5000cc hand built

1-2-11 This is the smaller diameter version of the Ford dizzy. An air scoop in the bonnet or an MGC bonnet facilitates the frontal location.

1-3-1 The slightly canted gear/shift lever tells us this is a Ford T5. It has an aluminium case and bellhousing which guarantees it will always be lighter than ...

1-3-2 ... the cast-iron case of the Rover LT77. The Rover bellhousing bolts to the gear-casing and is made from aluminium.

1-3-3 Another view of the T5 – a Ford version judging by the extra length of the bellhousing. Its all-aluminium construction is clear from this shot. The twin pipes exiting the clutch-lever opening are, in this case, for an HTOB (hydraulic throw-out bearing) which actuates this car's clutch.

WHAT GEARBOX?

In most cases the choice of gearbox will follow-on from your engine selection. While you can fit almost any gearbox to any engine, if you elect to follow an unconventional route you will add cost to the project, often for very little benefit.

Ideally the gearbox you choose will be the standard/stock manual gearbox for that engine – and where possible this is certainly the most practical gearbox selection method to follow. Rover, Ford and Chevy engines all have manual gearboxes attached to some variants and this 'pre-coupled' approach has many advantages. The clutch and marriage of engine to gearbox is resolved for you so you only need to provide a rear crossmember to properly support the tail of the gearbox and sort the speedometer cable/drive and the hydraulic actuation/line to the clutch. We will explore solutions in chapter 4.

Unfortunately it may not always be possible to purchase an engine and manual gearbox as one unit. All the engines we are considering have a high percentage of auto-boxes fitted behind them and it is not practical to pass-up an absolutely first-class engine just because it does not come with a pre-coupled manual gearbox. If your engine is without a suitable manual gearbox, you may well be able to cast around and find a manual version.

If you are forced to buy the engine and gearbox separately, ensure your prospective gearbox comes with all the appropriate fittings. The bellhousing is the most obvious, but there are numerous other parts required – the flywheel, clutch, clutch bearing carrier, clutch slave cylinder and arm, and the gear-change extension

all need to be included in the deal if it is to be the simplest of marriages. Furthermore, be very careful that the gearbox and fittings come from an identical engine. The bellhousing, flywheel and clutch carrying components can look the same at first glance but vary in detail. For example, a Rover 5-speed box from a straight-six (2600cc) engine will not fit a Rover V8 without extra change-parts. Consequently care is needed. The next most practical method is to retrofit another assembly, e.g. the Ford T5 (see 1-3-1) to a Ford 302.

Getting the box to fit

All MGBs will need the gearbox tunnel under the dashboard/fascia area modified to some degree regardless of gearbox selection. Without exception you will also need to replace or modify the gearbox supporting crossmember to some extent. In the case of the Rover engine/gearbox combination, it is possible to buy and fit an MG RV8 crossmember since it provides the correct mounting for the LT77 and R380 gearboxes and the capability to bolt directly to the existing MGB chassis. However, all the mainstream engine/gearbox combinations have a well-proven gearbox crossmember design that can easily be purchased or fabricated.

Assuming you have avoided buying an early three-synchro MGB with its narrow tunnel, the extent of the bodyshell modifications depends upon the choice of gearbox. If you are fitting a 3500/4000cc Rover engine, the Rover SD1 LT77 5-speed gearbox (pic 1-3-2) is the natural 'follow-on' gearbox. The bigger capacity Rover engines will probably require the LT77's successor – the newer, stronger R380 with the advantage of synchromesh on all gears. Both these gearboxes have the added attraction of requiring the least tunnel changes. A sheet-metal upward extension is all that is required (detailed in chapter 9) to provide space for these taller Rover gearboxes.

1-3-4 These days you will be routing the exhaust manifolds/headers through the inner wing/fender, so will see very similar holes to those pictured regardless of your choice of V8 engine. However, it was the arrowed changes to the footwells that I wanted to highlight – these are for a Ford. Were this a Rover transplant, these alterations would not be required but if we were fitting a Chevy they would be rather more drastic than what we see here.

The Ford and Chevy engines were both fitted with BorgWarner (now Tremec) T5 gearboxes (seen at 1-3-3). Consequently the easiest and most effective solution is to find and fit the relevant T5 gearbox. These gearboxes are shallower than the Rover units and don't require an increase in the height of the MGB's gearbox tunnel. However, you will need to alter the inner-faces of both footwells (pic 1-3-4) to allow for the T5's larger bellhousing (pic 1-3-5).

Alternative choices

If you are thinking of fitting a very big capacity engine there will be an understandable temptation to fit a 6-speed gearbox. The size of a gearbox usually increases as the number of gears is increased. Furthermore, the size of the gearbox increases with its power handling capacity – thus, as a rule of thumb, a very powerful engine demands a larger gearbox. Choosing one or both of these options brings with it an escalation in sheet-metal alterations to accommodate it. The BorgWarner (now Tremec) T56 is probably the most readily available 6-speed and its

1-3-5 With little to scale this Ford T5 bellhousing against it is difficult to tell its size but it does look bigger than the Rover bellhousing. However ...

1-3-6 ... the T5 in the foreground is dwarfed by the size of the T56.

size can be judged by comparing it to a T5 in photograph 1-3-6.

So you need to select the smallest gearbox with a power/torque handling capacity adequate for the engine you plan to fit. We'll explore the detail in chapter 4

but when looking at the specification of any gearbox remember that it's power/torque handling will have been specified with the weight of its original vehicle in mind. The MGB you restore/convert is likely to weigh less than the vehicle your gearbox was originally intended for and this could provide you with some degree of safety margin. However, you may also be increasing the power and/or the torque of the engine above standard/stock which reduces the safety margin or requires that you upgrade your gearbox specification.

Like the Rover LT77, the T5 gearbox has successors – some of which are available only via aftermarket outlets. Several of these Tremec manufactured units, upgraded versions of the T5, are explored in chapter 4 and bear consideration partly because they are new units but more particularly because of their superior torque capacities.

A Toyota Supra gearbox is another worth considering provided your power is below 400hp. It can be strapped behind any of the engines we are considering and can be sourced locally or in fully reconditioned form from Australia. It was never fitted to any of our short-listed engines and consequently there will be no point looking for a suitable bellhousing or clutch arrangement but these are available from Dellow Automotive in Australia.

CONCLUSION

There are lots more details for you to think about, not least the front and rear suspension arrangements, the brakes and the wheels/tyres you plan. However, I feel that the bodyshell, the engine and the gearbox are the heart of the car and the starting place for your planning. We will look at the many other details as the book progresses **but I strongly recommend you read the whole book before rushing into buying parts and bashing metal about**.

Chapter 2
The Buick/Rover aluminium engines

The Buick, Oldsmobile, Pontiac and Rover (BOPR) engines all stem from the same General Motors 1960s 215in^3 (3528cc) stock and, although there have been many subsequent developments and numerous increases in capacity, they remain the engine of choice for the majority of MGB V8 conversions. For simplification, I will generally refer to the original trio of aluminium engines as 'Buick' – if only because of the Buick's original numerical superiority. Although the choice of capacities and tunes varies considerably these days, these Buick/Rover aluminium engines are undisputedly the easiest V8 to install in the MGB. We will look at the engine choices available to the converter shortly but first I think we should explore what engine bay changes are required for each of the MGB models.

ENGINE BAY CHANGES

The 1976-80 model MGBs were actually made to accept this engine, albeit with the now superseded block-hugger

exhaust manifolds/headers, without any modifications to the car at all. Today we would prefer to fit the rather stronger Rover 5-speed gearbox in preference to the original V8 4-speed/overdrive gearbox/transmission that BL used. This necessitates that a small sheet-metal extension be welded to the top of the tunnel as shown in picture 2-1-1

The cooling of water, oil and engine bay is also enhanced by your fitting RV8-style exhaust manifolds/headers – an innovation developed by Rover for the MG RV8 – instead of the block-huggers. Consequentially you'll be wise to cut a hole in, and strengthen, each inner wing/fender – but that's it! You will need to replace the radiator, change the electrics slightly and maybe add an electric fan in some locations, but there are few cars you can transform so easily. And it is a transformation, for you can fit a 3500cc/215in^3/200bhp engine (itself providing an increase in power of at least 100 per cent) or a 4600cc/282ci/300bhp Rover unit, or

2-1-1 The full details appear later in the book but you will need to weld this tunnel extension in place before a Rover gearbox can be fitted.

any specification in between – all without any increase in weight or front-to-rear balance.

The 1974-77 MGB models are almost as easy. To fit any of the Buick/Rover V8s to these cars you will need to move the radiator forward. This is best accomplished by fitting a pair of late/pre-formed radiator-mounting brackets/panels.

The 1967-75 chrome-bumper cars need all the above changes effecting along with some changes to the bulkhead/firewall

2-1-2 The heart of a huge number of Buick/ Rover V8s is this 3500cc/215in³ block. Later engines had differing ancillary fittings (the front timing cover in particular) but this casting remained virtually unchanged until the increased bore sizes generated more torque necessitating increased rigidity.

2-1-3 This 3500cc ex-Rover Defender engine uses an identical block to that seen in picture 2-1-2, but the front cover, water pump, crankshaft pulley and position of the alternator may render this engine too long to squeeze into the MGB's engine bay without changing most of the front-end ancillary components.

to allow the cylinder heads some room when fitting or removing the engine. In my first book I suggested you reshape the inner/wing – the RV8 exhaust manifold/ headers now mean that you do not have to effect that change. However, you will need to fit the later/longer steering rack/shaft and the smaller steering u/j.

1962-67 chrome-bumpered (fitted with a three-synchro gearbox) cars need the gearbox tunnel increased in height and width – and are probably best left in 1800cc form. However, if you are prepared to tackle the sheet-metalwork involved, then the car still has conversion potential.

Engine options

I outlined the history of the BOPR (which I generally refer to as Buick/Rover) engines in *How to Improve your MGB* (Veloce Publishing). The detail does not bear repeating here but the briefest of summaries may help some readers. The list of potential donor vehicles for this aluminium V8 engine is amazingly long. Many engines, indeed the majority, will have been fitted with an automatic gearbox/transmission but this need not present much of a subsequent flywheel/ clutch/gearbox problem, as we will see in a later chapter. Look, therefore, for:

Buick (Special and Skylark models), Oldsmobile (F-85, Cutlass and Jetfire models) and the Pontiac Tempest through 1961, 1962 and 1963. The normally aspirated versions gave 155-200bhp. The engines were 3500cc/215in³ generated by eight 3.5in (89mm) bores and 2.8in (71.1mm) stroke.

1967-1975 Rover P5B/P6 3500cc units. Initially with 10.5:1 compression ratio, these engines were a slight improvement over their US predecessors, in particular from 1973 when the rear crank oil seal was improved and the compression ratio dropped. A typical block from this era can be seen at 2-1-2. These units employed the ideal (narrow) front pulley arrangement for MGB conversions but the oil pump capacity, crankshaft oil seal design and cylinder head efficiency for these pre-SD1 engines is poor.

1976-1993 Rover SD1, Discovery, Defender, Sherpa models used a 3500cc/215in³ engine which had better breathing (improved cylinder head/valve arrangement) and increased oil-flow (longer oil-pump gears). (Pic 2-1-3)

1988 US Range Rover was fitted with a 3947cc variant with 94mm bores as a response to ever tightening emission

requirements. This engine capacity was standardized in the UK and other markets in 1989, and in 1993 for the Discovery. The RV8 used a fuel-injection 3947cc unit with the MG plenum chamber and oil pump base. A 4227cc engine, using a long throw crank with the 94mm bores was also available – though in somewhat limited numbers.

1995 to date Rover 4000cc and 4600cc/282in³ engines are probably the best base for an MGB conversion. My favourite would be for the smoother 4000cc engine. Although designated 4000, to differentiate it from its elder sister, this generation of engines still use the same 94mm bore as the previous generation and the smaller engine is still of 3947cc capacity. The 4600cc unit has the same 94mm bore but achieves its enlarged capacity by a longer throw crankshaft.

2-1-4 As a comparison to photograph 2-1-5 which follows, this picture shows a '4000' V8 block. In this case you will note the cross bolts are conspicuous by their absence (as is the case with all 3947cc engines).

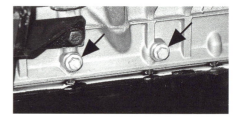

2-1-5 The 4600cc cylinder blocks have five pairs of cross bolts that go through the blocks into the side of the main bearing caps. This picture shows two in close-up. Yes, it also shows that the sump is not quite 'nipped-up' yet.

Both these engines have the advantage of a more stiffly constructed block (further stiffened on the 4600cc version by five cross-bolted main bearing caps). However, the original front timing cover had no provision for a distributor and, consequently, you will also need to acquire an earlier front cover for this engine if you buy second-hand, or specify that one be pre-fitted if you buy new. Although the engines identified by photographs 2-1-4 and 2-1-5 are now out of mainstream production by Rover, surprisingly they are still available new for as long as stocks of parts last, and we will explore that option in more detail a little later.

Like the other engines explored in later chapters, the ease with which you can acquire a used Buick/Rover engine depends to some extent upon your geographical location. There are a number of US specialists who stock a wide range of later used engines and there are still a number of the earlier engines to be found in numerous breakers' yards and at swap-meets. However, there is no doubt that the UK has the advantage when it comes to acquiring a used Rover engine.

The most frequent and easily available engine is the ex-SD1 (£40-£100 at most breakers). We are still only talking about 3500cc – nevertheless this is the route to follow for the most cost-effective way of doubling the power available to your MGB. The SD1 engine gives you an opportunity to make your converted car superior to an original BGT V8 in terms of power and reliability. The front oil seals are far superior and the daily benefit of the SD1's improved cylinder heads and oil volume should not be discounted. The original BGT V8 engine produced 137bhp with twin SU carburation and cast manifolds; the standard SD1 engine is rated at 155bhp, but this is easily increased to 175bhp with the tubular exhaust manifolds and carburation discussed in more detail in Chapter 4. No particularly special tuning is required,

therefore, to make your converted MGB and MGB GT 30 per cent more powerful than the original using a standard SD1 V8 engine, and you can easily achieve 200bhp with only relatively mild tuning. However, today the choice is very wide indeed and it might help if I summarized the standard Buick/Rover engine capacities available:

3.5-litre/215in^3 – 88.9mm/3.5in bore + 71.1mm/2.8in stroke. Where it all started.

3.9-litre/243in^3 – 94.04mm/3.7in bore + 71.1mm/2.8in stroke. A 3.5-litre crank with new, larger liners.

4.0-litre/243in^3 – 94.04mm/3.7in bore + 71.4mm/2.8in stroke. Stiffer block, cross-bolted mains, bigger bearings.

4.2-litre/258in^3 – 94.04mm/3.7in bore + 77.0mm/3.03in stroke. A stroked 3.9-litre engine.

4.6-litre/283in^3 – 94.04mm/3.7in bore + 82.0mm/3.22in stroke. Standard engine, gives approximately 200bhp and 300lb-ft torque.

An engine from an automatic-gearboxed SD1 is just as usable in your conversion as an engine with a manual gearbox. The snag being you will need to swap the flywheel/flexplate and crankshaft spigot bush on the automatic version (and buy an SD1 clutch, of course) suitable for a manual gearbox – whereupon your manual Rover gearbox will bolt straight on.

SUPPLEMENTARY COMPONENTS REQUIRED

Bearing in mind the number of V8s that were produced with an automatic or four-wheel-drive gearbox, you should not be surprised if the V8 Buick/Rover bellhousing (for a Rover 5-speed gearbox) and manual flywheel are hard to find. We will go into acquiring the bellhousing, clutch and gearbox in a later chapter. I consider the flywheel part of the engine and intend to look into procuring and lightening that component later in this chapter. However, it will not be easy to find and, in the USA, you

2-2-1 This shot shows the P5B/P6 front crank pulley and demonstrates the need for a slim, shaped, front pulley. The minimal clearance with the anti-roll/sway bar shows that a wider pulley would either necessitate moving the engine backward, or procuring a cranked RV8 anti-roll/sway bar from, say, the MGOC spares department.

2-2-2 This is how an SD1 pulley comes apart …

2-2-3 … allowing you to turn your own P5B/P6 lookalike front pulley.

may need to consider buying one from the UK or using one of the (US-made) billet-turned ones.

Today, the Discovery, Land and Range Rover models are a ready source of used, later-model engines. These have the added advantage of enlarged capacities and maybe the greatest improvement of all – stiffened cylinder-blocks. They can

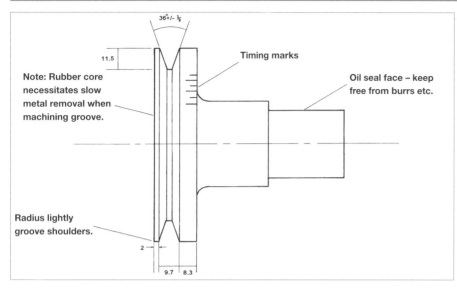

36°+/- ⅓
11.5
Timing marks
Note: Rubber core necessitates slow metal removal when machining groove.
Oil seal face – keep free from burrs etc.
Radius lightly groove shoulders.
2
9.7   8.3

D2-1 Machining detail for fanbelt groove in SD1 crankshaft pulley.

2-2-4 Later Rover front pulleys may consist of differing components but should still provide ...

present a problem in that their front covers need replacing and you will need to find a distributor or the body for a distributor. The former is no problem as Clive Wheatley (MGB V8 Conversions) is having them re-manufactured but the latter are now quite scarce and you may have to resort to a Mallory twin-points dizzy.

The front pulleys for any post-Rover P6 will be difficult to find too given their popularity in conversions and kit cars. The SD1 and later crankshaft pulleys are all too long in standard form to enable you to fit a radiator once you have the engine in place, consequently a shorter pulley is essential.

The P5B/P6 Rover pulleys seen in picture 2-2-1 are ideal but in very short supply. Consequently you may need to remove the bolts that hold the various parts of most bottom pulleys together as per the SD1 pulley shown in photo 2-2-2. Throw the front and rear sections of the assembly away but keep the cast section with a rubberised, bonded, outer circular casting (photo 2-2-3). Have this machined as per drawing D2-1 to accept a fanbelt (photo 2-2-4). Incidentally, Land Rover and Discovery pulley assemblies are even more complex as picture 2-2-5 shows.

2-2-5 ... the vital harmonic rubber-bonded balancer you need.

The shortage of P5B/P6 front pulleys and the difficulty of finding a matching set of crankshaft, alternator and water-pump pulleys (all of which need to line up if the fan/drive belt is to run consistently) may

lead you to consider bespoke/custom pulleys. As shown in picture 2-2-6, there is no disputing they enhance the appearance of any engine bay and are a necessity if you have no other way of aligning and sizing

2-2-6 A set of these aluminium billet-turned pulleys will resolve your problems and may save you from changing front timing-covers and water pumps. These wide-belt ones are made by D+D Fabrications in the USA but conventional V-belt pulleys are equally readily available and have the advantage of being narrower than wide or serpentine drive belts.

2-2-7 The P5B/P6 water pump seen here is shorter than all later derivatives. You will note that the heater water hose connects to the water pump's horizontal outlet, and thus necessitates the cranked alternator tensioning arm also shown here.

2-2-8-1 This later water pump is mounted noticeably higher on the front of the timing cover than earlier versions, and has both heater hoses connected to the rear of the timing cover which …

2-2-8-2 … allows the use of a straight alternator tensioning arm. Note the six fastenings that hold this front pulley assembly together.

the front pulleys. Incidentally, fanbelts are measured and specified via their outside circumference.

The water pump on an MGB GT is from Rover's P5B and P6 cars, and is shorter than the SD1 (and later) water pumps and is a necessity. They are readily available new or service-exchange from Clive Wheatley. The pulley for the water pump is also from P5B or P6 Rovers and these are also in short supply. A few years ago I managed to find one at a Land Rover dealer.

The alternator-mounting bracket and adjusting arm, as taken from the SD1 and later engines, are too large for most MGB V8 conversions. Most will have to replace them with P5B/P6 parts from your scrap-yard or a V8 conversion specialist. Photograph 2-2-7 shows the P5B/P6 cranked adjusting arm while later Land Rover/Discovery timing chain covers and water pumps employ a different

hose arrangement (pic 2-2-8-1) and permit/require the alternator tensioning arrangement seen in picture 2-2-8-2. You will almost certainly have to move the engine backwards to accommodate these front ancillaries

COMPRESSION RATIOS AND CYLINDER HEADS

If you are offered a V8 engine without information as to its original specification, do look at the identification plate on the left side of the engine (below the dipstick). It should have '9.35' stamped at the top if the engine is from a standard SD1 Rover. However, this can vary from 10.5 for the P5B Rover engines to little more than 8:1 if the engine has come from a Range or Land Rover vehicle, a TR8 or MGB GT V8. This number signifies the compression ratio and is the result of a combination of components – principally (assuming the cylinder head is standard/stock) the pistons

2-3-1 The Rover pistons are lightly stressed and can usually be reused. Wear a pair of stout gloves for the cleaning operation and use this picture to help you reassemble the new rings in the correct order, starting from the bottom.

2-3-2 The, to my mind, preferable steel shim gasket ...

and the material the cylinder head gasket is made from.

This is a shoehorning not a tuning book, so I am leaving tuning to the specialists, some of which you will find detailed later in the chapter. However, I must tell you that you must not machine the cylinder heads in an effort to increase the CR, you will destroy the relationship with the inlet manifold. Using differing pistons is the route to changing the engine's compression ratio. If the engine you have acquired is in good shape and has a CR of 9.35:1 it is unlikely you will have to fit new pistons. You can have the engine bored and fit new pistons, of course, but this is rarely essential. The engine is lightly stressed and, if you are on a budget, just clean everything very carefully (particularly the ring-grooves seen in photo 2-3-1) and fit new rings. It's even worth looking for another second-hand engine if it transpires your first

acquisition does need new pistons. If you are re-using the original pistons ensure your reconditioning machinist hones your bores to break the bore glaze before you reassemble the pistons/rings.

However, with so many engines having low compression ratios, you could find yours has a CR of below 9.35 – in which case you will probably wish to increase the CR and will consequently need to buy a new set of pistons. In that event, select 9.75:1 (Vitesse) pistons for, with today's fuels, it is unwise to try and increase your CR beyond 9.75:1.

Composite/shim steel gaskets affect both the engine's CR and the register of the inlet manifold to the cylinder heads too. The standard head gaskets, up until about 1994/1995, are the thin, all-metal shims seen in pictures 2-3-2 and 2-3-3. Rover, no doubt mindful of the engine's tendency for head gasket leaks, then introduced (as standard) composite and relatively thick gaskets reputed to be much more reliable. Simultaneously, Rover reduced the number of cylinder head securing bolts from 14 to 10. The composite gaskets do provide

excellent sealing properties, the trouble is that they reduce your compression ratio by about 0.7 to 1. So, for example, if you have 9.35 to 1 pistons in your engine and change from shim to composite head gaskets, you will lower the compression ratio to 8.65 and lose a corresponding degree of performance. It is not so bad if you have 10.5 pistons fitted to start with, but for lower compressions I would recommend you stay with the original steel

2-3-3 ... fitted without any sealer. Note the pistons are being reused and that their crowns have been cleaned before reassembly.

shim gaskets. I suggest you pre-coat them with an excellent sealant called Wellseal to improve the gasket's reliability and reduce the number of head fastenings you fit.

As already stated, the later blocks (4000cc and 4600cc) will not have provision for the lowest row of (four each side) cylinder head bolts so, even if you are marrying a pre-1996 cylinder head to a 4000cc or 4600cc block, you will have to omit these two lines of bolts. If you are fortunate enough to have a post-96 head, you will find this does not have the bottom row of 4 bolt holes seen in photographs 2-3-4 and 2-3-5 forcing you to omit these bolts. In fact, current thinking is that you should omit these bolts from your head-to-block assembly even if your block and head has provision for them. The 10 main bolts per head provide for a 'ring' of four cylinder bolts around each cylinder. Experts feel that the extra bottom row of bolts do little more than distort the head slightly and reduce the pressure on the head gasket at the top of the head/block interface – where the majority of head gasket leaks occur. Seek advice from your preferred V8 engine specialist, Burgess Automotive Performance (UK) or RPI if in doubt – but my advice would be to lightly slip the bottom row of four bolts into the head just to keep the dirt out. Do not torque them beyond finger-tight.

2-3-5 This photograph shows a late block with a late cylinder head which now also omits the holes for the bottom row of bolts! Note: the three (of five) cross bolts at the bottom of the picture show this to be a 4600cc engine.

The cylinder heads on the Buick and early Rover engines deserve our attention because they suffered from asthmatic performance mostly as a result of their cylinder head and valve design. The valves were too small and, along with the combustion chambers, were improved when the SD1 models were introduced. You can, of course, gain much by having your early cylinder heads reworked and gas-flowed, and RPI in the UK and D+D Fabrications in the USA will be happy to help, but the most cost effective improvement is to fit ex-SD1 cylinder heads to your early block. Better yet, of course, get the ex-SD1 heads reworked and gas-flowed similar to that shown in

2-3-6 This cylinder head has been prepared by Peter Burgess under his Ecotune system and is about to be dropped onto my MGB GT V8.

picture 2-3-6 before you fit them.

However, even the SD1 heads with their 1.57in inlet and 1.18in exhaust valves are really only suitable for engines up to 3500cc. The valves are not on the centre-line of the bore, which limits the scope to increase their size. In any event, as you increase the size of the valves over a 3500cc/215in^3 engine, you will find that the cylinder wall 'shrouds' both valves, thus limiting the value of any incremental diameter. The close proximity of the cylinder-wall-to-valve-lip can be seen in drawing D2-2, where you will note the reduction in shrouding that occurs when you increase the bore size to the 3.7in that all post-3500cc engines enjoy. This is one reason why a 3.9/4.0/4.2 or 4.6 block is much the better bet. However, getting back to the cylinder head itself, the ports are too small and the thin walls prevent your

2-3-4 This photograph shows a post-1996 V8 block with an earlier cylinder head, and is included to illustrate the omission of the bottom row of cylinder head bolts (they were not tapped into the cylinder blocks!).

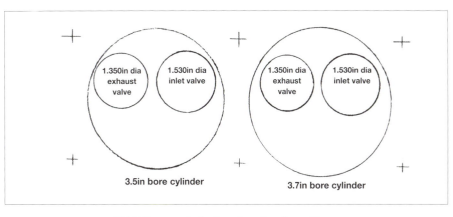

1.350in dia exhaust valve   1.530in dia inlet valve
3.5in bore cylinder

1.350in dia exhaust valve   1.530in dia inlet valve
3.7in bore cylinder

D2-2 Rover cylinder head's valve disposition.

increasing the ports sufficiently. In the USA D+D Fabrications can supply Buick 300 cylinder heads which are an improvement over the Rover SD1 heads but are really not adequate as the capacity of the engine and the gas flow-rate increases. The very latest Rover heads are a shade better and if you can find a pair of these you are starting with (almost) the best available.

Let's spend a moment looking at the 1964 Buick 300in³ aluminium cylinder heads. The 1964 aluminium heads weigh only 18.5lb each, complete with valves, springs and retainers which is ideal but they were fitted with restrictive valves of 1.625in intake and 1.313in exhaust. Thus the standard/stock 300 heads will not breathe sufficient air and fuel to keep up with the demands of the larger engines unless fitted with enlarged valves. The intake valve can be replaced with a 1.72in diameter piece from the 1988-92 Pontiac 'Iron Duke' 151in³, 4-cylinder engine (Federal Mogul P/N V2530). The 300 head's exhaust is opened up using Manley P/N 11667-4 Volkswagen 38mm (1.496in) stainless steel intake valves. The larger valves will require new seats, such as Precision PC 1500-31 (exhaust) and PC 1750-39 (intake), which any competent machine shop can easily install. The new valves and seats need a three-angle grind to help the gases follow the contour of the seats more readily while the valve-stem lengths will need reducing.

Whatever your cylinder head, I strongly recommend you have them professionally gas-flowed (ported in the US). This might cost you £750 or so – but it will be money well spent. If yours is a budget conversion, while you may not achieve the full effectiveness of professional gas-flowed heads, there are improvements you can effect at home.

You will need to buy some relatively low-cost special but simple tools which, in the UK, Peter Burgess can supply. Work carefully using a hand grinder, initially

opening both the inlet and exhaust port pockets to match the valve seat diameters. The face of the boss supporting the valve guide needs to be smoothed and shaped to minimize air flow restrictions. If you are fortunate enough to have found a pair of Buick 300 heads there is usually a pronounced lip immediately behind the valve-seat insert; this acts as a restriction that needs to be smoothed out. Remember that the head is relatively soft aluminium and it is easy to remove too much material. You want to match the edges of the insert and the port and not enlarge the port itself because this will slow down the charge velocity.

The next area for attention is the aluminium boss holding the valve guide. The step from the boss to the smaller diameter guide adversely affects a smooth flow so, with a long shank on the grinder, taper the boss gently down to the guide, being careful not to touch the guide itself.

Examine the walls of the ports behind the valves because these are sometimes excessively rough. You should not need the grinder but carefully lap-sand the walls, smoothing them and removing any flashing but not actually enlarging the ports. Many think polished walls improve gas-flow but a smooth finish is all that is required and you will spend hours bringing them up to a polished standard to no good effect. In fact, there is a school of thought that argues that a certain degree of port wall roughness is needed to keep the mixture in suspension.

The ultimate cylinder head

There is a better, if more expensive, cylinder head solution – Wildcat Engineering's bespoke casting.

I haven't explored them here as the information is widely available elsewhere, but there are now steel cranks, forged steel con-rods and forged aluminium pistons available at reasonable cost to strengthen

the bottom end; the main obstacle to extra power remains the cylinder heads. Wildcat Engineering has developed a new head casting for the Rover engine that bolts straight on and uses the same pushrod arrangement. The best fully-worked Rover race-head manages about 105cfm but in its most basic form the Wildcat heads will flow 130ft³ per minute of gas as the result of its 1.85in diameter inlet valves, 1.55in exhaust, enlarged inlet port (2.1in²) and a 1.7in² exhaust port. The Stage 2 Wildcat Cylinder Head for race-cars has flowed over 150cfm, and helps a 5-litre Rover V8 to just under 450bhp.

Therefore, at the top-end of the Rover's capacity, there is huge potential both for power and expenditure. However, an MGB V8 conversion does not have to be at the top, even the middle, of the power bands to offer great fun and exhilarating performance, so let us go to the other end of the scale and look at the improvements the early engines need to maximize their 3500cc potential.

UPGRADING THE EARLY ENGINES

By 'early engines' I mean the American GM 215 and the Rover P5B and P6 – all of which would benefit from the following upgrades before you fit the unit into your MGB.

Oil pressure/flow

These engines had low oil flow volume and pressure, consequently upgrading the oil system becomes a serious consideration, particularly in warmer parts of the USA.

Beginning with oil flow improvements, most US MGB V8 converters drill out the 215's two main oil galleys to half-inch diameter. You'll see this in progress at 2-4-1 and 2-4-2. Naturally the benefit will be reduced unless you also replace the standard 0.43in diameter oil pick-up tube with a half-inch diameter unit from a 1979-86 Buick V6. Some converters maximize the improvement by enlarging the oil pump pick-up pipe to 0.62in diameter (15mm). The vast majority increase the volume pumped by their oil-pump. The Rover SD1 achieves higher volume by using longer oil pump gears in a deeper housing than our early engines and kits are available from Kenne-Bell and others that increase the oil flow by about 40 per cent. The details depend upon the engine and kit in question, but typically, a spacer plate (seen in picture 2-4-3) is inserted between the base and the oil pump housing. This, in effect, increases the depth of the oil pump housing, whilst longer (ex-SD1) pump gears are used to match the deeper housing.

Oil pressure increases are purely a question of a stronger pressure-relief valve spring. The springs come in a variety of strengths, from 35 to 60psi, and are available from numerous specialists, including Kenne-Bell in the USA and several Rover V8 specialists (e.g. Real Steel, RPI, etc.) in the UK.

Flywheels

Chronologically we need to discuss the US Buick and Oldsmobile flywheels first. There were Pontiac 215 flywheels made in the 1960s too, but they were different

2-4-1 Opening out the two primary oil-passages in the early blocks can be done by hand but you risk scrapping the block and for the cost involved it is best to …

2-4-3 This shot is a Buick 215 timing cover with a spacer fitted between it and the oil-pump base which, in this example, is a Buick Metric pump base and a D+D Fabrications filter adapter. The spacer is about ¼in thick and must be matched with correspondingly longer than standard oil-pump gears.

2-4-2 … leave it to professionals with the appropriate equipment.

and relatively rare so we will explore just the Buick and the very similar Oldsmobile flywheel. All were manufactured from cast-iron and individually balanced before being fitted to their respective crankshafts and balanced again. GM employed two styles of manual gearbox flywheels: a light and heavy version. The light version (seen

2-4-4 The front of an Oldsmobile light flywheel. This flywheel not only offers increased acceleration but is balanced more carefully than the Buick versions via ...

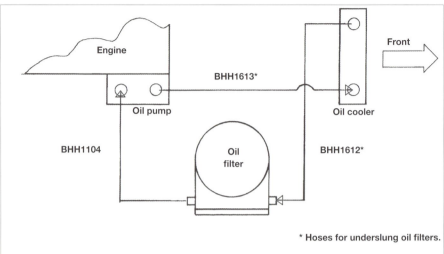

* Hoses for underslung oil filters.

D2-3 Oil circuit diagram.

2-4-5 ... an additional balancing hole drilled top left in this shot.

in photo 2-4-4) weighs in at only 23lb, is flat faced on the clutch side (pictured at 2-4-5) and would be the ideal unit for an MGB V8 conversion. The heavy version flywheel incorporated an integral cast inertia ring around its circumference which boosted the weight to 32lb. It is possible to machine the width (and some of the weight) of this inertia ring to ¼in.

There was only one version of the

Rover V8 flywheel although it does look very similar to its 2.3- and 2.6-litre sister-engine versions. The Rover V8 manual flywheel weighs 35lb in standard trim and, like the US 215 units, you are unlikely to regret having a specialist take yours down to 27lb, possibly even a pound or two lighter. But take care not to take too much off and ensure you use a specialist who knows how to take the material off in the right places.

LUBRICATION UPGRADES
Regardless of the year of your Rover engine, consider incorporating the following improvements as you rebuild or fit your Buick/Rover unit.

Oil-filters and locations
All converters have no choice but to change the oil-filter arrangement on any V8 engine they propose installing in an MGB. The reason for this is that the standard arrangement will foul on the MG's front crossmember. A remote filter housing connected by flexible pipes from the new oil-pump base (seen in photograph 2-5-1) is the solution, usually with the oil-cooler 'in series' as we see in diagram D2-3. The

detail varies slightly depending upon your location.

US converters can procure an oil pump base from a Buick 231 V6, with the word 'metric' cast into the bottom of the base (seen in photograph 2-5-2-1). The metric base bolts directly to the

2-5-1 The usual bottom half of the SD1 oil-pump needs to be replaced by this more compact but filterless base. The twin outlets are the flow and return connections for a pair of flexible hoses; the flow one feeds the remote filter and, usually, an oil cooler fitted in series with the filter.

2-5-2-1 Buick V6 metric pump base, viewed from the bottom. This provides an alternative for US V8 MGB installation.

2-5-2-2 A rotatable oil-filter mount shown on a Buick V6 oil pump base.

2-5-2-3 In this comparative view the Buick V6 oil pump base is on the left and the original Buick 215 (and Rover) base is on the right.

Buick/Olds/Rover oil pump and points the oil-filter mounting horizontally. A remote oil-filter kit with a 13/16-16in thread, such as Transdapt's (part number 1420 90), spins onto the metric pump base and has NPT female threaded ports for the inlet and outlet hoses to the remote oil-filter. If you prefer not to use a remote oil-filter, D+D Fabrications offer a special oil-filter mount which spins on to the Buick metric oil pump base (2-5-2-2 and 2-5-2-3). The oil-filter position can actually be set straight up, straight down, or in any position in between, and is certainly the simplest solution to the V8's oil pump/filter clearance problem. It could help oil pressure and flow, too, if you eliminate some fittings and the two oil hoses. Note! Horizontal or inverted oil-filters usually allow much of their contents to drain away when the car is standing, resulting in a most undesirable few seconds delay in getting oil to the engine bearings when the car starts up.

The usual V8 remote oil-filter location is normally as far forward on the right side of the engine bay as is practical, however, remember you will need to unscrew the oil-filter every 3000 miles or so. This engine is prone to build-ups of sludge probably because of its relatively low oil flow, consequently if longevity is of any interest to you, you'll need to change oil and filter with higher than normal frequency. Consequently take a little care when mounting the oil-filter near the alternator.

One proven location for the remote filter is under the wing/fender close behind the right side headlamp. This location keeps the engine bay uncluttered and probably makes oil changes easier (more on this in a moment!) although a sheet-metal guard then needs to be fabricated or the cover we see in picture 2-5-2-4 (overleaf) fitted to protect the filter from stones thrown up by the wheel.

Some converters bolt the oil-filter housing straight onto the inner wing near the alternator within the engine bay in the manner of photograph 2-5-3 (overleaf). This has merit for you do need to exert considerable pressure on an oil-filter to unscrew it and the inner wing provides a nice strong foundation for the base-casting.

I would guess however, that most converters follow the GT V8 style of oil-filter

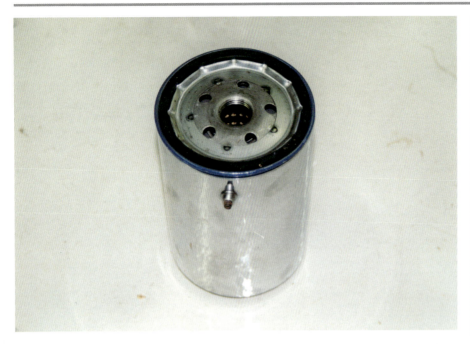

2-5-2-4 This is a chromed version of an oil-filter cover/protector. It's sold primarily for aesthetic purposes from numerous outlets but works well in a protective capacity when you fit your oil-filter under the front wing/fender.

2-5-3 The simplest mounting for a remote filter is to the inner wing/fender like this. Take care to ensure there is sufficient room between filter and wing to remove the (often stubborn) filter which ...

mounting and fit a special bracket welded to the right side inner wing shown in photo 2-5-4 and drawing D2-4. This location does require care as it is hard to get to. The size of the filter you intend to use is important: the MGB V8 unit is designated GFE 121 and, of course, fits, however, you will find there is insufficient depth to fit the slightly longer, and more easily available, Rover SD1V8 cartridge here. The outside diameter

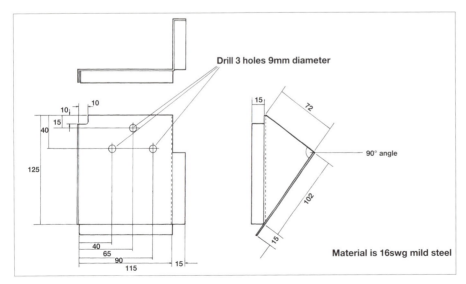

Drill 3 holes 9mm diameter

90° angle

Material is 16swg mild steel

D2-4 Oil-filter base support bracket.

2-5-4 ... the standard MGB GT V8 location probably does something to alleviate provided you use the GT-V8-length filter.

2-5-5 I found I needed to increase the rigidity of the GT V8 filter mountings I was using with this additional plate – which you will see in situ if you look closely at the preceding shot.

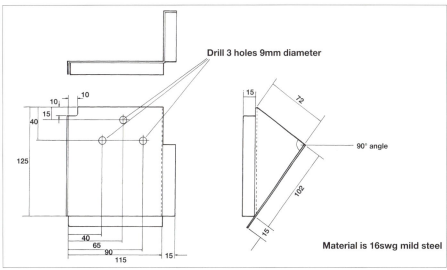

Drill 3 holes 9mm diameter

90° angle

Material is 16swg mild steel

D2-4 Oil-filter base support bracket.

2-5-6 Perhaps this simple solution is best – although I do wonder about its rigidity when removing a stubborn filter.

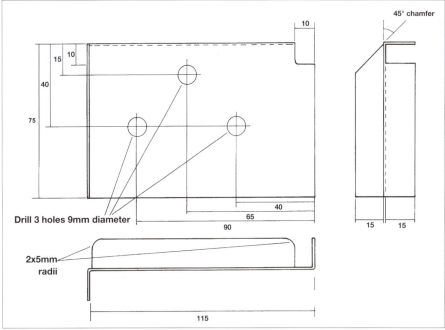

45° chamfer

Drill 3 holes 9mm diameter

2x5mm radii

D2-6 Oil-filter base support stiffening plate.

of the MGB V8 cartridge is actually larger than the filter base diameter. This is good news in one sense because one imagines they have a greater filtration area than a smaller diameter of cartridge. However, the location is confined and you need to allow sufficient space to get a filter gripping tool on the cartridge – so give yourself that little extra clearance (15mm, if possible) over the original sized oil-filter base support bracket by extending the bracket forwards. Neither the original nor replica supports are available, so you will have to make something. The accompanying drawing D2-5 gives the correct (extended) dimensions. Even in 16swg, the bracket is

not up to the job of removing a stubborn used filter. Original MGB and MGB GT V8s have the top lip of the bracket turned over and you should consider whether to add this strengthening feature. You could bolt a second flat 16swg plate 'inside' the bracket

or, better still, make up the multi-flanged additional support plate as in photograph 2-5-5 and drawing D2-6 – end of problem!

Clive Wheatley can supply a support bracket as depicted in photograph 2-5-6 (which also shows the filter base outlet

2-5-7 The typical early oil pick-up arrangement where the oil is drawn to the pump through the block through …

2-5-8 … this strainer. Note the windage tray.

2-5-9-2 … externally there are differences too with, bottom, the earlier design of sump fitted to camshaft driven oil-pumps. Note the gearbox support plate to the left of the earlier sump is omitted from the later sump.

2-5-10-1 This is an example of a front cover from a serpentine drive-belted engine. The width of the serpentine belt is going to make it difficult to shoehorn this complete engine into an MGB in spite of this cover having provision for a distributor and, in this case, even the securing stud for the distributor.

point relative to the front right side radiator mounting plate).

The 3500cc SD1, Defender et al and 3.9 Discovery engines use a camshaft-gear-driven oil pump with the sort of oil pick-up arrangement seen in photo 2-5-7. The oil is transferred via passages in the block and a pipe/strainer in the middle of the engine (pic 2-5-8). The later engines used the best oil-pump system of all the aluminium V8s – driven off the front of the crankshaft. Unfortunately, not only do these later engines have a different crankshaft but also the oil pick-up arrangements differ so you basically need the whole bottom end of a 4.0/4.2/4.6 engine to benefit from the improvement. They collect their oil via a pipe from the sump direct to the pump that is still located in the front cover but driven off the crank. There was a consequent change in sump design as seen in pics 2-5-9-1 and 2-5-9-2.

Not only do the oil pump arrangements change, so do the water pumps. The Range Rover/Defender water pump is different in detail and mounted higher up on

2-5-9-1 From inside the engine, the two types of sump. Top in this picture is the later sump with windage tray which is fitted to engines with crank-drive oil pumps while …

the front cover than say an SD1. However, provided you change the whole cover/water-pump assembly, they will fit (see 2-5-10-1 to 2-5-10-3).

Speedier return

You will increase the volume of oil over the timing chain (enhancing longevity) and reduce the amount of oil in the top-end of the engine by getting it back to the sump quicker if you drill two holes in the front of the block down into the timing chest (pic 2-5-11.)

Priming the oil pump

Follow the workshop manual's instructions regarding filling your new oil pump with Vaseline (petroleum jelly) pictured at 2-5-12-1 and 2-5-12-2 before you bolt the new base to the oil-pump housing. Without the

2-5-10-2 Here is another example that, with its provision for a dizzy, at first sight looks very promising. However, the P6 style front pulley will not fit this cover. If you are prepared to fit a cranked anti-roll/sway bar and/or fit the engine back in the engine bay and/or move the steering rack (definitely not recommended!), you could use this and the preceding front cover. However, as attractive as these covers appear, they probably need to be binned and replaced with the correct (SD1) front cover from Clive Wheatley, unless …

2-5-11 Once you have found the best front cover for your conversion, drill these holes to allow extra lubricating oil to drain into the timing chain compartment.

2-5-10-3 … you can reduce the depth of this front pulley and find a thin water pump.

petroleum jelly your oil pump will not prime and you'll be without oil pressure. Do not use any form or grease as only petroleum

2-5-12-1 At the top of this shot you can see the original oil-pump base which will prevent all Buick/Rover engines fitting in the MGB's engine bay. This is the UK replacement base with the essential petroleum jelly needed to pack the oil-pump gears …

2-5-12-2 … tight, like this.

jelly subsequently melts. Grease could clog the oilways generally and the pressure gauge take-off in particular.

The following tip may help in the event of zero oil pressure, assuming you have not blocked the oil-pressure gauge take-off with grease! The standard initial start-up procedure with any new engine is, of course, to remove the spark plugs and turn the engine over on the starter until oil pressure is established. The V8 is no exception, although there is an additional option. In fact, you may want to follow this

2-5-13 Not very startling from this view but care in fitting the sump/oil-pan is worthwhile and the thicker gasket shown here is very helpful in preventing leaks. Above all, do not over-tighten the numerous sump fastenings.

2-5-14 This is a Buick 215 sump. Its low frontal section might have been designed with MGB conversions in mind. If you have a Buick/Rover with a deeper front section the problem is easily resolved by fitting one of these slim-fronted sumps/oil-pans.

route anyway to ensure your lovely, newly-reconditioned engine gets oil right from the first turn of the starter motor. Remove the oil pipe going from the front of the oil-filter base to the cooler and, using a funnel, prime the pump by filling this pipe with engine oil. Reconnect the pipe. Remove the distributor. Cut a 3mm wide slot in a piece of 10mm diameter steel rod and fit to your electric drill. Turn the oil pump drive tang with the slotted end of your rod and electric drill until oil pressure is established, remove drill, refit distributor – and start the car.

Sumps and gaskets

Use a competition thickness sump gasket as the standard Rover gasket is too thin and oil leaks will probably result between sump and block. The considerably thicker competition gasket is available from JE Motor Engineering in Coventry and seen at 2-5-13. An alternative is to apply lots of silicone gasket/sealant – but with great care to ensure no surplus globules are allowed inside the engine.

If your Rover sump is badly distorted around the mounting bolts, place it upside down on a flat surface and tap out the worst of the imperfections.

The vast majority of Buick/Rover sumps/oil-pans have a wonderfully low frontal section to their profile as seen from picture 2-5-14 (previous page). This provides for plenty of front crossmember clearance. However, ex-Rover P5B and P6 sumps have a deeper frontal section for some reason that can cause interference problems with the MGB's front crossmember. You can modify the front of these sumps to allow adequate clearance over the MGB's front crossmember and steering rack. The best solution, though, is to pick up an SD1 sump from a breaker's yard: and, for £15 or so, is the most cost-effective remedy.

OTHER UNIVERSAL IMPROVEMENTS
Camshaft

I believe the standard SD1 camshaft is the ideal camshaft for UK applications and will give up to 200bhp without loss of torque or drivability. However, the standard 3947cc camshaft (available from RPI) is reputed to be even smoother, and good for an extra 10bhp even in 3500cc engines. A range of aftermarket alternatives are available, in addition to replacement original GM camshafts, to the US V8 converter. The shortlist for MGB V8 uses might be the Crower 50232 for manual transmissions or the Kenne-Bell KB Mark 2A. Another Kenne-Bell option is the KB 1XA with a slightly earlier power/torque curve (1000-5500 rpm). Kenne-Bell particularly recommends the 1XA with a Carter carburettor, but points out that the 2A does give superior mid-to-top-end performance.

Camshaft drive

The plastic camshaft driving/timing gear seen at 2-6-1-1 should be simultaneously upgraded to something more substantial. You may lose out slightly with respect to noise levels but, more importantly, your timing will be much more reliable and your timing chain less likely to stretch. In fact, this improvement is uniform across the range of GM and Rover V8 engines (including most of the later units) and involves fitting hardened steel gears and a double-row roller chain. Edelbrock or JP Performance Products (part number 5984) seen in photos 2-6-1-2 and 2-6-1-3 are available from RPI and both are suitable.

Transplanting EFI engines

The work required to get an injected V8 under an MGB's bonnet/hood will be explored in chapter 11 (Induction). The majority of second-hand 3947cc units will come from Range Rovers (and will probably be fitted with a Hot-wire Injection system). Be aware that such a system's ECU has a speed limiter built in at 110/112mph to cope with the vehicle's S-speed-rated tyres. You can have a specialist eliminate the problem by re-chipping the ECU (RPI or an EFI specialist can carry out this work quite cheaply). If you want a new 3947cc short engine, they are available from RPI.

Starter motor

Although slightly longer that the original MGB GT V8 starter motor (pic 2-6-2, overleaf), the normal standard SD1 Lucus 3M100PE unit is all you need. If you use a tubular (fabricated) 'Block-hugger' exhaust manifold you should just be able to get a faulty starter motor off. However, it will sit very close to the exhaust pipe and heat the exhaust generates. In this circumstance the starter motor will require a heat shield between it and the exhaust to ensure the motor performs reliably. You can make your own (photograph 2-6-3-1, overleaf) but the moulded insulating ones seen at 2-6-3-2 (overleaf) are available from Clive Wheatley. However, all such space and heat problems are eliminated if you use RV8-style exhaust manifolds/headers.

You may be better advised to fit a modern 'gear-reduction', high-torque starter motor. These dual-geared motors use less power to develop more torque

2-6-1-1 The larger sprocket drives the camshaft and on the Rover engines is made from plastic so is consequently susceptible to wear.

than the conventional starter motor – and they are much more compact too. Earlier motors all suffer interference and/or torque-generating limitations when fitted to an increased capacity engine – particularly a high-compression one. These starters are explored in more detail in chapter 13.

Anti-roll/sway bars

With a 4.6-litre engine, you'll need to allow more space between the front pulley and anti-roll bar – even to the extent of using an RV8-style cranked anti-roll as this engine moves slightly forward under breaking.

Engine mounts

The engine is mounted each side via a circular rubber flexible mount bolted to the fabrication seen at 2-6-4-1 (overleaf). Clive Wheatley's cast alternative to this fabrication can be seen at 2-6-4-2 (overleaf).

2-6-1-2 This JP Performance Products timing gear set is one of several worthwhile upgrades providing a duplex chain and hardened steel sprockets. This is a universal set and the multi-position crank sprocket needs care and some thought in order to get its position correct for the Rover engines but ...

2-6-1-3 ... once in place will provide years of hard use.

Always use RV8 flexible/rubber engine mounts, seen in place at 2-6-4-3 (overleaf). They will be more expensive than, but look very similar to, rubber-bumper 1800cc

2-6-2 The original MGB V8 starter motor, seen here on the right, was a slightly shorter unit without a front connection to its solenoid. The SD1 starter (on the left) will suit most V8 conversions even if block-hugger exhaust manifolds are to be used. Take care with later Rover starters, particularly when the solenoid is mounted on the side of the motor, because you will then find it interferes with the MGB's chassis rails.

2-6-4-2 A recent development is the availability of cast replicas of the original V8 engine mountings, shown here. Clive Wheatley also has the special flexible V8 engine mountings, shown at the top of this picture. They are made from a different, firmer, rubber compound which is more resilient to heat.

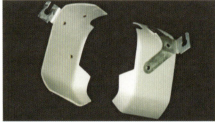

2-6-3-2 ... Clive Wheatley started having these neat moulded shields made.

2-6-3-1 As you can see a block-hugger exhaust manifold passes very close to the starter motor and, consequently, some thermal protection is essential. I fabricated this steel shield and put fibreglass insulation inside it before ...

engine mounts. However, they are made from harder rubber and are more resistant to elevated temperatures. These days the RV8 flexible rubber engine mounts vary in thickness – which may help you out of bother or, if you don't know about it, could get you into bother. One is 40mm thick while there is a 30mm one available. The thinner one is fitted to the passenger side of the engine leaving the thicker one

2-6-4-1 Cast engine mounts were not available so I fabricated this mounting and bolted it to the existing mounting holes in the block.

to provide added clearance between the driver's side exhaust manifold/header and the steering shaft. If you position your

2-6-4-3 The flexible engine mount goes here. Note the hole in the rear of the fixed engine mounting bracket where, were this a LHD car, the steering shaft would pass. Note, too, the clearance between this rubber-bumper front crossmember and the sump of the SD1 engine – no problems here.

2-7-1 Whatever the state of tune of your engine, it is important to align the exhaust ports and gasket with the manifold/header, and to smooth the interfaces between head and manifold.

engine mounts a shade too wide you could always use two 40mm flexible mounts to lift the engine slightly.

I have found further constraint unnecessary, but there are those who find an engine steady bar helps prevent the engine touching the steering shaft under hard acceleration. This will only concern those with 'Block-hugger' exhaust manifolds/headers. Often fixed to the top of the left-hand chassis rail, a rubber-bushed bar is then bolted to the front of the left-hand cylinder head. You can make your own steady bar or use an ex-Morris-Minor unit, which, with the right rubber bushes, should not transmit any noticeable engine noise to the car. As I recall, the BL Mini also used a steady bar and could, therefore, be a more recent donor/source. Be very careful to design and weld the chassis bracket in such a way that fatigue cracks are not induced and do not fasten the bracket to the inner-wing/fender – you will fatigue a hole in such thin material very quickly.

Crankcase breathers & filler

These are available as spare parts from your local Rover dealer. Check out part number ERR 3473A for your breather and ERC 247A for the filler adapter. Items screwing to the rocker covers require an

2-7-2 This is an EFI inlet manifold/track but whether it is EFI or carburettor induction you are using, the internal gas passages need to be free of casting marks ... but it is unnecessary to polish them.

O-ring/seal. Watch for and correct anything that extends through the cover and thus poses a danger of fouling the rocker gear below.

ENGINE UPGRADES

There is a lot of excellent tuning information available some of which I have suggested as further reading at the conclusion of this chapter. Nevertheless, the following tips may be interesting:

2-7-3 The good old SU carburettors were used on the original MGB GT V8 and have a undeserved reputation for poor performance. They do not, however, have an accelerator pump but can be tuned easily and provide cheap and remarkably effective induction – so, if you have a pair of HS6s, think twice before investing in expensive replacements. The air-cleaners seen here do need upgrading.

The Buick, Rover P5B and P6, and the 3500cc ex-SD1 all offer the opportunity for a low cost/great fun, moderately-powered MGB conversion. The cylinder heads are (again) the key, particularly early cylinder heads. The first thing those on restricted budgets should contemplate is to use 'mid-size' valves discussed elsewhere in some detail. JE Engineering (in the UK) offers 'Sport' or '2A' heads which, when fitted in conjunction with a JE '101' cam, will give very good performance from a 3500cc engine. Naturally some track polishing is required and the manifold(s) must be aligned with the head-ports (picture 2-7-1). If rally/track day performance is required, try JE's enlarged valve heads with a Piper 270 or 285 cam on a non-catalyst car, or a Crane 218 or Piper 270i profile if the engine has a catalytic converter.

The EFI single throttle plenum is quite adequate up to 200bhp, but the internal trumpets and the inlet manifold ports can be advantageously enlarged by gas-flow work to match the work in the heads (picture 2-7-2). Fitting a larger throttle will help top-end power where more than 200bhp is required, although this is now getting expensive for our 'low-cost' concept. You will need to ensure the injectors are capable of flowing enough fuel and raise the fuel-rail pressure (up to 3.5bar above manifold) as necessary. You will need to have the injection system adjusted/chipped to compensate for these changes, particularly if you expect reasonable idle and low speed cruise performance.

There is little point in using carburettors larger than the 1.75in (44mm) SUs (picture 2-7-3, previous) on the standard carburettor manifold. Nevertheless the standard Buick/Rover manifold can be internally ported/polished and with suitable heads, cam and carburettor tune can occasionally offer 250bhp. However, for those aiming at over

2-7-4 This dual-port Offenhauser manifold is more expensive than some competitive high performance inlet manifolds but it offers two advantages: the dual tracks help generate good low-down torque from the engine, while the carburettor sits as low as any manifold allows. Such manifolds are essential if you want maximum performance from your engine and to fit ...

2-7-5 ... a Holley, which we will see more of later in the book, or this Edelbrock aluminium four-barrel carburettor.

200bhp, a dual plane Offenhauser manifold (2-7-4) with a 390cfm Holley or 500cfm Weber (2-7-5) will work well, allowing more top-end power on the higher-tuned engines.

The standard valve train is limited to 6000rpm, so if high power outputs are required for track days (where higher engine speeds are likely), it is important to use a reinforced rocker shaft. Also applicable where higher engine speeds are to be used, are forged pistons. However, I think the value of increasing the capacity of a 3500cc engine, particularly an early one, by stroking it is dubious. Nevertheless we will explore the method under *Increasing the capacity,* but with the stiffer, later 4000cc blocks principally in mind .

MG rocker covers
Purely an aesthetic improvement, but a pair of the replica MGB GT V8 rocker covers (illustrated at 2-7-6) from Clive Wheatley V8 Conversions certainly sets the engine bay apart from the usual SD1 covers.

Increasing the capacity
There are two ways to increase the capacity of an engine – increase the length of the stroke (colloquially called "stroking) and by increasing the cylinder bores and thus the piston diameters. When starting with a 3500cc/215in^3 BOPR block (i.e. anything with 3.5in bores), you should approach capacity increases with a degree of caution and certainly avoid targeting the top-end of the capacity increments if you want longevity. You would be much better served spending your money on a block with a 3.7in cylinder bore and, if a capacity increase is still required, work from a more worthwhile base. Rover added webbing and four/cross-bolted mains bearings to later engines to counter the earlier lower-block tendency to flex at high rpm. Various engine tuners resolved the inherent weakness in the early blocks by adapting the steel girdles you see at 2-7-7 to the main bearing caps and lower end, or by incorporating special 4-bolt main bearing caps. However, the cost today of a late block, even a late full engine, is such that increasing the capacity of any of the early engines is not cost effective. If you have a later engine block, some thoughts

on modification are listed below.

You can bore your engine oversize to +0.030in, which will increase the capacity and the engine's performance – although you would be prudent to ensure that the

2-7-6 These rocker covers may be replicas, but very good ones that will really 'set-off' your engine bay.

relevant pistons are available before you commit yourself, and take a look at picture 2-7-8 before you try opening the standard/stack bores further. There are tuners who specialise in increasing the bore (much) more than 0.030in but we are moving into a different order of cost scale. Nevertheless,

2-7-7 The flexibility of the earlier Rover blocks can be reduced by fitting the main bearings with these additional steel girdles.

2-7-8 This cross-sectional view of a late 4.0-litre Rover engine will help you appreciate why you cannot overbore the cylinders by more than 0.030in, and why re-sleeving is possible but difficult and not cost-effective for the average V8 conversion.

2-7-9 This stroker kit comprises a Rover 4.0-litre block, Buick 300 head(s), Buick 300 crankshaft, a bespoke flywheel and rear crank seal, a Rover 3.5/3.9 con-rod and Ford 255 piston.

2-7-10-1 The Rover 4.0-litre crankshaft seen on the right of this shot differs quite considerably from the Buick 300 crank that necessitates ...

2-7-10-2 ... this D+D Fabrications bespoke flywheel when the Buick crank is used within a Rover block and ...

JE Engineering in the UK specialises in the following engine upgrades using only very latest (i.e. stiffened) Rover blocks:

4.5-litre (96mm bore, 77.7mm stroke)

4.6-litre (96mm bore, 79.4mm stroke) – Fast road should give 260bhp with flat torque curve peaking at 300lb-ft

5.0-litre (96mm bore, 86.3mm stroke) – Fast road should give 280bhp with a flat torque curve peaking at 328lb-ft

5.1-litre (96mm bore, 88mm stroke) – Fast road/track day spec gives 355bhp and 320lb-ft at about 5000rpm

All utilise the special 96mm cylinder bore. This requires replacement liners be fitted with a special 'top-hat' lip to prevent the liner moving in the block; this is an expensive operation even before the rest of the high-quality engine rebuild starts. However, JE Engineering gets some impressive results from its fully assembled enlarged capacity 'turnkey' engines.

D+D Fabrications in the USA has also perfected a range of increased capacity engines using a Buick 300 crankshaft, a bespoke flywheel, a Buick 300 timing cover and a variety of con-rod/piston combinations. D+D will assemble a turnkey engine for you or prepare the components for home assembly, thus reducing the cost. The kit is shown at 2-7-9 (previous). D+D Fabrications' catalogue contains very detailed options, components and assembly information. The use of a combination of differing components warrants the folllowing summary.

The finished engine weighs 340lb including flywheel and incorporates the crankshaft from a 1964-67 Buick 300 cast-iron block. This crank increases the stroke by 0.600in over a standard/stock Buick/Rover 215/3.5/3.9 crankshaft. However, the Buick 300 crankshaft (picture 2-7-10-1, previous) necessitates changes in the main bearing journal sizes and compensation for the Buick's extra length. The latter is accommodated a specially machined new flywheel (pic 2-7-10-2) designed to fit within the Rover bellhousing and align with the starter. Further, the Buick's rear oil seal location requires changing to align with the 300 crankshaft (pictures 2-7-11-1 and 2-7-11-2, overleaf).

There are numerous proven head/piston/con-rod combinations available but if the original Rover con-rods are to hand, since they are forged and therefore strong enough certainly for road-use, they will usually be re-fitted (picture 2-7-12, overleaf). There are five proven piston/con-rod combinations but 2.8 Chevy pistons provide a 10.08 CR and are a popular choice, as are Ford 255 pistons which can also be seen in picture 2-7-12.

The harmonic balancer, which goes on the front of the crankshaft, is more

2-7-11-1 ... this special rear crank oil-seal housing that ...

2-7-11-2 ... comes as part of this D+D Fabrications kit.

important than it looks and will need to be procured before balancing the engine can be finalised. It is not just the drive pulley for the fan/drive belt but damps-out harmonic cycles within the crankshaft. Since the Buick crank is employed, it is necessary to use a complementary Buick front pulley – ideally that from a Buick 300. It is important to accurately balance a stroked engine – indeed, the greater the stroke of any engine the greater the importance of the balancing operations.

There are two ways to balance the rotating parts of an engine: internally by balancing each component individually; and externally when the parts are bolted together and balanced as one. Buick/Olds/Rover 215/3.5L engines are usually internally balanced while the Buick 300 is usually externally balanced (picture 2-7-13). I favour the internal method because you

2-7-12 The Ford 255 (truck) piston is worth a closer look.

can subsequently change the clutch and/or flywheel and, provided the replacements are balanced before fitment, you should not upset the overall balance of the engine.

The mix of manufacturers is not confined to the bottom half of a stroked D+D engine. The valve springs can be upgraded by using early, small block Chevy springs. These are of the same dimensions as the 215 but yield 100lb force as opposed to the 215's 60lb.

There are literally dozens of camshaft options, Rover, Buick and aftermarket. For road/street use in the UK the standard Rover 3.9 camshaft is hard to beat while in the US the Crower 50232 offers best all-round performance. The 50232

2-7-13 Note the balancing holes in this late front pulley/harmonic damper.

carries Crower grind number of 276HDP. Advertised lift is 0.488in, with 1.6:1 rockers. 276° of intake duration and 281° of exhaust duration. Lobe separation is 112°.

The valve-train components are fairly straight forward. Use stock Buick 215 or Rover push rods and rockers, along with Crane 99849 small block Chevy springs. Hold the valves in place with stock VW (Sealed Power P/N VK204) and Pontiac (Sealed Power P/N216) keepers meshed with '87-'91 GM P/N 10040230 2.5L retainers. Either Buick 215 or Rover lifters will work.

Bolts vs studs

A normal Buick/Rover V8 engine uses bolts to fix the main bearing caps, the cylinder heads and the exhaust manifolds/headers. When increasing the stress on your engine by increasing the power it is prudent to fit new studs to both the cylinder heads and the main bearing caps. Studs are inherently better than bolts when torqueing important fastenings within an engine because you eliminate the drag of the bolt shank when pulling down the resultant (high-tensile) nut onto its stud. Consequently you get more consistency when fastening your key components to the block. Perhaps more important when it comes to an aluminium block, there will be less force applied to the block threads, which contributes to block longevity. Automotive Racing Products fastenings use material, manufacturing techniques and precision heat-treatment methods to ensure stud quality of the highest order.

The main reason for using a stud kit to secure the main bearing caps is that the standard bolted mains are not sufficiently stiff for the power now available from these engines. As unlikely as it sounds, the main caps rock to a certain extent and the standard bolts fret the threads in the block. For the £60 involved, the ARP mains cap studs seen in pictures 2-7-14-1 and 2-7-14-2 are worth the investment.

2-7-14-1 The block looks quite different with the main bearing cap studs in place but …

2-7-14-2 … perhaps not quite so unique once the main caps are bolted down.

ARP can provide a cylinder head stud kit too which includes head-washers and offers a choice of conventional hex nuts or compact 12-point nuts. Whether you use bolt or stud fastenings, provided you follow my 10 fastening recommendations explained earlier, you should not experience head gasket problems.

Exhaust stud kits are available too but I would recommend fitting 'cap-head' (allen-head) screws because in the small space available in an MGB you will find it difficult to get the manifolds/headers on and off studs for want of space and/or movement in the exhaust system.

Checking the pre-loads

When you are reassembling the top-end of a Buick/Rover, particularly when this is the final phase of a full rebuild, you do need to check the cam-follower pre-loads. This operation also needs to be carried out after fitting a new camshaft and cam-followers, a new head gasket, a replacement cylinder head, etc.

Always fit new cam followers when you replace the camshaft and **always** check the followers' pre-loads. The engine has been in production for 30 years and there are many new and re-manufactured components with differing tolerances, and the wrong combination can bring about reduced or lost compression on one or more cylinders, and/or noisy tappets and/or premature wear to the cam-lobes (which wear quickly enough already!).

Tappet pre-load is the distance between the pushrod seat in the lifter/cam-follower and the circlip. This clearance or pre-load can only be checked if the lifter/follower is on the heel of the cam and the valve is closed. The simplest way to measure the gap is by using round wire. Use a piece 0.020in for the minimum acceptable clearance check, and a piece of 0.060in for the maximum clearance check. Check all 16 lifters individually – you will see a check of one cam-follower in photograph 2-7-15.

There are various ways to adjust the pre-load on the Rover V8. To decrease clearances, use a 'rocker pedestal shim kit' to lift the rocker shaft. The kits contain a selection of shims. If the opposite applies, you will need to lower the rocker-shaft by machining the base of each rocker pedestal.

Alternatively, adjustable push-rods are available but are normally only necessary in race-spec engines. You will need to plan ahead in that they are $\frac{3}{8}$in diameter (10mm) and consequently will require the guide holes in the cylinder head to be opened out – work that obviously needs to take place before the heads are fitted to the block. When calculating pedestal height adjustments remember to take into account the rocker arm ratio of approximately 1.6:1 and make absolutely sure that any shims you fit do not block-off oil feeds.

2-7-15 Using 0.060in diameter wire for the high tolerance cam-follower pre-load check.

Engine fitting

I find the fitting of the V8 engine and Rover 5-speed gearbox easier than fitting the original MG 1800cc engines, MG gearbox and overdrive. The latter extends backwards over the B's central chassis cross-rail, whereas the Rover box is shorter and does not involve this complication.

Raise the rear of your B on a pair of ramps under the rear wheels, then apply the handbrake and chock the car so it cannot move. You should have about a 20° forward angle on the car. Assemble all rubber mountings and any shims you think appropriate to the engine and gearbox. Now sling your Rover engine and gearbox assembly so that it hangs safely from the engine hoist at about a 20° angle (gearbox lower than engine). The point of balance is about two-thirds back from the front of the engine. It's then a question of 50mm down, 50mm back, 50mm down, etc., until the gearbox is close to the floor. Jack up the gearbox, support it on wooden blocks ... and concentrate on getting the two front engine-mounting studs into their respective slots.

Offer the gearbox crossmember to the prelocated gearbox cotton reels and, with these in place, use a trolley jack to lift the gearbox crossmember (and hence gearbox) up into position. Affix four gearbox crossmember-to-chassis bolts, remove engine slings and measure-up to ensure engine position is satisfactory before applying washers, nuts, etc., to engine and gearbox-mounting studs.

ACQUIRING AN ENGINE

Rover P5B, P6 SD1 and Land/Range Rover vehicles were exported to the USA, so, whichever side of the Atlantic you are on, your local breaker may provide a used engine for your MGB V8 conversion. Naturally US 215in^3 engines are still available in the US. US sources of second-hand or rebuilt V8 engines include TS Imported Automotive, Towery Foreign Cars and the already discussed, D+D Fabrications.

In the UK, again your local breaker will be the most likely source but there are several specialist Rover breakers listed in the classic car magazines. RPI is probably the biggest source of used and reconditioned V8 engines. At the time of writing, costs of a bare reconditioned engine were as follows:

Short engines – £1450 (3500cc), £1750 (3900)

Long engines – £1950 (3500), £2350 (3900cc) They can be bought without exchanging a core unit for a modest extra charge and are exported all over the world.

The 3500cc engines can give an MGB performance that will get your attention and are certainly not to be dismissed, particularly as they have become a shade cheaper to buy since 3947cc and 4600cc

units became the preferred choice for most performance car enthusiasts. However, at the time of writing you can also buy brand new 4000cc and 4600cc Rover crate engines – either as bare short, bare full or as ready to run turnkey engines. How long this situation will continue remains to be seen but currently all are available with the stiffer blocks and, frankly, for as long as RPI's prices remain at the levels detailed below, these units make reconditioning and/or stoking engines a questionable pastime. These cross-bolted main bearing units include new block, crank, rods, pistons, rings, timing gear and camshaft, fully assembled. All are hand built and dynamically balanced, employing the latest, stronger block casting, bigger journal crankshaft, fully enclosed main bearing caps, stronger rods and rod stud fixings. The short bare engine costs £1695 ex-works while a full bare engine includes fitted heads and rocker assemblies is currently available for £2695.

New 4000cc and 4600cc fully assembled turnkey engines come complete and are fully fitted out and ready to run. Also from RPI, they are fitted with starter, wiring, alternator, 'serpentine' pulley belt system, fuel-injection system, clutch, flywheel, rocker covers, breathers, fillers, timing cover, etc. They too are hand-built and balanced and come with a 'Lifetime care warranty'. Complete engines of either capacity cost £4895 ex-works but this excludes the ECU and Air Mass-meter.

Furthermore, RPI will assemble your engine with two further stages of tune if you so wish. Stage 1 and 3 upgrades are available on all completely rebuilt engines. Stage 1 concentrates on maximising the engine's torque, efficiency and economy,

adding 10-15 per cent torque and power to the standard levels of tune. Torque-max or RP4 Cam and stage 1 gas-flowed cylinder heads are the main changes and add £600 to the basic engine building costs.

RPI's stage 3 upgrade is as per stage 1 but with more head-porting coupled to hi-flow enlarged valves, an RP285 cam (or other appropriate cam), duplex timing chain and gears, vernier timing gear on pre-1995 engines. This all adds bhp and torque to the engine and £1100 to the basic engine costs.

FURTHER READING

How to Power Tune Rover V8 Engines by Des Hammill (Veloce Publishing, 2005), *Tuning Rover V8 Engines* by David Hardcastle, *Increasing the Displacement of Buick-Olds 215 and Rover Aluminium V8s* (9 informative pages within D+D Fabrication's catalogue)

March 1985 issue of *Hot Rod* magazine. A six-page summary of the numerous combinations of components that have been used to extend the stroke and therefore the capacity of the basic 215in^3/3500cc engine to (amongst others) 245, 262, 289, 298 and 305in^3! The latter is as near 5000cc as makes no difference. To obtain a reprint send a $5.00 cheque to *Hot Rod Magazine*, Peterson Publishing Co., 8490 Sunset Blvd., Los Angeles, CA 90069 USA (213-782-2000) asking for a copy of Marlan Davis's *Affordable Aluminium V8's* article on D&D Fabrications and Baker's Auto Repair respective work, experience and specialities. The contact details for both these experts can be found in the appendix.

Chapter 3
Small-block iron V8s

OVERVIEW/ COMPARISONS

We are talking of two engines here – the Ford 302 (4956cc, referred to as 5.0L in the USA) pictured at 3-1-1 and the small block Chevy. In most cases it is the Chevy 350 (5740cc) seen in shot 3-1-2 (overleaf) that is used, although other capacity options are available. Both engines have their respective advantages and disadvantages and we will examine these over the chapter, starting with a few comparisons.

Both engines will require some engine bay bodyshell changes. In fact all the engines we are considering, including the Buick/Rover, require the provision of inner wing/fender exhaust outlets seen in picture 3-1-3 (overleaf). The Ford engine is commendably compact and consequently the engine bay alterations are identical in concept (but not necessarily in location) to those required by the Buick/Rover engines. In fact, the Ford is about the same size as the Buick/Rover and MGBs, and from 1976 models onwards the only other engine bay

3-1-1 This Ford 302 crate engine fitted with Edelbrock single-point fuel-injection system will perform superbly. However, as the chapter progresses, we will refer to a number of potential problems that can also be seen in this shot. The following will require solutions before the engine will fit: the position of the distributor, the diameter of the distributor cap, the oil-filter position, the front of the sump, the crankshaft pulley and the length of the water pump.

3-1-2 A Chevy 350 crate engine – although from the exterior, any of the Chevy small-blocks will be indistinguishable from this unit. The gearbox appears to be a Muncie 4-speed that was the transmission to have at one time, and was used extensively by drag racers. In one version, it was known as the 'rock crusher' – in part because of its strength, and in part because of its noise.

3-1-3 The advantages of this RV8-style of exhaust exit route are such that any current MGB V8 conversion will be advised to use it regardless of the engine used, even if it necessitates cutting and strengthening the inner wing/fenders. (This is a Ford 302.)

changes involve the engine mountings. A 1974-76 rubber-bumpered bodyshell would need to have the radiator mountings moved forward, as would be the case when fitting a Buick/Rover engine.

The Chevy engine is the biggest and heaviest of our three engines and consequently the only one that requires that the heater platform (and consequently the heater) be removed. Partly as a consequence of the bulkhead/firewall/heater platform changes, the Chevy also requires the greatest degree of footwell changes (this alteration is applicable to all MGB bodyshells) (picture 3-1-4). Even with this additional space there is unlikely to be room for fan/drive belt and pulleys at the front of the engine. The deck height of the Chevy block could also bring with it steering installation difficulties. However, these penalties are offset by the fact that the Chevy's sump, like the sump on a Buick/Rover, requires no alteration to the front crossmember and is therefore easier to cope with in an MGB than Ford's equivalent.

Fitting the gearbox on a Chevy is probably, on balance, the more difficult.

The distance from the back of the engine to the gear shift/lever on a Ford 302/Ford T5 is 26.5in, about the same as the 27in on a Buick/Rover/GM-T5. The Ford bellhousing is 7in deep while the GM one is 6in – the shorter length being an advantage.

Chevy engines were made by the million and, outside MGBs, are the most frequent donors for an engine swap. The interchangeably of parts within Chevy engines is very broad and also contributes to their popularity. Thus used Chevy parts, adapters and ancillaries will be the easiest and cheapest of any engine to find. Used Ford part prices are not far behind, particularly with the growing popularity of the Mustang. The relative rarity of Buick/Rover engines in the US makes finding used parts for them a bit more difficult and costly.

Iron-block Chevrolet V8s were built from 1955 to 1992 with, in standard trim, cast-iron cylinder heads. They

3-1-4 This shot will give you some idea of the extent of footwell modifications required when installing the Chevy engine. Certainly the big (Tremec TKO) gearbox planned for this very powerful Australian car will have done nothing to reduce the amount of metalwork changes, but even with a more modest T5 gearbox the changes would be considerable.

were available from the factory with displacements of 265, 283, 302 (yes, Chevy really did make a 302 for a few years in the late '60s – but few realise that now), 307,

3-1-5 Even with its substantial inlet manifold, this Australian 302 Chevy-engined conversion looks unlikely to have any bonnet interference problems. The engine develops about 485bhp at the flywheel.

there are stroker kits available for Fords. This increases cost by about $1500 and capacity by 45in[3] (to 347in[3] or 5695cc).

One final point of comparison – the Chevy's distributor is at the back of the engine – more or less at the point of greatest headroom within the MGB's engine bay and presents no problem, as seen in picture 3-1-5. The Ford's dizzy is right at the front of the engine bay, as seen in picture 3-1-6, just where the bonnet/hood is starting to reduce in height. However, as picture 3-1-7 shows, the problem is not by any means insurmountable.

3-1-6 There is no question that the Ford's dizzy appears to be right where you don't want it – at the front of the engine and therefore posing a potential bonnet-closing problem. However ...

3-1-7 ... this is a chrome-bumper radiator diaphragm temporarily replaced in order to help us gauge the extent of our bonnet-closing difficulty. Sharp eyes may just spot the very tip of the dizzy cap showing over the top of the diaphragm and obviously the high-tension leads have yet to be fitted, but if an MGB bonnet will not close, an MGC one certainly will.

327, and 350in[3]. They can be taken up to 400in[3] but the engine weights are virtually the same, regardless of displacement. They came in a variety of guises including, from 1985, throttle-body and the highly desirable multi-point fuel-injection. 1992 saw the introduction of the LT1 generation of engines with their essential aluminium heads. The cooling was improved by reversing the coolant flow and they were fitted with electronic management controls. A redesigned Corvette came out in 1997 to coincide with a new design of engine featuring an aluminium block – but few MGBs will be fitted with this version for a while yet.

Particularly for US converters, availability of both engines is superb. The Ford began life in 1961 as a 221in[3] engine for use in the Fairlane. It was almost immediately increased to 260in[3] and, in this form, was the original engine used by Carroll Shelby for the Cobra. The 289in[3] followed soon after and became the engine of legend in the Shelby Cobra. The

302in[3] was introduced in 1968. Needless to say. Ford introduced numerous detailed improvements to the 302 over the years, but the engine has stayed basically the same as its 1968 version. Consequently, parts from one engine will usually fit most other 302 engines. The more significant changes were in 1980 – balance weights on the flywheel changed necessitating matching the crank damper and flywheel to your particular engine. 1984 saw throttle body fuel-injection introduced while the cam was changed for hydraulic roller operation in 1986. 1988 saw the volumetric multi-point EFI introduced, although the next year this was upgraded to the preferred mass-metering air flow measurement.

There is no doubt that a Ford powered MGB will be great fun to drive – the engine regularly gives 300/320/350bhp, with 375bhp available if you want it. So you do not have to go to the Chevy's larger capacity if it's performance you need. If you have some sort of 'cubes' hang up,

The last comparison I want to make is that of the differing firing orders – if you think the firing order for all V8 engines is the same you will find drawing D3 invaluable, as Ford use a different order to Rover and Chevy.

3-2-1), the overall length of the Chevy ensures there is no room in the MGB's engine bay for the water pump or any drive belts. Consequently you have no choice but to use an electric water pump and some have found it necessary to fit

this frontal extension down to the 5.32in we see in 3-2-2 and 3-2-3.

3-2-2 Not only has this Ford 302's engine bay required less surgery at the firewall end, but you can fit a conventional water pump and drive belt system at the front. Admittedly the water pump is a Ford Motorsport short version and the pulleys are billet turned specials – but they do go in where they are supposed to.

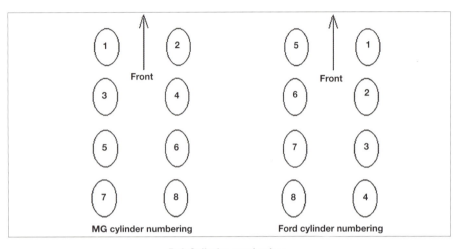

D-3 Cylinder numbering.

WILL IT FIT?

The 26in length (crank front pulley to the face of the bellhousing) of the Chevy engine makes for a very tight squeeze in the MGB when the length of the water pump and pulley are added. Even with the MGB's heater platform removed (picture

the alternator under the car and to drive it off the propshaft. What would happen if you were to have a bespoke/custom short water-pump made up I do not know – but it might be worth enquiring of Margus Auto Electrical (Los Angeles) how short a water pump can be fabricated.

The overall length of the Ford engine, from the bellhousing-mounting surface to the front tip of the water pump, is 29.75in – just a shade longer than the Buick/Rover. Consequently, you will likely find the standard Ford crankshaft pulley comes very close to the back of the radiator. However, this would also occur if you tried dropping a Rover SD1 engine and front pulley into your MGB. With both the Ford and Rover engines you need to pre-fit narrower pulleys and a shorter water pump – whereupon their respective lengths are manageable. The short Rover pulley is available from the P6 Rovers. Ford and aftermarket short-nosed water pumps and aftermarket thin (billet-turned) pulleys keep

The Ford engine is slightly smaller externally than the Buick/Rover – not enough to provide a significant advantage, but enough so that if there's room for the Buick/Rover, there will be enough room for the Ford. To be a little more specific, the maximum engine width, excluding exhaust manifolds, is 19.25in. Since the tops of the valve covers extend beyond the mounting flange for the exhaust, the width for the exhaust flanges will be less than the overall width of the engine.

Height depends on the choice of sump, inlet-manifold, carburettor and air-cleaner. The Ford is 20in from the centre of the crankshaft to the top of a typical aftermarket air cleaner. Below the crank we need to add the depth of the sump/oil pan, depending on which one you use. The best option is the dual sump that adds 7.5in, thus, at the rear of the engine, the Ford's total depth is 27.5in. These dimension could vary by as much as -2in/+7in or more, depending on your choice of intake, carburettor and air cleaner. A high-rise intake with a circle track air filter might

3-2-1 Nearly ready for its 302 Chevy engine, you will note that this engine bay has lost most of its heater platform, and that the footwells are widened to the extent that the steering column now enters the cockpit on the corner of the footwell. Note the Chevy engine mounts, too.

3-2-3 These thinner Ford front pulleys are off-the-shelf Ford racing pulleys (part number M-8509-Q) and are made for the short neck water pump (part number M-8501-E351S) we see here. D+D Fabrications and March also do a range of billet-turned aluminium crank, water-pump and alternator pulleys.

add as much as 10-12in. Interestingly, the height of the air cleaner mounting flange on the Edelbrock EFI set-up is the same height as the flange on an Edelbrock carburettor/ intake set-up, so the clearance will be the same.

The Chevy engine is 17.7in from the centre of the crankshaft to the top of its distributor which, apart from its air-cleaner, is the highest part of the engine. Below the crank we need to add the depth of the sump/oil pan – only about 3.6in at the front and no more than 4.5in as far back as the centre of the engine. Even at the rear, the Chevy sump/oil pan only extends 7.5in below the crankshaft centreline – making the sump perfect for an MGB. Total depth is therefore going to take up only slightly over 25in. Width across the Chevy's rocker-covers is 20in and will not pose a problem, either, although the exhaust manifold/ headers will extend this to circa 24in.

THE WEIGHT ISSUE

The Ford is the easier of these two engines to shoehorn into the MGB bodyshell, which is possibly why about twice as many Fords are fitted to MGB V8 conversions as Chevys. However, there are other factors to consider. The Chevy engine is, in my opinion, too heavy to fit in an MGB unless you have aluminium heads fitted. Even then its weight is questionable and could generate undesirable handling characteristics as the result of excessive weight on the front wheels.

However, the Ford too must be fitted with alloy heads for both its optimum performance but more particularly to reduce its overall weight. Standard/stock engines are made from cast-iron and, I believe, too heavy to be suitable for an MGB. Even when fitted with alloy heads a complete 302, with aluminium heads, intake, water pump, a lightweight starter

and a 27lb flywheel will still weigh about 435lb – some 40lb more than the original 4-cylinder engine. A T5 transmission helps reduce the excess because it weighs 50lb less than the original MGB overdrive/ gearbox/ transmission, although this welcome reduction comes from the middle of the car.

The resultant overall weight of the car will be about 2250/2350lb – an increment of 25/100lb over a standard MGB. With 5000cc/302in^3 available, this incremental weight is not going to affect the car's acceleration but you could bear it in mind when considering your braking and, possibly, your handling. Typically a Ford-engined MGB will substitute the original ideal 50:50 front to back weight balance for something between 54:46 to 53:47 ratios while a Chevy engined car will be more likely to be in the order of 55:45 front-end heavy.

In my view a 55:45 front/rear ratio is not unmanageable, although I think it is best corrected as far as possible by weight reductions. A TR6 has 55:45 front/rear balance in standard trim and superb handling characteristics. However a TR6 has a totally different suspension arrangement to an MGB. The MGB suspension is more comparable to the MGC's – that failed because of its poor handling characteristics brought about by its front/rear balance of roughly 55:45. I also believe that the MGC's rear-spring defects played a part in its downfall. The compromise is perhaps to think that this front/rear balance maybe just acceptable in a chrome-bumpered car with its lower ride height. However, you may need to think seriously about the consequential handling in a standard/stock rubber-bumpered car with its higher ride height and inferior handling even with its 50:50 balance.

There again, in the intervening years we have learnt a thing or two about MGB suspensions and anti-tramp bars in particular. Chapter 8 explores some improvements that, had BL introduced them to the MGC, may have prolonged its life. Additionally you can reduce the front-end weight of both cars by over 100lb by fitting an aluminium radiator in place of a brass one, an aluminium bonnet/hood (standard/stock on early MGBs) and one of Fast Cars Inc's lighter (by 80lb) bespoke front suspension set-ups (covered in more detail shortly).

Then there is the small consideration of the type of roads you expect to drive upon. In the UK, many of the roads are continually twisting and consequently offer minimal forward vision yet are bogged down with nose-to-tail traffic density. Thus a road car with very rapid acceleration, deceleration and superb handling characteristics not only makes for fun driving but (more) rapid progress through congestion than a lower-powered car, particularly one that does not inspire confidence through its sure-footed agility. The wider, straighter roads I experienced in the USA put less emphasis on the handling characteristics of a car and maybe account for our differing emphasis on suspension designs.

CREATING THE FORD SUMP/CROSSMEMBER CLEARANCE

As I have already intimated, the Chevy presents no sump/oil-pan/crossmember interference problems. However the Ford sump/oil-pan will necessitate some alterations to both the Ford sump and the MGB crossmember if the engine is going to fit within the MGB's engine bay.

The sump(s)

Three Ford sumps are available and we first need to select the best one of the three in order to minimise the depth of the Ford sump in two critical areas – at the front where the sump needs to clear the crossmember, and centrally to provide

adequate ground clearance. In all Ford engines the oil-pump sticks straight down into the front of the oil-pan. Most engines have the pick-up attached directly to the bottom of the pump and consequently the major depth of the sump is at the front of the engine – just where you do not need it for an MGB conversion. There is little you can do to reduce the overall engine depth of a front-sump engine and, consequently, engines with a front sump (seen in photograph 3-1-1) will need both the sump and oil pick-up replacing.

Fortunately there are two alternative oil pan designs available – rear sump and dual sump. Logic says you need the rear sump design of oil pan for an MGB conversion and indeed this has the shallowest front depth of any Ford oil-pan. It also has the all important rear mounted oil pick-up point. This pan can be seen in picture 3-3-1 and was standard/stock on 302 vans, 4x4 Broncos and pick-ups and

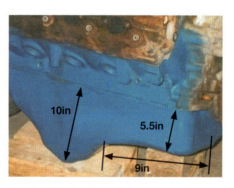

3-3-1 This is the initially attractive rear sump/oil-pan which becomes less attractive when you appreciate that the 10in deep sector may prevent you dropping the engine as far into the engine bay as you could if you were using ...

10in

5.5in

9in

would seem best suited to a MGB Ford V8 conversion. However, even with this sump the front will still cause problems with MGB conversions because the pump body still requires a significant depth at the front of the sump and will necessitate modifications to (or a change of) MGB front

3-3-2 ... a modified dual sump. From its description you will appreciate that the sump in the foreground is the original dual unit, while the one at the back of this shot has been modified ...

3-3-3 ... by cutting out the centre of the dual-sump oil pan. A cardboard template was formed and transferred to a piece of sheet-metal. The metal was then hand-shaped to get it to conform to the pan, and then welded in place.

crossmember. Nevertheless the depth of the front of the sump may be immaterial because of the very deep rear section of this 'rear' sump. With the engine fully dropped into the engine bay, the rear sump will almost certainly sit too close to the ground for comfort, and if there is one part of a car you do not want to leave behind when you go over a stone, curb or hump it is the oil-pan/sump.

So what of the third option – the dual sump – does that offer any advantages? Two in fact – its oil pick-up is located at the rear of the engine while its main sump is 2.5in shallower than the rear sump design. However, these pans are ¾in higher at the

3-3-4 It was finally painted so that the changes do not look at all out of place.

you are with your Ford sump acquisition/ modifications, the MGB's crossmember still needs to be cut down to allow the Ford engine to sit fully into the engine bay. A notch needs to be cut out of the middle of the crossmember and, with a Ford sump being 9.5in wide, the slot seen in photo 3-3-5 will need to be at least 11in wide. Furthermore the notch might extend so

3-3-5 This picture shows the sort of change that is essential to an original MGB front crossmember. There is more detail in chapter 7 but I would recommend you assign this modification to an accomplished fabricator/welder, and also suggest you refrain from jacking up the car at the centre of a modified crossmember.

front of the sump and also have a notch built into them. For most V8 conversions the notch is a complication you ideally want to avoid but in fact the advantages of the dual sump outweigh the notch problem. In fact, some would say the notch is no problem and ignore it. They may regret that each time it comes time to change the lubrication oil as the front drain plug will be inaccessible.

However, you get the best sump of all if you are prepared to have a dual sump modified as shown in pictures 3-3-2 to 3-3-4. This arrangement lowers the front as far as the pump allows while simultaneously removing the central hump. The front drain plug needs to be tightened and welded in place to simplify oil changes. Furthermore, these modifications will slightly increase the engine's oil-capacity to advantage. Surprisingly therefore this makes the dual-sump Ford engine your preference – provided you are comfortable with having it modified. If you want to avoid a sump modification, go for a rear-sump

engine but do not overlook any dual sumps you come across in the mean time for you may well change your mind when you see the engine in the car.

So what dimensions are involved? The measurements are, in effect, from the centre-line of the crankshaft. Read the Sump Dimensions table below in conjunction with pictures 3-3-1 and 3-3-3.

The front crossmember

The Chevy engines, like the Buick/Rover power plants, have an ideally shaped sump that causes no interference problems with the MGB front suspension crossmember. However, regardless of how successful

far down that only 2in depth is left across the bottom of the original crossmember. Consequently it is **essential** that you weld a substantial inverted U-channel to the inside of the crossmember before welding a new top cover in place and plug-welding through the top cover to the U-channel.

However there is an alternative solution to the crossmember interference problem. Fast Cars Inc has developed a custom front suspension design for the

Sump dimensions		
Sump design	Depth at front	Maximum depth
Rear	5.5in	Starts after 9in and reaches a max of 10in
Dual	6.3in	Starts after 13in and reaches a max of 7.5in

MGB. This not only works well from a handling point of view but is 80lb lighter and has also been designed to allow the Ford sump to be fitted without interference problems. The steering is lighter, ride height is easy to adjust and camber/caster are adjustable too. This would be my preferred solution to the Ford engine's sump/front-weight/crossmember problems.

Photograph 3-3-6 neatly shows the end result of a very well modified rubber-bumper front crossmember and an equally well modified dual-sump. The picture also shows that the Explorer's serpentine drive belt and pulleys allow space for what I would regard as an obligatory anti-roll/sway bar.

expensive than the Chevy but cheaper than a Rover and with good bargaining skills you might be able to pick up a good used bare engine for under $200. However, budget for the overall cost to at least double as you acquire the numerous ancillaries needed, although they are in plentiful supply. Even if your bargaining skills are less practised you still should be able to buy a good late model engine, complete with all ancillaries including fuel-injection for under $1500. However, not all the ancillaries nor the sump fitted to your used engine may be useful and thus there is bound to be some further expenditure before the engine can be fired up in the car.

If you want to fit a new engine in

3-4-1 Unless you have access to sophisticated mandrel tube-bending equipment your only route to exhaust manifold/headers is to subcontract them to specialists or, as seen here, to fabricate them yourself.

manifold, 8in crank/torsional damper and cast-iron water pump. This sort of purchase provides 355bhp @ 5250rpm with torque peaking at 3500rpm @ 405lb-ft – but for MGB applications, the water pump will be discarded in favour of an electric one. You will still need some of the ancillaries listed below for a Ford engine, so prepare your budget accordingly.

There is a great deal to be said for the Ford 302 crate engine too. The Ford Motor Company sells eight different 302/5000cc crate engines – four with the essential aluminium cylinder heads. All aluminium headed engines retail for $3195 and should produce circa 350bhp while torque varies from 300 to over 360lb-ft. When ordering you must get the sump and oil pick-up details correct and will still need to budget for **all** the ancillaries, which might include: Edelbrock Performer EDL-2121 intake manifold; Edelbrock 600CFMEDL-1405 carburettor; Edelbrock EDL1207 air cleaner; GM7127 alternator; Ford lightweight, hi-torque starter M-11000-A50; Accel ACC-71202E distributor; Ford clutch M-7560-A302; clutch slave cylinder; and Ford motorsport (short) water pump M-8501-E351S for V-belts.

The Ford ancillary costs can run the total up to around $4500, making the Ford a shade more expensive in total. However,

3-3-6 Lovely job, Larry Shimp – thanks for sharing it with us.

COST CONSIDERATIONS

Costs are extremely variable and much depends upon your geographical location. Obviously the USA is the place to be for the best deals – if only because there will be some sort of useable Ford 302 in almost every breaker. Compared to the two alternative engines we are studying, the Ford probably falls in the middle of the trio – at least in the USA. It will be more

your car (and who wouldn't?) and you are based in the USA you are spoilt for choice. I counted eight variants from one supplier alone but a typical Chevy crate engine is available for $4000 and comes with a cast-iron block and four bolt mains, the essential aluminium cylinder heads and 10:1 compression ratio. It will have some ancillary equipment fitted including a distributor, dual plane aluminium intake

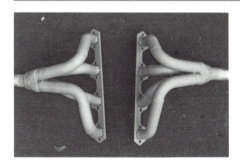

3-4-2 Designs differed in detail but pretty much all Ford and Chevy manifolds/headers used the 'through the inner wing/fender' exit route that proved so successful for the MGR V8 production run. These headers look as if they have been 'jet-coated' – a process we will explore in chapter 11.

Ford users will need to give consideration to V-belt pulleys. Either you will have to use those that came with the MGB, buy used Ford ones or go for a set of billet-turned custom pulleys.

Another custom part to consider is the exhaust manifold/headers. Up until recently you would have had to fabricate your own manifolds (picture 3-4-1), difficult for anyone without the essential tube bending equipment. Ford 302 'through the fender' manifolds/headers (similar to the RV8 design and seen at 3-4-2) have recently been put into production by Coyote Conversions. Initially only in mild steel, they should also be available in stainless by the

homemade or comissioned from a bespoke exhaust fabrication specialist with the inevitable consequential cost.

The alternator securing brackets seen in picture 3-4-3 will have to be fabricated or adapted from scrapyard finds – but they should not prove too difficult nor costly for most readers.

SOME FITTING DETAILS

● Looking at the more popular Ford engine mountings, note that mounting points on the engine block are not symmetrical – on the left side they are set back by $7/8$in from the holes on the right side. I understand that all 289-302 engines have the same offset, but you should measure yours to be sure. You also need to get the rear of the engine the correct distance from the MGB's firewall. To achieve this the holes in the chassis mounting bracket holes need to be positioned 18in in front of the firewall/bulkhead (or back of the heater), also shown in picture 3-4-4. This should position the rear of the engine block 5.5in from the firewall.

● The Ford flexible rubber mountings can

3-4-3 The detail will vary with the alternator you choose and with where you choose to locate it; here, Pete Mantell has wisely elected to fit the alternator in front of the left cylinder head. His three-point mounting arms are well displayed in this shot ...

3-4-4 ... while these are his chassis engine mounts for the Ford that looks about ready to drop in. Note the well located MSD ignition system, minimal changes to the bulkhead but the, currently, very large apertures for the exhaust manifold/headers.

all of the above parts are available at discount prices and some parts can be bought second-hand – which might be a good idea as there are also some custom parts to acquire and cost.

time this book is published. However, the volume for MGB/Chevy headers is unlikely to make it worthwhile for a fabricator to make even small production volumes thus Chevy headers would either have to be

be viewed at 3-4-5 to 3-4-7 (overleaf). They usually fit but if not consider Caterham 7

3-4-5 The Ford flexible engine mountings will fit the 45° mounting bracket seen in the preceding picture providing ...

3-4-6 ... you get them the right way round. It is not an illusion – the right side 'leg' of this mounting is longer than the left leg in order to counteract Ford fitting the block mounting positions asymmetrically.

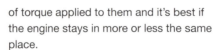

3-4-7 Here we see the right side Ford flexible mounting in place on Pete's plastic engine block awaiting a trial fitting. They are Pioneer Inc Automotive Products part numbers 602220 (left side) and 602221 right side.

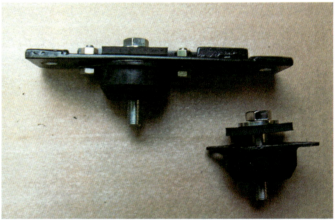

3-4-8 Caterham engine mounts require a different chassis mounting bracket but are only about 2in (50mm) in diameter. They are meant for heavy-duty racing use so have an internal stop to prevent separation and a bolt hole all the way through the rubber mounting.

mounts pictured in 3-4-8. I also understand that Chevy S-10 truck mounts are 2in (50mm) diameter with studs on both ends and should fit – although you do need to ensure they are strong enough for your application. Ensure too that your whole engine mounting installation is made from adequately thick material and that it is gusseted to guard against fatigue stresses and fractures. There is going to be a lot of torque applied to them and it's best if the engine stays in more or less the same place.

● There are various specially fabricated front crossmembers available (discussed in detail in Chapter 7) which will do nicely too, but as a minimum, with either of these engines, you are best using a rubber-bumper front suspension crossmember and, if yours is a chrome-bumpered car, lowered, front, road springs. The position of the steering rack on this readily available crossmember provides for minimum interference problems.

● One detail that will be of great benefit to Ford users is that, to ease fitting, P-AYR makes a plastic replica engine block. This accurate, full-size block comes with threaded metal inserts to allow all accessories to be bolted in position.

These blocks can be bought at a discount on eBay and then sold again when you are finished and will meanwhile prove invaluable as you carry out your initial bespoke engine bay alterations.

● Post-1985 Fords come with factory-installed roller cam. However, with these engines it is imperative that you use either a bronze or a special steel distributor drive gear on the distributor. Use a standard cast-iron distributor gear and both the distributor gear and the cam gear will be destroyed very quickly. However, some aftermarket roller cams are made of a different alloy to the factory cams and can use any distributor gear – check with the cam manufacturer as to which dizzy-drive gear to use.

● The V-belt system seen at 3-5-1 and 3-5-2 usually takes up less space than a serpentine belt and, consequently, is often the preferred route if only to allow fitting a front anti-roll/sway bar. Nevertheless, do note that the water pump for a serpentine belt drive system rotates in the opposite direction to that of a V-belt installation. Stock and aftermarket pumps are available

for both types of belt but ensure you are fitting the correct pump for the belt drive system you are using as the pumps rotate in different directions.

● The Explorer front cover with its short reverse rotation serpentine belt drive (seen in picture 3-5-3 and 3-5-4) also allows a front anti-roll/sway bar and is available as a kit from Ford (#M-8501-A50). It comes as standard on all Ford high-performance crate engines but if you've bought a used engine it will be cheaper to get it off of an Explorer in a scrap yard. This does have another advantage – it allows the use of an Explorer front pulley/harmonic damper. Unlike most Ford front pulleys, this one is part of the Explorer damper, but no other damper/pulley combination is short enough for this MGB application. The toothed sensor ring on the Explorer damper can be removed (it is only a press fit) to increase the steering rack clearance, but this may not be necessary in many installations.

● Any Ford front cover/water pump assembly will fit on any engine but 289 and smaller engines have a 28oz counterweight in the front damper, while 302 and larger

3-5-2 ... although the anti-roll bar is still not present, I thought this front-on shot interesting both from a drive pulley point of view, and when I tell you that this is a plastic engine block.

3-5-3 This shot of an Explorer serpentine drive belt is no less informative – this time with the roll/sway bar in place.

3-5-1 Although we don't see the anti-roll/sway bar in this shot, nevertheless it is clear that you cannot move the drive belt much closer to the engine than these V-pulleys permit and ...

3-5-4 Here is another take on the serpentine drive belt system.

engines have a 50oz counterweight. Thus, the Explorer damper/front cover/water pump cannot be used on a 289 engine.

● Before you settle on your Ford engine position and weld the engine mounting brackets in place on the chassis rails, do try the radiator in place (not applicable to Chevy engines). This is to ensure there is sufficient clearance between engine and radiator for whatever fan, be it fixed or electric, you plan. We will look into fans in more detail later but remember that a shrouded puller fan (fitted between the radiator and engine) is the preferred option and that to fit such a fan a thin water pump will be essential. Rather than buying a new fan, it should be possible to find one in a scrap yard, although you are looking for a powerful, shrouded yet thin unit.

● A Chevy engine in an MGB will leave insufficient space for a mechanical water pump and a drive belt system. This removes one problem but poses others – where to put the alternator and how to fit an electric water pump? Picture 3-5-5 is, perhaps, the answer.

● Ford uses a cable to operate the clutch

3-5-5 This is Paul Knott's Chevy powered 'B, showing his alternator driven off the prop shaft.

but there is insufficient space between bellhousing and chassis rails in an MGB to accommodate the cable mechanism while significant changes to the MGB pedal and master-cylinder would also be required. Two proven solutions are explored

3-5-6 Autoworks International's solution to activating the clutch on a Ford or Chevy engined T5 gearbox looks very neat and effective to me.

in Chapter 4 but picture 3-5-6 shows a superb solution with an external slave cylinder.

● If you need to buy a gearbox separately from the engine, note that you need the appropriate T5 (assuming this is what you're going for) gearbox. The Ford T5 was slightly different in detail to the Chevy T5. In particular the gearbox is designed to go in at a 5° left-side down angle. On the garage floor the gearbox-mounting pad **appears** to be positioned at a right-side down angle

3-5-7 Obviously this is not in an MGB, but you can see this Ford T5's 5° lean towards the left of the car.

3-5-8 The oil-filter on the far side of this Ford will clearly foul the MGB chassis rails. In fact it is a tight fit …

but ends up horizontal once engine and gearbox are in the car – as you can see in picture 3-5-7. The Chevy requires an 18° inclined mounting pad and thus a GM T5 behind a Ford engine makes for a more difficult installation.

● As picture 3-5-8 shows, the Ford 302 oil-filter sticks out from the left side of the engine and will be a problem when the engine is relocated in an MGB. Consequently, a remote oil-filter is required. Its position and importance is made clear in pictures 3-5-9 to 3-5-11.

● On the subject of remote oil-filters, remember that the Ford remote take-off does not incorporate a filter bypass valve to prevent the inevitable pressure drop that occurs with a clogged filter. The Rover pump base incorporates a relief-valve that allows oil to go around the filter if you allow the filter to become clogged. However, neither the Ford lubrication system nor the remote take-off contain a filter bypass valve. Consequently, for Ford remote filters you need to specify a bypass cartridge when buying new oil-filters. If in doubt as to the filter type, the valve in the bypass filter can be seen at the bottom by looking down through the central mounting hole.

● The oil dipstick on transplanted Ford engines can cause a disproportionate amount of problems. Early Ford engines were all front sump design and the dipstick was inserted in the front cover. Obviously,

3-5-9 … even with a Trans-Dapt #1413 adapter in place. Some adjustment to the engine position or the chassis rail will be required. This engine was moved about 1 inch to the right while …

3-5-11 … here. Note the filter location on the left inner wing. The parts are available separately (in which case note that it uses ½NPT tapered pipe threads) or in a kit with a filter holder and hoses (seen here too). This shot is also valuable as it shows the chassis mounts for Caterham flexibles and the line of the steering shaft. This is a rubber-bumper, front crossmember rack and, consequently, smaller rubber-bumper steering u/j. The inner wings have been opened out for the RV8-style exhaust manifold/headers for the Ford that will shortly fill this space.

3-5-10 … this engine was kept central and the chassis rail bent slightly away from the engine as we see …

this will not work with a rear sump engine. Early rear sump engines had the dipstick mounted on the oil sump pan itself. Later engines all have a dipstick hole towards the rear of the block as seen at 3-5-12. This hole is blocked off on front sump engines. If you build your engine, fit a Lokar flexible dipstick – also on view in picture 3-5-12. However, if buying a crate engine, it will have a dipstick boss in the block, and will generally only fit a Ford dipstick tube. Unfortunately, this tube is too long and will have to be cut. The dipstick itself will also have to be cut and new oil level lines marked on it. Be sure that the tube is not too long or it may be impossible to install the manifolds/headers.

● The alternator on a Ford engine is usually mounted on the right side. However, the left cylinder head is mounted slightly to the rear of the right side, so there is slightly more space available if you mount your alternator on the left side of the engine (picture 3-5-13).

● For V8 conversions where there is minimal under-bonnet clearance, the engine-steady seen in 3-6-14 may help.

● If rebuilding your own Ford, choose the camshaft with care. There are many options but XE (Xtreme Energy) Comp Cams XE264HR comes highly recommended. It is mild yet capable of producing 384bhp at 6000rpm with the appropriate supplementary equipment. It also has a

3-5-12 The dipstick position tells us that this is a later rear-sump Ford. The picture also shows a Lokar flexible dipstick and an oil-filter adapter plate on the side of the engine.

3-5-14 This is an ex-Morris Minor anti-torque restraint you may find helpful. I have not found this necessary with my modest 3500cc conversions, but obviously as engine capacity increases so does the torque and so may the engine twist that that torque induces.

3-5-13 We have seen the alternator mounted on both sides of the engine bay but this is the preferred location. Note the twin 10in Summit Racing fans (part number SUM-G4910) rated at 850 CFM each, and the excellent coolant access/sealer cap located in the top hose of this Ford. Almost every V8 conversion suffers from airlocks in the top hose and this is an excellent solution as the cap can seal the opening.

useful power range that begins at 1500rpm, that I think is very important. It takes full advantage of roller cam technology and gives a smooth idle and good low speed response. Duration is 264° intake and 270° exhaust.

● Give some thought to the flywheel, particularly if the one you are planning to use is of advancing years – they have been know to explode. A new flywheel is the safe option because, even with a rev limiter, it is very easy to upgrade the rest of the engine

and subject the flywheel to forces it was never designed for.

ACQUIRING AN ENGINE

US based converters will need no help finding sources of Ford and Chevy engines (Summit is one of many sources), but UK enthusiasts may appreciate a few starting points in their search for a US V8. The classified advertisements in the CHP magazine *American Car World* are one starting point or you could visit www. yanktanks.co.uk for a comprehensive list of US car specialists based in the UK. To my mind, two stand out as shortlist potential suppliers – Ultimate Spares of America which is based in Norfolk for used parts and British American Engines for new turnkey/crate engines.

FURTHER READING

Ford – Back issues of the magazine *Street Rodder* for February and April 2004. Two issues from this three part series will be of great interest to MG converters. Part one (February) covers engine choices, water pumps and front covers, pulleys, mounts and oil pans. Part three (April) gives some details on motor mounts and transmissions.

Chevy – *How to Build Chevy Small Blocks on a Budget* or *How to Build and Modify Chevrolet Small-Block V-8 Cylinder Heads*, both by David Vizard.

American Car World magazine published by CH Publications Ltd.

Chapter 4

Gearboxes, clutches & propshafts

Within reason, any gearbox (transmission) can be married with any engine. However, the gearbox needs to be selected with care – there will be subsequent problems if you fit an inadequate gearbox. Over-specifying the gearbox has its drawbacks too – usually incurring space, weight and cost penalties. So, selecting a gearbox with the right power/torque-handling capabilities must be the first priority – thereafter ease of fitment becomes our principal interest. Every gearbox we consider these days must have an internal fifth (overdrive ratio) gear within the box.

When it comes to fitting a gearbox, its size is very important. The width of the bellhousing will need to be accommodated within the footwells and firewall/bulkhead of the MGB, and the height of your intended gearbox will need to be accommodated within the gearbox/prop-tunnel. In both cases, some modification to the original sheet-metal panels is to be expected and the work involved in these changes increases the larger the gearbox becomes.

For this reason I will mainly focus upon 5-speed boxes.

The parentage of your gearbox will influence the ease of the marriage to your selected engine. As I said earlier, any gearbox can be fitted to any engine but the wrong combination can increase your costs and even present an engineering challenge. Better to minimise the cost and problems where you can: selecting a gearbox/bellhousing/clutch combination that is compatible with your engine is the best approach. Thus I strongly recommend that you try to buy a mating engine/gearbox combination simultaneously if possible. This ideal is not possible in some cases, in which case, if say seeking a T5 gearbox, go shopping for a Ford T5 if fitting a Ford engine to your MGB and, conversely, a GM T5 if you have a Buick/Rover up front.

You also need to consider your rear axle ratio and overall gear ratios when selecting a gearbox. You may have minimal choice with used gearboxes but this consideration is particularly important when

buying a new gearbox. The first gear and fifth gear ratios are particularly important. If you are thinking of retaining the MGB's original rear axle ratio of 3.9:1 you will not be making the most of your engine upgrade, and will compound the problem if you fit a gearbox with a low first gear and/or a low fifth gear ratio. In fact, you will hardly need a first gear at all. On the other hand an overly tall rear axle (say 2.75) coupled to an overly high first gear will make you slow off the line. I personally aim for a modest rear axle ratio (say 3.07/3.3) with the tallest fifth gear (0.63) I can find; this makes for a good compromise between lively acceleration and relaxed high-speed cruising.

MODERATELY-POWERED ENGINES

There are numerous choices here but two gearboxes in particular offer the availability, capability and fit we seek. They are largely divided by geographical considerations.

Rover gearboxes
In the UK, using the Rover LT77 ex-SD1

5-speed manual box identified by photo 4-1-1 is the easiest route to take for Buick/Rover-engined cars because, with the correct bellhousing, this gearbox will bolt straight to the engine. Furthermore, the SD1 clutch assembly is more than capable of handling this degree of power and requires no modifications to engine, gearbox or flywheel – although I would have a professional machine-shop carve about 7lb off the periphery of the flywheel to reduce the rotating inertia of the engine and thus improve the car's acceleration.

Furthermore, the SD1 box is actually narrower than the MG box, so width limitations pose few problems. The bellhousing requires a couple of thumps on the left side with a club-hammer whereupon it will fit. This box is, however, higher than the original MG box (as photo 4-1-2 shows) and thus the propshaft tunnel needs the sheet-metal upward extension detailed in Chapter 9.

The LT77 gearbox was fitted to many unsuitable vehicles too but gearboxes from the following models are ideal – Rover SD1 2000, 2300, 2400 turbodiesel, 2600 and 3500 models, to later TR7s and all TR8s. These should be relatively easy to obtain from your local breaker's yard. They may even be available from breakers' yards in the US. However, several Rover parts dealers are listed from both sides of the Atlantic in the index (under 'Rover') and there will be alternative sources too, so the gearbox itself should not be difficult to procure. The quality of what is available might be another problem and you should look opposite for some checks. Some associated components may also be harder to find, and we will explore these shortly.

The UK's Ministry of Defence also used the LT77 gearbox in its freight Rovers. These have D, E, F and G suffixes to indicate the approximate age of the box. The latest box in the Rover SD1 saloon/sedan was the 'D' suffix so the E,

4-1-1 The Rover LT77 gearbox fitted with the essential V8 bellhousing necessary to marry it to a Rover (or Buick) V8 engine.

4-1-2 The original MGB four synchro gearbox is nearer the camera with the marginally taller Rover box immediately behind it, thus demonstrating the need to slightly raise the top of, at the entrance to, the gearbox tunnel.

F and G are later boxes with the largest rear bearings and correspondingly are

difficult to come by. As attractive as these gearboxes may sound, bear in mind that they have been put to heavy-duty use in a heavy vehicle, so do not expect too much.

The bellhousing and flywheel you need to fit to your Buick/Rover V8 are unique to the V8 and in short supply in the second-hand market. They are available new from Clive Wheatley, RPI and other specialists, so all is not lost. When buying a gearbox from a dealer/specialist make sure that you specify you want a gearbox, V8 bellhousing, flywheel and all clutch release mechanics, etc. in one package deal if possible.

Assuming you plan to use a conventional Rover clutch release mechanism, check you are given the correct V8 ball (upon which the clutch-release lever pivots). It is available new at little cost so it is not a disaster if you get the wrong one but you MUST use the one shown in drawing D4-1 when assembling gearbox to engine. You will need a clutch-release arm too – preferably one that is not worn at its pivot/pressure points. If yours looks fragile, weld strengthening patches to it before fitting.

You will need a V8 clutch-release-bearing carrier. This is the carrier upon which the clutch thrust bearing sits, is unique to the V8 and is virtually

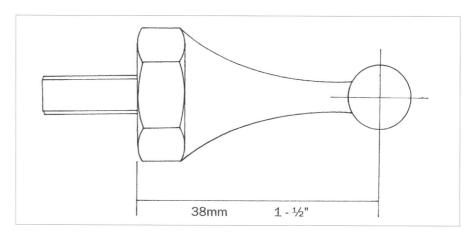

38mm   1 - ½"

D4-1 Identification of V8 clutch arm pivot post.

unobtainable. There are two solutions. One is to weld an extension to a more readily available shorter carrier – best carried out by a specialist, as it is very hard to get to once engine and gearbox are in the car. Another is to buy a one-piece plastic (yes, really!) carrier/release-bearing from a Rover dealer. They are not as robust as the original metal carriers but adequate, still available and a lot cheaper. MGOC (Spares) do a kit of conversion parts including a dust-cover, shortened remote change, speedo, etc.

If you encounter major procurement difficulties you may need to resort to the hydraulic annular throw-out bearing to activate the clutch that we will explore in more detail later.

An advantage of using the Rover 5-speed gearbox is that the standard Rover SD1 starter motor (Lucas model 3M100PE) can be used. Furthermore, the clutch can be easily assembled using the Rover's standard V8/3500 slave cylinder – although the result is an increase in pedal pressure. It's quite usable, but possibly requires twice the effort of a standard 'B clutch pedal. The V8 Conversion Company can supply a new slave cylinder which, it says, reduces the pedal pressure required, but my wife drives the car very happily with the SD1 slave so I think this upgrade is unnecessary. I would fit the MGB V8's clutch master-cylinder – available from Moss (part number GMC 1011) or any reputable MG spares stockist.

Assessing the condition

Before you fit the box, drain the oil and use it to help you establish the likely condition. A slight brassy look is normal. If the oil is very grey in colour or particularly if grey coloured steel chips are obvious, remove the top cover casting and look for damaged gears. You may need to revolve them but it is likely you will find some teeth are missing or chipped.

A thick grey sludge means the layshaft and/or gears have disintegrated,

confirmed by a telltale hiss when driving. Check the input shaft; it is held into the front casing of the transmission using a taper roller-bearing and slight movement is pre-set at the factory with shims. A very common fault with a used box is that the input shaft becomes slack within the front cover, which adversely effects its meshing with the layshaft. If caught early enough, it is possible to fit new shims to the correct tolerance and give the box/transmission a new lease of life. However, the problem is rarely caught in time and brings about excessive wear of the input shaft and layshaft teeth. The resultant swarf contaminates the oil, which damages the fibre oil pump, synchro rings and the gearbox bearings, etc.

Brass pieces signal broken synchro rings or bushes which will also have been obvious when driving, but any or all the above imply you need a major overhaul or that an exchange or replacement box is required.

The Rover 5-speed SD1 manual box usually runs best on automatic transmission oil. Dexron II is the ideal but any good quality ATF will probably work well. Not all workshop manuals have been updated to include this information and you may find your manual recommends a thick gear-oil which makes engaging gears difficult when cold and risks wearing, and even stripping, the pump's nylon gears, which is one step away from bearing failure. Modern thinking advocates using ATF. I have used Castrol TQF satisfactorily for some years although the LT77 box can still be difficult to engage when cold.

If you are already using ATF but still find gear selection difficult, try renewing the ATF and adding a dose of Slick 50in gearbox treatment. Opinion varies but if gear selection is still difficult, there are those that believe ATF lacks adequate lubrication properties; some gearbox specialists recommend synthetic-based 5 x 75 W 90 gearbox oil. A more specific

suggestion (by other specialists) is to use Castrol SMX-S – a fully synthetic manual gearbox oil rated at SAE 75W-85. Gearbox SAE ratings bear no relationship to engine oil SAE ratings so I tried it and can report that it improved the feel of my Rover box.

A few final details

Rover, in its wisdom, has made the pressed V8 manual bellhousing dust cover obsolete for SD1s and, to the best of my knowledge, MGB V8 catalogues. However, it is still available from Triumph specialists under its TR8 part number: FRC 142.

The Rover's gear lever/stick will be about 30mm taller than its MG predecessor and might be too far back in the MGB's propshaft tunnel for comfort. You can remedy the problem by cutting 25mm off the top threaded section and extending the M10 threaded section downwards by 25mm as depicted in photo 4-1-3.

However, this does not help reposition the gear lever but you can solve both

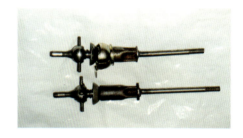

4-1-3 The original SD1 Rover gearbox change/shift lever is at the bottom. The shortened version has had a new retaining cup added as it is susceptible to breaking its securing tabs.

the over-long and positional problems simultaneously by carrying out the modifications to the gear lever shown in drawing D4-2. This requires you cut the gear lever off the ball and lop 25mm off the plain bottom of the gear lever. Before re-welding the gear lever back together, make up a flat intermediate plate which allows you to reposition the centre of the

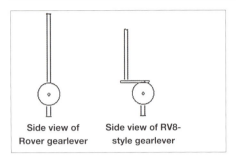

D4-2 Diagramatic view of gearlever modification.

Side view of Rover gearlever

Side view of RV8-style gearlever

gear lever/stick an inch (25mm) or so further forward than the original. You'll see a couple of addition shots in photos 4-1-4 and 4-1-5.

The Rover gear knob looks out-of-place. However, any gear knob with a soft rubber shock-absorbing insert will fit easily. I chose a wooden one. You may prefer one with the gear change pattern molded into the top, if so the Ford Sierra's (5-speed) knob might have been made for the job.

The T5 gearbox

Although there is nothing to stop UK enthusiasts fitting the T5 gearbox, as long as the Rover boxes are available, most will not regard this as their first choice – unless

4-1-4 The standard Rover box has a bias spring, arrowed, to provide some feel as to where you are in the gearbox. If you shorten the change-housing by ...

they are fitting a Ford engine whereupon the T5 may well be the best option. However, based upon its availability, US converters will almost certainly regard this

4-1-5 ... cutting and welding it here (arrowed) you will also need to alter either the mounting or shorten the spring – neither of which is as easy as it sounds. Thus the best solution for a gear lever that sits too far back is to copy the cranked RV8 gear lever, which is how Rover got around the problem of a rearward gearbox position.

gearbox as their first choice. Made initially by BorgWarner, and latterly by Tremec, this 5-speed gearbox has proved very popular indeed. Many were fitted to Camaros, Firebirds and Mustangs and many of the boxes available in breakers yards will come from these. Currently, the T5 is being fitted to Ford Mustang, the TVR Cerbera and Tuscan, Chevy Blazer and S-10 Pick-up, and the Ssangyong Musso and Korando models – so many (but not all) examples will be strong enough to use in all power/torque categories of MGB V8 conversions.

It is probably true to say that all T5 boxes will handle the power from our 'moderate' category of V8 power plants. Nevertheless, I would avoid all pre-1985 pre-'world-class' T5 boxes.

The later, better 'world-class' units are readily available in most areas and are the result of the manufacturer re-engineering the transmission to increase torque capability and smooth gear-changing/shifting. This took place in the mid-eighties and included tapered bearings on main and countershafts to reduce noise and improve durability. Needle bearing under 1st through 4th gears improves high speed performance and reduces gear-changing effort. There is also a reverse synchromesh option (allowing immediate access to reverse), 3-piece non-metallic cluster synchro/blocker rings and a change to automatic transmission fluid (ATF), rather than gear oil, for lubrication. These uprated gearboxes are designated 'world-class' to distinguish them from earlier models.

It is generally accepted that a T5's longevity is more a factor of its mileage rather than the torque that it has been subjected to. A high-mileage, ex-high-performance T5 will probably shift poorly and die much sooner than an early T5 that came out of a low-mileage car.

The T5 weighs 30lb (14kg) less than the Rover SD1 gearbox since it has an aluminium case and consequently will become more popular in the UK, particularly as the Rover box and clutch fittings get harder to find. Furthermore, the T5 avoids the complication of an oil-pump and thus has less to go wrong than a Rover box.

The T5s all have the same gear case dimensions, but, as demonstrated by picture 4-1-6, the extension housings vary according to the gearshift position requirements of the original application. 1994-95 Ford models can be used but are less desirable for use in an MGB because they were fitted with slightly longer bellhousing and first motion/input shaft. That said, an ex-Mustang box would be an excellent acquisition for any Ford engined MGB.

Ford began using the 'world-class'

4-1-6 The slightly longer first motion/front shaft of the GM-style T5 at the front of this shot is hard to see, but you cannot miss the 1½in (38mm) difference in change arrangement with the Ford T5 positioned in the middle of this trio. The Rover box is positioned furthest from the camera.

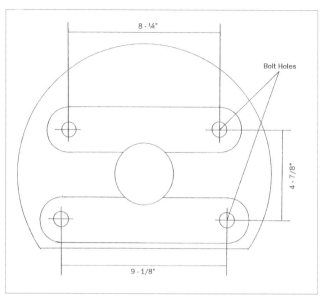

D4-3 General Motors 215 4-speed bell housing rear bolt pattern.

T5 in 1986 and GM followed with 1988 vehicles. If you have a Ford engine in mind then the simplest marriage will be by using a Ford T5. A Ford T5 would require an adapter plate if used with a GM 215 bellhousing; adapter plates for all eventualities are available from D+D Fabrications. Furthermore, Dellow Automotive in Australia can supply a special bellhousing, clutch and ancillary parts to directly couple any V8 engine to any T5 gearbox.

The GM version of this gearbox (seen at 4-1-7) is the one converters should choose for Rover/Buick/Olds engines. The 215 4-speed or dual pattern bellhousing effects the marriage and can be identified by the bolt pattern shown in photo 4-1-8 and diagram D4-3. It's possible to use the GM T5 with a 215-type, 3-speed bellhousing, or indeed a Rover bellhousing, but these require an aluminium adapter plate. A stock Buick bellhousing, with the removable bottom inspection cover marries engine to gearbox without requiring special adapter parts and/or machining.

Another circumstance where a D+D

4-1-7 Another shot – this time the GM-style T5 is on the right (note the gear lever's length and angle), and can readily be compared to the Rover LT77/SD1 box.

Fabrications adapter plate may be helpful is when marrying a T5 to a Rover engine – the Rover crank and the T5 first-motion shaft prevent the bellhousing fully closing with the back of the engine my some 0.375in (9mm). A spacer (preferably aluminium) will correct the problem and is my preferred solution. However, if you are still rebuilding the engine you could consider cutting the dowel off the rear and shortening the Rover crankshaft's rear spigot by 10mm.

4-1-8 This is a later stock Buick/Olds 215 bellhousing, drilled for both 3- and 4-speed transmissions. When the 215 first came out it was offered with a 3-speed gearbox, although a 4-speed was soon added as an option. The 4-speed needed a different bellhousing with larger bolt pattern so, in early 1962, the factory started drilling the bellhousing for both 3- and 4-speed transmissions: the 3-speed took the four inboard holes and the 4-speed took the four outer holes. The dimensions of the more useful 4-speed gearbox holes are shown in diagram D4-3.

A temporary plug will be required to allow the lathe's tailstock to steady the crank while the spigot's length is reduced.

4-1-9 An ex-Camaro T5.

Another way to marry your T5 to your V8 is via a stock Buick bellhousing with removable bottom inspection cover. This joins engine to gearbox without special adapter parts and/or machining. The removable bottom offers the opportunity to eliminate the conventional clutch thrust bearing, actuation arm and external slave cylinder by fitting a hydraulic throw-out bearing instead (discussed later).

However the GM T5 gearbox is built with an 18° twist to one side to allow installation into various Camaro (pictured at 4-1-9) and Firebird cars. This twist does not prevent it being bolted to the bellhousing, although the rear gearbox-mounting bracket must accommodate the twist, and it should be appreciated that the shift lever will exit the tunnel at this angle. The first four gears in all GM T5s are identical (2.95:1 first and 1:1 gear ratio in fourth). The fifth gear ratio can vary between a 0.73:1 or 0.63:1 overdrive gear. For very high speed cruising, the 0.63:1 gears are preferred but might be a little too high if using a 3.00 or 3.07:1 rear axle ratio. Maybe the 0.73 ratio is the best compromise, allowing use of a high ratio rear axle (and thus a useful first gear) and a practical top gear (i.e. overdrive).

To select the T5 most suited to your engine, first check the casting numbers on the gear case. The GM model number for the T5 is 1352 and is included in the number cast into the case. Next, weed out the T5 gearboxes which were not installed behind V8s; the V8 gearbox has 26 splines on the input shaft and 27 on the output shaft. On your short-listed gearboxes, look for the metal identification tag which should be attached to one of the lower gear case extension housing bolts. The tag will carry four lines of numbers and letters, which are, respectively, the BorgWarner part number, GM part number, gearbox serial number, and build date. The only numbers we should concern ourselves with are the BorgWarner and GM part numbers. Those gearboxes with a 0.73:1 fifth gear carry BorgWarner part number 1352-212 and GM part number 1019-2297. The 0.63:1 fifth gear gearbox carries BorgWarner part number 1353-213 and GM part number 1019-2298.

For a more complete source of T5 identification and torque ratings take a look at www.fordmuscle.com/archives/2000/09/t5swap/index and/or www.moderndriveline.com/Technical_Bits/transmissions_spec.htm.

The stock 215 flywheel is recommended in any T5 installation with a 9½in Chevy clutch. The 9½in friction plate should cope with 250bhp, thus all moderate- and medium-powered conversions – which makes it favourite for most road-going US V8 conversions. Above 250bhp, a machined flat flywheel and 10in Chevy clutch will be required – but that takes us into the 'high-power' category!

Ford dealerships across the US will have them, of course, but the rear-mounting pad for the T5 is also available from most parts stores such as Advance Autoparts or Autozone for about $20. Try a pad for an '87-93 Ford Mustang with a 5-litre (302) engine. For special racing mounts, Summit Racing is your best bet.

MEDIUM-POWERED ENGINES

We have already dealt with the most suitable and available US medium-powered gearbox and clutch in the T5. Provided you choose a world-class model, the T5 should be very satisfactory, although you may like the sound of a brand new gearbox.

In the UK there is an updated and also uprated Rover 5-speed gearbox that came on the scene about a quarter of the way into MG RV8 production. Up to car number 643, MG RV8s used the Rover LT77 5-speed gearbox but later cars switched to the R380 Rover gearbox. Both weigh 110lb (50kg) and the R380 has the following ratios: 1st – 3.321, 2nd – 2.132, 3rd – 1.397, 4th – 1.0, 5th – 0.77. This gearbox provides synchromesh on reverse gear, as well as on all five forward gears and is capable of handling 280lb-ft torque.

That may not sound a very high torque-rating, but remember that the rating is set based on two factors – engine torque and vehicle weight. In the case of the R380, it was developed mainly for Discovery and Range Rover vehicles – which weigh in the region of 4500lb. The rating is set so that the maximum loading and maximum torque input should not exceed the rating for the gearbox. In fact, MG Rover has allowed engine torque delivery to exceed the actual torque rating on some smaller and lighter vehicle applications such as the MG ZR and MG ZS. MG Rover clearly feels that the maximum weight of the vehicle doesn't come close to the weight aspect of the rating and so the actual gearbox loading still falls within the capability of the R380 gearbox. Transpose the same thinking to the R380 when fitted in a vehicle of potentially half the weight of that it was designed to be used in, and the load on the transmission drops dramatically. Therefore, the engine's input torque can be correspondingly increased yet still be within an accepted tolerance. In reality I see that this means that the R380 will easily cope with over 300lb-ft and I would expect it to be comfortable at 350lb-ft as long as vehicle weights are kept below, say, 3000lb/1500kg.

Remember that you can apply the same principles to any part of the transmission and this includes the clutch. Therefore, a Range Rover clutch designed to control up to 280lb-ft of torque in a 2.5 tonne 4WD off-roader will easily handle a 350lb-ft 1.2 tonne sports car that will easily spin out any excess torque, even with the stickiest of tyres. Thus, if you seek a suitable clutch for the R380 box, the related clutch set would be a good choice.

The easiest engine to fit this superb gearbox to is the Buick/Rover range of engines in virtually whatever capacity you choose. You just need the V8 bellhousing (which is not supplied as part of the new standard gearbox package but can of course be ordered simultaneously if required) and the SD1/TR7 gear lever/stick and remote casting assembly.

At the time of writing the new boxes were available from Clive Wheatley V8 Conversions and from RPI Engineering for about £950-£1000 new, including the V8

bellhousing. I have heard that production has recently ceased and thus stocks are limited to what dealers have in store. This fact, coupled with the T5 being cheaper (certainly in the US), may lean you towards the Tremec box but if you can find an R380 gearbox, it will be easier to fit. The clutch, bellhousing, speedo drive, overall length, prop flange and the gear change remote assembly and lever are common to the SD1/TR7 gearboxes. The mounting also appears similar. Photograph 4-1-10 shows the R380 gearbox and you will note the close resemblance to the SD1 gearbox depicted in photograph 4-1-1.

HIGH-POWERED ENGINES

A new R380 box is still feasible, at least for Rover engined cars, but may become progressively harder to find now that production is coming to an end. However, there is much to be said for a carefully selected used BorgWarner T5. The 1985-89 Ford (mostly ex-Mustang) boxes, rated at 265lb-ft, are probably marginal for most high-powered MGBs. These T5s can be identified by their short-throw gear lever/shifter and gold/cadmium coloured base-plate. These boxes are possibly satisfactory for road use but need an uprated countershaft, second and third gear if track days or other really enthusiastic motoring is on your mind. The 1990-95 T5 was rated at 300lb-ft when new and consequently is a better choice. The countershaft, second and third gears were made from superior material while the gear pitch is straighter and therefore stronger. However, they were not unbreakable and I suggest they still need to be used with care if your engine is capable of more than 275/300lb-ft.

The best-used T5 is that from a 1993-95 Cobra and is rated at 310lb-ft. A tapered roller bearing assembly replaces several roller-bearings and greatly improves durability. Non-Cobra T5s of that era retained the roller bearings and

4-1-10 The R380 box is indistinguishable from its LT77 predecessor. You will have to reuse an original 5-speed TR7 (or TR8) bellhousing.

are consequently less desirable for very powerful conversions.

Further T5 options became available following the 1995 sale of BorgWarner's gearbox interests to Tremec. Remember right through the range that these gearboxes can be purchased for Ford or GM applications and consequently you need to specify your preference when ordering any of the new gearboxes.

The Toyota option

It is possible to use one of several of Toyota's excellent 5-speed gearboxes behind a wide variety of engines, including all those we are focusing upon here, provided power does not exceed 400bhp. Additional Toyota gearbox options are available but the gearbox of choice must be the Supra with its alloy case, weighing (77lb/35kg). I mentioned Dellow Automotive earlier in the chapter and it is perhaps worth adding here that if you can't locate your own second-hand Toyota box, an in-house refurbished one can also be supplied for about A$900 by Dellow Automotive which has a production line refurbishing Toyota gearboxes.

If you are ordering a Toyota gearbox with your bellhousing and clutch you have some choice over gear ratios. The W58 looks ideal for MGB V8 conversions, but is available only occasionally. The W55 is usually in stock and is possibly the one to go for.

Certainly anyone with a Supra box lying in the garage will wish to marry that box to any of the engines on our shortlist and will want to know how that can be achieved for modest cost and maximum reliability. Dellow Automotive is the answer as it makes a wide variety of components and kits to achieve just such a marriage. It can also provide parts and kits to achieve any possible combination of engine/ gearbox discussed. Furthermore, where a manual flywheel is required Dellow can usually supply that too. Where a Supra box is being fitted into an MGB, the necessary rear/transmission pressed crossmember (fitted with twin exhaust pipe holes too) is available for A$100.

AFTERMARKET GEARBOXES

The T5 is available in numerous guises, each with its own ratio and/or torque rating. The lower ratio of 3.55:1 may be attractive because the car will take-off quicker than a higher-geared 2.95 ratio gearbox, however, D+D Fabrications points out that the higher ratio gearboxes are about 10 per cent stronger than a comparable 3.35 unit as the result of input-to-countershaft gear ratio. Consequently, for serious track use, or with rear axle gearing over 3.55, the 2.95 first gear is the way to go offering 305lb-ft torque capacity. That said, Cobra aftermarket units have been rated at 330lb-ft rating since 1993.

Tremec's 3550 handles 350lb-ft – but weighs in at 100lb, about 23lb more than a T5. This stems from its larger gear and shaft mass, which in turn allows the higher capacity – although some high-vpowered applications have still managed to break a few of the early units. Hence the introduction of the Tremec TKO with its changed input shaft – increased from 1¹⁄₁₆in and 10 splines to 1⅛in and 26 splines, while the output shaft went from 28 splines to 31.

4-2-1 The T56's six forward speeds must be every converter's dream (after a powerful engine!) – but ...

4-2-2 ... check out its size before you jump in. The (much) smaller comparison is a T5.

D+D Fabrications recommends Tremec gearboxes are given at least a 500-mile running/break-in before hard driving use as a consequence of their brass synchro/blocker rings. These same brass rings mean aftermarket Tremec's should always he filled with GM synchromesh fluid and not the Dexron used by the T5 and T56. The brass rings require the extra viscosity of the synchromesh fluid, whereas the carbon-fibre rings in the Borg-Warner units work best with the lighter Dexron.

The T56 6-speed gearbox seen in picture 4-2-1 is the ultimate gearbox/ transmission option particularly in view of its 440lb-ft capacity. It also enjoys an enviable strength/quality reputation but expect it to set you back over $2000, perhaps best left for the highest-powered engines. Its strength is partly derived from the 85mm distance between the main-shaft and countershaft, which controls the

size of the gears. All else being equal, as this distance increases, torque capacity goes up by the square of the increase. By comparison, theT5's centre distance is 77mm as is the Rover LT77's. However, take a look at picture 4-2-2 before you plump for the T56. It's a great gearbox but it is big and will necessitate a lot of sheet-metal changes before it will fit in an MGB.

The T56 is currently used in the Dodge Viper, Chevy Corvette Z06, the Pontiac GTO, Ford SVT Mustang Cobra, Aston Martin DB7 Vantage and V12 Vanquish, and the Holden Commodore and Monaro. However, approach buying a T56 with care since the bellhousing is integral with the gear-casing and consequently you must get one that marries to your selected engine. You have a choice of gear ratios – 2.66/1.78/1.30/1.00/0.74/0.80/0.50, or 2.97/2.07/1.43/1.00/0.80/0.62. Either suits a high-output V8 but be aware too that the box is 115lb, much heavier than the T5, the bellhousing is bigger and it is slightly taller too – so significant tunnel modifications will be required to install it in an MGB.

The super-duty T5

In 1993 Ford started offering a new super-duty motorsport box called the Z spec T5.

4-2-3 The Chevy 302 (out of shot) develops 475bhp so needed a strong gearbox to transmit all that 'go' to the road. This Tremec TKO does just that. Note the dual earth/ground leads bolted to the especially fabricated crossmember.

The T5 Z is a 1993 Cobra T5 with a 2.95 first gear set and 0.63 overdrive. It has the best of everything. Hardened gears, short throw shifter, steel front bearing retainer, and tapered output shaft bearing. Best of all it has a torque rating of 330lb-ft. This T5 can handle up to 450bhp and would be the box of choice for MGBs with top-end engine power and torque.

T5 Zs are only available from aftermarket suppliers such as Summit Racing (part number FMS-M7003Z), it will fit behind a T5 bellhousing and is available in four versions, each costing roughly $1000. If you are buying new you can also consider some 3550 derivatives. For example, the TR-3550II rated at 375lb-ft, a TKO (pictured at 4-2-3) rated at 425lb-ft or the TKOII rated at 475lb-ft. Gear ratios are 3.27/1.98/1.34/1.00/0.68.

BELLHOUSINGS & CLUTCHES
Bellhousings

The bellhousing does more than house the clutch; it provides a link between the rear face of the engine and the front of the gearbox. I have mentioned some particular bellhousings but you may have an unusual combination; Dellow Automotive specialises in supplying bellhousing and clutch actuation kits that marry the vast majority of engine and gearbox combinations. US converters will need to contact Dellow Automotive direct (details in the Appendix) but interested UK conversion enthusiasts can probably save some freight costs by ordering via Classic Conversions.

The conversion kits supplied by Dellow Automotive are comprehensive. They include bellhousing, crankshaft pilot bush, clutch fork, 3-piece clutch set, slave cylinder and speedo-cable and a typical kit costs A$1200 ex-works. Airfreight costs to the UK or USA range from A$500 to A$750 depending upon the contents of the crate but although modest, this additional cost makes it worthwhile weighing-up what you

are going to need and ordering everything simultaneously to facilitate one shipment.

Size rule of thumb

For moderately-powered street/road cars a 9½in clutch will be adequate, while you might be prudent to use a 10in clutch for medium-powered engines. However, when you move up to high-powered applications, 10½in is what you probably need. Bear in mind the weight of the car; a marginal clutch in a 2000kg (4400lb) monster will be perfectly adequate in your 1000kg (2200lb) MGB. The lower weight not only means less stress and wind-up in the transmission, but that tyre grip is lost earlier and the wheels can spin away the excess torque, although tyre grip makes only a small difference to the overall effect.

However, much depends upon how you intend to use the car. Sprinting, drag-racing or hot-starts at track days may necessitate a heavy-duty clutch such as those supplied by McCloud. Be aware that these can require very heavy pedal pressures to disengage and, in a predominately road car, such clutches can be very uncomfortable to drive in traffic. Alternatively, an uprated AP (Automotive Products) clutch (probably just the driven plate to start with), could be of use to sharpen the grip of the clutch. Take advice in respect of your engine, gearbox and the clutch most suited to your application and

on the hydraulic cylinder sizes you intend to use. You could use a remote Lockheed brake servo to give servo assistance to your clutch pedal, but this is a complication best avoided.

Hydraulic line

A flexible hose will be required to connect the bottom of the MGB's pipe to the slave cylinder. The end fitting on the gearbox may vary but in all cases I recommend you use a stainless steel braided flexible hose to activate your clutch. Seen in picture 4-3-1, they are less susceptible to heat than plain rubber hose. I would personally cover any part of the clutch pipe run that passes near an exhaust pipe in rubber hose (or other heat insulating material) to minimise heat take-up.

You may well need to relate the chassis mounting bracket for these clutch lines (picture 4-3-2) and connect your flexible hose with a line coupling to one of the lines exiting the HTOB (hydraulic throw-out bearing – more soon, but meanwhile see picture 4-3-3).

Chevy clutches & flywheels

Chevy used two slightly different flywheels – 168-tooth and 153-tooth. The 168-tooth flywheel was fitted with either a 10½in or

4-3-1 Seen from below, this Goodridge stainless steel braided clutch hose fastens to a relocated ...

4-3-2 ... chassis mounted bracket, the position of which will vary according to your engine/gearbox/clutch combination. I ended up keeping the same location but angling the bracket towards the front before welding it in place.

4-3-3 Although the line arrangement looks quite different at first sight, HTOBs require the same hydraulic line feeding the bottom of these connections. The top line here is no more than a bleed nipple.

11in clutch – either of which will be suitable for a relatively light car such as your MGB V8 conversion. Flywheels from family cars are drilled for 10½in clutch but ex-truck and performance car flywheels are drilled for an 11in clutch. You need to take a little care with the 153-toothed flywheels for while they can be fitted with an acceptable 10½in clutch, some were fitted with 8, 9, 9½in clutches depending upon their original application and their suitability needs to be weighed against the power of your engine. When acquiring a Chevy engine you are as well to try for one with the flywheel attached because there is a further complication with pre- and post-1986 engines. The clutch bellhousing is interchangeable but the crankshaft/flywheel mounting flange bolt pattern changed, thus pre-1986 cranks will not accept older flywheels.

There is a large variety of clutches available for the Ford engine/T5 transmission but Ford Motor Sports M7560A302 clutch can handle 40 per cent more torque than a standard 5.0 Mustang clutch and sounds a good bet. Ford claims it is designed to have a shortened operating throw which is advantageous to our application because it allows the use of a smaller clutch master-cylinder which, in turn, provides a lighter clutch pedal. However, Ford makes another clutch, M763C302, that is claimed to have

the same capacity and short travel as the previous clutch, but requires 10 per cent less force to disengage.

While in the UK most readers will opt for a Rover SD1 (9½in) clutch set, in the USA Buick/Rovers use an aftermarket Chevy clutch with an HTOB. In both cases the clutch is moderately heavy; I would guess it requires about twice the pedal pressure needed in an original MGB while at the same time the full travel of the pedal is needed to just barely disengage the clutch. I keep meaning to experiment with master-cylinders and you may care to read the section on the effect of cylinder sizes later in the chapter before you settle on your Buick/Rover arrangements.

Actuating a T5 clutch arm

As mentioned in the previous chapter, the Ford cable-operated clutch requires several changes partly because there is insufficient space between the T5 bellhousing and the MGB's chassis rails for the cable mechanism and, in any event, you would be faced with significant changes to the

'B's clutch-pedal if you wanted to use a cable to activate the clutch. Therefore, the simplest overall solution is to retain the MGB's original pedal/master-cylinder arrangement that already utilizes a hydraulic master-cylinder and use one of the two options explored shortly to activate the T5 clutch. However, the MGB's original ¾in bore master-cylinder may possibly move enough fluid to fully disengage larger clutches. Much will depend upon the bore of the clutch slave and the distance you need to move the release bearing. Consequently, you may need to experiment with master-cylinder bore sizes to find the best trade-off between pedal pressure and travel – which will vary with the diameter of the master-cylinder.

A ⅞in (22mm) bore master-cylinder moves about 35 per cent more fluid for the same stroke than the original MGB master but with a corresponding increase in pedal-pressure. In the UK, Demon Tweeks sells a range of AP master-cylinders with 'remote' (i.e. non-integral) reservoirs. These compact master-cylinders are suitable for all brake and clutch applications and are

4-3-4 There are alternatives but this is the ⅞in bore version from the Tilton 'short' series of hydraulic master-cylinders fitted to a rubber-bumper pedal box. Note the side exit, hydraulic line feeding the clutch.

especially useful where space is restricted as in an MGB chrome-bumper pedal box. They are flange mounted and have bore options from 0.55in (14mm) diameter through to 1in (25.4mm). There are various push rod options for both the thread and length and they can be fitted with a screw-in reservoir adapter that accepts a push-on hose of $\frac{5}{16}$in (7.9mm) inside diameter.

In the US, the $\frac{7}{8}$in bore Tilton master-cylinder we see in photograph 4-3-4 comes in four versions, regular and short, with and without a remote reservoir. A rubber-bumper pedal box has enough room within it to use the short (series 75) Tilton cylinder with reservoir for the clutch actuation because the (dual) brake master-cylinder is close-coupled to the front of the servo and out of the way. The Tilton cylinders come in eight bore sizes from $\frac{5}{8}$in to $1\frac{1}{8}$in, so if you need to make some adjustments, you can vary the master-cylinder bore accordingly.

The chrome-bumper's pedal box is too large to accept the 'with reservoir' Tilton and the brake master-cylinder so you will need to use a remote reservoir Tilton, contact Demon Tweeks for an AP unit or consult your local brake/clutch specialist if you are converting an early MGB.

The Tilton cylinder bolts in the standard/stock position and allows you to refit the banjo, special bolt and clutch line. You will need to increase the size of the central hole in the pedal box to clear the OD of the Tilton cylinder, transfer the MGB's original push rod clevis fork assembly to the Tilton or buy a replacement MGB rod/clevis if yours is worn.

Don't forget (another 'rule of thumb' coming!), for a given size of slave cylinder – the bigger the bore of the master-cylinder, the greater the amount of fluid displaced, the greater the stroke of the slave cylinder and the heavier the clutch-pedal will feel. In general, the clutch should engage about $\frac{1}{3}$ of the way off the floor. If yours engages a lot nearer the top of the pedal's travel you

4-3-5-1 HTOBs mount to the front of the gearbox inside the bellhousing like this. The annular hydraulic cylinder sits nearest the gearbox and advances the thrust bearing we see at the front of this example into the 'fingers' of the clutch pressure-plate in order to release the clutch. HTOBs are more complex than a straightforward piston-like hydraulic cylinder. The lack of accessibility makes a remote bleed nipple essential and the top line (protected with plastic wrapping) leads to the nipple situated outside the bellhousing.

could find it worthwhile trying a smaller bore master-cylinder since this should reduce pedal pressure and help the clutch 'Bite' closer to the floor.

At the gearbox end of the hydraulic line, two solutions are available to you:

1 – fit a throw-out/clutch-release bearing to the nose of the box;

2 – fabricate a new bracket and use the existing mounting holes in the T5 gearbox to mount an external slave cylinder.

Hydraulic throw-out bearings

The HTOB is an annular ring slave-cylinder mounted inside the bellhousing as we see from photographs 4-3-5-1 and 4-3-5-2. It probably provides for the simplest installation but in the event of a subsequent problem they have the major disadvantage of requiring engine and gearbox removal to effect even the most minor repair. Such throw-out bearings eliminate the possibility of clearance difficulties in the area of the starter

4-3-5-2 This shot shows a T5 with HTOB actually inside the bellhousing. Note that both lines are protected from chaffing by rubber hose sleeves.

4-3-6 Various types of HTOBs are available from a variety of manufacturers. Buy the correct one for your application from a manufacturer with a reputation for quality and reliability.

motor/external clutch slave cylinder and the MGB's chassis. Versions are readily available for virtually any gearbox/clutch combination from Tilton Engineering, McLeod Industries or Weber Performance Products, and a couple of comparisons can be seen at 4-3-6.

External slave cylinders

There are options as to how this can be achieved – the quickest, simplest and neatest solution is to buy the Larry's Autoworks assembly pictured in the previous chapter. However it is perfectly feasible to use picture 4-3-7 to help make a mounting bracket and fit a propriety slave-cylinder – typically a ⅝in bore unit. As we can see from this picture, CNC make suitable cylinders (part number 305B), which, with a push rod adjusted to activate the clutch arm/fork, will work just fine and not interfere with the MG's chassis rails. It mounts to the outside of the T5 onto the existing bolt-holes highlighted in picture 4-3-8. You will need to order the adjustable

4-3-7 The basic shape of the mounting bracket for this external slave cylinder is an 'L' – with the vertical leg visible here and the second leg passing under the bottom of the T5. The hydraulic cylinder is attached to the bracket while ...

4-3-8 ... the bracket attaches to the casing here, here and here.

push-rod (part number 1312) additionally to your the cylinder but this fits in the seat in the clutch arm where the Ford cable normally sits. The only problem is that there is no way to seal the hole in the bellhousing where the clutch operating arm exits. Ford uses a sheet-metal box with a forward opening, but this cannot be used with the slave cylinder. You may be able to make-up a rubber flap if you deem closing the opening that important.

Speedometer

The speedo drive can be electronic but most MGB V8 conversions will continue to use a conventional inner/outer cable assembly. The length will probably vary from the original cable fitted to the car, but you can at least use that as a guide to the length needed in your converted car. If you intend to retain the original speedo, then the original cable will also provide a guide as to size of coupling needed at the dashboard-end of the cable. However, the gearbox will dictate the lower end coupling arrangement.

Your friendly V8 conversion specialist will supply you with the correct speedo cable for about £15 if you are changing to an SD1 gearbox. He will need to know which MGB speedometer you intend using. There are two sizes of MGB speedo, each of which has its own rear cable fitting: if your speedo came from a rubber-bumper MGB it will be the smaller diameter (80mm), or the larger diameter (90mm) if from a chrome-bumper car. Speedy Cables Ltd (in the UK) or your V8 conversion specialist would, in my experience, quickly resolve any difficulties.

If you are fitting a T5 gearbox to your conversion then a different set of speedo-drive solutions are called for. D+D Fabrications will have the answers and parts you need. Lokar also offers a variety of speedo cables and accessories and its catalogue may be worth exploring.

Gear lever/stick location

Supra boxes have four gear lever/stick positions from the front of the box/rear of the bellhousing – 18in, 19in, 20½in and 21in. The 21in version looks preferable for MGB V8 conversions but I believe the 18in to be the most prevalent.

The Rover box is 22½in from the front face of the box itself to the centre of the gear lever/stick – which is perhaps 1in to 1½in too long to be ideal. Drawing D4-2 showed a remedial solution to a misplaced gear lever/stick, which should work for small adjustments to other gearboxes too.

The T5 lever/stick distance from the rear bellhousing face depends upon the version you are thinking about – the GM/Camaro is 21in, the S-Truck 12¼in, while the Ford is an almost ideal (for MGB conversions) 19½in.

GEARBOX REAR CROSSMEMBERS

The removable crossmember that supported the rear of the original MGB's gearbox can generally be modified and used to support the new gearbox. The fine modification detail will depend upon the gearbox in question, its position within the chassis and the actual flexible mounts

4-4-1 The T5 uses a rubber block to support the rear of the box which makes for easy fitment using the original MGB crossmember after clearing off the original bracketry. Note, it's always better to mount a gearbox slightly low rather than high as you can always, and easily, shim it to the correct height.

4-4-2 Top is the normal MGB crossmember and flex mounting arrangement while below we see my V8 modified version. The Rover gearboxes use a pair of cotton-reel mounting rubbers, one of which is in view. The cotton-reel will appear off-centre here because I was not planning to relocate my crossmember and was, consequently, using the width of the crossmember to accommodate the slightly different mounting centre.

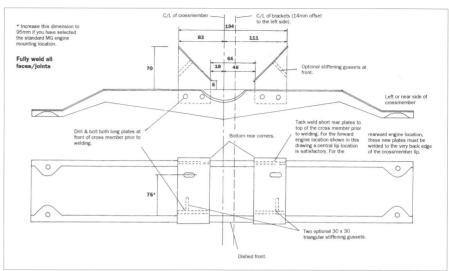

D4-4 SD1 gearbox mounting components.

to be used. We will look at the general modifications necessary to support the Rover and T5 gearboxes in a moment, but let us first explore the relocation of the crossmember along the chassis rails. This will be necessary with T5 and other non-Rover gearboxes but most conversions using a Rover box manage to adequately support the box without moving the crossmember.

Whether you are planning to move the crossmember or not, your first task is to fit the appropriate flexible mounting block (T5 pictured at 4-4-1) or cotton-reels (Rover seen at 4-4-2) to the crossmember. In the case of the T5, photo 4-4-3 could provide a little more detail. The modifications for the Rover box are a bit more complicated but drawing D4-4 and photo 4-4-4 using the plates shown in drawing D4-5 should help.

Mind you, there are short-cuts to resolving issues with both gearbox crossmembers. With the Rover 5-speed gearbox, the easiest solution is to buy an RV8 gearbox crossmember from Clive Wheatley V8 Conversions and fit it without modification. In the case of the T5, a D+D Fabrications pre-made replacement

4-4-3 The T5 requires no more than a couple of bolts to secure the flex mount to the MGB crossmember.

crossmember (pictured at 4-4-5) takes the worry out of the job – although you still have to relocate D+D's crossmember.

If you are carrying out your V8 conversion concurrently with general renovation work, and floor replacement in particular, get the gearbox crossmember relocated before you fit new floor panels. In the case of a Rover gearbox, this approach enables you to use the MGB's gearbox crossmember largely unaltered, but involves relocating the gearbox crossmember's four captive nuts (pic 4-4-6) which are clenched into the two main chassis rails. These will need moving backwards by anything from 1in (25mm) to

4-4-4 This Rover boxed conversion shows the crossmember in its original place but note that the cotton-reels are on the limit of their location. The cotton-reel rear edges are actually overhanging the rear of the crossmember slightly and ideally the crossmember would have been better placed had one new captive nut per side been fitted (arrowed) to the chassis-rails and the crossmember indexed back one hole.

6in (150mm) depending upon the engine/gearbox combination and where you have positioned the engine. Establish the exact location by welding your front engine mountings in place and offering the engine and gearbox up.

Assemble the crossmember to the gearbox and then spot-drill the chassis rails in four places to coincide with the new captive nut locations. Remove the

4-4-5 D+D Fabrications can supply this T5 mounting crossmember. It carries the T5 flexible mounting pad but also (thinking ahead!) makes provision for a pair of exhaust pipes to be raised up to the floor in order to protect them from damage by grounding. I would reverse the 'U' clamps we see at the very bottom of the picture in order to minimise the chance of them getting 'hooked-up' too.

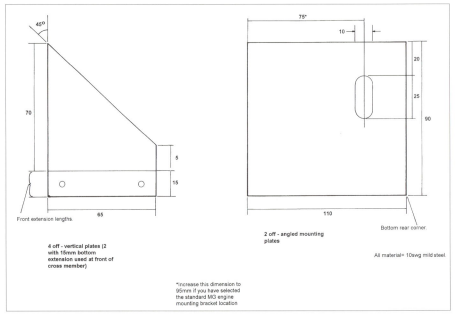

D4-5 SD1 gearbox mounting assembly.

4-4-6 Often the MGB chassis rails has three captive nuts per side allowing you some latitude with the crossmember location. I've arrowed the front unused one here on my heavily waxoyled underside. This latitude may help your conversion too but will be insufficient for many non-Rover-engined conversions.

4-4-7-1 This modified MGB crossmember augments the standard part at the top of this shot with a pair of braces welded to a channel that is bolted to the chassis rail that crosses the car between jacking-points.

4-4-7-2 This is the view from below the crossmember. The arrangement stiffens the gearbox crossmember and adds strength to its fixing to the chassis. I think this is particularly helpful if/when nutserts have been used to relocate the crossmember.

crossmember. Drill four clearance holes through the chassis rails and fit four nuts welded from the inside or make up a tapped plate (which drops into each chassis-rail and is tack-welded) before finally replacing your floor-panels. If you are relocating the crossmember from under the car you need to use four correctly-sized 'nutserts' – which are pushed up through a blind hole and then expanded inside

the chassis-rails to form captive nuts. However, bearing in mind the torque being handled by some of our engine/gearbox combinations, I wonder whether the 'nutsert' modification is up to the job over the long term and so was very pleased to receive Pete Mantell's suggestion pictured at 4-4-7-1 and 4-4-7-2.

If you have no reason to replace your

floor panels, it is possible to relocate the captive nuts from beneath the chassis without disturbing the floor pans. However I do not recommend cutting substantial holes in the structural chassis rails/channels and think you would do better to remove a small section of floor, effect the crossmember relocation and patch the floor as professionally as possible. You will

4-5-1 This shot is included to show the propshaft spacer. Such inserts can have two purposes: that of a straightforward spacer to increase the length of a propshaft – the bolts then pass through the spacer as we see here. However, they would normally be used as an adapter, in which case the fastenings would be offset and screwed (and locked) into the adapter.

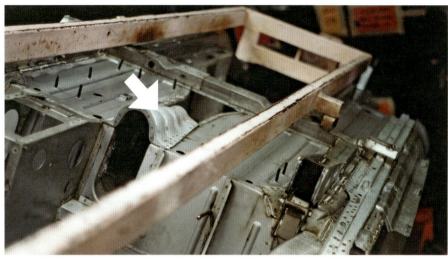

4-5-2 The heel-board stiffener, arrowed here, comes in two sizes. This is the deeper, rubber-bumper version shown fitted to an RV8 bodyshell.

not see the floor once the car is trimmed and will not have introduced a potential structural weakness.

PROP/DRIVE SHAFTS

It goes without saying that most conversions will need a new propshaft. Four details require some thought.

● The length of the shaft will vary from that originally fitted to the car – the extent of the variation differing with the engine and gearbox fitted and the position of the engine. Consequently I cannot provide you with a length to buy to, but I can advise that you only measure the 'at rest' length once all the main components are finally fitted to the car. It does not take the specialists long to make a prop/driveshaft so leave measuring and ordering it until you are sure there are no final positioning tweaks required. Photograph 4-5-1 may give you some ideas.

● The flange sizes and pcd of both the gearbox and rear axle drive flange require careful measurement. Some flanges are square, most are round – but you need to offer the right information to the propshaft

manufacturer and if you are using a slightly unusual (a Toyota gearbox or Commodore rear axle for example) component, may even need to send the respective flanges to the manufacturer.

● To some degree the size of the u/js is dictated by the diameter of the main drive shaft – but get the largest possible and best quality u/js fitted and specify u/js with grease nipples (many come without grease nipples under the guise of being maintenance-free).

● The diameter of the shaft is very important and dictated by the torque of the engine. However there can be two potential problems as the shaft diameter increases to the 2 to 3 inches (50-75mm) necessary for most conversions: the heel-board stiffening plate (shown in picture 4-5-2) if your car is a chrome-bumper model, and that part of the handbrake that is 'hidden' within the propshaft tunnel. Only the most moderate of V8s will be able to re-use the original MGB propshafts – and I will be surprised if the shaft lasts more than a short time. Almost every conversion will need to increase the diameter of the shaft

– many substantially, to the extent that the vast majority of chrome-bumper cars will need to replace its heel-board stiffening plate with the later deeper rubber-bumper version.

With a 3in diameter propshaft, if your prop-tunnel handbrake lever fouls the shaft, you probably have the tail of your gearbox a shade too high. In any event, you need to check the alignment of the gearbox with the nosepiece of the rear axle in order that the u/js on your propeller shaft are symmetrically aligned. Any propshaft out-of-symmetry will result in a jerky drive as the front and rear u/js transmit the engine's revolutions in pulses.

In the UK, GKN Driveline (for many years known as Hardy Spicer) makes bespoke propshafts to any specification you require and are well placed to advise on the specification. There are numerous other specialists in the UK and US too. I used TVR Tuscan propshafts in my conversions and, over tens of thousands of miles, they have proved faultless.

Chapter 5
Cooling

One of the major concerns with running a V8 MGB is the difficulty of keeping the coolant under control when traffic slows to a crawl. We will need to consider oil cooling too, but the focus of this chapter is on keeping the engine coolant at an acceptable level. I think this is largely a consequence of building the car correctly in the first place, which is why the first part of the chapter explores what to fit where – some details of which you may not initially give much thought to. About 30 per cent of the heat generated by combustion will be transferred to the coolant and subsequently (hopefully!) to the atmosphere. There are some tips for resolving any subsequent overheating problems, but most should be unnecessary in a well-built and properly maintained car.

INITIAL BUILD DETAILS

There is no doubt that one of the ongoing anxieties when running a V8 converted MGB is the coolant temperature, particularly when stuck in slow-moving

or stopped traffic. If stopped you can at least switch off. Re-starting may not do the battery charge much good, but prolonged use of the electric fan does nothing for the battery either. There is much to be said for initially fitting lots of battery capacity. Converters working on chrome-bumpered models can fit two 12-volt batteries. You'll also need to enlarge alternator capacity as electric fans and/or electric water pumps can singularly or collectively discharge even a high-capacity battery. We will discuss these matters in more detail in chapter 13.

When you fit a bigger engine, there will inevitably be more heat to dissipate. Furthermore, the greater the degree of tune the greater volume of fuel used, which will in turn generate much more heat and further increase the volume of hot water that needs cooling. In high ambient temperatures, cooling these beasts can prove to be a real headache.

Starting off with a well-built, cooler-running engine is undoubtedy a good idea,

and those with engine building experience will usually do so, although the advantages over an amateur build (purely in terms of internal build quality) may well decline as the internal friction in an amateur's engine eases with use.

Build quality can, of course, extend to other temperature reducing factors: an unrestricted (or correctly routed) exhaust system, for example, or the correct fuel/air mixture and timing, and even to the lack of obstructions to the air flow through the radiator.

Some overheating problems are difficult to handle in that they are partly out of your control and relate to modern fuels. If your engine already has a high compression ratio and you run the car with low-octane fuel you run the risk of generating lots of heat but not that much additional power. The ideal CR will depend upon the fuel available to you and the intended use of the car. The USA's 90 octane 'street' fuel could require lower compressions than I am about to mention

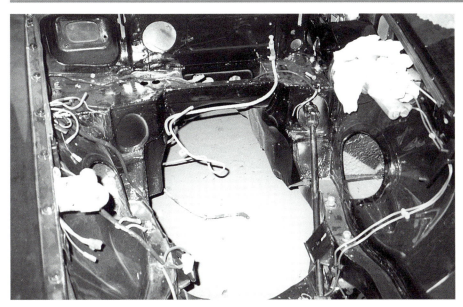

5-1-1 The engine bay of a left hand drive MGB, photographed principally to show the inner wing apertures for the RV8 exhausts manifolds that will be fitted later. Note the route of the twin caliper brake lines.

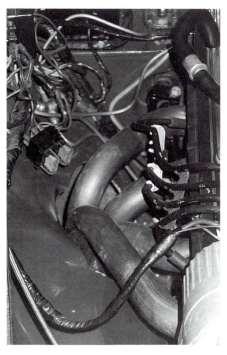

5-1-3 This excellent view shows the RV8 exaust manifold/header exiting the engine compartment as swiftly as possible, just behind the (unseen) front suspension.

for UK and European cars, some of which have the benefit of 97, even 98, RON octane. I would expect the majority of UK fast road engines to be running with a compression ratio of between 9 and 10 to 1, but the CR is very much something that needs resolving locally – different countries use different methods to calculate their octane rating.

An RV8 exhaust system is a particularly helpful build feature in that the exhaust pipes are routed away from the engine sump/oil-pan thus reducing radiant heat reaching the engine's lubricating oil. Some relevant features of the RV8 exhaust system are covered by photographs 5-1-1 to 5-1-4 and make further comment here superfluous except to point out that the pipes do not lie under the sump/oil-pan as would once have been the case.

An important detail concerns the heat transfer within the engine, starting with the transfer of heat from cylinder to coolant. Obviously engines need to have a good flow of water around them and the waterways on most engines can silt

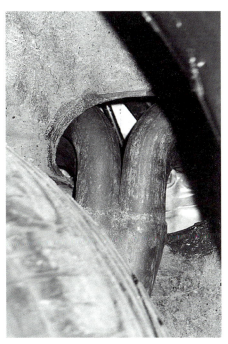

5-1-2 This photograph shows that the inner wing has been strengthened, in this case by turning down a lip. Most inner wing strengthening for RV8s is achieved by welding a "ring" of steel around the aperture.

5-1-4 This is the Clive Wheatley system, which is somewhat different in detail. The manifolds can be fitted and removed with the engine in situ, which means there are more junctions than alternative systems. Note the absence of clips: the system just pushes together with very little sealing compound. Very smooth. However, did you spot that the gearbox bottom dust shield is missing near the clutch slave cylinder?

I will bet the dust shield came from an automatic. Manual ones are available via a Triumph TR8 dealer, part number FRC 142.

up. Consequently, always have the block pressure-washed before it is assembled. If you are fitting a used/assembled engine, take the trouble to flush the block though with one of the numerous de-scalers. The two-part ones usually work best but must be thoroughly rinsed afterwards.

You **must** fit a reliable and accurate means of monitoring the coolant temperature. This basically means deciding between electric and mechanical temperature gauges. There will be lots of high-quality, accurately calibrated electrical temperature gauges on the market – I can only tell you that I have found nothing more accurate than the original MGB mechanical, expanding-alcohol temperature gauge. They can be purchased with differing dial calibrations if you are

5-1-5 This photo illustrates the correct way to install the capillary tube for a dual gauge MGB. As the pipe seems too long for the car (the excess length is intended to act as a flexible joint between a vibrating engine and static body), it sometimes gets routed round the side of the engine bay and then straight to the front of the engine. The correct way is to clip it to the side of the rocker cover, coil as much as possible into the 2-3in diameter loops you see here, before fastening it to the top of the footwell. It adds a touch of class – as well as providing a little added support – if one of the heater water pipes is threaded through the coil. With the capillary installed this way, the engine can jump about as much as it likes since the coil takes up the vibration.

prepared to search outside what the MGB spares stockists offer. If properly installed they can give years (in my case 15, 13 and 10 years so far with my three working examples) of highly accurate information. If poorly installed, the capillary tube seen in picture 5-1-5 will be broken by engine vibration, the contents spilt and the gauge will stop working. At least 50 per cent of those installations I've studied have been badly installed.

There is an almost unlimited variety of inlet manifolds for the Buick, Rover and Chevy, and many for the Ford as well. The original engine builders will have a selection of inlet manifolds and aftermarket ones, including Edelbrock and Offenhauser, are available too. As far as I know, they all come with provisions for temperature senders/fittings. If the manifold fitting doesn't match the sender you want to use, there are adapters available that will adapt anything to anything.

Engine cooling usually only becomes a major issue at the two extremes of the car's operation – dead stop and flat-out. Nevertheless, I have tried to cater for all eventualities and there are a surprising amount of contributory factors to consider. Nevertheless, the obvious starting point is the radiator itself.

THE RADIATOR

There are two ways to assess/compare the effectiveness of a radiator – those with the greatest tube surface area are best at dissipating heat to the fins while the higher the fin-count the better that radiator's cooling capacity.

The standard/stock MGB GT V8 radiator is available new but, unmodified, will have limited applications beyond a very modestly-powered V8 conversion used in a fairly temperate climate. Fortunately there are numerous improvements that can be made to the standard/stock units or you can fit a different type of radiator if you wish. You can use an ex-RV8 radiator and

its cooling fan as a 'first-level' upgrade. The advantage of using an RV8 or modified MGB GT V8 radiator is that you can retain (or fit as appropriate) the standard/stock rubber-bumper radiator support-plates, simplifying the radiator mounting. The radiator support plates are already in place on post-1976 rubber-bumper cars but need to be positioned as explained in chapter 9 if your car is chrome-bumpered.

Size

Since the size of the radiator you fit is slightly flexible, I think an enlarged bespoke unit is the best option for most conversions – certainly for those with medium-to-high-power. The width is restricted by the chassis rails and the height above the slam-panel by the bonnet/hood, consequently there is little you can do to increase the size of the cooling area of standard or bespoke radiators in these directions. However, you can and should increase the overall depth of the radiator by some 4in (100mm); this will increase the frontal area of your radiator by about 25 per cent but the ST (special tuning) front valance detailed below will be essential in order to utilize the extra radiator area.

In the US, ex-Mustang radiators are a popular choice for MGB converters but these can extend too far down. In fact, once you go below the front crossmember or bottom of the ST valance you run the risk of 'curbing' the radiator and even speed bumps can cause ex-Mustang radiators damage.

Increasing the radiator's depth takes the bottom tank down to the level of the front suspension crossmember and this can be achieved by having a standard radiator re-cored and having a couple of extra side supports fitted. This radiator will still fit standard/stock rubber-bumper radiator mounting panels, consequently I would recommend this increase as a routine improvement that every converter should adopt, even if it means having a

5-2-1 Actually this is not an extended MGB V8 radiator but a Griffin aluminium radiator of the same size. However, note that it has been positioned before the support plates have been welded to the engine bay – a practice I would recommend if fitting a non-MGB radiator.

5-2-2 I used a standard MGB GT V8 bottom hose here but cut it (just out of shot) and inserted a 6in length of stainless steel tubing to extend the hose by the increased depth of the radiator.

new standard radiator re-cored before it even goes in the car. The photo at 5-2-1 will give you a better idea of the effect.

Re-routing the lower bottom hose around the anti-roll/sway bar might look like an awkward task but is easily achieved as picture 5-2-2 shows.

You can also increase the front-to-back thickness of the radiator. An example can be viewed at 5-2-3 which necessitates a completely new radiator as the standard/stock header/bottom tanks would be too narrow to fully cover the ends of a thicker core. If you are mounting the increased thickness forwards of the mounting panels, you will have to reduce the front-back depth of the radiator duct panel fractionally. You can allow the increase in thickness of the core to sit back into the engine bay – but if space is tight then the loss of even ½in can be undesirable.

The benefits of an extra row of tubes are often over-stated. The air flow through these radiators can be slower while the extra tubes (located at the back of the core) do not proportionally add to the cooling capacity of the radiator since they are 'running' in hot air. So, here too, careful enquiries are recommended. There are, however, some really effective ways to improve the core.

Increasing core efficiency

The number of fins per inch of radiator core can have a dramatic effect of the cooling capacity of a radiator. The conductivity of a standard/stock MGB GT V8 radiator can be increased by 15 per cent by fitting a high-pack core or by 30 per cent by fitting an 'S' pack core. Currently all V8 radiators purchased from Clive Wheatley V8 Conversions are of standard MGB GT V8 size but fitted with an 'S' core that presents the cores to the incoming air flow in a staggered 'S' shape thereby increasing the core's cooling capability. Although this increases the cooling capacity of the radiator one wonders whether it would not be possible to produce an 'S'-cored radiator that was also some 4in deeper than the standard MGB V8 radiator. I would think you would then be looking at increases in capacity of over 50 per cent.

The tube-design of the core also effects the transfer of heat because the cooling fins only make contact with the

5-2-3 I would guess this is a bespoke/custom brass radiator that has been eased forward by perhaps ½in (12mm). Note the Rover engine, what looks like a commendably flat top hose and the mechanical fan mounted on the nose of the water pump.

flat sides of the vertical tubes, not on the rounded ends. For example – a single 1in wide tube is better than two ½in wide tubes because the 1in tube only loses fin contact at two ends compared to the losses incurred by the four ends of two ½in tubes. The lighter weight of aluminium allows 1in wide tubes to be fitted with wall thicknesses that can withstand the coolant pressures. Copper is the better conductor but, if 1in wide tubes were fitted, the wall thicknesses necessary to prevent 'Ballooning' (and thus the weight and the cost) would be completely unacceptable. Thus aluminium radiators are more effective than copper (and brass) units as they have wider tubes and, consequently, more heat transfer area.

Furthermore, a thick radiator with multiple rows will provide more heat transfer than a thin radiator. Thus re-coring your three row radiator with a thicker five row core may improve heat transfer but the added two rows will not be proportionally as efficient as the first three. The first three will have heated the air flowing through the additional rows, so their heat transfer capacity will be reduced.

While core design has more bearing on heat transference than the material the core is made from, the core's fabric does make an important contribution to the effectiveness of a radiator. Brass is the material used in the vast majority of radiators (including the standard MGB GT V8) because it is easy to work and relatively cheap. However, both copper and aluminium have superior heat transfer properties. Copper is heavy and very much more expensive than brass and consequently you find few radiators made from copper. Furthermore, copper radiators have smaller tubes and soldered joints that reduce their effectiveness despite copper's superior conductivity. Aluminium is cheaper than copper and much lighter than brass but usually necessitates a thicker core – nevertheless, it is the material of choice for performance cars because the weight of a radiator is outside the wheelbase where weight reduction is doubly important. A Griffin aluminium cross-flow radiator can be seen at 5-2-4.

Although expensive, an alloy radiator offers both weight reduction and, by way of its construction, improved heat-transfer. In the USA – where ambient temperatures are higher than in much of Europe – Afco, Allstar, Griffin, Howe, Modine 3- and 4-core aluminium radiators are very well thought of and also cool some pretty hot MGBs. However, I think you would be prudent to use a specialist with 'hot' MGB experience. In the USA, Towery Foreign Cars can supply a six-row radiator which, it claims, will cool the hottest V8 engine while D+D Fabrications is confident it can solve most overheating problems. Alloy radiators are available in several designs and some offer the chance to mount the radiator in a cross-flow configuration – which you may find makes plumbing it in easier, particularly with an electric pump.

However, these days there are also coolant additives or alternative coolants that improve the ease with which heat is absorbed and discharged – thus aiding the effectiveness of the radiator. We will explore those a little later.

MAXIMISING AIR FLOW

Possibly the simplest of the solutions is to maximise the air flow through the radiator. You do need to approach this solution

5-2-4 This performance racing, cross-flow Griffin radiator is part number 2-25135-x and cost (at the time of writing) $220 from Summit Racing. It fits neatly between the MGB's chassis rails on its side, which also aligned the inlet and outlet necks with the Ford engine.

mindful of the fact that air is being forced into the air intake, at least when the car is on the move. However, you must get every ounce of air flow out of the engine compartment that enters it if you are to avoid a build-up of pressure that will, in turn, restrict the air passing through the radiator. So exit is every bit as important as entry air flow – if air cannot get out, it cannot get in.

The primary contributor to good air flow is getting lots of air into the radiator, less obvious is ensuring the air can escape easily from the rear of the radiator without building up pressure. Most hot air from the radiator/engine bay escapes down the propshaft tunnel, which is not a problem provided there is at least as much cross-sectional area for it to escape down as the front air intake. In fact, you really need a larger escape area than the intake. I suggest you check and maximise your air flow as your first priority.

● Ensure that there are no unnecessary obstructions (such as badges, auxiliary lights, horns or an accumulation of dirt/bugs) preventing the absolute maximum of air flow to the front of the radiator. Make sure the front number-plate neither obstructs the air nor deflects it from entering air intakes. If in doubt, fit an adhesive number to the bonnet or body (taking care not to contravene the law in your location).

● Ensure that all the air that enters the front grille is directed to the front of the radiator. The B has natural ducts each side of the radiator but rubber seals around the edges of the radiator ensure ALL the air entering the grille reaches engine coolant. Additionally if you have followed my suggestion and fitted a front spoiler/air-dam to increase the air-flow to the radiator, you will maximise the spoiler's effectiveness by fitting a short duct between the spoiler intake and the radiator.

● The inner wing/fender holes we see in 5-3-1 are part of the RV8 exhaust system

5-3-1 This photograph clearly shows the right side inner wing aperture for the RV8 exhaust system. Sharp eyes may see the spot welds around the aperture showing the strengthening lip/rim has already been added to the underside of the inner wing. The rear of the front wheel is clearly seen but you may not notice the slightly flaring and angled style of the headlamp mounting (top left) declaring this also to be an RV8 replica bodyshell. The beneficial side effect of these two inner wing exhaust apertures is a significant increase in airflow through the engine bay.

and minimize the under-bonnet/hood resistance to air flow and thus maximize the flow of air through the radiator. Even if you are using a block-hugger exhaust system, you can cut, strengthen and temporarily mesh-over similar holes to increase your air flow.

● Assist air flow through the radiator, particularly at slow speed, via fan(s). Mechanical and electric fans are explored later in the chapter.

● The volume of air feed to the radiator will be enhanced by a front ST (Special Tuning) air dam. Available in plastic or fibreglass, these dams bolt on as a substitute for the original front valance and an example is shown in photo 5-3-2. Take care parking front-on to any high curbs, however, and I recommend the fibreglass material since, while it may not look as pretty, it is much easier to repair. A not insignificant additional benefit of a front air-dam is that front end stability is also enhanced making this a **must**. If, for some reason, you do not plan to employ the ST front valance, it is important that you ensure that the later

MGB front valance with twin ventilation slats is fitted to the car, as is clearly shown in photo 5-3-3.

● Bonnet louvres are really only effective when the car's speed is above 30mph and then only when they are positioned in an area of (relatively) low air pressure. The area in front of any car is a high-pressure area due to the car's movement compressing the air and pushing it out of the way. The air that is forced up over the front is deflected upwards, and so a short area behind the leading edge of the bonnet is actually at low pressure and some of the louvres seen in picture 5-3-4 may be of considerable help. At the other end of the bonnet we find that the windscreen generates another high-pressure area which is why most motor manufacturers place the heater intake there. Consequently, the vents shown in photograph 5-3-5 may help air exit the engine bay at slow speed but could actually allow air to enter it at high speed.

● The high pressure area in front of the windscreen is about one-and-a-half windscreen heights forward from the base of the screen. Clearly the louvres need to

5-3-3 The vented front valance fitted as standard to later chrome-bumper MGBs. I initially fitted this to my GT V8 conversion, but changed to an ST spoiler in the interests of additional air flow though the radiator and better front-end stability.

5-3-2 This is Pete Mantell's superb Ford 302 conversion with an ST front valance/spoiler. Note the MGC bonnet which increases the space available for the front mounted Ford distributor.

5-3-4 Because they are located in a low-pressure area, these forward (arrowed) louvres may be very helpful in extracting hot air from the engine bay. The rear pair is, however of less certain benefit. Rather than go to the expense of having a specialist punch louvres in your bonnet, the same air flow can be achieved more cost effectively by cutting two, or four in this example, suitable holes in the bonnet and fixing standard pre-louvred panels to the underside.

5-3-5 These Pontiac Trans-Am air vents, in plastic, about $15 each, provide for very simple installation using silicon adhesive. Louvres or vents positioned too near the windscreen may only be effective at slow speed due to a build-up of air pressure in front of the screen at high speed.

be behind the radiator so, consequently, I would suggest the best place for louvres is just in front of the bonnet's crossmember, remembering to avoid electrical items.

MAXIMISING COOLANT FLOW

Coolant temperature is a balancing-act and you can over-cool an engine. When you first start an engine, particularly on a cold day, it is often necessary to inject extra fuel by 'choking' the mixture in order to get the engine to run reasonably well. The thermostat provides an essential restriction in the coolant flow to speed the warm-up and allow the engine to operate without additional fuel and the consequential emissions that result from a low coolant temperature. Too low an operating temperature is not good for either the engine nor the environment and the thermostat is there to keep the temperature at the optimum.

In fact, engines generally operate with progressively improving efficiency as the coolant temperature increases.

Most engines will not run efficiently below 82°C/192°F and many only minimise their emissions if they are operating at 88/200 (°C/°F) degrees. In fact almost all fuel-injected engines need 88/200 (°C/°F) degrees to operate effectively. So you need a thermostat that is hot enough to ensure your engine runs well but one that is cool enough to keep the coolant temperature within bounds when driving/traffic conditions slow you down. You will find the temperature that yours starts to open stamped on the top – in Europe 82°C is 'normal' with 76°C and 88°C alternatives being available depending whether you want to run your engine hotter or cooler than normal. I run my winter car hot and my summer car with a cold thermostat. In the US there are, I believe, 170, 180, 190 and 200°F choices.

Fit the most suitable thermostat for your engine and conditions. However, the volume of coolant flowing through the system clearly also has a major impact on the effectiveness of the coolant and the following details need exploring:

● You can drill three (increasing to six if necessary) $\frac{3}{16}$in (about 4mm) diameter holes around the base of your thermostat to increase the continuous flow of water

around the system. Unless you are fitting an electric water pump, do **not** remove the thermostat completely – it provides some back pressure which keeps the water in better contact with the block and consequently aides heat transfer. As an alternative to drilling holes to increase the coolant circulation you can remove the central piston – but expect warm-up times and pollution to increase.

● The anti-corrosive properties of coolants deteriorate with age and the system needs to be drained, flushed and re-filled with new coolant/antifreeze every two to three years. This is particularly important when aluminium components come in contact with the coolant as would be the case with most V8 conversions.

● The core of the radiator is vital in that it must not be obstructed by corrosion or silt which not only degrade the core's ability to act as a heat exchanger but also restrict the volume of water passing through the radiator. If you have the slightest doubt as to the cleanliness of your radiator's core, either replace the whole unit or have the existing one re-cored. I re-core my Stag radiator as a matter of routine every four years.

● A loose but slipping fan/drive belt can cause engines to overheat and alternators to undercharge. A worn fan belt can appear adequately taut but still slip because it is driving on the bottom flat of the pulleys not on the sides of the 'V'. Be careful not to over-tighten the belt.

● The original MGB heater valve restricts coolant flow to the heater and, if you ever use the heater, the original valve is best replaced by, in Rover parlance, the water flow-control valve – part number ZKC 5119 (shown in photograph 5-4-1). Used on the RV8 it is operated in the same way as the MGB's valve (Bowden cable) and, when combined with half inch pipework, will undoubtedly increase the effectiveness of your existing heater matrix. The valve is still available new in the UK for about £30

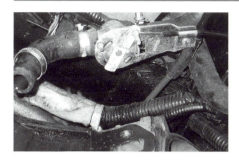

5-4-1 The RV8's in-line, larger capacity heater control valve. Note that the water hose to the left of the picture is noticeably larger than anything you will see on a standard MGB. A similar Bowden cable operated valve can be found on other Austin-Rover vehicles as detailed in the text.

from Rover dealers. However, Austin Minis, Marinas, Itals, Princesses and all modern Rovers and saloon/sedan MGs in your local breaker's yard are other potential sources, probably all costing much less than an RV8 one.

● If overheating only occurs at high speed (when frankly I'd least expect it), check the bottom hose is rigid enough to prevent it collapsing at high engine revs. Bottom hoses collapse when the water pump moves coolant faster than the radiator can supply it and the problem is very hard to detect. Today, reinforced silicone hoses are available and are worth fitting for their longevity and strength.

● The diameter of the crankshaft drive and/or water pump pulley influences the rotational speed of the water pump. You will increase your water pump's speed if you increase the diameter of the crankshaft pulley but it may be more practical to reduce the size of the water pump pulley. However, you need to be careful when considering this solution. If the pump is running too slowly then increasing its rpm will help. However if the pump is already operating at a reasonable speed, increasing its rpm will likely do more harm than good as you could provoke 'cavitation' around the impeller reducing the water flow.

● If all else fails, check that neither cylinder head gasket has been installed incorrectly. For some reason, Ford gaskets in particular are incorrectly installed with some frequency and the error results in overheating symptoms. Rover gaskets are stamped 'top' and Ford 'front' and both instructions mean exactly what they say.

CONVENTIONAL WATER PUMPS

The problem with a conventional water pump is that you need to satisfy space (forward length) criteria, rotational and water flow requirements while ensuring you choice fits your engine. I hope a few notes will help.

The effectiveness of the water pump is crucial, and upgraded mechanical pumps are available but so too are electric pumps which we will discuss in a separate section. Replacement water pumps vary in quality and efficiency. If you have temperature increments when driving, it's a good idea to consider an Edelbrock or a Weiand high-flow mechanical water pump. A Weiand Team G water pump was tested and shown to be 100 per cent more effective than the standard/stock pump it replaced.

FlowKooler also tells me that its water pumps produce 20 per cent more gallons per minute (GPM) at 2000rpm and 100 per cent more GPM at 900rpm than any other pump on the market today. Not only will this result in better water circulation it will also generate more water pressure inside the block helping to suppress engine hot spots and steam pockets. Furthermore FlowKooler claims its pumps are very mechanically efficient meaning less power is lost turning the pump. These claims make checking out the product range worthwhile.

As a general rule, engines with 'V' belt drives have a clockwise rotation and serpentine belts run anti/counter clockwise.

If you fit a mechanical fan to

your water pump its blades MUST be appropriately pitched to suck air through the radiator, not blow it forward

For Buick/Rover engines, the standard Rover P6/MGB GT V8 water pump is 4.5in between engine face and the front of the nose where your mechanical fan (if used) would be mounted. Alternatively, you could use a short water pump from an air-conditioned Buick Special or Olds F-85, as shown in photograph 5-5-1. Simco's 1353A measures 3.8in from the gasket surface to the front of the pulley and a '64-67 Buick 300 water pump, which also measures 3.8in, fits Buick, Olds and Rover V8 blocks.

Ford certainly make water pumps with differing nose lengths – as discussed in chapter 3.

MECHANICAL PULLER FANS

A mechanical fan works best at high revs, just when it is not required! It also consumes power. Estimates vary from a

5-5-1 Buick 215 with Buick/Olds 215 water pump and seven blade plastic ex-1800 MGB fan. This is the pump furnished with the air-conditioned cars referred to in the main text and is about 0.75 inches shorter than the 'standard' 215 water pump. The metal inserts in the fan were drilled out and the fan bolted directly to the water pump to accommodate the Buick's slightly larger fixing bolt. The radiator consists of 1972 MGB tanks spliced to an American fabricated core using the same dimensions as the factory MG V8 radiator. The inlet was moved to the left side to be nearer the water pump outlet.

5-5-2 An extra fan guard cowl covering the engine driven fan is highly recommended – here is an excellent example.

couple to 5bhp, but it definitely reduces the power you have to drive the car. Nevertheless, in locations where high ambient temperatures are the norm, cooling can be aided by an engine driven 'puller' fan fixed to the nose of the water pump, as shown in photographs 5-5-1 and 5-5-2.

A shrouded mechanical fan running about 1in from the closest part of the fan to the radiator will pull air through the core while the clearance allows for movement in your engine mounts and some flexing of the fan. Generally speaking, all fans are most effective when fitted about halfway within a peripheral shroud. Lightweight and relatively thin mechanical 'puller' fans such as seen in photograph 5-5-3 are available from most mail order equipment dealers, such as Summit Racing Equipment, and a fan diameter of 14in should clear the radiator hoses. Avoid flimsy plastic or fibreglass fan blades, though, since these have a tendency to flex under heavy load and chew a hole in the back of the radiator.

Flex-a-lite fan spacers have a dual bolt pattern that fits Chevrolet and Ford water pumps.

You do not have to install a clutch when you fit mechanical fan – in fact, I think that if the ambient temperatures in your area are such that you need a mechanical fan to supplement a pair of electric fans then you should not install a clutch. The

clutch is really only for situations when a mechanical fan will only be required from time to time. The electric fans fulfils that role making the mechanical fan's clutch an unnecessary complication.

If you doubt the wisdom of omitting the clutch, consider the following synopsis of clutch fan problems starting with noise. Fan noise is sometimes evident during first few minutes after start-up until the clutch can redistribute the silicone fluid back to its normal disengaged operating condition after overnight settling. It can also occur continuously under all high engine speed conditions (2500rpm and up) if the clutch assembly is locked up due to an internal failure. You can check for clutch failure by trying to rotate a static cold fan by hand. If it's locked-up or if there is a rough grating feel as the fan is turned, the clutch needs replacing.

Then there is the opposite problem – looseness. If the fan revolves with no drag (say it spins through four or five revolutions) the clutch needs replacing. If you can feel slight lateral movement at the end of the fan blade (say $^3/_8$in or 5mm) this can be a normal condition (due to the type of bearing) for a clutch – although I must say it would concern me because of the proximity of the radiator.

These clutches are normally filled with silicone fluid and small leaks are probably

of little consequence in the short term. If, however, the leakage increases you can expect the unit to fail in the near future.

ELECTRIC FANS

You will probably not need me to remind you that these days electric fans cool the vast majority of cars and that is because they are only in use when needed. In that sense the original MGB was ahead of its time with its twin electric fans – although by today's standards they were of low performance.

5-6-1 Adequate in their day but superseded by advances in fan technology, I really should replace these original MGB GT V8 fans.

The original MGB GT V8 parts, including the fan blades seen in picture 5-6-1, are all readily available. You need to budget for at least £150 by the time you've allowed for relays, some form of thermostatic controller and an override switch but frankly this money is better spent on modern fans. The controller/relay will still be needed but I recommend you buy a modern, aftermarket fan(s) as seen in picture 5-6-2, ideally mounted behind the radiator. The effectiveness of today's fans are enhanced by being close coupled to the radiator (they are usually held in place by thin plastic 'ties' to the radiator itself), by the use of a peripheral shroud and superior blade-shape technology.

The specialist electric fan companies have a couple of 'rules of thumb' that may interest you –

5-5-3 An excellent example of a fixed fan, but its effectiveness would have been increased had a shroud/cowl been fitted around its periphery.

5-6-2 An excellent example of a modern electric fan awaiting close-coupling to its radiator. These blades are straight but some of the very latest fans have curved blades which, the maker claims, further increase the effectiveness of the fan. Note the bottom hose with its integral thermostatic fan switch (which I would couple to the fan via a relay).

● For primary use, fit a puller fan, however, if you have a mechanical primary fan and the electric one is for auxiliary use, fit a pusher.

● They recommend 70 per cent of the radiator core be covered by an electric fan.

Various MG specialists prefer different makes of fan and you have a wide choice. Base your selection on the fan(s) that will fit in the space available, move the highest volume of air (measured in cfm), are close-coupled and shrouded. It is an added advantage if the blade of the fan(s) can be easily reversed.

While we will look at the circuits themselves in chapter 13, there are a couple of details that need emphasising here. A relay is essential to control the fan. Most of the fans we are thinking about will take 15-20amps current; without a relay you will grossly overload not only the thermostatic switch that automatically controls the fan but the manual override switch too.

Speaking of thermostatic switches, I personally think you are best fitting an adjustable thermostatic controller/switch such as that seen at 5-6-3 (available

from Kenlowe). A 20/30amp relay is also required and part number 2193956 is available from Lucas. I think you should initially set the Kenlowe controller to trip about halfway between 'normal' and 'hot' or about 90°C. You do not want the fan(s) to cut in too early or too frequently, and many make the mistake of having the fan come on at 'normal'. That is too early.

However, there is an alternative to think about as non-adjustable thermostatic switches with (about 5) different trigger-temperatures are also available. We see an example in picture 5-6-4 – which is a stainless steel bottom water-pipe with the thermostat switch mounting welded in situ. This raises the question as to the best place to trigger your electric fan. The top hose has been the traditional point but it has to be pointed out that modern cars tend to trigger the electric fan from the cooler bottom hose.

Pusher fans

There are too many makes of electric fan to evaluate them all but as one example, Kenlowe recommends its 10in and 8in fan combination to fit in front of the radiator

5-6-3 The adjustable thermostatic control of an aftermarket fan.

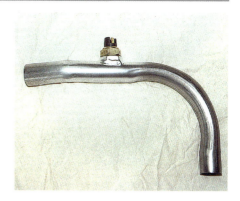

5-6-4 The modern approach is to fit the control switch for electric fans into the bottom hose, thereby controlling the temperature of the water as it goes into the engine.

and, in effect, replace the original MGB GT V8 twin 8in units. Kenlowe's advanced forward curved blades drive through secondary stator vanes on the 10in fan to maximize pressure and air flow and this is further aided by twin plastic housings that seal both units to the radiator. It is time I upgraded my fans.

Electric fans that are mounted in front of the radiator are notorious for their vulnerability to the elements. Failure due to water and debris ingress over the years brought the car manufacturers to increasingly mount electric cooling fans on the engine side of the radiator. Your engine may do the task for you but, if your 'pusher' fan(s) get very little exercise, you would be prudent to operate the manual override switch for a few minutes each time you take the car out in an effort to prevent the motors from seizing up.

Puller fans

Provided you have planned for their installation and left sufficient space, there is much to be said for puller fans. You can fit a much bigger diameter fan behind the radiator and a 16in puller will provide for about twice the area that the best combination of pushers generates. Furthermore, in this location the fan motor

5-6-5 A vertical view of a 'close coupled' fan with the radiator on the left. The fan blade housing and the electric drive motor are on the right of the photograph.

5-6-6 This is an RV8 electric fan positioned behind the radiator 'pulling' cooling air through the matrix. The fan is particularly valuable because it has no motor protruding backwards into the engine bay to interfere with the fan belt, water pump or the various pulleys.

is in a warm air flow from the radiator which quickly dries out any moisture that has managed to penetrate it.

Perma-cool's 16in fan generates 2950cfm air flow and is the highest volume

fan I've seen so far; it would solve all sorts of problems if you can fit it into the space between engine and radiator. The problem is that it is 3.75in front to back – which is likely to be too wide for most conversions. If space here is a problem, consider an RV8 electric puller fan with its 'thin' profile shown in pictures 5-6-5 and 5-6-6. Summit, in the USA, offers what looks like a suitable range of fans in its catalogue and MRG 1987 looks a good bet. In the UK you could consider the range of Pacet engine fans in Demon Tweeks' catalogue. Models CF88, CF99 or PF1606 are worth discussing – but do ensure you have adequate space as the motor on these units can extend backward by 3 or 4 inches (75 to 100mm).

ELECTRIC WATER PUMPS

12-volt Davies-Craig electric water pumps are available from MAW Solutions in two sizes. The larger pump not only circulates water very effectively but also allows you to eliminate the original thermostat, water pump (housing and impeller) and of course the associated pulley. The smaller electric booster pump is hermetically sealed and features a robust magnetic (ie brush-less) motor. The makers claim it is ideal for use as a booster for car cooling systems where it improves water circulation throughout the engine block. It is intended to supplement the existing mechanical water pump but nevertheless has a flow-rate of 13.3 litres per minute (175 gallons per hour) and will operate over a range of –40 to +130°C. The unit is roughly 2in x 2in x 4in (50mm x 50mm x 100mm), has ¾in (20mm) hose connections and weighs slightly over ½lb. The centrifugal pump's motor has an impressive 15,000-hour life and draws 1.3amps at 12v. I have yet to fit one but plan to do so and wire it in to run when the electric fan cuts in – usually at low engine revs and in slow moving traffic.

The larger (5.1in x 5.1in x 3.1in or 128mm x 131mm x 77mm) pump seen

5-7-1 Davies-Craig's electric pump kit which does for coolant circulation what an electric fan does for air circulation! The pipework will be approximately 2in (50mm) in diameter, which should help you 'scale' the size of the pump. The pump can be purchased with or without ...

5-7-2 ... its electronic control unit/kit shown here.

in 5-7-1 is more powerful – Davies-Craig claims flow rates of 20 litres to 80 litres per min (300 to 1300 gals per hour). It says that it increases cooling capacity while simultaneously giving you more engine power – claiming up to 20bhp (15kW) more power. Certainly the hose fittings are larger – accommodating 1¼in to 2in hoses – and current requirements are up to a maximum of 7.5amps, while motor expectations are reduced to 2000 hours.

The unit can be utilised in two ways –
● Installed as a complete replacement for the existing mechanically driven pump, in which case an electronic sensor/controller (available separately) must be fitted too.

The existing pump is deactivated or, in many cases, removed and a shorter drive belt fitted. The controller electronically senses engine heat and adjusts the rate of flow from the pump to maintain the coolant temperature you set, even after engine shutdown if you wish. Converters with space problems between timing cover and radiator may care to think about removing their mechanical water pump completely, fitting a flat cover with water take-off over the aperture and fitting one of these units elsewhere in the circuit. This installation will cost circa £300.

● Alternatively, the pump may be fitted to provide a very significant boost to the existing mechanical water pump in which case it can be controlled either by a manual or automatic on/off thermal switch. The thermal switch (seen at pic 5-7-2) recommended for this purpose is part number 0401 from Davies-Craig. This installation saves about £100 but saves nothing by way of mechanical efficiency or pulleys, belt etc. If you are going to follow this route you are as well buying the smaller pump/cheaper unit and fitting that as a manually controlled auxiliary unit.

Incidentally, whenever the electronic controller is fitted, it should be fitted away from the harsh conditions often prevalent in the engine bay. The cockpit is favourite. If you replace your conventional water pump with an electric pump you automatically remove any possibility of fitting a mechanical fan.

I do not know any details but understand the Weiand division of Holley also does electric water pumps.

EXPANSION/HEADER TANKS

There are two types of coolant tanks for your consideration – pure expansion tanks, which is the minimum you should contemplate, and preferably large header tank. Both are best fitted as high as possible, usually near the bulkhead. This

5-8-1 A BL expansion tank. The tank is from a Rover SD1, and coolant from the radiator is fed to the bottom of the expansion tank. The pipe leading from the filler neck is the overflow.

improvement increases the coolant volume, allows the radiator to self-bleed any trapped air and increases the head of water over the water pump.

The easiest solution requires you acquire an expansion tank from an MGB (post-Sept 1976 cars use tank BL part number ARH250 with pressure cap number GRC 110) but Dolomite, Rover SD1, TR7 and no doubt many other cars of the 70s and 80s use a similar tank. Expansion tanks (some are metal, many are plastic) have one small inlet pipe and all those I have seen have the slightly necked central waist we see in 5-8-1 to facilitate mounting via a band. The pipe must go to the bottom of the tank to ensure that water is sucked back into the main coolant system whenever the system cools down. This pipe is connected to the top of the radiator using a suitable length of small-bore water-hose. A jubilee clip should be sufficient to secure the new hose to either the special outlet provided for the purpose or, in its absence, the overflow outlet on the filler neck. If you use the latter you will need to buy a new (blanking) cap for the top of your radiator – the type that seals the top lip but has no-pressure spring/sealing washer. The top of the expansion tank will be sealed via the traditional spring-loaded pressure cap transferred from the top of your radiator if it is in good condition and of the correct

5-8-2 The fact that this Vauxhall Nova header tank is on a Stag makes no difference to how one would fit it to an MGB. The pipe draped across the top of the tank is not relevant, but note the large bore bottom hose and the top air bleed pipe that comes from the top of the radiator. I installed this extra coolant capacity/head before heading off to Italy via the Alps in the height of summer, and can report 3000 trouble-free miles.

pressure for your car. Once the coolant settles down it would be normal to run an expansion tank about half-full, thus adding approximately one pint of coolant to the capacity of the system.

You will get the advantages of at least twice that extra coolant capacity coupled with the benefits of a self-bleeding system by utilising a more recent header tank. I have never seen one made from anything other that plastic and there are numerous examples to be found in 1990s cars. I have used a Vauxhall Nova header tank (pictured at 5-8-2) but, were I carrying out the change again, Volvo and Ford Granada tanks look to offer good alternatives.

5-8-3 This header tank has two pipes. The air bleed can be seen quite clearly on the top left of the tank, but the larger diameter pipe feeding into the bottom of the tank is slightly hidden, so I've highlighted it with an arrow.

The installation will be a little more difficult since these later tanks have two connecting pipes, one of about 20/25mm bore and one smaller diameter pipe, usually roundabout the same size as those used for expansion tanks. You can see both pipes and their differing sizes in 5-8-3. There are similarities in the installation in that the small pipe still needs to be coupled to the expansion outlet at the top of the radiator – but this time the other end is connected to the top of the header tank. This pipe now acts purely as an air bleed and needs to be routed accordingly. You still need to fit the same new top-lip-only sealing cap to your radiator. However, it is connecting the large diameter pipe that will exercise your mind the most. When fitting mine I welded a 'T' piece to the stainless pipe that coupled to the bottom of the radiator. I used a stainless tube of an identical external diameter to the bottom header-tank outlet but the tricky part was getting the 'T'-angle just right. The main coolant flow/expansion takes place though this larger diameter-connecting pipe – and I was very surprised at the volume of flow and turbulence through the header tank. These tanks usually have a sealed top cap – i.e. the system is sealed with no opportunity for expanding water to escape. Consequently the tanks all have a 'maximum when cold' line marked on

the side and it is important that you never over-fill the tank beyond this line or you risk busting a hose due to over-pressurisation of the system as it warms up.

OTHER COOLING AIDS

Not every contributing factor to keeping the beast cool is obvious –

Exhaust wrap

Another major reduction of under-bonnet temperatures can be achieved by the use of Thermo-Tec exhaust insulation (available in the UK from Agriemach Ltd or Demon Tweeks). Summit Racing Services stocks the product in the USA. I do not think it a good long-term idea to fully wrap mild steel manifolds/headers (shown in photograph 5-9-1). If you have a pair of good, fairly new, mild steel exhaust

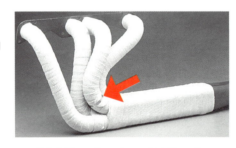

5-9-1 The exhaust manifold/header wrapping tape shown in this photograph is said to reduce under-bonnet temperature by 70 per cent. Note the stainless steel securing clip on number three pipe's wrapping (arrowed).

manifolds/headers, and are reluctant to buy new, you could have the outside of your mild steel ones metal sprayed before applying the wrapping tape. Alternatively, I would suggest you leave about 30 per cent of the metal unwrapped unless you can get assurances from the manifold's manufacturers that it will take a 100 per cent cover. This will, of course, diminish the effectiveness of the wrap.

However, if you are still in the planning and budgeting stage, do assume stainless

steel manifolds/headers will be required as they are ideal for this excellent wrapping. This insulation is so effective, I am told, as to make it possible to touch the exhaust manifold without burning yourself (take care if attempting this experiment!).

You will be effectively moving the heat down the exhaust system and not into the engine bay thus aiding the engine cooling. I have insufficient personal experience but the manufacturer assures me the exhaust system is more effective as a consequence of the higher temperature exhaust gases being able to move faster through it. An aerosol of Hi-Heat Coating is available which preserves and protects the insulating wrap after it has been installed. Extra resins and binders toughen the surface of the wrapping by sealing the pores to minimize the penetration of any external liquids.

Do not be alarmed if the wrapping smokes and smells when you first use the car; this is quite normal. In damp climates you may also find that the wrapping emits water vapor each time you start up, having absorbed it from the atmosphere while the car is not in use. Finally, don't take your wrapping so far down the pipes as to risk dirt/water from the road getting onto it (this is best avoided).

With most vehicles the wrapping operation can be accomplished with the exhaust manifold(s) in place (even if it is necessary to remove other equipment to gain access). However, with the MGB V8's block-hugger style manifolds/headers, you will almost certainly need to do the actual wrapping with the manifolds off the car. Offer the manifolds up (to ensure they fit and to note where to fit the wrapping's securing clips so they do not subsequently get in the way), then remove and wrap them. RV8-style manifolds probably provide enough clearance to wrap the tape in situ.

Agriemach distributes the silica-based tape in a variety of length and widths, though one 50ft roll of 1in tape should be enough for one manifold. The tape contains no asbestos but, nevertheless, can withstand temperatures up to 2000°F!

You will also need to purchase some special self-assembly stainless steel securing clips, called 'snap-strip', to hold the wrapping in place at the beginning and end of each run. Do take care with these clips since they are very sharp indeed. The tape is wound round each exhaust pipe with a 0.25 inch overlap on each turn.

The cost of a tape wrap kit for a V8 engine is about £150 in the UK. Readers with original style manifolds/headers may care to think about a cheaper alternative which is easier to install. A 'Blanket' is available which, as the name implies, covers each manifold with one piece of insulating material. Since each pipe has quite large areas of its surface uncovered (but still under the blanket) it will be appreciated this method does not reduce the under-bonnet temperature quite so efficiently (the manufacturer claims a 50 per cent drop).

Air locks

Try and ensure the top hose lays as flat as possible between the engine thermostat housing and the top of the radiator. Some conversions have a big 'loop' of water hose that encourages air locks. The airlock problem is more common than you may

5-9-2 Actually fitted to a (Rover-V8-engined) TR8, nevertheless, this simple airlock bleed arrangement is a good idea for any engine with a looped top hose.

5-9-3 Alternatively this filler-cap location neatly fitted to a Ford perhaps solves more than one problem.

5-9-4 This photograph is of an MG RV8 engine bay, and is incuded to demonstrate the improved route of the radiator's top hose (part number GRH 1324), and the necessarily different thermostat housing (ETC. 6135A).

imagine but avoidable by initially fitting a bleed nipple (an example is at picture 5-9-2) or a filler cap (picture 5-9-3) in the top hose if it has a 'loop'.

The flatness of the top hose depends upon the thermostat cover you are using – some make it very difficult to get the hose to lay flat. Buick/Rover engine users can fit the MGR V8 arrangement pictured at 5-9-4 to reduce vulnerability to airlocks.

Coolant additives

I have come across two coolant additives that are reputed to improve the speed at which the coolant collects and gives up heat.

Water Wetter is added to the coolant after the system, including any antifreeze,

has been drained. In operation in very high ambient temperatures it seemed to work well for me and reduced the engine's operating temperature – although that is very subjective. The instructions said it worked best if the system was drained of antifreeze and I was slightly concerned that without its antifreeze and corrosion inhibitors the water passages in my Rover aluminium engine could be corroding. Consequently I drained the Water Wetter as soon as possible after the holiday in question, refilled with new antifreeze (always a good idea to replace the corrosion inhibitors), and water. Water Wetter works by breaking down surface tension in the coolant to improve heat transfer. The resultant improved thermal conductivity reduces hot spots and vapour bubbles as well as lubricating water pump seals. I note the latest publicity says the product can now be used with antifreeze.

Agriemach claims its product, Radiator Relief, to be the best coolant system additive on the market today, and can be used with or without antifreeze. It is designed to function in two ways. First and foremost by reducing operating temperatures by as much as 30°F. As an additional bonus it speeds warm-up times by about 50 per cent. 32fl oz is sufficient for 15 litres of coolant.

Alternative coolant ('For-Life')

Developed during the Second World War for cooling radar installations, this ethanediol-based coolant stays liquid down to -40 (thus antifreeze is unnecessary) and only boils at about 180°C. Furthermore in its For-Life form, it is mixed with an excellent detergent that keeps water passages clean and rust-free. Available from Demon Tweeks in the UK, it **must** be used undiluted after first ensuring the coolant system is flushed clean. An additional bonus is that it warns of head gasket failure by changing colour from red to yellow. For topping-up, keep a small container of For-Life in the boot/trunk and avoid adding any water and/or antifreeze. To fill your system the cost will be circa £30 in the UK – but For-Life is effective for 10 years.

Radiator cap

Modern radiator caps increase and simultaneously regulate the pressure in the cooling system. Each cap will have a pressure rating in lb/in^2. For every additional pound of pressure, the coolant's boiling point increases by 3°F.

Carburettor spacers

All V8 carburettors sit in the 'V' of the engine atop a water-heated inlet manifold. If they do not get overly hot while running most will suffer from heat-soak after the engine is switched off and consequently can be difficult to re-start when hot (the fuel just evaporates when pumped into the hot carburettor). A Phenolic spacer/insulator between the inlet manifold and carburettor base will reduce heat-soak and aid hot starting. It could also improve the air/fuel distribution and consequently top-end performance.

The final thought

As an overheating 'long stop' – run with the heater and heater fan. That has saved me on countless occasions and the resulting sauna got some weight off the driver too!

COOLING THE OIL

An oil cooler also contributes to lowering the engine-temperature. However, if you have utilized the RV8-style of exhaust manifold/headers, unless you live in a particularly warm climate or have a particularly 'hot' engine, you may not need an oil cooler. This is important not because it saves on installation cost and

complexity, but because it removes one not inconsiderable obstruction from in front of your water radiator.

If you have retained a block-hugger exhaust system, a 10-row oil cooler connected by flexible pipes to the engine and filter is a necessity. An external oil circuit/pipe diagram is shown in drawing D2-3 in chapter 2, which gives oil line part numbers for the rubber-bumper's under-slung oil coolers.

For chrome-bumper cars, when fitting an oil cooler there is an option in respect of location: above or below the radiator duct panel. The location has a bearing on which oil line hoses are needed. For rubber-bumper cars the location question does not arise as the oil cooler is already mounted centrally below the radiator duct as we saw in photo 5-3-3, away from the radiator cooling fans, thus allowing for maximum air flow to the main bulk of the water radiator.

The easiest location for the oil cooler in a chrome-bumper car with a 'puller' electric fan is above the radiator duct. In this event use pipes BHH 1103 to connect the front oil pump outlet to the cooler and BHH 1341 to connect the oil-filter (through the right side radiator panel) to the oil cooler. BHH 1104 connects the rear pump fitting to the filter in all cases.

However, the central/under panel location (i.e. copying the rubber-bumper cars location) is definitely best if only to allow pusher fans full operation; it does require two additional 38mm diameter holes in the radiator duct panel. For Buick/Rover engines it also requires the use of pipes BHH 1613 (pump to cooler) and BHH 1612 (filter to cooler). The easiest way to achieve this location for chrome-bumper car owners is to change the radiator duct panel as described and recommended in chapter 9.

In the higher ambient temperatures of the USA it may be too drastic to totally omit an oil cooler. You may even feel an enlarged oil cooler important if you live in the warmer areas of the US, in which case a higher capacity cooler from Summit Racing Equipment could be used. 'Perma-Cool' units come in four sizes, the smallest of which is designated PRM 201 and copes with 450bhp engines. It is 1.5 inches deep, 6.5 inches wide and 18 inches long.

If you fit an oil cooler after installing RV8 exhaust manifolds, it would suggest that you live in a very hot climate. That being the case, you do not need to worry about over-cooling your lubricating oil. However, if you fit an oil cooler and live in a moderate/cool climate there could be occasions when your engine oil does not need cooling and you are doing the engine no good at all by over-cooling the oil. In these climates the thermostatically controlled oil valve seen in photograph 5-10-1, fitted in line with the oil-cooler, is a very good idea. The valve will not pass oil to the cooler during start-up or whenever the oil is below a good operating temperature but will allow it passage to the cooler when necessary.

5-10-1 This thermostatically controlled oil-valve recycles the engine oil until the oil reaches its operating temperature, whereupon it allows oil to pass through the oil cooler.

Chapter 6
Wheels & tyres

This chapter may appear rather earlier in the book than you might have expected, but the wheels and tyres are so important to the conversion that I felt they deserved our early attention. They dictate what brakes and rear-axle ratio you fit, they are instrumental in the car's roadholding, steering and stability, they affect several bodyshell alterations and may change the suspension spring ratings. The width of the wheels allows the use of wider tyres which benefits both handling and ride. More rubber on the road will also improve stopping as the brakes stop the tyres and the tyres stop the car. However it does not stop there for the diameter of the wheels affect the size and thus the stopping power of the brakes!

The MGB front suspension was basically designed in the very early 1950s for the MG TD 'Midget'. In those days it bolted straight onto the TD's chassis rather than to the front crossmember enthusiasts of the MGB are familiar with. Nevertheless, the similarities in the designs

and the differences with what today we take for granted, are startling. It was designed with 5.5in (138mm) wide tyres in mind and maybe the designers were far sighted enough to realise that tyre widths, technology and design would advance, but I doubt they envisaged today's wide wheels, low profile tyres and radial construction. Consequently, as we plan our conversion, we need to bear in mind the close links between the car's suspension and its wheels/tyres and not take our wheel/tyre improvements too far without corresponding suspension improvements. The wheels and tyres also influence your suspension considerations and I thought we'd best resolve the wheel/tyre issue sooner rather than later.

As you get towards the end of the chapter you may wonder if I forgot wire wheels or 'knock-on' alloys. The answer is no, I have not forgotten them but feel that neither have a place in a car with 200-300lb-ft of torque. In fact, once you get to the medium range of engine torque

you need to be thinking whether the 5-stud wheel fixing seen at 6-1 is not essential! So 'wires' are not even on my list of options. We will touch on 5-stud wheel fixings

6-1 16 x 7J wheels with, I guess, 55 or 60 profile tyres. However, it is the 5-stud bolt pattern that I really wanted to emphasise.

again when we look at front and rear suspensions, but let me prompt you here by mentioning that the MGC had 5-stud mountings with 150bhp at its disposal. If it were my car, I would go to 5-studs long before the 'high' power-band was reached and consider high-powered cars running on four studs a potential hazard.

The improvements modern wheels and tyres can make to an MGB can be dramatic. Indeed, I believe that the biggest single improvement you can make to your MG's handling can be achieved by using modern wheel and tyre technology. Increasing the width of the tyre that comes into contact with the road can extend the road holding benefits offered by the modern tyre. This is achieved by increasing the size of the wheel and decreasing the aspect ratio of the tyre – but within reason if you plan to retain the original MGB suspension.

You must be comfortable, of course, with the aesthetic qualities of your selected wheels – a detail that is completely personal and consequently one that I am not going to even discuss other than to show a few (of the dozens) of options. Your wheel selection must be chosen with gear ratios, tyre size, bodywork, brakes and unsprung weight very much in mind – and we do need to explore those details. It is hard to know where to begin. However, since stopping seems fairly important I will discuss first how brakes should influence wheel size selection.

WHEEL DIAMETER

The size of the front brakes generally, and the disc diameter in particular, has a major impact upon the size of the wheel you can choose. As a rule of thumb, the bigger the engine and the faster the car, the larger the brake capacity one needs. Braking capacity is dictated by front disc/rotor size, which in turn requires progressively bigger wheel diameters. So, with moderately powered cars up to say 3500cc, those on a tight budget could stick to the MGB's standard/stock 14in wheels. I feel this size, when fitted with a lower profile tyres (185 x 70 x 14), is adequate and allows 270/273mm diameter front discs to be fitted. You may still prefer 15in wheels, of

course. These allow for 195 x 60 x 15 tyres and thus put more rubber on the road, while larger wheels will fit over the 273mm discs and even allow for an increase in disc/rotor size at some future date.

Medium-powered conversions need at least 15in diameter wheels to allow for both increases in brake disc size to 295mm and the opportunity to select a tyre size that gives you the long legs and the road holding such an engine deserves. There is, of course, nothing to stop you using 16in wheels but, for the majority of medium-powered road-going conversions, 15in diameter wheels will be adequate.

High-powered V8s, particularly if they are heavy cars, do need the brake capacity provided by a 16in wheel and, of course, the grip provided by a compatible rim/tyre width. Remember, however, that you cannot go on increasing the rim/tyre width without eventually getting into trouble with tyre contact. Bodywork is the obvious contender, though front anti-roll bars shouldn't be entirely forgotten. Almost certainly the first problem you will encounter is interference (probably when going over a bump) between the outside of the tyre and the MGB's rear wing 'lip'. If the interference is minimal and/or intermittent you will probably be able to grind about half the lip's width away to effect adequate clearance. If your selected tyres are over 195 section, more drastic remedial measures may be necessary, such as flaring the rear wing or a change of body-style. In any event, it is prudent to get this potential problem resolved before you paint the car.

RIM WIDTH

Rim width will be most improvers' next consideration and, while engine capacity and available power must be factors, the preferred tyre width will be the most influential factor (since tyre widths must be married to compatible rim widths). That said there is some relationship with wheel

6-2 A 15in diameter 7J rim with quite some offset and the evergreen 'Minilite' pattern.

diameter because you will find that, for a given rim width, you will be able to fit a wider section tyre to that same rim as the wheel diameter increases. A 6J rim on a 16in wheel with take a slightly wider section tyre that a 6J rim on a 14in wheel. Take professional advice, however, for an incorrect marriage of rim and tyre could be lethal.

A final thought on rim widths with today's powerful engines in mind – 225 section tyres on 7in rims are progressively becoming more and more common place. However, you will not get a 7in (177mm) rim under a standard MGB

6-3 The wheels on this Chevy powered 'B are 17 x 8J, but look, I think you will agree, completely in place. I would be concerned that 40 per cent ratio tyres would make the steering over-sensitive – in fact, I would advise driving a car with tyres with a lower than 60 aspect ratio before you rushed out and bought a set.

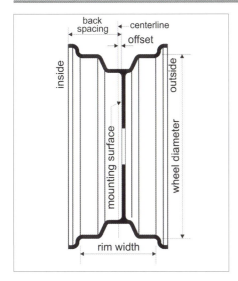

D6-1 Difference between the centreline & offset of a roadwheel.

wheelarch. Consequently, our wheel and tyre selection also affects body shape and style. Flared wheel arches and RV8 and Sebring styles allow for wider wheels/tyres – and are explored in chapter 9 – but do not forget the simultaneous suspension improvements required. Picture 6-2 shows a 7J wheel, while pictured at 6-3 is a rather special MGB created by Australian Paul Knot of PK Automotive Repairs with 17x8 HSV wheels shod with 245/40 tyres This gives you an idea of the available scope.

ROAD WHEEL OFFSETS/ SPACERS

The offset of a road wheel is the distance between the centre of its rim width and the back or mounting face of the wheel-boss. The offset is (usually but not always) said to be positive when the wheel 'sits-out' from the centre-line of the wheel and to be negative when the rim moves closer to the centre of the car. Offset is always measured in millimeters regardless of the rim being measured in inches. Diagram D6-1 is drawn with positive offset and may help you picture the critical nature of road-wheel offsets. I have occasionally heard the amount of space required from rear

rim to the mounting face as 'Backspacing' and have used this diagram to record what backspacing means and to specify several other terms commonly used when talking road-wheel sizes.

If you have a problem with the inside of a wheel/tyre fouling the inside of the wheelarch or suspension and become tempted to fit a set of spacers – don't, or at least think twice! Picture 6-4 shows a typical proprietary spacer. The central bore size of the wheel-centre is (or should be) a load carrying component and it should be a reasonably tight fit on the boss machined onto the centre of each hub. This is another reason for not using wheel-spacers, as the dissipation of loads through this central boss becomes lost and its contribution is instead carried by the wheel studs. I will return to the importance of this central boss very shortly; sticking with this spacer issue, you are better to buy a set of wheels with a different offset to correct the problem because spacers put additional load of the wheels studs. Furthermore,

6-4 Proprietary wheel spacers, one of which is shown here, come in quite a variety of thicknesses. The majority of these is intended to be used between a bolted wheel and its hubs. Care needs to be exercised, and the wheel studs correspondingly increased in length. However, in the context of spacing a wire wheel adapter away from its hub, to obviate cutting down over length studs, a 6mm thick spacer will do.

most fail to extend the length of the studs to compensate for the 'lost' wheel-nut threads.

If you are still contemplating spacers (albeit with lengthened studs), consider the effect that spacers have on tyre scrub radii. Drawing D6-2 examines positive, negative and zero scrub-radii. You have no control over the angle of the king-pin but the width and diameter of the tyre, the offset (or backspacing) of the road-wheel and any spacers you fit can and will alter the scrub-radius. You need to maintain a positive scrub-radius, but do not want to over-do it. You are unlikely to approach negative scrub-radius (unless you fit very large tyres) but you will affect the steering if you extend the offset and/or fit spacers and consequently need to approach this part of your conversion with caution. Rather like several other conversion details, there is much to be said for using the same combination of wheels and tyres (without spacers) as a previous successful conversion.

You cannot assume your selected wheel size will automatically provide adequate offset for front brake caliper clearance. Differing makes and styles of wheel offer differing caliper clearances. A look at photo 6-5 and you will notice that the internal diameter of the wheel is quite satisfactory and clears the caliper comfortably. However, the side clearance between caliper and wheel is down to an

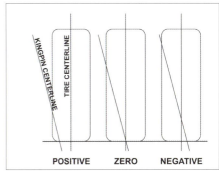

D6-2 Scrub radius.

6-5 Compare and contrast the very close clearance between this 14 inch MGB Rostyle wheel and the Princess caliper which, again, can be viewed through the wheel slots.

6-6 These superb Compomotive wheels have 7 inch rims and are running 205x50x16 inch tyres. These show off the brake calipers very well indeed (in this case, SD1 Vitesse), which are considerably wider than the Princess caliper shown in the preceding shot.

absolute minimum, even though the brake upgrade in this picture is not particularly startling (12.8mm solid discs, unspaced Princess calipers).

The alternative brake/caliper arrangement shown in photograph 6-6 uses 22mm thick ventilated discs with ex-Rover SD1 calipers. Consequently, before buying a full set of alloy wheels, I would strongly recommend that you borrow a friend's example, or buy a wheel on a returnable basis, and try them on your preferred front brake set-up before settling upon a certain design, and certainly before having tyres fitted to them.

WHEEL MATERIALS

The change in wheel technology since I wrote the first edition of this book has been amazing. The growth of alloy wheels with the attendant reduction in unsprung weight has effectively made steel wheels obsolete and it is today just a question of which alloy wheel suits your needs best.

However, there are complications when it comes to selecting materials – for while the majority of wheels are made from aluminium there are those that are made from magnesium alloys. Magnesium wheels are primarily intended for racing and are more expensive and lighter without losing strength. Aluminum wheels are excellent – I run all my cars on these – but you need to take care to buy the road-going version of any selected pattern because some aluminium patterns are also available in a thinner racing version which I would not advise in a big-engined V8 conversion.

CENTRAL WHEEL PATTERNS

The main focus of this section is to assess the aesthetic shape of the wheel centre and the associated brake-cooling considerations. Remember the central boss of the wheel should be a tight fit over the boss of the hub. After that you could be forgiven for thinking that the only things that matter about the central part of a wheel are its bolt pattern and whether it appeals to the eye. In fact, wheel design (and therefore, air flow) might have a major impact on the car's braking characteristics. Alloy wheel patterns that use a thin spoke design allow high volumes of air to pass through them and this provides a significant cooling effect on the disc and, to a lesser effect, on the caliper. Do not underestimate the value of these cooling air flows and the contribution they make to efficient braking. However, in very wet weather the brakes can prove to be too exposed, causing a momentary dead response period until the water is cleared from the discs.

A friend's recommendation is the best way to select a central wheel pattern but I've added a few pictures at 6- 8 to 6-10 to get you started – but there is a lot more out there, even with 5-stud mountings.

6-8 This is a 14 inch x 6J alloy wheel called Stealth. It is made by TSW but marketed by the MGOC – very smart too.

6-9 A 15 inch x 6J variant available from the MGOC with or without Yokohama Tyres.

WHEEL CENTRING

Earlier I mentioned the importance of the central boss and how it both centred the road-wheel on the axle hub and dissipated some of the stresses. There are other wheel-centring factors to think about when buying new road-wheels. Wheel-nuts with tapered/beveled faces are probably the most common method but a number of alloy wheels use a plain (parallel) shank to the wheel-nut as it passes through a

6-10 This excellent Compomotive wheel lets us see the (cast) Wilwood Superlite front brake caliper.

tight and precisely-bored hole through the wheel centre. These methods, particularly if the central boss engages on the hub, will give safe wheel location and centring – provided that they are properly fitted and maintained.

However, there is danger for the unwary. If you inadvertently fit the incorrect wheel-nuts with too small a shank there will be excessive clearance between wheel and nut – demonstrated by drawing D6-3 – and you will lose the initial centring register and the retention capability of the system. If there is play between the shank of the wheel/lug nuts and the mounting holes you will be relying on friction to locate the wheels. No matter how tight you get the wheel/lug nuts, the wheels **will** move around as you drive which will wear the nuts and/or the wheel surface and loosen the nuts. Consequently, it is imperative that you buy and fit new wheel/lug nuts simultaneously with your new alloys in order to ensure you have the absolute minimum clearance required for this system.

TYRES
Profiles

The profile is governed by the aspect ratio of the tyre. Originally, all tyres fitted to MGBs would have an aspect ratio of at least 80 per cent, which is to say the wall height is only 80 per cent of the declared tread width. If you have a '165' radial tyre on your MGB with no additional aspect ratio figure shown, then you may assume the tyre's wall height is 0.8 x 165 or 132mm (5.2in).

If your tyre is marked (on the wall) as say 185/70 you will gather that this tyre has a 70 per cent aspect ratio and a wall height of 129.5mm (5.1in). The RV8 uses a 65 profile tyre and this provides reasonable steering stability. The design of the suspension and the MG's basic limitations, however, even with the RV8's modifications, still means that to fit tyres of less than 60 profile (e.g. 55) could start to over-sensitize the steering, necessitating constant steering corrections. Tyres below 60 profile are therefore best treated with caution if you are staying with the MGB's original front suspension set-up. When enquiring about a change of front suspension design, include some questions about recommended tyre widths and profiles in an effort to be sure your wheel/ tyre plans are compatible.

Diameter calculations

It may help you to know how to calculate the overall diameter of any tyre size you are contemplating. Not only is this relevant to the gear ratios on your car, you may find it helpful to estimate the accuracy of your speedometer after a tyre size change. The overall diameter of a tyre is 'wheel diameter + twice the tyre wall height'.

We calculated the tyre wall height earlier using its aspect ratio, so as an example let us calculate the overall diameter of a 15in wheel fitted with a 195 x 60 tyre:

15 + (2 x 195 x 0.6mm)
or 15 + (2 x 117mm)
or 15 + 9.2 inches
or 24.2 inches (diameter)

You can use the resulting diameter to work out your approximate road-speed per 1000rpm in 4th gear (not 5th gear). Multiply the tyre diameter by 2.975 and

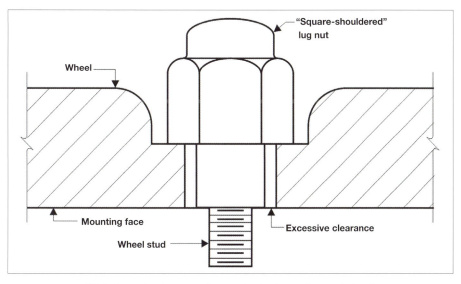

D6-3 An undersize securing nut in the bore of a roadwheel.

then divide by your rear axle ratio. For the above tyre with, for example, an axle ratio of 3.5, you would get 20.5mph/1000rpm or about 72mph at 3500rpm. Keep in mind that tyre size data is only approximate and varies slightly from manufacturer to manufacturer and, of course, as the tyre wears. Nevertheless, this may help you decide not only whether your speedo needs re-calibrating but whether you have the right combination of rear axle ratio and tyre size. We will look at rear axle ratios in chapter 8.

Speedometer re-calibration

A change in tyre size may necessitate your understanding the consequences on your speedometer's accuracy. Dramatic tyre changes may even require the speedometer be recalibrated. However, any change to the rear axle ratio will, without delay, necessitate the re-calibration of your speedometer.

To re-calibrate your speedometer with any degree of accuracy you will need to have your wheels and tyres on the more or less finished car (to get the weight about normal) and the tyre pressures at their correct level. Measure the rolling radius of your rear wheels – i.e. the distance from the centre of the rear wheel to the ground.

Next you need to mark the speedometer cable at the dashboard end with a 'flag' of sticky tape and put another piece of tape on a rear wheel. Get some friends to push you forward six revolutions of the road wheel while you count the revolutions of the speedo-cable. Send the rolling-radius and cable-revolutions information together with the speedo to any re-calibration shop (there are a couple of suggestions in the Appendix) for a refurbished and re-calibrated speedometer.

Speed rating

A cautionary word on the legal speed rating the tyres on your car must comply with to satisfy both the law and insurance regulations, never mind your own safety considerations. Here is an abridged list of the speed rating letter codes and the respective maximum speed capability. You must ensure the rating on your tyres are comfortably adequate for the maximum speed capability of your car, whether you use the full capability or not.

In the UK the following are the principal ratings of interest:

T	118mph
U	125mph
H	130mph
VR	over 130mph
V	150mph
ZR	over 150mph

As an of example, an original standard 3500cc MGB V8 should sport absolutely no less than 'H'-rated tyres.

In the USA the abridged list is as follows:

T	118mph
U	124mph
H	130mph
VV	150mph
Z	over 150mph

Obviously, you would be prudent to increase the speed rating of your tyres as your engine power increases the car's speed potential.

Tyre tread patterns

I doubt there are any poor tyres made today – the competition would ensure that a manufacturer of poor tyres would not stay in business long. However, the car, its driver, intended use and owner's preferences make suggesting tyres very difficult. Furthermore, tyre technology advances at an amazing pace so any suggestion I make here today might be out of date by the time you read the book.

Nevertheless, the tyres are so important to the car's performance that you are probably best talking not only with friends with similar cars but several retailers in your area. Your tyres need to be considered in parallel with your suspension spring rating. A low profile tyre (say 50 per cent aspect ratio) will have much less 'give' in its wall than a tyre with a 70 per cent aspect ratio, and consequently a slightly softer spring may be appropriate for the 50, or similar low-profile tyres.

You need to bear the hardness of the compound in mind as this effects wear-rate and grip dramatically. A soft compound will generate wonderful grip but everyday use of the car may necessitate a harder compound and thus a different tyre to what you might select if you were thinking just of a blast on dry Sundays. If you are lining up a few track days each year you may need to think again about make, compound and tread pattern.

Watch for directional tyres – a consequence of advancing tyre technology. These have their inside and outside and direction of rotation stipulated. I have a close association with the TR Register racing scene and can tell you that Yokohama's A008R tyres were the choice of the vast majority of participants although supposedly superseded by the A032R some years ago.

Whatever the make/compound/pattern of tyre, you are best to buy your tyres at the last possible moment. Neither engines nor tyres appreciate being stood around for months or years while a car is modified/converted/restored. Tyres actually harden with age thus a tyre bought yesterday will perform better than exactly the same tyre bought a year ago. They also need to be stored upright and ideally in the dark – so do not leave your intended road-tyres on a car undergoing an extensive conversion outside. Fit a set of slaves. Your retailers maybe pleased to give you an old/bald set of the chosen size against your agreement to buy the road-going set when the car is near finishing.

Chapter 7
Front suspension & steering

Suspension arrangements for the MGB have undergone considerable development by aftermarket specialists in recent years – almost to the point that the options available are confusing. Throughout your deliberations on the front suspension you think most suited to your engine conversion you need to bear a few things in mind:

● First, the front suspension must be compatible with the rear suspension. Consequently, if you are modifying your front suspension (e.g. lowering it) you need to carry out a compatible modification to the rear suspension.

● If you plan on buying a front suspension kit or package from one supplier you need to at least talk to them about a compatible rear suspension set-up. If the supplier also makes a rear suspension package, he is going to try and sell you both. There is much to be said for a front and rear package that has been proven and tested as a pair and that you can test drive. Therefore, ideally you are advised to buy all your conversion components for the front and the rear suspensions simultaneously and from one supplier.

● Bear in mind the stresses that you will be introducing upon the wheel hubs. The stresses not only come from the torque of the engine, mostly through the rear hubs, but from the increased braking effect of bigger calipers and increased vehicle weight mostly through the front hubs. Thus there will come a time when 5-stud wheel mountings are essential. Incidentally, one easy route to 5-stud wheel mountings is to fit MGC front hubs in place of the original MGB hubs and then to ensure the rear studs follow the same pattern. Front hubs from an Australian Commodore are 5-stud and use similar wheel bearings to MGB.

● You may be able to live with different front and rear stud patterns but identical patterns are worth planning into your conversion. Note that in these days of imperial and metric measurements you need to take care to ensure your front and rear stud patterns are absolutely identical.

This is best double-checked by offering a wheel to the selected studs to ensure that all the studs are on precisely the same PCD as the wheel's.

● The extra stress that greater vehicle weight brings when stopped by more powerful brakes not only feeds into the hubs but into the front suspension generally and front crossmember in particular. Do not be too quick to carve lumps off these or the surrounding components. When braking hard they are very highly stressed and need to be professionally modified and tested if they are changed at all.

● As a rule of thumb you need to run your car at the ride-height of a chrome-bumper car so we will first address this issue, but we also need to ensure that the car actually can be fitted with a steering column.

CHANGES FOR MODERATE CONVERSIONS
Ride heights

The ride height/ground clearance of

7-1-1 This is a standard (5⁄8in diameter) anti-roll/sway bar. The proximity of the Rover front pulley makes it clear that there is insufficient clearance to fit a significantly uprated bar without a simultaneous change in its position, or you could fit a cranked anti-roll/sway bar.

chrome-bumpered MGBs differs from that the of the original V8 and rubber-bumper models. The latter is about 1in (25mm)

higher than the former and is the reason for the original V8 and rubber-bumper models having inferior road holding and cornering qualities. Lowering kits from Moss-Europe can improve the adverse handling qualities of the V8 and rubber-bumper models but need to be fitted simultaneously at the front and rear of these cars. Such kits involve fitting a pair of shorter road-springs to the front and a pair of cast spacers between the rear leaf springs and the axle.

Don't be tempted to cut down your front coil springs – fit new ones. Road-going 218kg CAHT 21 springs will do nicely, although to achieve my ideal ride height, I had to make and fit a 10mm thick spacer each side. These days you can buy 5mm thick polyurethane spring cushions – two of which would have the same effect. Most MGB specialists offer a complete rubber-bumper lowering kit, which will enable you to also lower the rear of your rubber-bumper model to chrome-bumper levels. Around four different types and lengths of front springs are available so you should be able to achieve the ride and height you seek and Moss supplies the suspension-handling kits.

Handling kits

Even at chrome-bumper ride-height, all MGBs benefit from the most basic of handling improvement kits designed to reduce body-roll when cornering. These are called 'Evolution' and are available from almost all MGB specialists and/or Moss themselves and involve fitting a more substantial front anti-roll/sway bar and a compatible rear bar too. The kits come complete with rubber bushes (more in a moment) and fitting instructions, and, if you are doing little else to your suspension, they are an essential upgrade for all cars.

A stiffer (i.e. larger diameter) front anti-roll/sway bar will form part of any handling kit. My front roll bar is 7⁄8in with a 300lb/in roll rating – roughly six times the original bar rating and, with the rest of the handling kit, body-roll has been eliminated. However, the larger size of these bars can bring them very close to the front crankshaft pulley as we appreciate from photo 7-1-1. The engine's location and the size of the front pulley have a major bearing on whether you have lots of clearance or, as sometimes happens, an interference problem. With a narrow pulley

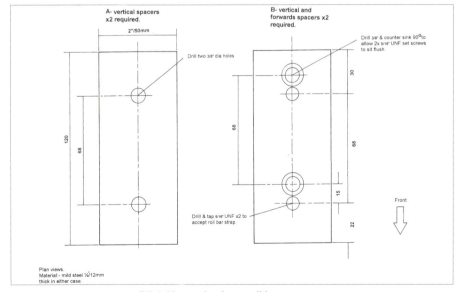

D7-1 Alternative front roll bar spacers.

7-1-2 The primary purpose of this shot is to show the anti-roll bar mounting packing piece designed, in this case, to move the roll bar both forward and down, away from the engine crankshaft pulley. The close proximity of the radiator and bottom water hose is evident. A side view of the underslung 10-row oil cooler – angled forward on the right-centre of the picture – can also just be seen.

7-1-3 This is a glimpse of the rear portion of an MGB handling kit – the rear anti-roll/sway bar mounting. The rubber mounting block ...

7-1-4 ... is bolted onto the corners of the boot/trunk floor. I have omitted the bounce strap because, out of shot, I have also fitted telescopic dampers.

7-1-5 The smaller u/j and longer shaft of the rubber bumper MGB steering arrangement is shown in this photograph. The earlier original chrome bumper rack, shaft and u/j is shown 'nearer' the camera and would have to be modified with an intermediate shaft to be of any use in a V8 converted MGB or MGB GT.

and an engine sited back far enough to fit an electric puller fan behind the radiator, you are very unlikely to have any difficulty fitting a conventional (i.e. straight) anti-roll/sway bar. Nevertheless, the RV8's crank pulley would interfere with a conventional anti-roll/sway bar (particularly under heavy braking) necessitating MG/Rover using a centrally cranked bar. So, if you do have a problem, option one might be to fit an RV8 front anti-roll/sway bar.

However, the RV8 bar's 'rating' may not be compatible with the rest of the handling kit, in which case you will need to move the bar's mounting points forward. It is possible to fit new captive nuts into the chassis rails but the spacers shown in drawing D7-1 may actually be the preferable solution. They give you two

options – straight down away from the pulley (option 'A') or simultaneously down and forwards (option 'B'). You will see the effect of 'B' in photograph 7-1-2.

Although not part of the front suspension, the rear roll bar shown in photos 7-1-3 and 7-1-4 is part of most kits and is included here to help you appreciate a little more about the rear-end changes resulting from fitting a handling kit.

Steering u/js & crossmembers

Like most details within an MGB V8 conversion, the combination of options is numerous and influenced by apparently irrelevant features. At first consideration it is hard to imagine how the exhaust manifold/headers you choose can affect the front suspension detail, but the headers are a factor if you are converting a chrome-bumper car. Then there are the various aftermarket front suspension designs to consider. We will look at those later in the chapter, first let us explore the most straightforward steering change – that of a rubber-bumper conversion – before we get into the more complex detail.

A rubber-bumper car provides for a very simple suspension/steering V8 conversion. It provides the best front

crossmember complete with the best steering rack (which in turn comes with the longer and more suitable steering shaft) already in place. Furthermore, the smaller/better u/j, its recess in the bulkhead/firewall, and the shorter steering column (thus compensating for the longer steering shaft) are also already in place. A further important safety point in favour of this rubber-bumper steering column is that it is designed to collapse in the event of an accident. You can see the differences in steering shaft length and u/js in picture 7-1-5.

It may surprise you to hear that the chassis's engine mounting brackets also enter this equation. In the case of the brackets needed for a Buick/Rover engine (seen at 7-1-6) they are in place and allow the steering shaft to pass through the driver's side, as we see in photo 7-1-7. If you are fitting a Ford engine, the steering

7-1-6 This is a perfectly standard/stock rubber-bumper engine mounting bracket in its normal position awaiting installation of a Buick/Rover V8 and ...

7-1-7 ... the rubber-bumper steering rack and shaft. You can see my V8 flexible mounting 'trial-fitted'.

7-1-8 The Ford chassis bracket is similar in principle but is positioned a little nearer the bulkhead/firewall. The Ford also uses the quite different flexible mounts we saw in chapter 4.

7-1-9 This is a close-up of the smaller u/j tucked out of the way in its cone, recessed into the bulkhead/firewall. The exhaust manifold is still close – just in shot in the bottom-right corner of the picture.

7-1-10 The size of the u/j makes a great deal of difference to the clearance available; here we see an earlier/larger u/j in very close proximity to the exhaust even though the bulkhead has been recessed.

7-1-11 The reason for the higher ride height generated by the crossmember of a rubber-bumper car (seen towards the rear of this picture) is clear when you compare its extended mounting bracket with the simpler, lower chrome-bumper version in the foreground.

7-1-12 Although the mounting face of the rubber-bumper crossmember (at the rear) is 1in (25mm) higher than its chrome-bumper predecessor, the platforms on which the dampers sit are identical in height.

shaft will lie a little differently because the chassis mounting brackets will have moved backwards along the chassis rails – as we see from photo 7-1-8.

The steering u/j is the key detail – it is smaller in size and fitted 3in (75mm) further back in the engine bay than a chrome-bumper u/j. These changes contribute to it missing the exhaust manifold/header even if you elect to fit block-hugger manifolds. The clearance between manifold and u/j is further enhanced if you fit RV8-style manifolds/headers. Pictures 7-1-9 and 7-1-10 should help you appreciate the necessity of the smaller, recessed u/j.

Before we move on to converting the steering on a chrome-bumper car to make space for the V8's exhaust, we had best illustrate the differences in the respective front crossmembers – see pictures 7-1-11 and 7-1-12.

There are two routes to converting the steering on a chrome-bumper car. To my mind the safest and best route is to copy the rubber-bumper design and fit an ex-rubber-bumper front crossmember, steering rack/longer shaft, smaller u/j, recessed bulkhead and shorter steering column. Admittedly this does bring knock-on changes within the cockpit – but the first priority is the integrity of the steering, and by this route it is not in anyway

compromised. The extra height of the crossmember aids sump clearance and the extra ride height is easily rectified. Later and much better chassis engine mounts (picture 7-1-13) can be used and the u/j location allows you to use whichever style of exhaust manifolds/headers you prefer.

The most cost-effective source for suitable second-hand rubber-bumper front crossmembers, steering columns and steering racks is likely to be the 'spares for sale' sections of club magazines but many trade spares stockists will be delighted to help.

7-1-13 The rubber-bumper chassis brackets are available and you will find the slotted hole for the flexible mounting invaluable. We explore positioning these brackets on the chassis rail in chapter 9.

7-1-14 A standard/stock steering rack is fitted with an integral steering shaft which, in the case of this interim shaft modification, is cut off short, fitted with a clamping bolt recess and splined. Its additional mating u/j is also in shot and is connected to ...

The front crossmember substitution is nowhere near as difficult as it sounds. The rubber-bumper crossmember sits on the 25mm extension welded to the top of the frame we saw earlier and, provided you use the two longer rubber-bumper mounting bolts (part number BHH 805) since the chassis holes are identically spaced, a straight exchange is possible. The various MGB manuals show the assembly sequence of spacer washers and rubber pads, as does the Parts Catalogue part number AKB 0039. Incidentally, the latter is a real asset to all restorers and is available for a very modest sum from Moss-Europe and/or Moss USA. Not only will it provide you with part numbering information, it also shows most assemblies in exploded view, which is a real help with reassembly and the correct sequence of parts.

The alternative chrome-bumper conversion route may be essential for Chevy-engined conversions, but for Ford and Buick/Rover swaps I think it is best avoided. In fact, I hear that in the UK it is becoming progressively more difficult to find suppliers for the essential intermediate shaft. The concept is based upon retaining the original crossmember and steering rack. It is, however, necessary to shorten/alter the rack as shown in picture 7-1-14 and to add provision for a bottom u/j. You also retain your original chrome-bumper

steering column, but this is shortened to recess the top u/j and provide the essential exhaust clearance we see at 7-1-15. The intermediate shaft shown in picture 7-1-16 bridges the gap down to the steering rack seen in picture 7-1-17 (overleaf).

The advantage of this approach is that there are no knock-on consequences in the cockpit, but the disadvantages are two-fold. Firstly you need an intermediate shaft with two u/js affixed to it, secondly (**WARNING!**) you need to take great care with the way the top column is shortened and re-splined. These are both critical safety components, and the top column is prone to failure if not modified properly. The column that goes from the bulkhead/firewall to the steering wheel has to be shortened to relocate the top u/j. The column consequently has to be re-splined

and cross-machined to accept the u/j and its retaining pinch-bolt. The problem and danger is that the shortened column becomes a thin-walled tube where the re-splining is required and it is therefore absolutely essential that a professional carries out this modification, either fitting a reinforcing steel plug (secured very carefully to the tubular column) and re-splining the plain end or cutting the column centrally and welding the shortened column together.

Suspension bush materials

All converters need to reconsider the suspension bushes used as the front suspension crossmember assembly goes back together. MG recognized the importance of fitting the original MGB GT

7-1-15 ... the usual top u/j by ...

7-1-16 ... the interim shaft that looks like this.

7-1-17 This shows (through a collection of oil pipes) the smaller u/j coupled to the now shortened chrome-bumper steering rack. These conversions are available from Clive Wheatley V8 Conversion Ltd.

7-1-18 The polyurethane bushes are much harder and more durable than the original rubber bushes, and come in various colours, depending on manufacturer and hardness.

V8 cars with upgraded 'metalistic' rubber/steel front suspension bushes. These are still available and can still be fitted to the inner wishbone pivots but technology has moved on and today we not only have polyurethane suspension bushing but it is available in varying 'shore' hardness too.

Polyurethane (seen in picture 7-1-18) is a synthetic material that does not flex in the same way as a rubber bush and can therefore be made harder than was possible with rubber bush technology. Some polyurethane bushes claim superior self-lubricating properties and all are resistant to fuel/oil corrosion – which is a long-term weakness of rubber. Some polyurethane bushes are further stiffened by having a stainless steel internal sleeve moulded in place. MG used soft rubber to provide a relatively quiet, smooth ride – but rubber distorts and the car's handling suffers. So polyurethane bushes offer numerous advantages when rebuilding your front suspension.

Polyurethane comes in varying degrees of hardness. In simple terms, the greater the shore the less the bush distorts under load but the greater the road noise and harshness transmitted to the car and occupants. Also a consideration with some of the bushes is the difficulty of fitting

– which increases as the bush gets harder. Different makes of polyurethane bush use different hardness of material. Generally Super-flex and/or Superpro seem to have got the balance between ride, noise, handling and fitting about right and are my suggested makes for most applications. At the bottom end of the power upgrade level I think you could fit a relatively soft polyurethane bush set but as the power available increases then so should the hardness of the poly-bushes. Superpro polyurethane bushes are imported into the UK by Revington TR and are impressive but only one manufacturer that I know of claims its polyurethane compound provides both better locationing and no additional noise – Powerflex suspension bushes. They are available via Demon Tweeks.

You will ease the fitting of even the hardest bushes if you put them in warm (but not boiling) water for five minutes beforehand and use lots of grease. Silicone grease is best.

Dampers

Next we need to consider the front shock absorbers. The original 'lever-arm' units are the same for all models and are

interchangeable from 1800 to V8 and from rubber- to chrome-bumper. As we will see in the next chapter, they are one of the first upgrades you need to make to the rear suspension because they are not up to the job and, at the rear, are easily changed. Substituting the front lever-arm dampers is more complex and expensive. Consequently, if you are on a tight budget, have a moderately-powered car in mind, have improved the bushes and your existing units are in A1 condition, then retain them. If you think you may need to spend significant sums of money on your lever-arm dampers, don't – use the cash towards upgrading your front suspension generally and fitting telescopic dampers in particular. We will look at alternative/aftermarket suspension upgrades very shortly.

MEDIUM-POWER CONVERSIONS
Uprating a handling kit

Handling kits generally come with rubber bushes. Two of these bushes (seen at 7-2-1) mount the roll/sway bar to the chassis and a further pair couple the ends of the bar to the front suspension. You can improve the effectiveness of your anti-roll/sway bar by substituting hard polyurethane bushes for the original compliant rubber bushes.

If you do not mind further increasing the noise/vibration levels, you can upgrade the effectiveness of exactly the same roll/sway bar by fitting 'solid' mounting bushes and rose jointed end-links. The solid mountings should come with grease nipples and match the diameter of your roll/sway bar. The end links have ball (rose) joints in place of any bushes and consequently they transmit even the smallest suspension movement to the bar, which does its best to restrict that movement. Moss-Europe part number is MGS30791.

Negative camber

The normal tyres available when MG designed the B were of cross-ply construction – which required some positive camber to perform well. However, modern radial tyres perform at their best with a straight-upward or slightly negative camber angle with the road. Very few, if any B's run cross-plies these days, hence the advantage of reconsidering the camber on your car. 1 to 1.5° of negative camber will make the most use of your radial tyre's grip.

The camber can be altered with relative ease by slightly extending the lower wishbone on each side of the car. Their construction makes them easy to alter using a set of old wishbone channels. However the task is so much quicker, easier and affords less opportunity for error if you buy and fit a set of longer, negative-camber lower wishbones. These will improve the handling and cornering but increase the 'weight' of steering. Negative camber can be seen at 7-2-2.

If you are reluctant to purchase the extra-length bottom wishbones before you've had a chance to experience the consequences, you can fabricate your own trial set very cheaply using standard MGB wishbones that have had their holes elongated by a seized-bottom pivot-bolt. Clearly you need to ensure that both the quality of the hole repair discs and the welding to each wishbone are of the highest order. Try increasing the pivot length, by say 2mm, and if you like the result make up another set with a further 2mm increase in pivot length. After you have decided what suits you best, buy the 'proper' set from your supplier.

Coil-over shocks

Full coil springs fitted over telescopic shock absorbers (or 'coil-over' shocks as they are usually called) are my preferred route to MGB front suspension improvements. The wider tyres that medium- and high-powered cars require make the improved road holding and steering these suspension systems offer essential.

We will look at two units, the first of which requires no modification to the car or crossmember, which can therefore be reverted to standard with ease. This kit is from Moss-Europe and is shown in photographs 7-2-3 to 7-2-5 (overleaf). You will note that the old lever-arm damper is replaced with a specially fabricated top wishbone and pivot and that a replacement bottom spring-pan is also supplied in the kit. The kit is offered with either Gaz or Spax dampers but either are adjustable for ride height – important in conversion applications. You will need a special collar-adjusting 'C' spanner. The Moss part number for MGB and MGB GT fast-road applications is TMG40751. The units cost around £600 and will transform your ride, steering and cornering and are strongly recommended.

Ford crossmember alterations

We will be exploring aftermarket front suspensions very shortly, one of which incorporates a specially fabricated crossmember centrally recessed to clear the Ford sump. However, the majority of front suspension improvements that will be explored here continue to utilize the MGB original unit that will necessitate additional alterations if the engine bay is subsequently to accept a Ford V8. As I have already mentioned, the crossmember changes for Ford engines are critical to your safety and should be carried out

7-2-1 Replacing these rubber bushes with harder polyurethane bushes will increase the transmitted road noise and vibration but also tighten the handling of the car very effectively by ensuring more of the roll/sway bar's effectiveness is transferred from suspension to chassis.

7-2-2 Mark Treadwell's TR6 has negative camber of approximately 1.5 degrees, as shown in this picture. With the slight body-roll that occurs when cornering, this negative camber presents the tyre to the road in a most advantageous manner.

7-2-3 This front suspension improvement uses coil-over shock absorbers. The photograph shows the new spring pan and lower mounting method for this type of front suspension. You should also note the route of the RV8 exhaust system.

7-2-4 Another view of the coil-over shocks front suspension system. Note the Wilwood Superlite cast alloy brake caliper and its intermediate mounting bracket marrying it to the MGB stub axle. Brake discs are 273mm, ventilated and most effective.

7-2-5 Finally, a third/top view of the coil-over shocks front suspension modification. Note the bolts still "pick-up" on the tapped holes originally used for the Armstrong lever arm damper, but the original MGB crossmember has nevertheless had to be modified to allow passage of the top shock absorber mounting. The top wishbone is a fabricated replacement.

7-2-6 A front crossmember for a Ford engine needs to be considerably strengthened internally to fully compensate for the structural strength lost when the top is cut away to provide clearance for the Ford sump. The compensatory strength is provided by a substantial inverted 'U'-channel, 'top hat' pressing or box-section fitted and welded within the crossmember. This pressing needs to be internally welded to the base of the open crossmember before a new, very substantial top cover fabrication is offered up. The top cover must be welded to the original crossmember and plug-welded to the top on the new (internal) channel. The welds must be of the very highest quality, before ...

professionally. Looking at pictures 7-2-6 and 7-2-7, I strongly recommend that you consider a Fast Cars aftermarket assembly.

HIGH-POWER CONVERSIONS
Fast Cars front suspension

This is, to the best of my knowledge, the only front suspension designed to accept a Ford V8 without further modification and can be seen at 7-3-1. It comes mostly assembled and complete with uprated brakes. It is intended as a true 'Bolt-on' conversion and conveniently the installation can easily be accomplished in an afternoon.

An important design objective has been to reduce the overall weight of the front suspension sub-assembly and ensure that the majority of the savings are in unsprung weight. Consequently, a complete new fabrication is incorporated into the kit that saves 75lb, much of which is in unsprung weight with a beneficial effect on ride quality and handling.

Modern state-of-the-art suspension geometry has been incorporated into this 'clean sheet of paper' design. Improvements in roll-centre, Ackerman and camber eliminate bump steer and give the light precise steering and handling of a modern European sports car. The caster is adjustable from 2° to 4°. Lightweight Carrera racing coil-over shocks make ride height and ride firmness easily adjustable. Camber is also adjustable from +2° to –2°. Incorporated into the set-up are Wilwood four-piston calipers and 11.75in (300mm) vented rotors providing world-class braking, but you will require 15in wheels.

Fast Cars can supply its front suspension with 4- or 5-stud wheel patterns and, at the time of writing, is only

7-2-7 ... turning over the crossmember and additionally welding the new internal channel to the bottom of the original crossmember. You can see the inverted 'U'-channel inside this crossmember through the bottom holes. You cannot carry out this modification too carefully or cautiously.

7-3-1 This Fast Cars crossmember is designed with all engine sump/oil pan configurations in mind, which is a particularly important feature to readers with a Ford 302 in mind. The design incorporates the dished centre we see here to provide adequate clearance for even the Ford's difficult (in an MGB fitting context) sump/oil-pan.

making the normal width/track version but I understand a wider unit is under consideration.

Hoyle coil-over front kit

Hoyle Engineering manufactures a replacement double wishbone coil-over front suspension based upon a largely standard MGB front crossmember. The front suspension can be purchased and fitted as a stand-alone improvement or purchased as part of a compatible and proven rear suspension upgrade should you wish to tackle both ends.

Seen at 7-3-2 and 7-3-3, the coil-over damper units are specially made 'click' adjustable, re-buildable units with adjustable spring seats to enable the ride height of the car to be changed. They are supplied with a 3-year warranty and individual test reports. The springs supplied are a 2¼in internal diameter and can be obtained in a wide range of stiffness.

This suspension set-up includes new anti-roll/sway bar links with spherical joints (rose joints, highlighted in picture 7-3-4, overleaf) to maximise the effectiveness of the roll/sway bar. The bottom stub axle cross shaft, always a weakness of the original MGB design, is replaced with a special high tensile bolt. This carries two snail cams that enable the camber angle to be adjusted simply and quickly while a small degree of castor adjustment is also possible via shim washers fitted at the top of the stub axle. Polyurethane suspension bushes can be supplied.

The kit includes replacements for the wishbones, spring-pans, damper, coil springs, bump stop/spacers and anti-roll/sway fixings. The MGB uprights/king-pins are retained, thus all MGB brake upgrades will fit.

Fitting the Hoyle kit is straightforward although it requires a small modification to each end of the front crossmember to provide clearance. This is best carried out off the car but it can be done with the crossmember still in place. You will need to angle-grind each rounded end off your crossmember and weld a 5mm thick convex plate back in place to give the new shock/spring unit clearance. Hoyle's instructions are quite clear and the task is not onerous, but nevertheless Hoyle offers a modified/powder-coated exchange service for those without welding experience or equipment.

If you remove the crossmember to carry out the modification, I recommend that the member mounting pads be replaced with polyurethane ones. You

7-3-2 The Hoyle front wishbones are fabricated using high grade tubular steel that improves structural strength and rigidity whilst ...

7-3-3 ... the springs are positioned closer to the wheel enabling a much softer spring to be used. Together with high quality damper units, Hoyle claims this results in a more supple suspension.

also need to be comfortable with the fact you are modifying a component on your car. Frankly, if you are carrying out a V8 conversion this should cause you no concerns whatsoever. However, replacement front crossmembers are readily available second-hand, and while it is most unlikely you or most subsequent owners will feel a need to return the car to originality, it is comforting to have the option. If in doubt, buy a second-hand original crossmember, pop it in the loft

7-3-4 We discussed 'solid' pivots within an anti-roll/sway bar earlier in the chapter, but here we see Hoyle's use of rose joints to achieve maximum effectiveness from the roll bar.

and explore coil-over shocks free of such reservations.

These kits are suitable for both chrome- and rubber-bumper MGB. The ride height of a rubber-bumper car can be lowered using the spring height adjuster but this will result in a similar amount of bump travel being lost. Nearly half of recent sales have been in the USA, where, like the UK and Europe, they are shipped direct to the customer by Hoyle, whose details appear in the Suppliers Appendix. The cost of a Hoyle Engineering complete kit is £675 at the time of writing.

The RV8 assembly

This spin-off from the MG RV8 certainly improves the MGB's road holding by the use of improved geometry and telescopic dampers, and also provides significantly improved braking. The complete preassembled package is shown in photographs 7-3-5 and 7-3-6 is available from your Heritage approved supplier or the MGOC. However, there is one problem for all potential users and two for those contemplating a Ford engine – cost and insufficient Ford sump-space. The price is circa £2200, but that does include a very worthwhile brake upgrade.

Our friends in Europe and the USA

may be pleased to know that the complete assembly is available in left-hand as well as right-hand drive variants. The part number for all models, chrome- or rubber-bumper, is HMP 213015 for right-hand drive cars and HMP 213016 for left-hand drive variants. The assembly comes preassembled and, via the Lockheed 4-pot calipers and 270mm diameter vented discs, will dramatically improve the braking efficiency for the same pedal effort (at least 20 per cent improvement is claimed). It will also reduce brake fade by at least 50 per cent, without changing the front-to-back brake balance and without seriously affecting pedal travel (about $\frac{1}{4}$in or 5mm additional pedal depression may be noticed). This can be corrected, however, since the majority of MGBs use a master-cylinder with a $\frac{3}{4}$in (19mm) bore size, whereas the RV8 and very late MGBs (1978 on) use a cylinder with $\frac{13}{16}$in (20.6mm) bore.

The unit is based upon a rubber-bumper MGB's front crossmember. Chrome-bumper cars can use the system, however, as assemblies intended for chrome-bumper cars have the steering rack mounting brackets welded about one inch higher on the front edge of the assembly than would be the case for rubber-bumper (and V8) cars. This allows for the continued use of the chrome-bumpered car's original steering rack. However, **(CAUTION!)** to my mind, it will alter the relationship between a chrome-bumpered car's steering rack pivot point and its wishbone pivot plane, and could therefore induce 'Bump-steer' so do get your Heritage dealer's prior assurance as to the suitability of this arrangement for your car.

Spares should be available via any Heritage-approved supplier or via Brown & Gammon (one of the UK's MG specialists). **CAUTION!** You should check with your Heritage supplier before ordering that the selected part number will have a ride height

compatible with your car. He should be able to select the right one from the 11 or so options that include both bolt-on and wire-wheel variants.

The RV8 front crossmember assembly does not come with an anti-roll/sway bar and so you will need to refit your existing anti-roll bar or a handling kit, or buy a new bar. If buying new, I suggest you order it at the same time as your RV8 crossmember. To the best of my knowledge, at the time of writing the RV8 crossmember only comes with MGB 4-stud wheel mountings.

7-3-5 An overall view of Heritage's complete front suspension assembly (just as it comes to you, ready to bolt to the car).

7-3-6 A close-up of the right side which shows the top fabricated wishbone, the cast shock absorber top housing, and the conventional MGB coil spring co-axially aligned as they should be. The large Princess-based four pot caliper is well in evidence, as are the 270mm diameter x 24mm thick ventilated discs and rather differently routed hydraulic brake hoses.

Chapter 8
Rear suspension

I have tackled rear suspensions before finalising the bodyshell because there could be some bodyshell alterations involved. You do need to consider this chapter in conjunction with your front suspension aspirations. A front suspension design from one supplier may work wonderfully well with an improved rear suspension set-up from a different specialist. However, because front and rear suspensions usually need to work in harmony with each other, there is much to be said for buying front and rear suspension upgrades simultaneously from one supplier. This removes any doubt about where responsibilities lie, and might save you having to do some unique development work in order to get the front and rear-ends of your car playing nicely together!

The rear suspension you plan is very much dictated by the type of axle/final drive that you feel appropriate. For my part I feel this is in turn influenced by the power of your engine, and so I have split this chapter into moderate-, medium- and high-powered suspension sections. We'll look at gear ratios and some other details a little later.

REAR-ENDS FOR MODERATELY-POWERED CARS
Anti-tramp bars

These bolt-on units can be seen in picture 8-1-1. They are fitted between the rear spring's front 'eye' bolt and the centre of the spring. They reduce the spring's tendency to 'wind-up' into a flat 'S' shape under high torque loads by constraining the front half of the spring to vertical flexing only. There are two types of anti-tramp bar currently available. The basic ones fitted with rubber bushes cost about £125. Bolt-on anti-tramp bars for heavy-duty applications are available fitted with rose joints and cost £300, but I would have thought that cars with sufficient grunt to be regarded as requiring heavy-duty bars would require the more substantial assistance discussed later in the chapter.

8-1-1 These bolt-on anti-tramp bars will help reduce axle-tramp, but you may need to modify the cross-bolt at the centre of the spring to allow a handling kit and telescopic dampers to fit, too.

Shock absorbers

There are some important changes that you need to make to a moderately-powered MGB – but they do not have to cost the earth. You can upgrade the rear-end by utilising something from later in the chapter if you wish. However, on the basis of the lowest cost/minimum requirement, I believe that it is quite in order to fit a moderately-powered car (up to 200bhp) with a well-located live rear axle and retain the leaf springs. However, a pair of telescopic rear shock absorber (dampers) is an absolute must. The choice of manufacturers, and features such as adjustable or non-adjustable shock absorbers, is relatively unimportant and is perhaps best dictated by your front suspension selection. However, the original MGB shock absorbers are quite unsuited even to this level of power and should be replaced with a pair of telescopic units such as can be seen a 8-1-2.

Ride height

The ride height/ground clearance differs between chrome- and V8 and rubber-bumper models. The lower ride height of the chrome-bumpered cars is preferable since it lowers the car's centre of gravity and reduces body roll when cornering. Consequently, as a minimum suspension improvement, those with rubber-bumper V8 conversions should at least lower the ride height at the front and at the rear of the car by about 1in. There is nothing to stop you reducing the ground clearance still further – except the dangers of a damaged exhaust system.

The easiest route to lowering the car is to use a rubber-bumper suspension lowering kit. All MGB specialists will be able to supply the necessary components to lower both the front and the rear suspensions in one kit. However, you can lower the front yourself purely by a change of road spring. I fit chrome-bumper GT road springs to both stiffen-up the ride

8-1-2 These are Spax adjustable telescopic shock absorbers fitted to the rear to improve rear-end road holding. Numerous manufacturers can supply similar products but buy from a trusted MGB specialist supplier to ensure you are getting the the best units for this important job.

and lower rubber-bumper roadsters ride height. At the back you need to fit lowering blocks between the axle and springs. This necessitates longer 'U'-bolts too.

Handling kits

We discussed these in the previous chapter so much of the detail and photographs have been covered, but a handling kit is an essential upgrade for most cars. You may recall that a kit consists of two anti-roll/sway bars – a much thicker one to replace the existing front bar and a modest but nevertheless important one for the rear. Moss-Europe's part number for a chrome-bumper kit is TMK002.

Note that while a live rear axle car will benefit from fitting the rear anti-roll/sway bar that comes within a handling kit, a car with IRS will be much less likely to benefit from a rear anti-roll/sway bar. If your car is

to be fitted with IRS do consult an expert and, if appropriate, buy the handling kit (which might be reduced to a front anti-roll bar) from the same supplier. Another example of why it is so important to buy suspension upgrades for the front and rear from the same supplier and simultaneously.

Leaf springs

Even with modestly powered engines, the MGB V8 or MGC leaf springs are inclined to wind up into an 'S' shape under torque which, when released by a change of throttle opening, gives you an exciting moment of rear-end steering. Interestingly there are two apparently contradictory improvements – note that I did not say 'solutions'. The traditional method would be to fit stronger leaf springs to help counter this unpleasant tendency. One extra leaf will help but replacement MGC/MGB GTV8 springs are the simplest solution particularly if the springs in your car are tired or sagging. I am using competition units on my Roadster (part number DMGR 4666) and MGB GT V8 O/E replacements on my GT (part number BHH1133). However, this only partly resolves the problem and consequently I also strongly recommend your fitting a pair of bolt-on anti-tramp bars discussed a few paragraphs ago.

8-1-3 This is an example of a twin-leaf parabolic conversion derived from Rover's RV8 single leaf rear suspension design. Note that the well-adapted lower spring bracket is being used to affix this telescopic damper.

More recently, Rover actually went in the other direction when improving the RV8's rear axle location, using better (than the bolt-ons) anti-tramp bars and a weaker dual-leaf spring combination. The reduction in leaves also reduced the internal friction within the spring, which increased the importance of the rear dampers but also improved the compliance of the springs aiding both roadholding and ride-comfort. An example of this sort of set-up can be seen at 8-1-3 and, if you are intending to retain leaf springs, you should consider using this arrangement on your conversion. Although this arrangement undoubtedly improves matters, there are even better ways of locating the axle.

TR7 axles

The later MGB axle is called a Salisbury axle (i.e. post-'Banjo') and is strong enough to cope with the power, although the ratio needs changing to provide higher gearing. We will discuss this in more detail later in the chapter. However, there is one alternative axle I would like to explore because it may simultaneously resolve several problems if you were to use an ex-TR7 5-speed rear axle in an MGB.

The TR7 came in two versions – the early, weaker, lighter 4-speed model and the preferable later, stronger but heavier models with ex-SD1 5-speed gearboxes and rear axles. The axle from the 5-speed cars is easily up to the power/torque from these moderate engines. Indeed, being of SD1 origin it should handle 300bhp/300lb-ft. Furthermore, the axle was fitted in a range of gear ratios including 3.45:1, 3.08:1 and even 2.84:1 – all of which are suited to MGB V8 conversions of various specifications – meaning you may be able to find an axle with a suitable gear ratio too. It is wider (55.5in across the drums) than the MGB by about 3.5in. You may see the extra 1.75in per side a major problem or, if you are prepared to widen the wheelarches, as an ideal way of widening

8-1-4 The TR7 did have the benefit of coil springs and telescopic dampers but ...

the track of the MGB. You can also buy offset rear wheels to reduce the track – but that, to my mind, would be losing one of the benefits of this change.

The four TR7 wheel studs are on the same PCD as the MGB so the wheels will bolt straight on. The rear brakes are bigger than the MGB's and may require a pressure regulator fitting to the rear brake line to prevent the rear wheels locking up.

You can get an overall impression of this axle and its installation in photograph 8-1-4. The method of location was infinitely superior to the MGB as the result of two differences: firstly, it uses coil springs to suspend the car and these have no part to play in locating the axle whatsoever; secondly, it comes fitted with two anti-tramp bars below the axle and two diagonal bars that are fixed above the axle. You will see these in pictures 8-1-5 and 8-1-6. The latter feed all sideways stresses into mounting points each side of the propshaft tunnel (picture 8-1-7). As un-classic as the TR7 is regarded, this suspension arrangement is very effective and might prove a cost-efficient alternative axle and suspension upgrade for an MGB.

However, there are downsides – I must point out that I have not tried the axle under an MGB. Even so I can see that you will need to fabricate the four sheet-metal axle location brackets on the MGB's heel-board in such a way that the inevitable repeated stresses do not fatigue the

8-1-5 ... a rear axle well located by these four bushed bars is key to its drivability even with a V8 engine in the TR8.

8-1-6 In closer detail two tubular bars seen at the top of this picture were fitted diagonally above the axle to prevent lateral movement, while the more substantial radius arms were mounted below the axle, located it fore and aft, carried the coil spring and the rear anti-roll/sway bar.

8-1-7 The heel-board was fitted with four mounting brackets – one of which is seen here.

brackets or the material they are welded to. Further, the original TR7 rubber suspension bushes are unsatisfactory and need to be replaced with the (8) polyurethane bushes we see in picture 8-1-8 as a matter of course. They are readily available and are a common upgrade by TR owners. Finally, you will find it necessary to reconsider the coil springs and their mountings. The MGB does have coil-spring mounting pads affixed to the chassis rails above the rear axle. They were never used in production. However, on the TR axle, the coil springs sit atop the trailing arms in front of the axle (picture 8-1-9) and are consequently not going to marry with the MGB's pads. This problem will need resolving and coil-over-dampers are almost certainly the solution. I would try 200lb-rated (possibly 250lb on a GT) rear coil springs over an adjustable-length damper fitted, at the top, to one or both of the MGB's damper-mounting holes.

MEDIUM-POWERED CARS
Anti-tramp bars

A few paragraphs ago we were discussing bolt-on anti-tramp bars. For medium-powered cars there is a slightly more sophisticated version that is better able to feed the greater stresses generated by medium-powered cars into the MGB's chassis. Using the RV8 as inspiration, a mild steel channel is welded between the car's existing front rear spring hanger and the chassis crossmember, as shown in photographs 8-2-1 to 8-2-6. Numerous

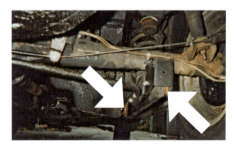

8-1-8 Good TR7 rear axle location depends on these bushes being in good order. Just one collapsed original rubber bush will degenerate the axle location to something similar to the MGB leaf-spring method.

plug welds are probably the most satisfactory route to achieving this extra depth of chassis, which is outlined in diagram D8-1 (p110). Do note, however, that this then becomes a highly stressed component, especially with high-powered engines, and so great care should be taken to dissipate the forces appropriately, select appropriate materials and above all to weld this load-bearing component appropriately.

The rear mounting bracket of the anti-tramp bar fits under the centre of the rear spring and can now be supplied to allow passage of a long and substantial crossbolt which will carry both the stresses of an anti-tramp bar and the lower mounting of a telescopic shock absorber.

8-1-9 The TR7 and 8 rear coil spring sits on this pad/locating spigot.

Trailing links

As a reference, trailing link rear suspension was used on early Aston Martins and dramatically improves the locating of the MGB's live rear axle. It also offers an opportunity to improve the ride and reduce the weight (by about 20lbs or 10kg, much of which is unsprung) of the original rear suspension.

The MGB's leaf springs locate the rear axle but their lengths vary as they flex up and down. We make matters much worse as we increase the torque from the engine. In fact, an 8-cylinder engine, even in modest tune, compounds the variations in rear spring length by causing them to take up a flat 'S' shape. With trailing link suspension, four parallel radius arms provide positive longitudinal and a Panhard

rod excellent lateral location for the axle. A pair of coil-over dampers provides the suspension and the arrangement seen in picture 8-2-7-1.

Normally you would fabricate the four equal length radius arms and fit polyurethane bushes – however, there is a case, particularly in very high-powered conversions, of fitting

8-2-1 This photograph shows the one-piece 'through' bolt that accommodates both the rear anti-tramp bar and bottom shock absorber mountings. Note the space to ensure the shock absorber is held clear of the bracket, and that the anti-tramp bar has, in fact, come adrift from its central bush. Two equal length spacers were subsequently machined and fitted each side of the anti-tramp bar end.

8-2-2 This is the tail end of the anti-tramp bar showing the centre bolt for spring locationing and two of the four 'U'-bolts' securing nuts. Note the rear disc brakes and the way Cox and Perry have accommodated the bottom telescopic shock absorber mounting.

8-2-3 This is a wide view of the strengthening member welded into both sides of the chassis between the central crossmember and the rear spring hangers. Note the two bolts: the top one goes through this extra piece and on through the front spring eye, whilst the bottom one provides the front mounting for the anti-tramp bars.

8-2-4 This is a closer shot of the non-RV8 fabrication. These anti-tramp bars have been fitted to a conventionally sprung car but with a further thickness of metal welded on both sides to give the spring and the anti-tramp bar plenty of solid material to push and pull against.

8-2-5 This is the RV8 equivalent. You can see the original spring eye has a bolt and spacer. Note the length of the strengthening piece running forward to the chassis crossmember.

8-2-6 Here is a close-up of the RV8 rear spring and anti-tramp location. Again, the original MGB front spring mounting has a bolt through it. Two additional mounting holes are provided beneath the original: the higher one for the spring, the lower for the RV8's anti-tramp bars. Note the extra material thickness with which Rover supplemented the mounting holes – for good reason!

8-2-7-1 The first of a series of three photographs showing a trailing parallel link rear suspension system. The lower link clearly fastens onto the original MG front spring mounting, whilst the top link locates onto an additional rolled hollow section vertical member welded to the heel-board just outside the battery frames.

8-2-7-2 If adopting trailing-arm suspension, it is imperative you provide a shell strengthening and stress distributing framework one side or other of the heel-board. This left-half shot is of a similar internal tubular/channel frame.

8-2-7-3 Frontline-Costello makes a 5-link rear suspension kit designed to completely replace the original MGB rear suspension with a bolt-on assembly. The conversion kit consists of four parallel training arms, bodyshell locating bracket, coil-over dampers and a Panhard rod.

a pair of rose/ball-joints to each end of the arms. Certainly the Panhard rod requires a pair of rose joints, and I think I would use one with a left-thread and one with a right-thread in order that the rear axle location can be adjusted using the rod as a turnbuckle.

This modification has many advantages but does require fabricating several highly stressed components, including (each) top and bottom link mountings. The heel-board (i.e. the almost vertical panel just behind the seats). The front of the lower links bolt to the car's normal front leaf spring mounting points (also clearly shown in photograph 8-2-7-1). If all this fabrication is daunting consider the Frontline-Costello prefabricated kits shown in 8-2-7-3. If still doing your own fabrication, you will finally have to fabricate a tower (photographs 8-2-8-1 and 8-2-8-2) on the chassis to provide the fixed-end for the Panhard rod (photograph 8-2-9).

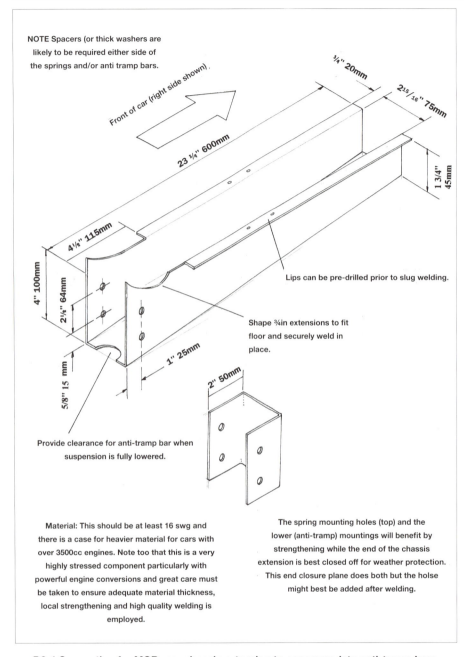

NOTE Spacers (or thick washers are likely to be required either side of the springs and/or anti tramp bars.

Front of car (right side shown)

¼" 20mm

2¹⁵/₁₆" 75mm

23 ¼" 600mm

1 3/4" 45mm

4¼" 115mm

4" 100mm

2¼" 64mm

5/8" 15 mm

1" 25mm

Lips can be pre-drilled prior to slug welding.

Shape ¾in extensions to fit floor and securely weld in place.

2" 50mm

Provide clearance for anti-tramp bar when suspension is fully lowered.

Material: This should be at least 16 swg and there is a case for heavier material for cars with over 3500cc engines. Note too that this is a very highly stressed component particularly with powerful engine conversions and great care must be taken to ensure adequate material thickness, local strengthening and high quality welding is employed.

The spring mounting holes (top) and the lower (anti-tramp) mountings will benefit by strengthening while the end of the chassis extension is best closed off for weather protection. This end closure plane does both but the holse might best be added after welding.

D8-1 Suggestion for MGB rear chassis extension to accommodate anti-tramp bars.

8-2-8-1 This photograph of the left side shows, at the very top of the picture, the chassis end of the Panhard rod and the bottom of the fabricated tower.

that parallel radius links slightly change the location of the axle at the extremes of suspension travel – when slight roll-steer can be introduced. This is especially true if soft springs allow large suspension movements, so do not specify overly soft coil springs.

One additional benefit you may care to consider were you using an ex-Rover SD1 rear axle – substitute the SD1's Watts linkage (in place of the Panhard rod) as your lateral locating method. You do not have this option if using an MGB axle. However, the SD1 axle actually has a Watts linkage pivot (seen at 8-2-10) built into the differential cover. You will need to shorten both linkage arms and fit two mounting points on your MG's chassis rails and I consider the latter an advantage as it halves the localized stresses. However, I think this the preferable lateral location solution. A Watts linkage always locates the rear suspension right on its roll centre, regardless of which end of its travel the suspension is, and therefore offers very

The Panhard rod works best if you set it up with as flat an installation as is practical – which is why a tower is worth the extra time and trouble. The coil-over damper units are a matter of choice – but ones with both an adjustable length and adjustable damping facilities may be worth paying a bit extra for. Choose a coil spring rated at about 200/250lbs and use the MGB's existing shock absorber mounting holes much as you would a telescopic damper installation/conversion. Be aware

8-2-8-2 A better view of the chassis-mounted 'tower'. Note the internal stiffening plate and the commendably flat (and substantial) Panhard rod installation.

8-2-9 This slightly different angle shows the right side coil spring and about half of the axle's lateral locationing method – a Panhard rod – and, in this case, the car's rear disc brakes.

8-2-10 This pivot is cast into the SD1's substantial axle cover plate and affords the opportunity to pivot your Watts linkage from here.

consistent locationing. With a Panhard rod you can sometimes get variations in roll centre, which can slightly alter the car's handling mid-corner. The cast SD1 rear differential cover will fit a TR7 rear axle too allowing the use of a panhard rod.

Stronger rear axles

If your car is aimed at the medium power band then, in the UK, you should upgrade the axle and its ratio all in one change. 3-litre Capri axles have been modified to fit but the good old SD1 unit is probably the best starting point.

Both these axles require shortening and a UK specialist like A1 Fabrications

can shorten the Rover V8 back axle (ratios 3.08:1 SD1; 2.85:1 Vitesse) to correct the track such that they are indistinguishable from an MGB Salisbury axle (picture 8-2-11). The Rover hubs and half-shafts are cut back, re-machined and re-studded to take the MG's brake drums and wheels. Rover hub bearings and oil seals are retained and the MG brake backplate welded to 25mm spacers which can be bolted to the Rover's axle flanges (photo 8-2-12, overleaf). Consequently, with the front extension tube (picture 8-2-13, overleaf)) removed from the Rover axle, you have, width-wise, an axle that is interchangeable with your MGB's and capable of handling 300bhp.

The beauty of the Rover axle is that the front oil seal and drive flange still need attention but any TR7 specialist will be able to help with the necessary parts seen in photograph 8-2-14 (overleaf).The oil seal (part number TKC 0302) and drive flange (part number UKC 3877) can be purchased

8-2-11 Nearest the camera is the standard MGB rear axle with bolt-on hubs. The 1800, V8 and MGC versions are indistinguishable from the outside, although the internal ratios vary. The axle behind is the modified Rover example. The track is now identical to the original 'B. Obviously spring pads and other changes have also been effected to allow the axle to accept standard MGB parts.

new at the time of writing, although a used drive flange is perfectly satisfactory. The SD1 brakes will be too big thus you may have to use your existing MGB backplates and drums as I did in 8-2-15 or buy new/

8-2-12 This photo shows the modified SD1 axle with the following points of interest (left to right): i) the remains of the old SD1 spring plate are just visible; ii) the substantial butt weld where the SD1 axle tube was cut, shortened and rewelded; iii) the fabricated replacement MGB spring mounting pads and bounce-strap mounting; iv) the original SD1 axle flange; v) the new fabricated spacer welded to an original MGB brake backplate and held in place by four high tensile steel 'cap' or 'Allen' screws.

8-2-13 A Rover SD1 axle as removed from a 3.5 litre V8 car. Note the front extension tube which unbolts from the nose of the pinion housing, and will be substituted by an oil seal housing and drive flange.

8-2-14 This photograph shows (top) the SD1 axle pinion extension tube as removed from the SD1 axle and (lower, from left to right) the replacement ex-TR7 gasket, oil seal/housing, drive pinion, washer and retaining self-locking nut.

used ones from your favourite MGB spares specialist.

However, this solution has one snag – Rover axles are rather notorious for whine after high mileage; I believe 80 per cent are likely to whine. SD1 specialist, RPI, offers two classes of second-hand SD1/V8 axles: untested for £40 and tested whine-free for £175. The company assures me that it will exchange the cheaper units until you get one you are satisfied with, but it's quite a job getting rear axles in and out of Rovers and impractical, of course, if you plan to modify the axle.

In the USA, however, converters are spoilt for choice. For reference, the MGB Salisbury axle weighs about 165lb. You may be surprised to hear that you can not only upgrade the strength of the rear axle but, in some cases, reduce the weight of it too. A shortlist of stronger US axles might be Chevy S10 (160lb), Ford 9in (186lb), Ford 8in (149lb) and the Dana 44 (195lb). Given the lighter weight and the strength of the Ford 8in this would seem to be the axle of choice, at least for medium-powered cars – all of the US axles will require width reductions to fit into the MGB wheelarches.

The USA's Ford rear-ends are preferred among performance car enthusiasts because of their strength as well as their availability. Almost any Ford rear-end, particularly the eight (picture 8-2-16) and nine inch crown-wheel (ring

8-2-15 This close-up principally shows the SD1 hub, which has had its 5 stud mounting re-machined to MGB 4 stud and the outside diameter of the hub also machined to accept MGB brake drums. We had not quite got the MGB brake/backplate assembly correctly orientated when this photo was taken – it was subsequently adjusted to the standard MGB orientation.

gear) units, will hold up to 300+bhp. Gear sets for these differentials are readily available, with ratios ranging from 2.47 to 4.10 to 1, and are relativity inexpensive. Lower ratios are available too but unlikely to interest V8 converters. Current prices are about $170 from suppliers such as Summit Racing Equipment and other mail order companies. Furthermore, Ford produced quite a number of limited slip diffs and these are available from almost any salvage yard. The few extra dollars for a limited slip unit will be well worth the expense as the option vastly improves traction. You may consider it an additional advantage that many Fords will come with disc brakes (or discs can be easily transplanted by

8-2-16 A Ford 8in shortened by D+D Fabrications for an MGB and fitted with discs/rotors and Wilwood calipers.

procuring them at a salvage yard or from aftermarket sources).

I do not see the necessity to change from the MGB's original rear drum brakes. However, I do accept that if an axle comes pre-fitted with rear discs and calipers, there is absolutely no point in throwing them away. All US Ford rear axles are too wide to fit an MGB bodyshell and, like the UK's SD1 axle, the Ford units must be narrowed to the MGB's standard 52in outside-of-drum to outside-of-drum dimension. Although many US towns have an autoshop capable of making said changes, Currie Enterprises will help if you are in any difficulty.

Before you consign the work you should have planned not only the width (brake-drum to brake-drum) you seek, but the wheel-studs, brakes (thus the drums and backplates), the handbrake cable fixing, the hydraulic hose mounting and the suspension mountings. No point in having MGB spring-pads welded in place if you are wisely going to use a more positive method of locating the rear axle. This might be your opportunity to handle both changes simultaneously.

The differential on the SD1 axle is offset away from the centre of the car and, if the shortened axle is to fit an MGB, you will need that anomaly correcting. In round figures this change alone requires about 3in

cut from one side of the axle but 6in needs to be removed from the other half to ensure the pinion drive flange ends up in the centre of the shortened axle. You may be lucky and find that by shortening only the longer half of your axle you simultaneously centre the pinion and shorten the axle to a width you can live with.

Assuming you wish to minimize the number of non-MGB parts on the car (particularly service items like brake shoes) you will also need to pre-mark the orientation of the brake backplates (i.e. where you want the handbrake lever to exit the axle). Consequently, take both MGB backplates with you to the axle shop as they will likely need to be spaced away from the axle flanges and orientated correctly for your brake lines and cables.

HIGH-POWERED CARS

The ease with which big capacity V8 engines now produce large amounts of torque demands you give serious consideration to the rear suspension from the roadholding and 'is it strong enough' points of view.

The size and the number of mounting studs on the front and rear hubs and their wheels bears reconsideration. Five studs seems to lie somewhere between prudent and essential.

It is possible that some engines in this power bracket will bend original MGB leaf springs, thus not only heavy-duty axles but the methods of locating the axle are required at this level of upgrade. We will start by reviewing some live axle upgrades but a strong axle will not solve all the problems, transmitting the power to the road and feeding the consequential stresses into the MGB's frame need your attention too.

TR7 rear suspension

I have already given the attributes of this rear suspension design plenty of space but need to add one caveat/further suggestion

for cars in this power-band. However hard the polyurethane suspension bushes you use for this or any similar suspension set-up, they will distort under the power available at this end of the power band. It is best to fit rose-bushes to both ends of each of the four suspension links. This will necessitate four new links being made from high-strength steel tubing. Further, each link needs to be made adjustable in the form of a 'turnbuckle' (i.e. with one end right- and one end left-threaded) and each fitted with a ½in x ½in rose joint. You will also need to further strengthen the chassis mounting points in deference to the force that will be exerted through these axle-link arms, as we saw in picture 8-2-7-2.

However, if you have a very high-powered car there may be preferable alternatives to a live rear axle. Read on.

Independent rear suspension

As stated at the beginning of this chapter, independent rear suspension (IRS) offers the prospect of a more comfortable ride than any live axle. Perhaps more important than the ride quality in a high-performance car, the road holding from IRS is superior as the result of one rear wheel's movements not affecting the other wheel.

Hoyle Engineering

My first suggestion is for those who want a 'Bolt-on' proven system. It is available both in the UK and in the USA from Hoyle Suspensions Systems (details in the Appendix). Designed by Gerry Hawkridge (of Hawk Cars) who is very experienced and already has the respect of the Cobra replica market with his IRS options, the design is actually a development of Gerry's Jaguar XJ6-based IRS, which was initially conceived for his Cobra replicas, where the structural integrity of the tubular construction (seen at 8-3-1 and 8-3-2) was essential given the power that was available. The product has been successfully designed to avoid any modifications to the car and with the concept that customers' MGs can be reconverted to original specification without welding or leaving any non-original holes behind.

In outline, the suspension is via twin tubular wishbones and AVO coil-over shocks – which can be seen at 8-3-3. Road holding is improved by a reduction in un-sprung weight of 120lb (55kg). This, and the fact that the rear springs no longer need to locate the rear axle, means that softer springs can be used, which, coupled to the high quality telescopic dampers, results in a more supple suspension. Unlike the original MGB suspension each wheel reacts independently to the change in road surface so not upsetting the balance of the car, and the unequal length double wishbones ensure that for hard cornering the small camber change induced keeps the maximum amount of rubber in contact with the road.

Picture 8-3-4 shows the details of the construction and front attachment point. Also attached to the subframe are the new stainless steel, braided brake pipes and the handbrake cables. All these parts plus all the necessary polyurethane bushes, and nuts and bolts make up the basic kit pictured at 8-3-5. Shims, in the form of quick-change 'C' washers, can be fitted between the wishbone pivot yokes and the subframe to make minor adjustments to camber and tracking. All fabricated parts are black powder coated, and the aluminium uprights are anodised. The dampers included in the kit are the same spec as Hoyle's front suspension kit.

There are donor components you will also need to budget for. The differential, drive shafts, hubs, stub shafts, drive flanges and disc brakes are from either a Ford Sierra or Granada. The half-shafts require shortening (by Hoyle if you wish) to maintain the MGB's standard track, whilst the Ford drive flange is replaced by a new

8-3-1 The Hoyle IRS system uses the existing MGB spring and shock absorber mounting points, and allows the car's existing battery box(es) and fuel tank to remain unaltered.

flange with the MGB stud pattern for bolt-on wheels. However, Hoyle makes things easy for you in that it can supply these donor parts new, reconditioned or as very cheap used – just as your budget dictates.

There is a range of differential ratios available – 3.1 or 3.9 ex-Sierra and 3.3 or 3.6 from a Granada. The Sierra unit has a 7in crown wheel and can cope with engine power up to 250bhp whilst the Granada's 7.5in will happily withstand higher output engines. For those with big V8 engine cars that want to drive them hard, or use

them for track days or competition, both differentials can be fitted with either the standard Ford Limited Slip differential or a Quaife torque biasing LSD.

Fitting the kit is pretty straightforward, helped by the fact that the new unit can be preassembled off the car. Once the original axle, springs and dampers are removed, the assembly is jacket up into position. It is attached to the original damper mounts (4 bolts): the rear spring front eyebolt mounts via the tie bars (2 bolts) and the check strap brackets (2

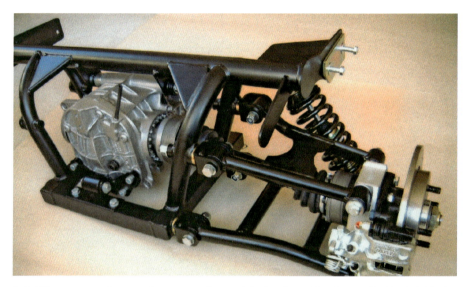

8-3-2 You can see the superb construction and design from this shot of the Hoyle IRS, the installation of which adds to the rigidity of the car's bodyshell, although the overall weight of the original rear suspension and this replacement are about the same, and ...

8-3-3 ... utilizes AVO coil-over dampers and a machined alloy hub carrier.

8-3-4 The system consists of a new subframe that supports the differential, upper and lower tubular wishbones, coil-over dampers, machined alloy hub carriers and tie bars to secure the assembly to the car's original spring eyebolt bracket.

8-3-5 The Hoyle kit looks pretty comprehensive.

bolts). The stainless brake hoses mate with the existing pipe-work and dual handbrake cables and their linkage attaches to the handbrake drop link.

At the time of writing the basic kit costs £1570. There is an extra charge of £85 for shortening your half shafts and a further charge of £1071 if you were to ask Hoyle to supply all the donor parts including a reconditioned differential and all other parts supplied new (i.e. cv joints, brakes, bearings etc). Hoyle deals direct and ships all over the world.

Hoyle has ensured that the comprehensive instructions cover setting up the geometry and adjusting the suspension to best effect but acknowledge that some customers find this a little

daunting. In such cases Hoyle stresses it is always available to discuss and advise but you are probably best starting with the springs and dampers set to their mid-points. A measure of this system's effectiveness may be gained by my mentioning that an MGB fitted with front and rear Hoyle suspension kits won the 2003 British Sports Car Cup championship. There were 70 competitors competing in slaloms, hill climbs and circuit racing across Germany, France, Austria and Switzerland.

Jaguar XKE/XJ6/XJS

An independent rear suspension will greatly improve handling, road holding, and ride quality. This is why so many of today's performance vehicles use IRS and the Jaguar unit has a well-deserved reputation as the strongest available. When fitted to an MGB it also improves the rear ground clearance, has better (inboard, disc) brakes, and some versions can be bought relatively inexpensively. Most come with a Posi-lock LSD differential and, with one exception, were built to withstand sports car use. The gear ratios are appropriate with 15in wheels and the hubs have the 5-stud wheel fixings that I believe important for this level of power and performance in an MGB.

There is one weakness within these assemblies – and we'd best get the correction out of the way – you need to replace the side bracket bolts with upgraded fastenings. Concours West Industries (CWI), based in Washington State USA, supplies a kit of stainless bolts and locking wire, and this is a 'must'. There are several companies that modify Jaguar IRS systems to whatever width you want but CWI specialises in all aspects of the Jaguar's IRS. However, you can modify an assembly at home with a little subcontracted welding and machine shop work – thereafter it is almost a bolt-in operation.

8-3-6 A Jag rear-end – try and get one with bolt-on hubs but if the assembly you most favour has wire-wheel splines, do a deal with the vendor and exchange the hubs for bolt-ons. Purchase a pair of MGC bolt-on front hubs too – they have the same wheel-stud PCD as Jaguar's rears.

Naturally you need to buy the complete Jaguar IRS assembly like that seen at 8-3-6 from your nearest used Jaguar specialist. There are two types of Jaguar IRS units – the XJ6/XJS and the revered XKE (in UK known as the E-Type). The former will require something like 4¼in (105mm) cutting off each side while Series 1 and Series 2 ex-E unit only needs 1¼in (30mm) off each side to bring the track back to the MGB's original. With these early E units you may elect to retain the

8-3-7 Inboard disc brakes make it easier to reduce the width because all the alterations take place outside the brakes. This shot helps with some parking brake information and shows how easy subsequent brake access is – through the battery box openings at the top of the picture.

8-3-8 A 1984 XJS cage cut to fit between the MGB's chassis rails.

8-3-9-1 While the majority of information you get from this underview will be helpful, do not, I suggest, copy this (arrowed) attachment method/location for the radius arms. (You will see this detail from a different angle in the next picture.) The prop/driveshaft installation angle is not as bad as it looks here, but note that the lower damper mounting has been moved outboard by about 3 or 4in so that it matches the original angle. This is not necessary if you replace the original shocks with aftermarket coil-overs with the proper spring rate. Furthermore, the spaced mounting brackets (fitted to compensate for relocating the springs) should not be required with properly installed rear dampers. The battery bin (a plastic item available from Moss and others) just clears the lower portion of the IRS cage. The bottom of the cage is not needed and can be cut away, giving a bit more clearance.

8-3-9-2 I am uncomfortable with this inflexible method of attaching the radius arms to the chassis. The perforated strap you see pointing towards the prop/driveshaft carries the cruise control speed sensor. This installation runs the exhaust out through each side of the car – which I do not favour either because you risk reducing the structural integrity of the sills.

8-3-10 This is a rubber-bumper Jag installation which only differs from the chrome-bumper to the extent of the battery box issue mentioned in the main text. Whether chrome- or rubber-bumper, there is just enough room to run the pipes under the diff, especially if you use twin (i.e. smaller diameter) pipes and do not lower your car too drastically. However, the best route is to run the exhaust pipes between the lower control arm and the axle shafts.

Jaguar track and simply flare the car's wheelarches. However, a Series 3 E-Type unit is wider and will need narrowing I think. If narrowing any of these assemblies, the inboard disc brakes seen at 8-3-7 (previous page) make it easier.

In the UK, most breakers yards will have a Jaguar and is the first place to try as the specialist Jag breakers tend to be more expensive. Avoid XJ40s though – they have IRS but it is different in many ways and also has outboard brakes. An XJ6 rear end should be obtainable for £50/£150 – albeit with a sttandard diff – but it will be worth looking for and paying around £350 for one with a power-lock (i.e. limited slip) differential. An E-Type's rear-end will be very hard to find in the UK and hardly worth looking for as quotes can be £800+ if you find one. It's better to get an XJ6/XJS and narrow it as shown in picture 8-3-8.

The welding involved in narrowing one of these units is critical to your subsequent safety. The work is certainly not suited to a low-powered, 'home'-standard mig-welder. Thus you are advised to either send the individual parts to a specialist or send the whole assembly for expert attention. Some suggestion follow shortly.

On chrome-bumper cars, the frame/cage assembly simply bolts in place and no modification to the battery boxes is needed. Pictures 8-3-9-1 and 8-3-9-2 give a view of this while a rubber-bumper car shown at 8-3-10, with its offset and larger

12-volt battery, will have to be changed one way or another. You have several options: the battery box can be shortened and one smaller 12-volt battery fitted or you can weld a second chrome-bumper battery tray in place, form a second opening on the other side of the car and fit a second small 12-volt battery. You can turn the original tray through 90°, enlarge the access accordingly and refit the original large 12-volt battery or even put the battery in the boot/trunk. I personally favour two 12-volt batteries in the chrome-bumper positions.

The Jaguar's frame or cage will then fit without serious modification. You will need to remove the Jag mountings and, if

you've mounted your engine with a slight downward tilt (as most are), the Jag cage will need to be mounted with the matching upward tilt/angle shown in D8-2. This will probably entail the use of metal packing pieces to ensure the propshaft installation angle is correct. This detail is relevant to

8-3-11 One of two boot/truck securing locations. Do make quite sure the frame is central by equalising both sides at the front and rear, and clamp it in place before you drill the holes for all your securing bolts. Use large load-spreading plain washers or a plate as seen here on both sides of the fastenings, and, if not aircraft grade fastenings, at least use high-tensile bolts and positive-locking nuts. The hole? There are two (one was an obsolete fuel-pump aperture) and they serve to allow access to the top mounting bolts for the rear/aft dampers.

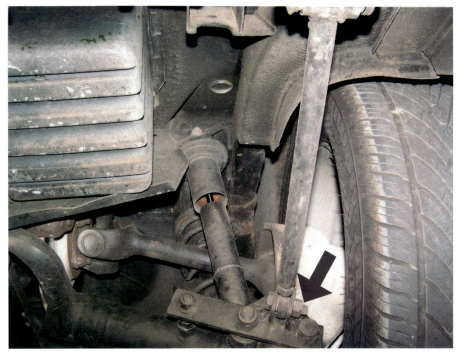

8-3-12-1 This view will differ from the usual Jaguar rear mounting arrangement because the dampers have been moved outboard by 3in (75mm). However, the rear radius arm mounting will be as you expect to find it. The arrowed bushes need replacing with polyurethane ones and, ideally in my view, the arm needs cutting and re-welding here to crank the front end of the arm over towards the centre of the car in order that the front pivot is axially in line with the inner wishbone pivot.

any IRS installation but in the case of a Jaguar unit you will need a pair of CWI adjustable side brackets to ensure the axis of the engine/gearbox unit and the axis of the differential are parallel (not aligned) with each other. These brackets are therefore an essential purchase for any MGB Jaguar installation – ask CWI for part number 1340-1342.

Fit a ¼in (5mm) heavy rubber pad between the cage and body to minimise road noise and vibration. You will need to through-bolt the cage to the MGB's flat body panels in at least four locations – two in the boot/trunk and two in the passenger

compartment just behind the battery box cover. You will see one of these locations in picture 8-3-11.

The XKE IRS is the easier to fit as the frame or 'cage' is narrower and requires little alteration. The XJ6 assembly requires more modification and therefore is more complicated.

8-3-12-2 A closer view of the unnecessarily altered bottom damper mounting. The spacing washers seen very clearly here substitute for the original space taken up by properly positioned dampers.

UK readers requiring a Jag modification service should give Ward Engineering a call.

You will need to fabricate a pair of

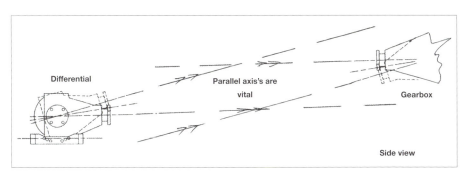

D8-2 Installing the propeller shaft with parallel axis.

8-3-12-3 This is the more usual bottom damper mounting arrangement.

control (or some may call them radius) arms. These could be made up from the original Jaguar traction bars – if they are long enough for your front end mounting location. I'd replace the rear rubber bushes with polyurethane replacements for the lower control arm fixing seen in the pictures at 8-3-12 (starting previous). However, the front mounting position and method needs discussion and great care.

Almost all Jaguar MGB rear suspensions slavishly, but understandably, follow the original Jaguar installation and fit the radius arm in a 'straight-out-in-front' manner. Jaguar certainly fitted them in this manner and "got-away-with-it" by using a soft, very pliable, front mounting rubber that could twist as the suspension adjusted to the road. You could provide an improved location by fitting fully flexible rose (ball) joints at the front as seen at 8-3-13-1 and 8-3-13-2. These pivot in all directions and should not overly stress the MGB's chassis spring-hangers. However, these radius arms are secured to the outboard ends of the wishbones – which, if you think about their movement, need to be constrained by radius arms that pivot on the same axis as the wishbones. In other words, the forward end of the radius arms should pivot in line with the centre wishbone inner pivot. Thus completely new longer radius arms are needed. I think rose joints at the front are still worthwhile but not essential if

8-3-13-1 These rose joints are being trial-fitted and, before being finally secured, will be spaced to sit centrally within the MGB's spring hanger.

8-3-13-2 The minimum front rose joint. But had you noticed this shot also shows the use of only one set of 250lb rated coil-over springs? Two 125lb springs can be used either side, but will increase costs.

the arms pivot as shown in drawing D8-3. Photographs 8-3-14 to 8-3-16 offer some further help with the detail.

Aldan shock absorbers permit

ride height adjustment and dampening adjustment, and offer a wide variety of spring ratings. They are a direct replacement for the OE Woodhead or

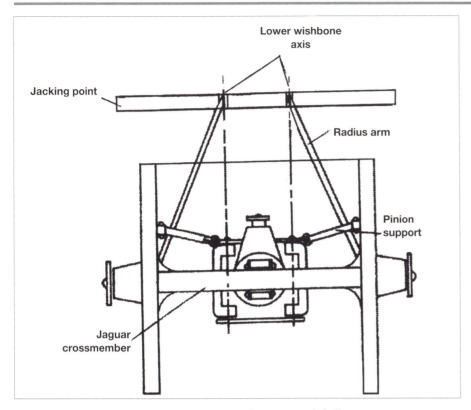

Lower wishbone axis

Jacking point

Radius arm

Pinion support

Jaguar crossmember

D8-3 Jaguar suspension pivots correctly in line.

8-3-15 From the rear this well-installed Jaguar rear might have been made for the MGB! Note the aftermarket replacement coil-over dampers and ...

8-3-16 ... here they are from the side, in close-up. The damper adjusting screw is just visible.

Girling shocks which enjoyed none of these adjustments.

With regards to the differential, the Dana 44 was available with many different ratios, so rear axle gear ratios can be changed reasonably cheaply.

SOME ADDITIONAL DETAILS
Rear axle ratios

There can be no doubt about the necessity of raising the V8's rear axle ratio from the standard 1800cc car's figure of 3.9:1. However, the car's intended tyre size needs to be taken into account. The MGB GT V8 uses 3.07:1 with 14in wheels and 175 section tyres. The RV8 uses a ratio of 3.3:1, very similar to the MGC's 3.307:1 ratio, but both the RV8 and MGC use 15in wheels. Both 3.08 and 3.3 ratios exist today as both SD1 and TR7/8 ratios and could be suitable for your conversion with appropriate tyres.

8-3-14 This is the main Jag wishbone which will require shortening. The amount of metal removed will depend upon which Jag donated its rear to you but note that your life may depend upon the integrity of this component and its counterpart – thus the cutting and welding is not for most home conversions. Get an expert to do the work for you.

A 3.5:1 ratio with 195/60/15 tires gives very nearly the same overall ratio as a 3.7:1 with 215/65/15 tires – 20.58mph/

1000rpm in 4th gear for the former, and 20.91mph/1000rpm for the latter. If you have access to the internet, you may want to download an MSExcel spread sheet and see exactly how the tyre size, axle ratio, and transmission gears interplay. The link is http://www.britishv8.org/swaps/chart.xls.

However, you need not only take the

wheels/tyres you have selected in chapter 6 into account – the gearbox ratios also need bearing in mind. There are other factors to consider too. The use to which you expect to put the car to is all-important. Generally a high-speed cruiser needs a high (i.e. 3:1) rear axle ratio whereas a sprint car needs a low ratio – perhaps 3.7:1. The power, torque and tune of your engine are also relevant. An engine with a hot cam and tune probably will not 'come on the cam' until perhaps 3000rpm, some even as high as 3500rpm. The car will be fun but very hard work to drive if you then select a combination of high-ratio gearbox, wheel-size and rear axle.

Overall, in my opinion, you will not go far wrong with a rear axle ratio of about 3:1 and certainly, assuming you want a gearbox/transmission with a useable first gear, you are better with a rear ratio of about 3:1 than the MGB's original 3.9:1.

Modestly-powered MGB conversions can have their original MGB axle ratio changed by fitting a new (usually 3.07:1) crown-wheel-and-pinion. Almost any UK MGB specialist or any rear-axle refurbishment company will be able to carry out this upgrade. However, such axles should always be of the later/stronger Salisbury or tube-axle, so, if the MGB you are contemplating converting is an early Roadster fitted with a 'Banjo' axle, you may need to first buy a second-hand Salisbury axle. Ensure it is a 'Bolt-on' wheel axle. They are readily available second-hand but original wire wheel axles are a shade narrower and are in shorter supply

second-hand and are consequently more expensive. Do not contemplate using a wire-wheel axle with bolt on hubs: you will get tyre-to-bodywork interference problems unless you are prepared to change wheel off-sets to compensate.

V8 converters in the US, like their UK counterparts, have the obvious route to a higher rear axle ratio by also fitting the 3.07 to 1 ratio gear set to their own MGB axle. Ian Pender or Towery Foreign Cars will be happy to oblige with the necessary parts, although V8 gear sets are also available by mail order from most of the UK's V8 conversion specialists.

Limited slip differentials (LSDs)

LSDs deserves a mention if only because of the improvement in adhesion and traction they bring about. Assuming we are avoiding the complexities and expense of electronic traction control, LSD works in one of two ways – Automatic Torque Biasing or Clutch/Slipper Controls. The former is much the cheaper and is a non-adjustable mechanical gear that allows more even power distribution both sides of the rear axle. For road-going use, Roadster owners with high power outputs should give serious thought to this option, for it has safety connotations too. Quaife Power Systems provide an excellent Automatic Torque Biasing LSD that became a standard feature on the RV8 and can be viewed at 8-4.

The Auto Torque Biasing does not, however, transmit power evenly if one

8-4 This is an LSD installation in an SD1 or TR8 and you can see the difference to a normal differential and the absence of planet and sun gears.

wheel were lifted from the ground – as may be the case were you to do some spirited driving on track days. If track days were likely to be part of your car's regular employment, you may do well to explore the 50 per cent more expensive, but adjustable, belleview washer tensioning clutch-plate LSD. Salisbury, Powrlok or Gripper systems all transmit as much power as possible to the road/track even if one wheel is 'off-the-deck', and can be adjusted to suit your driving style. Note that clutch-plate LSDs can cause understeer and will certainly affect the car's cornering. When the clutch operates, both wheels are locked into turning at the same speed making the car is more reluctant to turn corners because, when cornering, the outside wheel needs to turn faster than the inside wheel.

Chapter 9
Modifying the bodyshell

What has to be changed on the MGB bodyshell will depend upon the model in question as well as the engine, gearbox and rear axle/suspension that you choose for your V8 conversion. The permutations of alteration is therefore far too large to cover entirely but I have divided this chapter into four sections that I hope will cover the most common circumstances. I strongly believe that as many converters as possible should use a new MGB bodyshell – particularly as it is possible to buy a specific shell made for V8 conversions. Consequently we will open the chapter with information on the Heritage-produced V8 bodyshell.

However, I also recognise how hard it will be to have a solid MGB sitting in your garage, perhaps one that was restored not so very long ago, but feel you have to go out and spend a large amount of money on a replacement shell. Although I am uncomfortable with this solution for anything but the most modest V8 conversion, nevertheless we will also look

at the changes you would need to make to an existing shell.

Finally, in parts of the US and certainly in large parts of Europe, the bodyshell of our existing MGB may be beyond saving but the cost of a new shell puts the enjoyment of a V8 conversion beyond reach. Again, a potential solution for only the most modest of conversions, but we will look into where and how to buy a used, but hopefully sound, shell from a specialist restorer or from an ex-dry state. If you must go for a big capacity engine, take very careful note of the next section.

STRENGTHENING THE SHELL

Whatever the condition of your bodyshell, even if you have a new one, it is essential that shell strengthening takes place once engine size extends beyond 3500cc. You will be sitting in the shell so remember that, above 200bhp, you will be subjecting the shell to over twice its original designed capability. Furthermore, as you move up

the engine capacity range, the power that progressively becomes available is quite literally capable of tearing the body apart unless very substantial changes have been incorporated.

When fitting a bigger engine you may think that any strengthening of the bodyshell needs to take place in and around the engine and gearbox. To some extent this is true in that you must ensure the engine and gearbox mountings are indeed strong enough to handle the enormous torque some of these engines push out. However, the grunt is mostly transmitted to the bodyshell through the rear of the car. Therefore it is in the area of the rear suspension that doubling-up, sometimes trebling, the strength of the brackets and structural members that transmit the torque to the structure of the shell becomes essential. I have seen the leaf-springs permanently distorted and a modified 4.6-litre tear the rear spring hangers away from the shell, even after doubling the material thickness and seam welding the surrounding area.

NEW HERITAGE BODYSHELLS

The reintroduction of classic car bodyshells by British Motor Heritage (which has made Triumph TR6, MG Midget and, of course, the MGB and MG RV8 shells) has probably done more to enhance both the profile and affordability of classic cars than any other single item. Indeed, the availability of new MGB and MGB GT bodyshells has also brought the practicality of a home rebuild to many enthusiasts who had previously been daunted by the time, skills, tools and experience required to rejuvenate their original bodyshell.

In the past, those that could, employed a suitable bodyshop or restorer to do the work for them, but at considerable cost. For the last 10 years, for less cost than the major body rebuild, the amateur enthusiast has been able to buy a new shell and, at a pace, cost and quality that suits his circumstances, reassemble his car. Furthermore, the new shell's built-in corrosion protection can be augmented with modern rust proofing technology such that the rebuilt car should outlast the original.

This advantage extends to the V8 converter too for Heritage now makes a non-original shell specifically for the Rover V8 converter. This perhaps does more to illustrate how far the activity has come since I wrote the first edition of this book than any words of mine. If you are installing a Ford V8, there will still be some minor changes to the shell to carry out, but Buick/Rover engines of any capacity will just drop into any one of the four options available:
Chrome-bumper Roadster V8 – part number BMH 4011
Rubber-bumper Roadster V8 – BMH 9021
Chrome-bumper GT V8 – BMH 4012
Rubber-bumper GT V8 – BMH 9020

These brand new, completely dressed shells all cost around £4500 (unpainted) and incorporate all the requisite features for dropping a Buick/Rover engine and Rover

5-speed gearbox straight into the shell. They make marrying a Ford easier too as the shells incorporate:

● Exhaust tail clearances in the front inner wings along with inner-wing/fender holes for RV8-style exhaust manifolds/headers (see 9-1-1).

● Suitable late rubber-bumper radiator mountings along with oil-filter mounting point (illustrated by 9-1-2).

● Suitable rubber-bumper single-stud engine mountings along with recessed steering u/j mounting for collapsible steering column (clearly seen in 9-1-3).

● Cutaway bulkheads as per rubber-bumper models giving V8 cylinder head clearance (illustrated by 9-1-4).

● Upward extension to gearbox tunnel for SD1 5-speed gearbox (seen at 9-1-5, overleaf).

● Deeper (rubber-bumper) rear tunnel/heel-board strengthener (to accept a larger diameter prop shaft) (see 9-1-6, overleaf).

● RV8 bulged bonnet (see 9-1-7, overleaf).

● RV8-style rear suspension anti-tramp mounting bracket (shown in picture 9-1-8, overleaf).

Corrosion protection

Quite apart from the building advantages of a new British Motor Heritage bodyshell,

9-1-2 The radiator mounting line will be moved forward from about the arrowed (chrome-bumper) point to the later car's position while, if you order a V8 conversion shell, the oil-filter mounting bracket seen here will also be in place.

9-1-3 Not only is the recessed cone for the steering u/j clearly visible here, but so too are the engine mounting and clutch hose brackets. Note the slightly dished footwell, just sufficient to give the bellhousing a little extra clearance.

9-1-1 I have arrowed the secondary 'dish' in this inner wing/fender to highlight it for anyone thinking of 'Block-hugger' exhausts – although with the RV8-style holes in place the dished clearance for the hugger tails would be unnecessary. Note the strengthening lips around each RV8 hole and the later engine mounting.

9-1-4 An interesting top-down view of a new shell under construction, included here to show the relatively small cut-aways in the bulkhead/firewall to provide Ford and Buick/Rover cylinder head clearance. You also get a good view of the plenum chamber behind the heater platform.

9-1-5 This is how MG-Rover provides the extra space for the Rover LT77/R380 gearbox and ...

there are longevity advantages to be had from the new shell's corrosion protection. The structural panels in today's new shells are made from Zintec – zinc coated mild steel sheet. These offer huge long-term corrosion improvements over the original MGB bodyshells, even over the early 'Heritage' MGB shells.

Since the early Heritage or Steelcraft panels were not made from Zintec, the resultant restored original bodyshell was at a major corrosion disadvantage compared with Heritage's new product, no matter how skilful you (or your restorer) are.

MODIFYING AN EXISTING BODYSHELL

This section is dependent upon what you are starting with, chrome- or rubber-bumper, and what you want to end up with. A Buick/Rover or Ford engine, the intended gearbox, the rear axle and front/rear suspension all affect the modifications

9-1-6 ... the deeper heel-board stiffener.

9-1-7 This the bulged RV8 bonnet ...

9-1-8 ... and this another view of the anti-tramp mountings.

required. You will already have gathered that a rubber-bumper car minimises the work you are likely to have to do on the bodyshell but here we need to explore the worst-case – a chrome-bumper shell – and leave you to decide which of the following applies to your situation. Naturally I have not attempted to cover any restoration work – that is a separate issue for you to incorporate as required.

1 – Rear suspension provisions. Any Roadster owner seriously contemplating re-using an old shell should remember that Rover has seen fit to add stiffening members to the rear of its new shells, as we saw in a couple of the preceding pictures. You would be prudent to carry out this change both to stiffen the shell and also to provide for anti-tramp bars. A drawing of anti-tramp members will be found at D9-1 and we saw several pictures of an anti-tramp installation in chapter 8.

If you have alternative rear suspension plans then the changes in this area need to reflect your selected suspension. The permutations are too numerous to cover every eventuality but, for prudence, even with a modest conversion you could include additional members similar to this diagram in order to add strength to this area of the bodyshell.

If you intend fitting a very high-powered engine, you may also find it necessary to strengthen the inside of the cockpit in line with the points at which the stresses are fed into the shell by the rear suspension. On an un-reinforced shell you are likely to see alarming fatigue cracks around the heel-board, floor and sills, as well as pulled spot welds in this general area. You should certainly seam-weld all panel joints in this area as a matter of course, and possibly add tubular longitudinal members alongside the inner sills and cross-car, inter-connecting box section(s) with lots of gussets to ensure the stresses are not focused in one area. We saw such additional strengthening

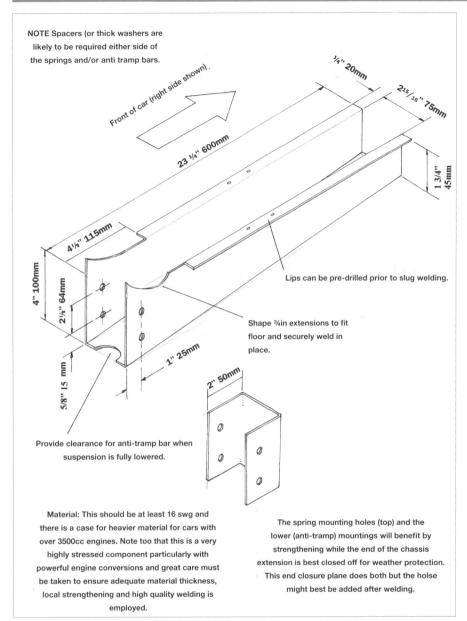

NOTE Spacers (or thick washers are likely to be required either side of the springs and/or anti tramp bars.

Front of car (right side shown)

¼" 20mm

2¹⁵/₁₆" 75mm

23 ¾" 600mm

1 3/4" 45mm

4¼" 115mm

4" 100mm

2¼" 64mm

5/8" 15 mm

1" 25mm

2" 50mm

Lips can be pre-drilled prior to slug welding.

Shape ¾in extensions to fit floor and securely weld in place.

Provide clearance for anti-tramp bar when suspension is fully lowered.

Material: This should be at least 16 swg and there is a case for heavier material for cars with over 3500cc engines. Note too that this is a very highly stressed component particularly with powerful engine conversions and great care must be taken to ensure adequate material thickness, local strengthening and high quality welding is employed.

The spring mounting holes (top) and the lower (anti-tramp) mountings will benefit by strengthening while the end of the chassis extension is best closed off for weather protection. This end closure plane does both but the holse might best be added after welding.

D9-1 Suggestion for MGB rear chassis extension to accomodate anti-tramp bars.

in picture 8-2-7-2. Form the ends of any reinforcing/fish plates with the usual rounded concave shape that dissipates stresses and carefully seam-weld all the additional material into the original shell. Triangulated structures are far stronger than similar un-triangulated structures.

Powerful conversions will also need to strengthen the MGB spring hangers if they are being used to dissipate any significant stresses from the rear suspension. Being in line with both the floor and sills the original hangers are well placed to feed stresses into the shell but were only designed with 100bhp (plus a safety margin, of course) in mind. It may be necessary to completely

replace them with much stronger material (perhaps a heavy gauge folded channel) and run that channel into a suitable dissipation point. It may be that the B's crossbrace that runs between the jacking points might be suitable, but remember that stress dissipating fish-plates and corner-gussets may still be essential.

If you are uncertain, take five minutes to look at Motor Sports Association's 'Blue' book (the UK's familiar term for the MSA's annual *Competitors Year Book*). Although you are not building a roll-cage, the stress-dissipation, joints, radii, triangulation, welding and mounting information within the 'Safety' section will get you thinking. I would be surprised if the book failed to yield a few other useful contacts too. If still in doubt about this stress issue, consult a racing expert or a company experienced in building roll-cages.

A pound or two of extra material in the car is not going to affect your performance but could save your life.

2 – Rover LT77 or R380 Gearbox provisions. The Rover 77mm gearbox requires about 40-45mm additional vertical clearance, as explained in chapter 4. This is achieved by cutting out the top front of the propshaft tunnel (picture 9-2-1-1) to accommodate the inverted channel-shaped insert shown in drawing D9-2 and photograph 9-2-1-2. The end result is shown welded in place in photograph

9-2-1-1 This cutout is further back than would be necessary for a Rover gearbox, but clearly shows the close proximity of this Tremec T5 to the top of the tunnel, and that a similar tunnel extension piece to...

9-2-1-2 ... this may well be necessary, resulting in ....

9-2-1-3 … something like this.

9-2-1-3. The task is made slightly more complex due to the necessity of cutting and welding the car's two internal structural braces to the top of the channel-shaped extension. You can weld 16swg right-angled supports if this makes the reconnection of the two internal braces to the extension any easier. Remember, however, that you are likely to want to fit your radio/cassette player in this area later in your rebuild program and the more metal you weld here the more difficult fitting your radio becomes.

3 – Change the front valance. As discussed under 'cooling' (chapter 5), replacing the front valance is a good idea for two reasons – improved cooling and frontal stability. The very least you should do as part of your V8 conversion is to fit the post-1972 valance (seen at 9-2-2) incorporating a pair of extra air flow ducts. The alternatives are a bolt-on front air dam or a Sebring front valance.

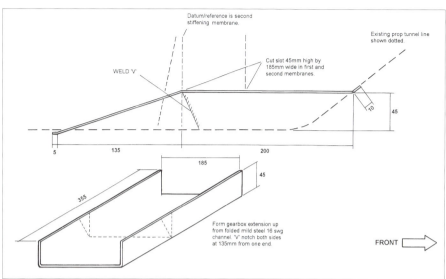

D9-2 SD1 gearbox propshaft tunnel modification.

Some detail on the latter is included later in the chapter.

4 – Alter the driver's side bulkhead. Do this to permit clearance for the cylinder head and make provision for the steering column. The extent of the work depends upon the engine you plan to fit. The Buick, Rover and Ford engines require no more alteration than that provided by the rubber-bumper bodyshell bulkhead detailed in the following paragraphs. However, the Chevy needs more space, an idea of which can be assessed from photograph 9-2-3-1 (overleaf).

9-2-2 This is the later front valance with its twin air openings. It is my oil cooler you can see through the nearest opening, not, as you may think, the radiator.

9-2-3-1 The amount of heater platform and footwell alterations required for the Chevy engine is substantially more than that ...

9-2-3-2 ... required to fit the Ford and/or the Buick/Rover engines into a chrome-bumper MGB.

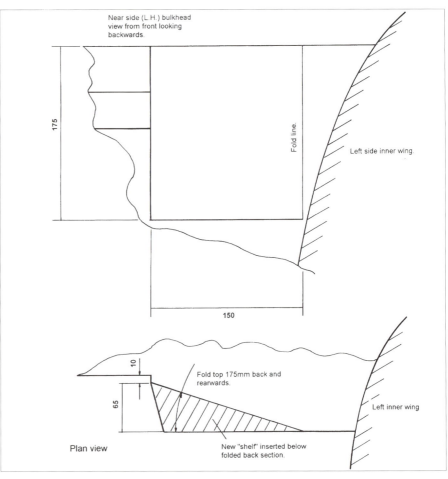

D9-3 Modification to left side bulkhead of chrome bumper cars.

If you have elected to utilize a modified chrome-bumper steering rack and double universal jointed steering shaft (explained in chapter 7), you will have only to cut back the bulkhead to provide clearance for the cylinder heads. These modification can be seen in photograph 9-2-3-2, while a similar cut-back is also required to the passenger side of the bulkhead to provide clearance for the cylinder head that comes very close to it, even after modification. The necessary dimensions for these changes are shown in drawing D9-3.

5 – The smaller universal joint we saw in chapter 7 was fitted from 1974 onwards to all rubber-bumper cars. The relocated universal joint fits into the recessed steering column cone that forms part of the rubber-bumper car's bulkhead. This recessed cone serves two purposes. Not only does it house the universal joint, but the top of the cone acts as the mounting point for the bottom of the collapsible steering column used on the rubber-bumper cars (part number BHH 1596). Three bolts secure the bottom of the column to the cone while a complex bracket simultaneously secures the top of the column to the inside of the bulkhead and to the square crossbrace that goes across the cockpit behind the dash.

If you are planning to use the (recommended) rubber-bumper steering rack and column, this modification requires you not only cut the bulkhead/firewall back but also provide a recessed bottom fixing for the rubber-bumper collapsible steering column. Panel HZA 5335 (RHD cars) is shown in photos 9-2-4-1 and 9-2-4-2 and offers two alternatives. If your driver's

9-2-4-1 The conversion of a chrome-bumper car bulkhead/firewall work can be eased by the purchase of panel (RHD cars) HZA 5335 ...

9-2-4-2 ... which is a standard rubber-bumper panel and incorporates both head clearance and steering cone changes.

9-2-6-1 Our US friends should end up with this, while ...

9-2-6-2 ... in the UK the steering cone will look like this.

9-2-5-1 You can use the whole panel but can alternatively separate the cone pressing here and ...

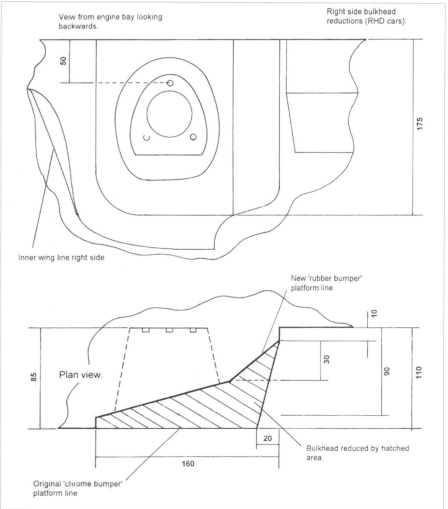

Veiw from engine bay looking backwards.

Right side bulkhead reductions (RHD cars).

50

175

Inner wing line right side.

New 'rubber bumper' platform line

10

30

90

110

85

Plan view.

20

160

Bulkhead reduced by hatched area.

Original 'chrome bumper' platform line

9-2-5-2 ... plug and seam weld it in place in the existing bulkhead/firewall.

D9-4 Right-hand bulkhead re-shaping.

side rear panel is corroded, fit the whole panel, or a very large proportion of it. That involves a lot of work, so if the rear of your wheel arch is sound you are advised to 'unpick' the top right portion of panel HZA 5335 shown in picture 9-2-5-1 and substitute that for your chrome-bumper original as seen in 9-2-5-2. Pictures 9-2-6-1 or 9-2-6-2 are your objectives, using drawing D9-4 for the critical dimensions.

6 – Alter the front inner wings/fenders if you intend to fit block-hugger exhaust manifolds/headers. This operation is not necessary for the recommended RV8-style exhaust system but provides clearance for the 'tails' of the block-hugger manifolds/ headers and the extent of the operation is shown in photograph 9-2-7-1. If your shell is in such a condition that new inner wing panels are required, fit rubber-bumper ones (part numbers HZA5324 and HZA5325) since they have the required profile and include relocated radiator mounts. Otherwise, dress your existing inner wing panels as per picture 9-2-7-2 and drawing D9-5.

Alternatively, you can avoid this whole 'dressing' modification and simultaneously improve your under-bonnet cooling by fitting RV8-style exhaust manifolds/ headers. These do not hug the block but pass out through holes in each inner wing/ fender and can be seen in photographs 9-2-8. We will look at this step in a little more detail shortly.

9-2-7-2 I wanted to be sure not to dress my inner wing/fender too far so left the front suspension dampers in situ, making it difficult to make a neat job of this beating operation. Heat from the exhaust has subsequently lifted the filler I made-good this rough dressing with!

9-2-7-1 This photograph shows the now bulged inner wing panel at the top of this picture very nearly coming into contact with the top of the shock absorber. There's also a view of the more efficient cross-drilled front discs recommended in the text and, almost dead centre, the heavy anti-roll bar supplied – in this case – by Hopkinson.

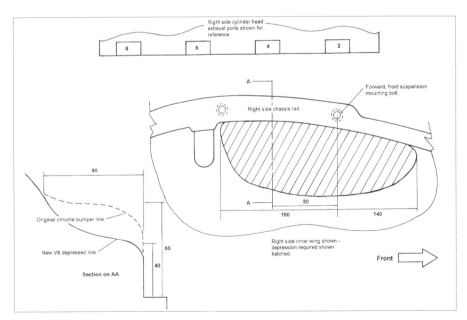

D9-5 Chrome bumper car inner wing dressing.

9-2-8 The RV8 manifold exit is much the better option but was not available when I carried out my conversions.

7 – Relocate the radiator mounting arrangements. Photographs 9-2-9-1 and 9-2-9-2 and the associated relocation dimensions in drawing D9-6) should help with the two mounting brackets.

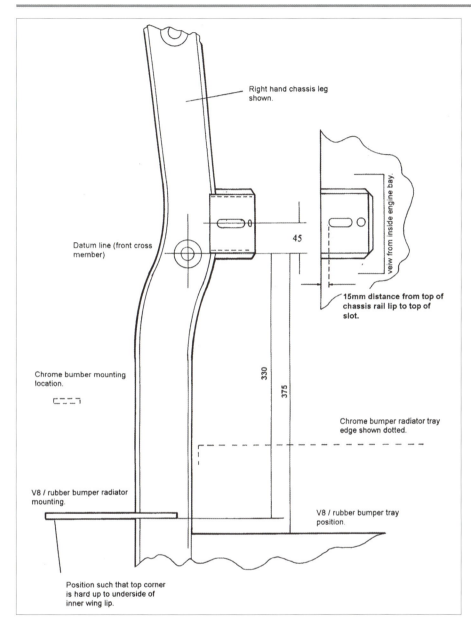

Right hand chassis leg shown.

Datum line (front cross member)

45

15mm distance from top of chassis rail lip to top of slot.

veiw from inside engine bay.

330

375

Chrome bumber mounting location.

Chrome bumper radiator tray edge shown dotted.

V8 / rubber bumper radiator mounting.

V8 / rubber bumper tray position.

Position such that top corner is hard up to underside of inner wing lip.

D9-6 Modification to left side bulkhead of chrome bumper cars.

9-2-9-1 The necessary radiator mounting panel numbers are available under part number HZA 4514/5 ...

9-2-9-2 ... and slot into place easily, although I used my radiator as a jig before tacking them in place.

9-2-10-1 This is the rubber-bumper radiator duct (part number HZA4851) that incorporates the necessary captive nuts and holes for an underslung oil cooler.

You will also need to either shorten your existing radiator duct and add a strengthening lip, or remove the longer chrome-bumper duct and replace it with the shorter rubber-bumper variant. Photographs 9-2-10-1 to 9-2-10-5 show the undertray in various stages of assembly.

Do trial-fit your radiator before finally welding these modifications in place. Furthermore remember that if you are upgrading the radiator with a thicker unit, then you may need to further reduce the front-to-back depth of the radiator duct and even adjust the position of the two radiator mounting panels to compensate.

8 – Fit rubber-bumper-style chassis engine mounts. This desirable change requires that two late single-stud engine mountings be welded to the chassis side rails as per

9-2-10-2. If you are fitting this shorter duct to a chrome-bumper car you will need to mark out ...

9-2-10-3 ... some cut-outs that must be made to the tray before ...

9-2-10-4 ... it is welded in position – assuming you want to be able to tighten the mounting bolts of your chrome-bumper, that is!

9-2-10-5 This is how the end result should look from below. The oil cooler mounting arrangements are clearly visible.

photograph 9-2-11-1 or 9-2-11-2. Drawing D9-7 should help you locate your Buick/Rover brackets correctly while the Ford ones need to be mounted 18in in front of the bulkhead/firewall. However, there is much to be said for the added insurance of tacking the brackets in place and using the engine block and steering rack as positioning aids. If this method appeals to you, remember that plastic replica Ford blocks can be purchased just for this purpose. Those fitting a Buick/Rover engine, particularly those who have to strip their engines for examination and/or reconditioning, can temporarily assemble the gearbox casing to the otherwise empty engine block before engine reconditioning commences. No flywheel is required, either, so the empty block and gearbox are significantly lighter than the complete finished assembly, which aids this stage of your V8 conversion.

9 – Relocate the clutch flexible hose-mounting bracket to a point about 200mm behind the rear front suspension mounting bolt. Photograph 9-2-12 shows the movement involved.

10 – Fine-tune the engine bay modifications.

   a) If you have not already done so,

9-2-11-1 The Heritage engine mounting brackets are handed so compensate for the slight taper in the main chassis rails: do get them on the right way round. It should not be necessary to worry about the angle of these brackets but ...

9-2-11-2. ... if you are making your own, as might be the case with a Ford engine, you do need to fit them with a 45° angle.

9-2-12 The relocated clutch pipe mounting, but angle yours forward, not backward as shown in this photo! The relocation is designed to ensure no starter-motor-solenoid-to-clutch-bracket interference occurs.

offer up your rubber-bumper steering rack with the longer shaft (photograph 9-2-13, overleaf) – it will almost certainly be necessary to dress back the top of the chassis rail to give it a small amount of clearance.

b) While dressing within the engine bay, dress the footwell inwards by about 20mm for around 75mm vertically to allow the left side of the gearbox bellhousing a shade more clearance.

c) Temporarily locate the engine block/gearbox at the front then fit/adjust the gearbox crossmember and 'cotton reel' gearbox flexible mountings as detailed in chapter 4.

d) Using D9-8 (overleaf) check that the vertical dimensions are such that you stand a chance of eventually closing your bonnet. You will appreciate that the distance between the chassis engine mounting brackets is vital and, if widened

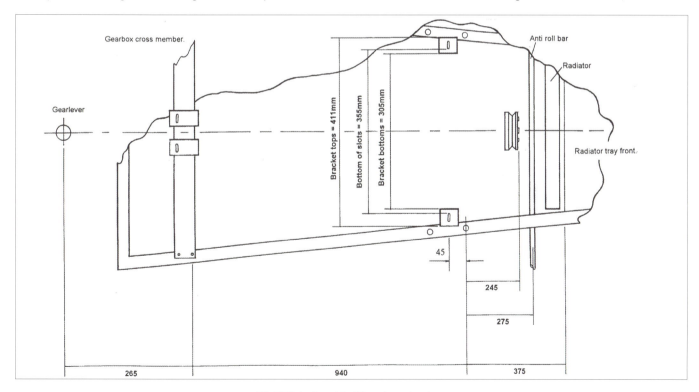

D9-7 Right-hand bulkhead re-shaping.

9-2-13 It will almost certainly be necessary to dress back the top of the chassis rail here, to give it a small amount of clearance for the steering shaft as it passes though the engine mounting.

slightly, will allow your engine block to 'sit down' as far as the block/chassis rails allow. You can use this to vary the height of the engine and, to aid you, I suggest

you get the driver's side bracket secured using the steering column as the criteria, then proceed to the passenger side mount and fix that with reference to the height of the engine. You may find this technique 'offsets' the engine by a very small amount – but this is not a problem.

e) If you've opened up the chassis brackets too much and the engine sits so low as to allow the block to foul the chassis rails, simply insert packing shims between the flexible engine mountings and the chassis bracket until the engine sits correctly.

f) While not strictly speaking an engine bay or bodyshell modification, the gearbox-mounting bracket drawings have also been dimensioned so as to allow

the gearbox to sit low for, like the engine, it is easy to shim it up but, if too high, impossible to easily lower.

g) Temporarily fix the new oil pump base to the engine, pop the oil pipes on and check they will clear the (right-side for the Buick/Rover, left for the Ford) chassis-rail even when the engine rocks over 10mm (towards the right side) on full torque. If in doubt, mark the rail-flange for subsequent dressing once the engine is removed.

11 – The top steering column bracket is identified by photo 9-2-14-1 and has to be accommodated if you are adopting the rubber-bumper rack and collapsible column. A small modification behind the dashboard is required as shown in drawing D9-9.

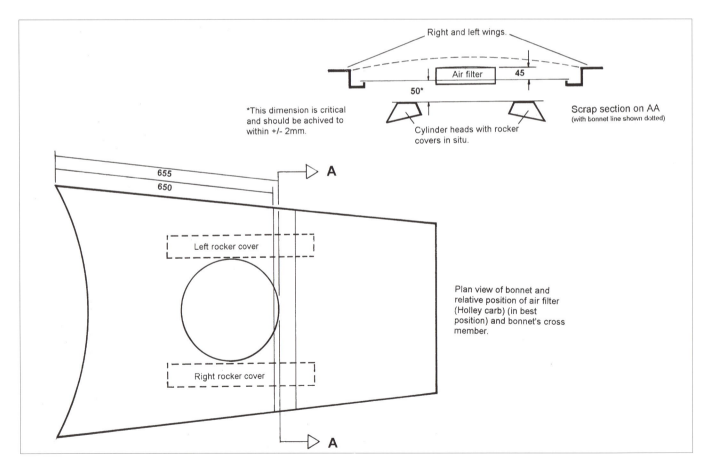

D9-8 Engine height checks and bonnet/air filter clearance.

9-2-14-1 This is the rubber-bumper car top support for the collapsible steering column.

After carefully scribing the centre-line of your chrome-bumper's steering column, grind off the existing twin-lobed bracket. Make up the 45° angled bracket shown in the drawing and tack-weld it to the car's square crossmember centred on your scribe line. This work is probably best carried out before your clutch/brake master-cylinder assembly is positioned

on the car for, having positioned the new steering column top bracket, you will need to drill the five mounting holes. The problem is that you are drilling into the almost closed void between the MGB's twin bulkheads (shown at 9-2-14-2).

After drilling, remove the bracket. You now have to get the bolts through from the blind side of the bulkhead box or, more realistically, from the cockpit side: use five threaded inserts that expand within the bulkhead to provide a captive nut. I used Avdel 'nutcerts' (pictures 9-2-14-3 and 9-2-14-4, overleaf), but there are other systems which I am sure are equally effective.

Weld the new 45° bracket in position and secure the main bracket with the appropriate bolts and washers so the finished bracket is like 9-2-14-5 (overleaf). If you run out of patience, I believe you could weld the top steering column bracket in place and, when appropriate, assemble the hydraulic master-cylinders and pedal

9-2-14-2 The inside face of the double-skinned bulkhead/firewall. Note the hole through which you can gain access to the rear of the hydraulic master-cylinders. A new shell may have three holes already in place and you will only need to add the bottom two.

assembly to the car.

12 – Time to fit and check the bonnet/hood clearance over the engine's ancillary equipment. The bonnet/hood clearance will probably require some work. Clearance will depend upon the position of your engine

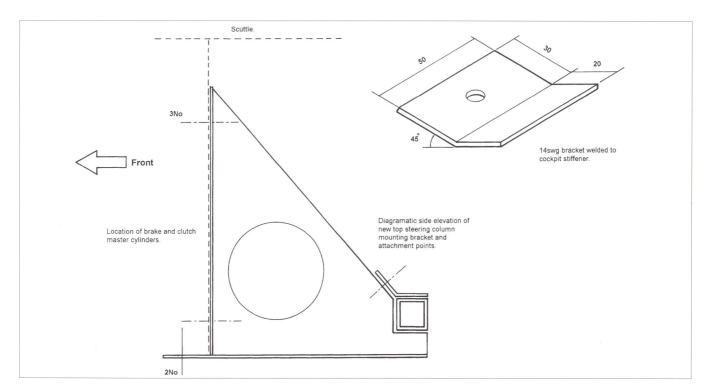

D9-9 Steering column bracket for the rubber bumper model.

9-2-14-3 These nutcerts come in a range of sizes. The plain end is pushed through a hole in a panel with an inaccessible rear. When squeezed the plain end expands outward to provide a threaded insert in the panel.

9-2-14-4 Try your local hire shop, body shop or MGB body shop specialist for these special pliers used to expand the nutcerts.

9-2-14-5 After the nutcerting operation you should be able to affix your new rubber-bumper top mounting for the steering column.

9-2-15 The edge of this bonnet crossmember has been dressed almost flat. This is much easier if you have an aluminium bonnet/hood and crossmember.

9-2-16. The RV8 bonnet (Rover part number ZKC 5425), at about £350, might seem an expensive option, but you could be saving the expense of an MGB bonnet and gaining increased clearance within the engine bay.

mounts, any shimming you have fitted, the induction method and the inlet manifold used.

Secure the bonnet/hood by temporarily bolting it to the hinges, but leave the front catch arrangement off the car so that the bonnet/hood fully closes without pushing/slamming. Check the satisfactory movement of the bonnet and fit the induction equipment and air cleaner. Place some thin towers of plasticine, blue-tack or other mouldable material on the highest induction components and **gently** lower the bonnet.

When you have gauged the extent of the problem, employ the solution most applicable to your circumstances. You will get a good idea of what you are likely to encounter by reading this chapter and the text relating to engine mounting. Here are some options for increasing bonnet clearance:

a) About half of the central crossmember interferes with the plenum chamber or air filter. Dress half the crossmember down as per photo 9-2-15.

b) Most of the bonnet's central crossmember interferes with plenum chamber/air filter. Your solutions vary according to the extent of the interference but, hopefully, the problem will be solved by relocating the central crossmember about 50mm further forward. This is most easily achieved if you have a steel bonnet/crossmember. Do not move the crossmember too far forward or water hose/distributor cap interference will result. Alternatively you can buy RV8 bonnets/hoods with the helpful bulge shown in picture 9-2-16.

c) If interference with the bonnet is so great that none of the above are likely to provide a solution (probably only applicable to cars fitted with hot-wire EFI induction systems) then I am sorry to say that you must think in terms of bonnet bulges. An MGC or RV8 bonnet might be one solution to bulging the bonnet/hood particularly for Ford engines with their forward mounted distributor. Fibreglass reproductions of MGC bonnets/hoods are available and these have the advantages of light weight and can easily be extended at home as necessary. We will see an example of a consequentially double-bulged bonnet/hood a little later in the chapter.

13 – The RV8-style of manifold/header needs to be offered up to find the centre

9-2-17 These RV8 strengthening lips (part number RGD-10048/9) are important. Hold each in place so that there is clearance right around where the manifold/header tail will pass through the inner wing, and scribe a final cut line on the inner wing before welding one in place on each inner wing/fender.

of each manifold/header and for this to be marked on the inner-wing/fender. The various engines differ in manifold position, the position of the engine in the chassis can alter, and the exact dimensions of the differing makes of manifold also vary; all of which makes the fitment of RV8 manifolds a trial fitting exercise, progressively opening up the small holes before removing the manifolds to reinforce each hole, as seen in picture 9-2-17. Be careful with this work as the inner wing/fenders are an important part of the front-end structure and you must only remove the minimum amount of metal to effect the opening. The most practical solution is for you to cut a **small** hole in the inner wing/fender – no more than 1in (25mm) at the centre-point of the manifold with a hole-saw, offer the manifold up again and enlarge the hole steadily. Once the tail of the manifold/ headers can just pass through the inner-wing/fender, consider the inner wing/fender reinforcing plates. The final welding of the strengthening pieces and trimming of any surplus material from them can be carried out once the engine bay is vacant.

14 – As the power of your engine increases so too must the strength of the propshaft and thus its diameter. On chrome-bumpered cars the diameter of the shaft will necessitate replacing the early/small

9-2-18 This is a (deeper) rubber-bumper heel-board stiffener, welded in place on my chrome-bumper car to make space for the larger propshaft I used. The EFI fuel pump can just be seen top of the picture, too.

heel-board stiffening pressing with a later, larger one seen in picture 9-2-18.

15 – Once any problems have been resolved, you should remove the engine/ gearbox. There may be some dressing and last minute changes required but basically the whole engine bay will then require preparation and painting.

OTHER OPTIONS
Rebuilt/converted bodyshells

Any MGB restoration specialist will be pleased to simultaneously restore, upgrade or convert your bodyshell to V8. I am sure this is applicable on both sides of

the Atlantic – the problem is cost, as you may find it more economical to buy a new Heritage shell than have your existing shell restored and converted.

It is possible that an approach used by John Hills has been replicated elsewhere. This UK MGB specialist was involved in the preparation of Lindsay Porter's original MGB restoration manual (recently republished) so the company knew a thing or two about MGB bodyshell restoration. It offered restored/converted MGB roadster body-shells on a no-exchange/outright sale basis. The shells were brought up to the specification of an RV8 undressed shell (i.e. without the removable panels) – although I am sure Hills would have been delighted to dress the shell for you. At that time, an ex-John Hills shell offers a worthwhile cost saving over a new Heritage shell.

Such shells were fully restored so there were no concerns about the structural strength of the resulting car and if you were buying a dressed shell it came fully painted.

I can only presume that Hills had a 'production-line' approach to body-shell restoration and that is where the cost-savings were made. Times change and it may be that other specialists have followed their example, so it may be worth contacting MGB restoration specialists in your area to see if they do a similar service and how cost-effective that might be. You

9-3-1 The most popular chrome grille is that used on the early chrome-bumpered cars (part number ARH218). As shown here, it has vertical bars.

may find it reduces your costs if you buy the basic shell and dress/finish/paint it yourself.

Rubber- to chrome-bumper conversions

There can be few that will disagree that the chrome-bumpered MGBs do look more attractive than a later rubber-bumpered model. The popularity of this opinion is born out by the fact that most MGB specialists sell a couple of kits to replace the front and rear rubber-bumpers with chrome replacements. In fact you will have a choice of two, one with all-chrome overriders and one with rubber buffer inserts (part number TMK70701). You will also need a front radiator grille, perhaps similar to those in 9-3-1.

However, this conversion will only change the aesthetics of a rubber-bumpered car. All rubber-bumpered cars will still sit about 1in higher off the road than their earlier chrome-bumpered sisters will with the attendant inferior road holding of the later cars. Consequently you also need a rubber-bumper suspension lowering kit. Again all MGB specialists will be able to supply the necessary components to lower both the front and the rear suspensions. The detail was covered in chapter 7.

Sebring valances

There is an alternative to chrome-bumper conversion kits for rubber-bumpered cars – you could do away with the bumpers completely by fitting Sebring style fibreglass front and rear valances. They look good too – at least to my eyes. Photo 9-3-2 will help but see the Sebring body kit section that follows shortly for more details.

Electrical provisions

The MGB usually has its electrical cables run externally beneath the bodyshell. The RV8 demonstrates that with minimal provision at this stage, it is quite practical to run the front to rear electrical harness internally. The RV8 uses small retaining clips welded to the top of the prop/drive shaft tunnel as seen in picture 9-3-3.

Dry-state bodyshells

I must say that a 20 or 30 year-old bodyshell that has spent all its life in a dry state or country has to be seen to be believed by us northern Europe residents. I guess the same is true of enthusiasts living in the non-desert states of the USA. The lack of corrosion is quite amazing and thus a Roadster from one of the world's dry countries or states forms an excellent basis for your V8 conversion project.

Be aware that it is a fallacy to believe that, for instance, all cars from southern USA states are always well preserved. Arizona is hot and arid – right? Well, a lot of it may be but you'll find that the northern half of this state is 5000-6000ft above sea level and, consequently, a lot less clement than you might imagine. Not all ex-US cars – even those from the southwestern states – are going to be rust-free, so be on your guard. If in any doubt at all, my advice is to revert to plan B and buy a new Heritage bodyshell for your MGB Roadster V8 conversion.

That said, a true 'dry-state' shell has to be seen to be believed. Resist the temptation to buy a supposed dry-state car that is in any way corroded. The one exception to this golden rule might be if the floor has corroded, provided the rot has not spread to the sills. In fact, it may even be difficult to find, say, a South African or Southern Californian Roadster without some floor rot. A rare rain shower can catch the car with its hood down, whereupon the carpets get wet, hold the water in contact with the floor and rot sets in. Nevertheless, floor pans are easily changed. Remember that the rubber-bumper shell will be a little less rigid than its chrome-bumper counterpart, so do not compromise on the corrosion question. If there is a shadow of doubt, either walk away or have the wax injection holes you are ultimately going to need anyway drilled and, with a special probe, take a look at the inside of the sills, pictured at 9-3-4 (overleaf).

Provided rot is not any more extensive than the floor pans, think about it ... but remember you may need some professional expertise to carry out additional modifications to any imported

9-3-2 A pair of Sebring front and rear valances will be lighter (much lighter than the rubber-bumpers) and cheaper (cost is £150 the pair) than a chrome-bumper conversion kit, as well as more aerodynamic and less prone to corrosion.

9-3-3 This is the RV8 'top of the tunnel' route – but you can run the cable internally down several routes of your choice to advantage. Tight to one sill/rocker may be favourite.

9-3-4 Inspecting the inner sills using a borescope.

vehicle you plan to purchase. You should therefore establish the cost of the following modifications if the car needs to be changed from lhd to rhd, or vice versa:

a) The need to buy a correctly handed steering rack and dashboard from a second-hand source, possibly together with some instruments.

b) The need to have the steering column bottom and top mountings re-sited on the other side of the car. The top bracket would be similar to the chrome-bumper shell modifications discussed earlier in the chapter. The bottom three-bolt conical steering column mounting has also been discussed within the chrome-bumper chassis modifications. However, an imported rubber-bumper car will have the bulkhead cutback and an aperture for the recessed cone will be in place. Nevertheless, the cone and three captive nuts need transferring, or additional ones found and positioned.

c) If the car you buy is an early rubber-bumper model, the 1974 to 1976 variants will need to have the radiator mounting brackets repositioned and have the bottom

radiator duct shortened, as, although the car is clearly rubber-bumper, the early versions retained these chrome-bumper characteristics.

d) If the floors on your imported car do need replacing and you intend using a Rover 5-speed gearbox, take the opportunity to have the gearbox crossmember retaining nuts repositioned as discussed in chapter 4. It is an easy task with the floor out, and saves you having to modify your gearbox crossmember so extensively.

e) Perhaps the most obvious difference between UK models (apart from which side of the car the driver sits) is the recessed dashboard employed on US and some other export models. The bottom square straight crossbrace is still there but the scuttle top or shroud panel has a much more recessed shape than UK models. Consequently, this needs changing if you are fitting a right-hand drive UK dashboard. The experts find this no problem: they remove the screen and cut the export style shroud panel at a radius that coincides with the Roadster's windscreen, cut the replacement (UK) scuttle panel to suit and weld round the joint – any minor ripples or height variations are very local and totally masked by the windscreen bottom seal.

At the same time, if your imported vehicle happens to have the three windscreen wipers seen at 9-3-5, the aperture holes in the very same panel will need to be closed and two new wheelbox holes formed.

f) Some export models (US) have four extra sidelights which UK converters will probably not require. These can be seen at 9-3-6-1 and 9-3-6-2 and their associated holes are best closed by butt-fitting and welding insert panels. (Use TIG welding to achieve the very best finish). As a matter of interest, most welding to automobile chassis is done by MIG welding, but the really professional outfits will use TIG (Tungsten Inert Gas) for these types of

9-3-5 Most post-1969 cars that went to the USA had three wiper arms/blades, as seen here and …

9-3-6-1 … were fitted with extra front and …

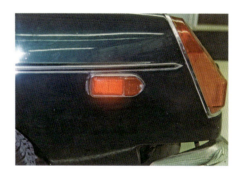

9-3-6-2 … rear 'side marker' lights, too.

modification. TIG is even cooler and thus distorts metalwork less than MIG.

So the purchase of an imported MGB does mean that certain skills and/or equipment are required. Most professional importers will be happy to quote for the work involved and, in my experience, the cost of a complete imported car with modifications is little more than a new but bare Heritage shell.

If you want a bit more detail before

going further, Murray Scott-Nelson wrote an explanation of converting ex-US chrome-bumper MGBs for the November 1992 issue of the MGOC magazine *Enjoying MG*. If you are a member, try the MGOC for back copies.

Centralising the fuel tank

My single pipe system provides a wonderful and unmistakable V8 exhaust note. Having the single silencer/muffler positioned where MG intended – alongside the fuel tank – maximizes my ground clearance. However, the RV8-style of exhaust manifolds/headers do present an opportunity to run twin exhaust systems, which we will explore in more detail Chapter 11, but may interest you now if you plan to retain the original tank. MGOC Spares sells special centralised tanks which require no body alterations but re-using the original tank necessitates the following body alterations. The picture at 9-3-7 of Larry Shimp's Ford/twin-pipe system may help you decide. There are two body-related changes that need to be effected – the rear valance (picture 9-3-8) and the centralization of the fuel tank. I have illustrated the main and probably first step by the pictures and captions at 9-3-9-1 to 9-3-9-4 – after which you will need to close the numerous tank mounting holes and re-drill them.

WIDENING THE WHEEL ARCHES

Surprisingly it will be the turned-in lip of the left-rear wing/fender that will first cause tyre/body interference problems as you widen the tyres on an MGB. This will likely start once you fit anything larger that 185 (7.3in) section tyres but can be resolved by turning the double-skinned lip of that wing/fender upwards. I also had to reduce the width of the lip as well and thus found it necessary to seam weld round the lip to prevent water ingress. Wider tyres

with their associated wider wheels will necessitate wheelarch alterations once you get past about a 195 (7.6in) section tyre.

Depending upon the width of the tyres your wheelarches need to cover, you can just flare the lips of the wheelarches an inch or so. One converter in the USA channelled the rear wings/fenders 4in to cover the 295/50/15 rear tyres. This requires some panel-working skills if you have retained steel wing/fender panels but becomes very

9-3-7 The twin systems have the main silencers/mufflers located centrally under the car, and use small secondary mufflers/ expansion chambers each side of the relocated MGB fueltank.

9-3-8 The rear valance requires more alteration than is obvious from this shot. The centred fuel tank puts the original exhaust relief in the valance in the wrong place, necessitating it be welded over and two new reliefs prepared. Do not make the new holes fullsize as smaller openings are better enlarged by turning in the lips with a pair of pliers to form a strengthening lip round each.

9-3-9-1 I thought this the most effective way to relocate the hole in the boot/trunk floor for the tank filler neck. If you seek to move the tank sideways by say 3in (75mm), measure and subsequently cut out a rectangle in the floor such that, when turned through 180°, the hole moves toward the centre of the car by the desired distance.

9-3-9-2 Position and lightly tack the piece of floor in its new location, and offer up the tank to check you have achieved your objective.

9-3-9-3 Weld, plenish and clean the repositioned piece of floor before again offering up the tank and marking out the new fixing holes.

9-3-9-4 The original fuel filler will not now fit, and moving the opening in the rear panel is neither practical nor necessary. However, a filler assembly from a Mk1 MGB (produced up to about 1967) will resolve the problem as we see here.

9-4-1 The fibreglass panels for a Sebring body style are available in three separate kits and you do not need to fit the front and rear valances if it is just the wing/wheelarches you wish to extend. In fact, this car retains its original style front valance. The bonnet/hood is interesting too – it's an MGC fibreglass panel with a Ford Capri 3000 bulge blended in.

9-4-2 This is a very neat installation of a perspex headlamp cover.

9-4-3 The RV8 body panels give this BGT a more individual and not unattractive appearance.

9-4-4 The same shell, of course, from another angle. It is difficult to appreciate, even from this angle, but the RV8 panels have the practical benefit of allowing wider track and/or tyres.

easy if you have fitted fibreglass wings or fenders. I personally do not favour fitting fibreglass panels as part of a straight restoration project but have to agree that they are easier to work with when it comes to this sort of change. You just need to cut round the outer lip of the wheelarch(s) with a jigsaw, temporarily hold the extended lip in its new location with a few external strips of metal and generously fibreglass the underside of the extended lips. After removing the temporary metal strips and self-tapping screws you are certainly left with a lot of filling, blending and shaping but with patience the end result will be indistinguishable from the original fibreglass wing/fender. Do not forget to extend the rear inner wheelarches to prevent water ingress into the boot/trunk.

Fibreglass front wings will also help to reduce the weight at the front of the modified car.

A Sebring body kit

This is one alternative, if more drastic, solution to accommodating up to 225 section tyres. Not everyone will agree but I think the overall effect of a Sebring body kit (seen at 9-4-1) is very pleasing and purposeful. A full kit costs a little less than £400 and was copied from the works GTS lightweight Sebring race-cars. The panels

were, I believe, designed to be fixed to the GT's original steel body panels and will not provide for more tyre width within the wheelarch unless you trim adequate amounts of material from the lip of the original steel wing. I would also think a Sebring kit could be made to fit a Roadster without too much difficulty.

Do not overlook the fact that whichever model you are thinking of changing, the inner wing/fenders will also require altering, strengthening and extending.

While not exclusive to Sebring body kits, the presence of the perspex headlamp fairing prompts me to mention that MGB's vertical headlights do create wind resistance. In fact some very late MGB's suffer wind noise from the slightly different chrome bezels fitted to them. You can change these bezels, of course, but by fitting the perspex fairing in picture 9-4-2, you resolve both problems and, to my eyes, add to the appearance of the car.

RV8 body styling

The RV8 is a very handsome car, as photographs 9-4-3 and 9-4-4 show, but the design is not only to be admired aesthetically, it has positive practical

implications too. It permits a wider track and just begs for broader tyres, with the associated improvements to the car's road holding.

RV8 panels are available in small numbers and simultaneously alter the car's appearance and widen the wheelarches while keeping the car with its intended steel bodyshell. This solution is the ideal route but the cost will be a problem to most readers. You are not only talking about the cost of four wings/fenders but the doors, sills and valances are also different, as are the bumpers and lights. The lights are a cost penalty on their own and will almost certainly have to be bought at spares prices from your Rover dealer.

When last in touch with Heritage I understood it was unlikely that they would be making RV8-style replacement bodyshells available through the Heritage network. Brown and Gammon took on the responsibility for RV8 spares upon the demise of the Rover dealership network, and you could enquire as to the availablility of them. John Hills MG Centre commissioned a set of fibreglass moulds for a complete RV8-style body-kit about 1997. The resultant kit comprises 12 pieces in all – front wings, rear wings, side sills, front and back valances/bumpers and bonnet being the main constituents. A drastic solution if you just want to enlarge the wheel arches, but if you are looking for an alternative eye-catcher to a Sebring body kit, the answer could lie with picture

9-4-5 if John Hills is still able to produce the kit.

You would be best only tackling such a wide-ranging job with some fibreglass panel-fitting experience. The biggest problem is where to cut the original (but presumably rusting) panels without going too far and without weakening the structural integrity of the undressed shell. In fact you may need to first restore the car's structure in steel before moving on to the body styling. Like any fibreglass body styling kit, the fit of the panels will mostly be close but by the very nature of the material, rarely 'spot on'. Don't let this put you off though as fibre-glassing is not rocket-science and consequently a degree of skill and patience will correct any problems.

The basic undressed bodyshell must be solid and the sills/rockers need to be of the highest integrity. The fibreglass-panelled car is lighter, has more room in the boot/trunk and indeed has more space within the wheel arches for wider wheels and tyres.

I would suggest that anybody wanting to go this route first check the availability and costs not only of the kit but of the lights (heads are Prosche 911) and other necessary fitment from Heritage/Rover. I would also order all the genuine RV8 parts you need simultaneously from your Rover dealer and not start work until they are all available. It would be dreadful to have everything else but then to find one part was no longer available.

The front and rear bumper/valance is one piece and bolts on but you will have to fabricate your own brackets. The front wings bolt on too but also need stiffening brackets around the area of the 'A'-post. It's a good idea to pre-bond the fastenings to the inside thus making the wings/fenders completely removable and allowing some panel-alignment adjustments. The side skirts require brackets to attach them to the original sills and some additional fibreglass

to blend them in. With the exception of the sills/rockers, no panels cover existing steel panels.

While certainly not obvious from the back of the car (picture 9-4-7), the rear-deck in front of the boot/trunk lid requires the ends be cut and opened up to allow the tongue on the fibreglass rear panel to be inserted and bonded.

The doors in the pictures are standard/stock 'B' doors but expect to have to give them a lot of attention to get the door gaps correct. Similarly the 'B'-post needs a lot of work as the new rear wing/fender has it's own 'B'-post facing which needs to be blended into the original steel 'B'-post. A lot of reshaping of the inner rear wing is required to accommodate the larger wheels and to marry up with the larger wheel opening.

PAINTING

By now you should have resolved all the bodywork alterations and be in a position to finish, prime and paint the bodyshell – because all further changes to the car are (hopefully!) bolt-on bits.

9-4-5 The total cost of these fibreglass RV8 panels was about the same as one genuine steel RV8 rear wing – around £750 – and they open up the available wheelarch space by a couple of inches each side.

9-4-7 A great deal of care is required when fitting the rear fibreglass panels – for example, the gutter that the boot lid sits in must be cut away from the old steel wing with enough lip left to bond the new wing/ fender to it. Similar care/skill is required where the rear wing/fender sweeps round at the rear light section as they must be bonded to the steel panel across the back where the original joints would have been.

Chapter 10
Brakes

There is no doubt that the brakes on an MGB with 3, 4 or 5 litres of engine are going to need upgrading. For 1800cc the original brakes were fine but with more power and, in some cases, more weight and therefore inertia too, we need more stopping power. That increased stopping power needs to largely come from the front and, depending upon the car in question, may necessitate increasing the wheel diameter. If you are carrying out what might be called a 'rolling conversion', do make absolutely sure you upgrade the brakes (and indeed the suspension) before you fit the higher-powered engine.

Although the main thrust of this chapter has to do with the specifics of the servo, larger front discs and more powerful calipers (and we will talk rear-brakes, brake-pipe routes and hoses too before the end of the chapter) there are a few general principles that are worth outlining first:

- 70 per cent of the car's braking comes from the front brakes.
- The brake pads retard the wheel rotation by friction between the pads and the discs. Differing pad materials have differing frictional characteristics.
- The further from the wheel centre that friction is applied, the greater the retarding force for a given pedal pressure. Thus the diameter of the front discs significantly influences the effectiveness of the brakes.
- Increasing the bore of the master-cylinder will reduce the pedal travel but will require a heavier pedal pressure to produce the same braking effect as a smaller diameter master-cylinder. Reducing the diameter will reduce the pedal pressure required and increase the required pedal travel.
- Most (but not all) calipers of the MGB era have one cylinder each side of the caliper to squeeze the pad onto the disc. These are called '2-pot calipers'. Longer pads perform more effectively if they are squeezed uniformly over their full length thus they benefit from an additional cylinder per side – making them '4-pot calipers'.
- It is usual to take advantage of the four cylinders to increase braking/squeezing by ensuring that the total surface area of the four cylinders in a 4-pot caliper is larger than the surface area of the two cylinders in the 2-pot caliper they replace.
- Increasing the rear slave cylinder bore will reduce the required pedal pressure and increase the pedal travel for the same braking effect. Reducing the diameter will increase the pedal pressure and pedal travel.
- Brake fade is caused by a boundary layer of gases that builds up between the pad and disc/rotor. This can be delayed by increasing the mass of the disc/rotor, by adding grooves and/or cross-drilling the disc/rotor by increasing the pad size to aid heat dissipation.
- It is possible to have too much braking power, particularly if the front/rear balance is incorrect. If the brakes are powerful enough to lock up the wheels, stopping distance is greatly increased. Thus you must ensure front and rear brakes work in harmony particularly in an emergency

stop. While it is possible to modulate the pedal pressure in an orderly stop, a panic stop will most likely cause a driver to apply maximum foot pressure on the pedal. If any of the wheels' lock up (usually the rears), there is too much braking power available and remedial action is essential.

PIPELINES AND ROUTES
Front pipe routes

Where permissible, I recommend you use copper-type brake pipes. The best flexible hoses are those with stainless steel braided outer covering. They resist abrasion better than normal rubber hose and, more importantly, they do not (minutely) swell under heavy braking pressure and therefore provides a more solid feel to your pedal. The same braided hose is best used for the clutch too but because the hose unavoidably passes in close proximity to the exhaust system, you could do worse than to wrap reflective thermal insulation around the hose and pipe to reduce radiant heating.

A helpful modification for chrome-bumper owners when routing pipes to and from a remote servo is to take the pipes over the top of the heater as per the standard routing for rubber-bumper cars.

The brake pipes or lines need to avoid passing within close proximity of any part of the exhaust system. For this reason V8 cars usually employ separate lines down to the front calipers in place of the single line used by 1800cc cars. Note that the right side front caliper is fed directly from a banjo junction that has been added to the front of the servo (seen at 10-1-1 – it will be the other way round for RHD cars). The reason for this alteration is that a brake pipe from the left side front wheelarch routed conventionally across the rear of the front suspension crossmember twice comes within 15mm of hot V8 exhaust pipes. This is not a good idea. The consequence of this change for chrome-bumper converters is that the later, three-way brake pipe/

10-1-1 Here you see special bolt (part number SSN101), copper washers, and extra banjo that allows you to route the passenger-side front brake pipe straight to the front wheel on V8 conversions.

junction (part number 90 577490) will be required in place of the four-way/brake pressure switch junction. Furthermore, this three-way junction should be moved away from the exhaust manifolds, and there is probably a convenient captive nut already positioned on your inner wing panel about 75mm above the standard location. Use that and photograph 10-1-2 as a further guide.

One snag about these brake pipe modifications to chrome-bumper cars is that the three-way hydraulic connection you need has been in short supply. Fortunately, it is identical to the three-way hydraulic connection mounted on the rear axle of chrome-bumper cars, so second-hand ones should not be difficult to obtain if you can't get a new one.

By now you will be wondering where the hydraulic brake light pressure

10-1-2 Although a chrome-bumper car, this photo shows the later brake light switch and three- (not four-) way hydraulic brake pipe junction mounted about 75mm (3in) higher than is usual for chrome-bumper 'Bs in order to avoid the worst of the heat from the exhaust manifold. Some converters cover these pipes in reflective aluminium foil as an added precaution.

switch goes. The answer is that it goes in your spares box, for you will need the mechanically actuated switch BHA 4675 and the early rubber-bumper car's pedal box cover – both available from a scrap-yard and also shown in photos 10-1-2.

Some V8 owners shield the brake pipes adjacent to the exhaust manifold with reflective/insulating material and, while I have not done so myself, I think the idea has merit.

Servo and master-cylinder

Of our major modifications, let's take the servo first. The MGB GT V8 used a remote Lockheed servo (as fitted to many chrome-bumper MGBs and MGB GTs between

10-1-5 The normal remote servo mounting bracket is shown left side of this shot, while the different hole pattern required to better orientate the servo is shown on the right.

10-1-3 The disadvantages of these dual circuit/close coupled rubber-bumper master-cylinders are the proximity to exhaust manifolds, and subsequent lack of maintenance access space to the starter motor (in the case of RHD cars), steering universal joint and rear half of the right side exhaust manifold.

10-1-4 Doesn't the earlier remote servo tuck in neatly out of the way of the washer bottle? Note the slant of the main barrel of the servo and the 8 o'clock location of the air valve, so positioned to ease brake bleeding. You can hardly fail to notice the fuel filter and flex fuel line which run up the inside of the nearside cylinder bank, well away from the exhaust.

1970-74). However, if you have purchased a rubber-bumper car this is most likely to have the combined servo/master-cylinder (photo 10-1-3) pre-fitted with the advantage of the safety that a dual line hydraulic brake circuit offers.

If you are starting without a working or reliable brake servo, I would recommend a remote servo (photo 10-1-4).

However, the mounting of the remote servos needs to be addressed at the same time. Every photo, diagram and mounting bracket of a remote servo shows the air valve located about 2 o'clock when viewed from the outlet pipe end. Abingdon got away with this position since there the car's brakes were bled by vacuum. You will be bleeding your brakes conventionally and will do so far quicker and more effectively if you site the servo so that the air valve is pointing downwards, between 8 and 4 o'clock. This ensures air is not trapped in the air valve outlet hole drilled in the main casting. Photograph 10-1-5 and drawing D10 of a revised servo main mounting bracket will help you with your 4 o'clock or 8 o'clock installation.

Rubber-bumper owners who elect to use the remote servo will need to visit an MG breaker to acquire a pedal box, pedal assembly and master-cylinders from a

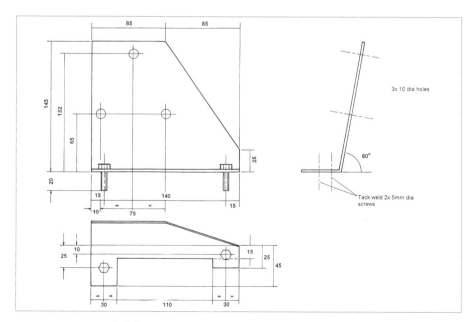

D10 Revised remote brake servo mounting bracket.

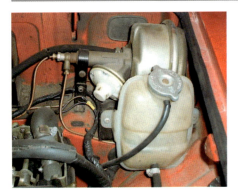

10-1-6 A wider shot of my extended bracket lifting the tail a little of this Lockheed type 6 remote servo. You could achieve the same effect with a packing piece under its foot to obtain the 10° slope recommended. Note the 4 o'clock air valve and coolant header tank.

10-1-7 I consider this one of the best brake master-cylinder upgrades I've seen. The MGB's single brake pedal operates (via the Tilton balance bar) a pair of independent master-cylinders – an AP Racing CP2623 short travel 7⁄8in (22.2mm) for front and 3⁄4in (19.1mm) for rear. Note that the necessary space is made possible by feeding these master-cylinders' remote reservoirs with Demon Tweeks hoses. The clutch master-cylinder is Girling 0.7in – although a 0.75in bore is readily available if required (both are Triumph TR6 options). I believe this pedal-box base has also been tilted to improve the angle of push-rod's travel using a 1in (25mm) aluminium wedge between frame and pedal-box.

chrome-bumper car seen earlier in picture 10-1-2. I recommend you replace both master-cylinders with new ones because the bottom of the master-cylinders can rust through leaking fluid over your paintwork and depriving you of your brakes or clutch. In any event, the V8's clutch master-cylinder is different and needs to be replaced with the V8 variant, as discussed in chapter 4.

Furthermore, you will also help yourself immensely if you ensure the outlet pipe end of the servo is raised at a slight (say 10°) angle to facilitate the outflow of air during bleeding. Later MGBs did have the servo installed at an upward angle, but many earlier cars had the servo mounted horizontally with consequential brake bleeding difficulties. You may need to extend your support leg as seen in picture 10-1-6.

Whilst on the subject of MGB brake bleeding problems, converters may find it helpful to bleed their servo-assisted systems in the fashion recommended by their workshop manual, and to follow this with a secondary bleeding operation in order to decrease pedal travel. During secondary bleeding, the engine must be running thus creating a vacuum in the servo.

With most improvements, there are numerous ways in which you can effect the change you need, and the master-cylinder set-up for the brakes is no exception. We have already discussed differing sizes of master-cylinder in the context of clutches (Chapter 4 – Actuating a T5's clutch arm) and similar brake master-cylinders offer you numerous solutions to your brake master-cylinder arrangement. I was particularly impressed with the arrangement seen at photograph 10-1-7 where two master-cylinders (actuated by a balance bar) have been fitted. This is made possible by the twin remote reservoirs. Clearly the master-cylinders are (hydraulically speaking) quite separate, offering the safety features of a dual-line system. However, this design

has the additional advantage of your being able to balance the respective front/rear operating pressures by selecting the bore of the master-cylinders and/or the extent to which the interconnecting linkage is pivoted off-centre.

The MGB pedal box will require modification by welding a cylinder mounting face and re-drilling two new holes (1.3in/33mm diameter) for the new masters cylinders 55mm apart. The brake pedal also requires modification by welding the pivot sleeve to the pedal's pivot point and fitting the balance-bar to the top.

You may be thinking that the arrangement prohibits the use of a servo. You can install a single (Lockheed Type 6) remote servo on the front brake-line if you wish, but the best solution is to fit a twin/remote servo available from various speed shops.

DISCS/ROTORS AND CALIPERS

There are numerous solutions to increments in disc/rotor diameter and caliper capacity. I've seen Chevy Chevelle discs/rotors and Dodge Dart calipers (a combination oft fitted to MGB/Cobra replicas) used. Speaking of Cobras, the arrangement seen in photograph 10-2-1 was originally fitted to a 1977 Chrysler LeBaron then adopted for a Cobra kit car and is now enjoying a third lease of life under MGB 15in wheels. If you want to go to 17in wheels you can follow Paul Knott's (PK Automotive Repairs) example and use ex-Nissan 200SX calipers with 330mm discs/rotors. The possibilities are endless and beyond detailed exploration here. We will just look at the more frequent solutions and, since 70 per cent of a car's stopping power comes from the front brakes, that is where we will devote at least 70 per cent of our time and, hopefully, your cash.

Moderate-powered cars retaining 14in diameter wheels are limited in the extra braking capacity they can incorporate within the original wheels. If you have fitted larger wheel go straight to the 'Medium-powered cars' section that follows. With 14in wheels, read on for your principal options.

MGB GT V8 standard brakes

The ½in (12.8mm) thick, non-ventilated, 273mm diameter discs and two-pot calipers as fitted to the original MGB GT V8 might be thought of as the first level of upgrade. These days however they are hardly adequate for even the lowest powered 3500cc cars and do not, in my view, offer good value for money compared to the alternative more satisfactory options that we will explore shortly.

10-2-1 At a time when most are fitting multi-pot calipers, this (massive) single piston caliper looks much heavier than an MGB caliper, but is, in fact, only 3lb heavier. Note the 5-stud hubs – they are from an MGC.

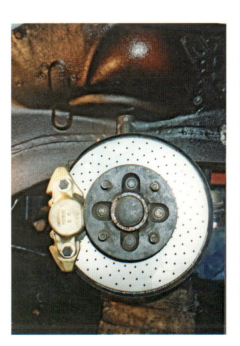

10-2-2. Disc cooling as well as gas and dust dissipation can be improved by fitting the cross-drilled discs/rotors seen in this picture.

Although the upgrade we see at 10-2-2 does not increase the capacity of the calipers to squeeze the disc, the disc's capacity to absorb heat is increased since the disc/rotor is some 25 per cent thicker than the standard 1800cc disc/rotors. You will need to shave the small corner off the

10-2-3 The small area shaded white will need to filed away to provide a little more space for the wider MGB GT V8 calipers.

10-2-4 The Princess caliper increases the length of the pad that comes in contact with the disc by 12mm beyond an MGB GT V8 pad – which will improve braking, although the squeeze pressure on the disc is about the same.

MGB dust shield shown in picture 10-2-3 before fitting these slightly wider-mouthed calipers. You will improve/maximize the 'grab' of the calipers on the discs if you fit EBC's MGB GT V8 Kevlar 'Greenstuff' brake pads.

MGB GT V8 discs with four-pot calipers

Today, I feel we must think of the first level upgrade as that provided by the ex-Austin Princess four-pot calipers and a standard GT V8 ½in thick disc/rotor. Both calipers and discs bolt straight onto the MGB with no more modification than the slight adjustment of the dust shield. The original Princess four-pot caliper was made to straddle a ½in disc/rotor and the only non-standard/stock changes I suggest would be to cross-drill the discs, use stepped mounting bolts and maximize the 'grab' by using Princess Greenstuff pads. You will see this arrangement in pictures 10-2-4 and 10-2-5.

However, if you are going to the extent of upgrading/reconditioning your calipers you may as well take the next step, delaying the onset of brake fade further still by fitting 22mm thick vented discs/rotors seen in picture 10-2-6. This will require the help of a brake specialist like (in the UK) Hi-Spec Motorsport but before we explore that solution, we need to talk about the calipers themselves.

Examples of original Princess calipers are very hard to find in the UK and are unobtainable in the US. If you are fortunate enough to find a pair remember that standard Princess calipers won't

10-2-5 On the right is the 4-pot Princess caliper while left side is an MGB GT V8 caliper for comparison. The increased pad size is clear from the lower pads. Incidentally, the caliper on the right is no more than an unspaced RV8 caliper!

10-2-6 These broader discs have internal venting for improved cooling but require careful selection to get an offset that suits your caliper. You also need to space most calipers apart to sit astride this type of thicker disc/rotor.

just bolt to your MGB hubs, although the mounting bolt holes are exactly the same pitch as MGB/MGB V8 calipers. The Princess calipers are made to metric standards and the mounting bolt holes are slightly larger than their MGB counterparts. Consequently, high tensile stepped mounting bolts are required to fix each Princess caliper to an MGB stub axle. Triumph TR6 (part number 158668) or GT6 bolts will both fit, or you can buy special bolts from Clive Wheatley V8 Conversions or Hi Spec Motorsport (UK).

Also bear in mind that the original Princess caliper is manufactured for a twin feed hydraulic pipe system. To overcome this you can make up, or have made, the small bridge from copper brake pipe seen in picture 10-2-7. However, if you buy the calipers reconditioned by either of the

companies mentioned above, the internal plumbing of the caliper can be rerouted during refurbishing. Consequently, one hydraulic feed pipe is all that is necessary – therefore the Princess calipers are no more complex to plumb into the car than the standard MGB/MGB V8 calipers.

You will need to buy a new pair of flexible hydraulic lines, though, since the metric female thread of the Princess caliper demands a compatible metric fitting on one end of each line. Clive Wheatley and Hi Spec Motorsport have the correct hydraulic lines and fittings. The other end requires the standard MGB Imperial thread to couple to the car's Imperial pipework at picture 10-2-8.

10-2-7 Princess calipers in their most cost-effective mode. The coupling pipe on the inside of the caliper reveals this to be an original caliper without internal modification. However, you will clearly see that these are 273mm ventilated discs with compensating spacers mounted within the caliper (the lower spacer is clearly visible).

You may think a lot of space has been devoted here to a caliper that is virtually unobtainable – and you would be right, were it not for the fact that replicas are now being made by Hi Spec Motorsports. I say replicas, but in fact the Hi Spec units are an improved version because they are made from aluminium and have slightly larger piston sizes than the original. Thus the Hi Spec units are lighter yet more powerful than original Princess units. That being the

10-2-8 The Imperial threaded end of the metric flexible line is easily identified as the longer of the threaded ends which fastens through the car's front crossmember. Note the bleed nipple is located at the TOP of the caliper and that it must be so positioned on ALL calipers to facilitate bleeding. Take care that you mount your calipers on the correct side of the car and that the bleed nipples are positioned to allow the escape of all air from the caliper.

case, let's move on to a really worthwhile brake upgrade.

Princess calipers and ventilated discs

Truthfully this upgrade should be the preferred choice of most enthusiasts with moderate and medium powered conversions. It uses the same four-pot Princess calipers just discussed but with a more appropriate disc/rotor. The onset of fade is delayed by increasing the thickness of the disc by over 80 per cent (to 22mm) and by the introduction of a vented disc centre for increased cooling. You can still cross-drill the disc/rotors for swifter dust, water and gas clearance. The disc/rotors remain 275mm diameter and will thus fit under standard/stock MGB 14in wheels.

The key change from earlier

suggestions is that the thicker disc/rotor proposed here necessitates spacing the Princess calipers. This is achieved by inserting two of the 10mm thick spacers seen in picture 10-2-9 and by securing the two halves of the caliper with 10mm longer bolts. You can carry out this change with your own original calipers or Hi Spec will do the change for you when purchasing a pair of its new aluminium calipers or a complete MGB/Princess caliper/disc kit, which is available with the correctly offset discs/rotors.

You will not need to worry about modifying your dust shields for this upgrade. Since they probably won't fit anyway, you should remove them completely from the stub axle. There is no need to be concerned about this since 90 per cent of today's cars don't have a dust shield fitted in the first place. Their absence will actually increase airflow and thus improve disc/rotor cooling.

Alternatives

There are alternatives using the same 22mm by 275mm diameter ventilated discs/rotors but with alternative calipers.

We start with RV8 calipers. These iron casting units are available from Rover or Lockheed as new parts and are the current production version of the Princess unit. The castings are clearly the same. A couple of bleed nipple bosses have not been machined, the pistons are the same size, the calipers come pre-spaced for 24mm discs and they have one fluid inlet position. The mounting holes and centres are the same as the Princess. Rover lists them as part numbers GBC 90182 and GBC 90183 for left and right fittings respectively. Lockheed lists them as LC5937 and LC5938 for the same left and right fittings.

Seen at 10-2-10, you could use one of the wide range of lightweight Wilwood calipers. These are marketed individually or as part of a complete kit. Rally Design in the UK is one such specialised kit supplier

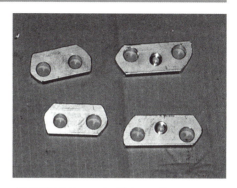

10-2-9 This is a set of inter-caliper spacers for a pair of Princess calipers. Two spacers have machined recesses for the essential "O" ring seals to prevent hydraulic fluid leaking from between the caliper halves.

10-2-10 Wilwood's Dynalite caliper with adapter bracket pre-fitted.

while Pitstop-USA or Summit are typical of several North American stockists. When lug-mounted these sometimes need to be spaced away from the centre line of the hub to provide space for the most advantageous disc/rotor diameter. This spacing is achieved by an expansion bracket of the type shown in picture 10-2-11 (overleaf).

Some MGB V8 converters re-use the ex-Rover SD1 calipers (picture 10-2-12, overleaf) that they acquired with their V8 donor vehicle – an excellent idea in principle. However, be aware that only post-1982 Vitesse and Vanden Plas models had four-pot calipers (with 41mm diameter pistons) but only 258mm diameter discs.

Rover SD1 calipers

Exploring the Rover four-pots further, with their 41mm pistons, you may well be disappointed with the amount of pedal travel you experience. Indeed, this is a potential problem when fitting transposed brakes to any new car, although if you are experiencing uncomfortable amounts of pedal-travel you can always fit a larger master cylinder. The MGB standard master cylinder is 0.75in (19mm or 0.442in^2) for single line and 0.813in (20.6mm, or an area of 0.519in^2) for the later dual line brakes. An SD1 uses a 0.875in (22.2mm) master cylinder piston and this should be the target size to aim for if pedal travel does prove a problem.

This may not sound a large increase in diameter but remember that it is the area of the master-cylinder piston that effects the volume of fluid displaced. If you have a chrome bumper master cylinder at the very least go for a late dual line MGB master cylinder increasing your displacement by 17.5 per cent. However note that the larger the diameter master cylinder you fit the more fluid you will displace but the harder the pedal will feel.

One other device that may help you reduce your first-application pedal travel – a Wilwood residual pressure valve. Generally used in the rear line to prevent the shoes retracting too far, a similar but different pressure variant can be used in the front lines if necessary.

Reverting to our exploration of fitting Rover brakes to our MGB, the discs you fit will again be from a Peugeot (504). So the best Rover caliper option would be to ask Hi Spec Motorsport (UK) to supply a pair of suitable 273mm diameter ventilated discs and a pair of caliper spacer brackets for your ex-Rover calipers. I would expect these to cost about £150. This would give you slightly more pad area and greater squeezing ability – superior front brakes, compared to previously mentioned combinations, for less cost.

10-2-11 As disc diameters increase each caliper must move a corresponding distance from the hub, and this outward movement necessitates an expansion bracket to join the existing caliper mounting bolts to the hub's mounting point. This is one example of such an expansion bracket.

High-powered conversions

You need a minimum of 15in diameter road-wheels and anyone with a mind to 'press on' or use the car on track days would be prudent to fit 16in wheels similar

10-2-13 You really do need to increase the diameter of the wheels (to make space for larger discs/rotors) and to select as 'open' a pattern as is practical (to aid air flow and cooling). These are not on an MGB but do illustrate my point.

to those seen in picture 10-2-13. The 16in wheels allow for the disc/rotor diameters to be increased to circa 300mm with the subsequent improved mechanical advantage and braking effect.

10-2-12 True, the SD1 discs were mostly ventilated but, on balance, these four-pot Vitesse calipers probably are not that much more powerful than the 'B's brakes because the 'B has superior (273mm) diameter discs/rotors – where size really does matter.

Wilwood offers a choice of calipers but the kits retain the 22mm thick, 280mm diameter, ventilated discs outlined earlier seen at 10-2-14. Avoid the cheapest Wilwood (cast) calipers – or at least ascertain that they will not flex open under heavy braking. The (machined from solid) 'billet' models are more expensive but worth the extra cost, although you still need to check with the retailer that the steel pad-backings are now adequately thick and will not warp. All Wilwood calipers are only about a third of the weight of cast iron equivalents. This has the advantage of keeping unsprung weight down to a minimum, as well as dissipating heat much more quickly than would be the case for cast iron. They are, understandably, much more expensive – the middle model SL II seen in 10-2-15 is about twice the price of a Princess caliper.

Hi Spec Motorsport

In addition to making the Princess calipers we discussed earlier, Hi Spec can also offer its own range of four and six-pot calipers from billet aluminium, each with a variety of piston sizes. One big advantage of Hi-Spec calipers for road-going cars is that the pistons all come with dust shields fitted as standard, thus preventing the ingress of dirt and water. These can be seen at picture 10-2-16. The aluminium dissipates heat better and reduces unsprung weight.

The beauty of Hi-Spec's design is that they can be tailored to any disc/rotor size by a simple alteration of the length of the bespoke mounting bracket. Consequently, they offer the ultimate brake solution for the serious MG'er and will get 295mm diameter, 22mm thick, ventilated discs (photograph 10-2-17, overleaf) under 16in wheels. The pads are seriously large too.

Automotive Products (AP) Racing

If you are into this level of braking, and can afford it, you would also be wise to discuss

10-2-14 This end-on shot shows the ventilated disc (included in the Wilwood kits), the home for the pads and the pin method of pad retention.

10-2-15 Wilwood has long supplied aluminium billet calipers to enthusiasts to upgrade the brakes of high performance cars.

10-2-16 'Four-pot' calipers refers to the total number of pistons per caliper. Here we get a view of one half of Hi-Spec Motorsport's 'Billet' caliper and can see two pistons and their dirt seals. The dirt seals are very important in fast road and ultra fast road cars. The two pistons we can see are of the same diameter, but most caliper manufacturers make 'differential' calipers where the sizes of these pistons vary.

your needs with AP Racing. It will be able to configure virtually any brake set-up for an MGB through any one of the many approved dealers. The resulting brakes will be from an original equipment (OE) supplier and, consequently, will be of a very high quality, in particular the design of the caliper usually allows a larger diameter of disc than most competitors. Furthermore, the caliper design is very stiff – probably as a result of AP avoiding spacers and using very substantial cross-bolts. The final plus point is that the ceramic pistons permit less heat transfer from the pads to the fluid. I have heard of AP CP5100 4-pot (38.1mm) calipers being successfully used in MGB racing applications.

As with most things in life you get what you pay for and they are probably the best – but the calipers seen at 10-2-18 (overleaf) are intended for racing and do not have dust seals fitted.

REAR BRAKES

When Rover developed the RV8 it saw no need to make dramatic changes to the rear brakes. True, the diameter changed slightly, but it stuck to drum brakes that

10-2-17 These are 295mm diameter brake discs/rotors – which are too big to fit within a 15in wheel. As a matter of interest, once you get to this size of brake disc/rotor you will find that it's actually a two-piece construction, perfectly illustrated here with 12 high-tensile fastenings securing the inner aluminium 'Bell' to the cast-iron ventilated disc/rotor. 16in diameter wheels will be required to fit over brakes of this size.

10-2-18 Automotive Products' racing division provides the four-pot caliper, and Racetorations the ventilated cross-drilled disc/rotor and special lightweight aluminium hub for this competitive machine. This alloy hub reduces the weight by about 50 per cent, which is doubly beneficial since this is unsprung weight.

are fundamentally the same as the original MGB/MGC ones. I believe this endorses my view that, in spite of the developments that have taken place, your MGB's rear brakes might not need changing. Only some 30 per cent of braking comes from the rear and the OE drums are more than capable of providing this for very long periods. I would, therefore, recommend you ensure your original rear brakes are in good order and spend any money that you are tempted to budget on rear discs on front suspension/brake improvements instead. Rear discs may look great but I am not convinced they are appropriate, except for a tiny minority of racing MGBs.

Naturally, if you are fitting a rear axle or rear suspension arrangement pre-fitted with disc brakes, retain them. A couple of interesting examples can be seen in photographs 10-3-1-1 to 10-3-1-3.

Rear disc brakes

The exposed nature of the rear brakes, along with the fact that they do not run very hot, means that seizure and disc corrosion is a serious problem for many cars fitted with rear discs. It may actually be the case that rear discs are simpler and cheaper for modern carmakers to fit, and it is this that dictates the move to rear discs, at least on the smaller, lighter cars. However, for the record, here's how it can be done (see picture 10-3-1-2).

There are two DIY routes open to you in the UK. Firstly, you can collect a pair of Rover 800 rear calipers from your auto salvage yard and buy a new pair of '800' discs. Alternatively, Ford Granadas from 1985 to 1995 use a similar rear caliper, though they might cost more than the Rover 800 calipers.

Remove the brake backplates and refix the hubs temporarily. You should find that the discs will just drop over your wheel studs in place of the original MGB drums and, via their centre line, show the mounting position for your calipers. You

10-3-1-1 A Jaguar independent rear suspension assembly with inboard rear disc brakes – retain them!

10-3-1-2 This is an Automotive Products AP twin-pot caliper. Note that the specially machined seal-retaining plate doubles as a caliper mounting and ...

10-3-1-3 ... the special rear hub with the numerous disc/rotor to hub fastenings. Probably this arrangement is only relevant to racecars or cars intended for frequent track use.

will need to make up a bracket to fit to the inside face of your rear axle and you may need to fit two slightly longer bolts through each oil seal plate. You will certainly also need to fit an adjustable brake limiter in the hydraulic line, new hydraulic pipes and twin rear handbrake cables and a different handbrake cable compensating arrangement. A Stag, TR5, 250 or 6 compensator attaches to the rear of the handbrake and will be difficult to squeeze into the MGB's prop tunnel, but would be ideal if you could mount it under the floor using bespoke cables from Speedy Cables.

In all cases, second-hand rear calipers are likely to be in poor condition and in need of a full reconditioning. Some parts, especially the handbrake mechanism, become so worn through contamination with dirt, water and salt that they are often beyond redemption. Do bear this in mind before parting with cash. I suggest that your best bet would be to speak with a reconditioning company before purchase and get tips on what to look for. You may even find that some reconditioning companies are able to do you a deal.

Rear drum brakes

If sticking with the MGB's original drum brakes you will probably need to fit new

rear brake cylinders as part of the re-building process. If so, make a virtue out of the necessity by reviewing the size of the rear wheel cylinders. Rear wheel lock-ups

are most undesirable and the diameter of the rear slave cylinders and/or the pressure applied down the line front the brake pedal affects the situation. A special cylinder is available (Moss part number GWC1101) but requires minor modifications to the backplate – a hole for the roll-pin – on some cars. Alternatively, you can fit Mini rear wheel cylinders while there are, naturally, a variety of shoe compounds available each with different frictional ('grab') characteristics. EBC, Mintex, Hawk and Ferodo have very popular rear shoe materials ... but maybe there is an altogether more flexible solution.

Whether you are fitting your own rear discs or staying with drums, it is a prudent precaution to fit a brake bias or balance valve in the hydraulic line. You can alter rear wheel cylinder sizes – but frankly I'd find that a pain, particularly as a change of front or rear friction material may necessitate an adjustment in front/rear bias. A variety of adjustable brake pressure valves are available which reduce the supply to the rear brakes. The racing guys fit these inside the cockpit for ease of adjustment, but for our road-going cars this is unnecessary and a location somewhere under the bonnet/hood perfectly should be adequate for the number of times you are likely to need to change the front/back balance. Some of today's valves come with metric pipe fittings, thus necessitating your altering the end connections on the relevant brake lines, but see what Wilwood and Tilton and other retailers have to offer.

MISCELLANEOUS BRAKING DETAILS
Brake and clutch pedals

Your chrome-bumper car brake and clutch pedals will both need slight adjustment if you have added the bottom steering column mounting cone detailed in the previous chapter. The clutch pedal has two 'kinks' pressed into it as standard, but will still foul the newly-added cone. Fortunately, a vice can straighten the kinks slightly, allowing the required clearance, but, unfortunately, in so doing, will bring the clutch pedal slightly too close to the brake pedal. I added a slight, right-hand kink to my brake pedal so that a 50mm gap was re-established between brake and clutch pedals.

Cooling ducts

I have recommended fitting a frontal 'ST' front valance to aid engine cooling and to increase front-end stability by reducing the air passing under the car. This could also reduce the volume of air flowing onto the calipers and brake discs/rotors. The resultant early brake fade is most undesirable and signals the need for a couple of flexible air ducts to be let into the front valance (another reason for using a fibreglass one!) to duct air to the front brakes.

10-3-3 This is an MGB rear axle/disc brake combination. The mounting bracket bolts to the inside of the rear axle flange. An interesting bonus is the view of the rose/ball joint on the end of this axle locating Panhard rod (top left of the picture).

Chapter 11
Induction & exhaust

There is an almost unlimited variety of carburettor manifolds for the Buick/Rover, Chevy and Ford engines. All have OE manifolds that are effective and should not be discarded without some thought. Of the aftermarket replacements, Edelbrock, Offenhauser/JWR and Wildcat offer some very effective products. However, I think the best approach to EFI induction is to, as far as practical, buy an engine with manifold and EFI in place.

When it comes to induction, a rolling road, gas analysing equipment and professional experience are essential to get the most from your set-up. Once you have the engine going and run-in, let the professionals do the tweaking, re-jetting, injector-cleaning and re-chipping.

That said, not everyone will be able or wish to fit an OE set-up whether it is carburettor- or EFI-inducted. Some may wish to change the carburettor or fit EFI just for the satisfaction of doing so and the resulting performance boost – and we therefore need to examine some of the options available.

AN OVERVIEW OF INDUCTION OPTIONS

On the face of it, V8 converters have a difficult choice when it comes to carburation but, as so many people opt for AFB (Aluminium Four Barrel) carburation, perhaps the choice is not that difficult. Naturally, the engine in question has a lot to do with your selection and Ford- or Chevy-engined cars will not suit twin SUs for, example. Nevertheless, let's explore the main options open to converters:

(a) SU twin HIF6 Rover carburation (Buick/Rover Engines only)

(b) Multi-SU manifolds and SU carburation (Buick/Rover Engines only)

(c) Aluminum four barrel carburation – all engines

(d) Single point electronic fuel-injection by Air flow meter (sometimes called 'Flapper') or hot-wire air-mass-meter control (Ford and Chevy engines only)

(e) Multi-point fuel-injection – all engines

(f) Aftermarket EFI – all engines

11-1-1 The twin SUs here are HIF6s on an original MGB GT V8 two-piece inlet manifold. If you were reproducing this induction system, I would recommend using a pair of HS6s. Note the shortened damper covers on the SUs and the secondary 'V' manifold, onto which ...

Of these options, I would estimate that the majority use option (c) although EFI in one form or another is becoming increasingly popular. Nevertheless, we will look at each method, albeit in some cases, briefly.

153

11-1-2 ... the carburettors bolt.

THE SU OPTIONS

SU carburettors offer two routes to V8 induction. Either or both can be used on other engines but I guess the vast majority will be applied to Buick/Rover engines and the smaller capacity Buick/Rover engines at that. The 2-carb method provides economic induction for moderately-powered conversions and has the not inconsiderable advantage of requiring less headroom under the bonnet than any other induction system. As photos 11-1-1 and 11-1-2 confirm, the original MGB GT V8s used twin HIF6 (44mm) SU carburettors mounted on a V-shaped cast adapter which, in turn, bolted onto the engine inlet manifold. Air filtration and temperature control was via an airbox and two filter assemblies (photo 11-1-3). Few of these original parts are now available, but you can consign your Rover P5B/P6/SD1 inlet manifold to your V8 conversion specialist for machining and, from the same source, purchase a reproduction cast manifold adapter. Photos 11-1-4-1 and 11-1-4-2 show Clive Wheatley's beautifully finished reproduction products.

Providing you have the Rover SU HIF6 (or a serviceable pair of the earlier and, many would say, preferable HS6) carburettors already available, this will be your cheapest induction option. Many British cars of this era used the HS6 carburettor so finding a pair should not be too difficult. Take care not to leave too much height on the manifold when

11-1-3 The airbox mounted between carburettors and heater carried two very unusual air filters and thermostatically controlled flaps. Today you would use a pair of high-efficiency K&N filters mounted on the airbox.

machining, or use too thick a base plate, or you could end up needing to 'Bulge' your bonnet and/or machine the tops off your SU dashpots. Clive Wheatley can supply the new SU HIF6 carburettors with short dashpots (seen at 11-1-5) for this very purpose.

Rover's twin SU carburettors can be mounted in different ways: both facing the rear bulkhead, as with the original MGB GT V8 and/or Clive Wheatley's reproduction equipment, or facing the inner wings on

11-1-4-1 Two views of a modified Rover SD1 'pent-roofed' inlet manifold machined flat, plated and powder-coated grey ...

11-1-4-2 ... with a specially cast reproduction 'V' secondary manifold cast, machined and powder-coated black.

11-1-5 A pair of new HIF6 carburettors with lowered dash-pots ready to mount on your reproduction 'V' secondary manifold.

11-1-6 Generally, the 'facing outward' Rover manifold will almost certainly introduce MGB bonnet/hood clearance problems – which is why MG introduced the slightly more convoluted secondary 'V' manifold. Triumph also had to introduce the double-bulged bonnet/hood in the TR8 because of the use of the Rover 'facing outwards' manifold/twin-SU approach. However, this cleverly executed solution uses the original Rover inlet manifold without bonnet clearance problems.

11-1-7 The throttle linkage is clearly in view but the operation of the choke via the cable seen at the rear of this shot is equally important and necessitates a second set of linkages hidden from view here.

an unmodified Rover manifold. You will almost certainly need to introduce an air-scoop or substantial bulge in the bonnet to accommodate using an unmodified SD1 manifold although photo 11-1-6 shows an unmodified manifold with an alternative method of using SUs.

If you are copying the MGB GT V8 original set-up, special inter-carb linkages are required. I know of only one source for these – Clive Wheatley V8 Conversions. You can, of course, make the various linkages yourself but a quick look at picture 11-1-7 will confirm it will be time-consuming.

Detractors point out that the SU carbs lack the accelerator pump facility offered by all the AFB carbs – and it's (partially) true. However, the SU dashpot acts in part as a accelerator pump (lifting to inject fuel when the throttle is depressed) and the SU is also ridiculously easy to tune. By finding a second pair of dashpots, fitting weaker

springs and reshaping the needles you will, in effect, have a pair standby carburettors. You can change the complete dashpot assemblies in about ten minutes making it practical to drive to and from a 'track day' on the 'road' dashpots yet go on the track with the track day tuned carbs. No other carburettor allows you to do that. Furthermore, they offer the advantage of

getting the top of the carbs well away from the bonnet crossmember which makes SUs less height-critical – a point that could be of particular interest to chrome-bumper converters reluctant to change their front suspension crossmembers.

Detractors also complain about the power producing capabilities of SU carburettors – but in my view the HS6 (I'm not so enthusiastic about the HIF6) produces the most power per £1 outlay. They may not be quite up to providing the same power from the very top-end as some very expensive carburettors, but for the majority of the rev-range the SU does not warrant the reputation it has been given. HIF carburettors do flow more air than the HS series and can provide a slight power advantage over them, though many dislike some HIF's auto adjustments features for things like fuel temperature. However the HS6's do not get things all their own way, as you will need to slightly modify the MG V8 style of air filter box to provide clearance for HS6's.

Furthermore all SU carbs run more efficiently with a radius at the entry of the carburettor air intake – so if using SU's, do ensure that the air entering each carburettor does so via a 'Stub Stack' to provide radius entries for the airflow. Opinions vary but this could be worth 5bhp, maybe a shade more, on a 3500cc V8 but needs thinking about if you are planning to bolt some air filters straight to the mouth of the carburettors!

Most standard SU needles have been shaped to provide economical motoring but a wide range of needles are available, or yours can be tweaked at home to consume more fuel and provide lots of urge. There is not a huge range of dashpot-springs available (which control acceleration) but those that are around can be shortened to reduce the piston's resistance to rising – which has the same effect as an accelerator/throttle pump.

V8 choke and throttle cables are

11-1-8-1 Known, I think, as a Boxer inlet manifold, the inlet tracks cross over so that the right side pair of carbs feed the left cylinder head. I note the four SUs have short dashpots which makes me unsure about the bonnet clearance implications of using this induction approach in an MGB conversion, and ...

11-1-9-1 A Road Demon carbuettor about which I have heard several good reports.

11-1-9-2 I like the fuel level sight-glasses in the float chambers but would much prefer a manual choke to the electric one seen in the previous shot.

11-1-8-2 ... while there will no doubt be many satisfied users, I must say that I doubt the cost benefits of buying the manifold and four decent modified SU carburettors. I think an AFB carb will be more cost-effective. Not sure of the vehicle shown in this shot but it's a Rover engine!

readily available from Clive Wheatley and/or virtually any MG spares stockist. However, I would bet the standard 1800 cables (if in good condition) are perfectly re-usable. Indeed, unless using SU carburettors on a V8 replica manifold, the official V8 throttle cable (part number BHH 1120) may actually be a hindrance because of its special end connection.

There are also induction systems that use four SU carburettors mounted on a fabricated manifold. I have shown a couple of examples at 11-1-8-1 and 11-1-8-2.

Air filtration would normally be via a pair of K&N high efficiency filters from your V8 conversion specialist mounted either off the air-box or when using an SD1 manifold, straight onto the carb. However, the airbox approach offers one interesting opportunity to feed cool air to SU carburettors. All MGB V8 conversions have, to one degree or another, a common under-bonnet/hood

11-1-10 A Rochester AFB carburettor from about 1963. Unfortunately, these do not suit an MGB conversion due to their unfavourable height requirements, although the manifold they sit upon is both effective and cheap.

11-1-11 One of the Weber trio of AFB carburettors – an Edelbrock. Most parts for these carburettors are interchangeable.

11-1-12 This is Holley's model 4150 – with its 390cfm flow capacity and twin metering plates/pannier float chambers.

11-1-13 Before unboxing your Holley carburettor, make sure it has 'List 8007' stamped on it: Holley makes other carbs that are identical-looking. This one is for 8-cylinder, 390cfm engines like your Rover unit.

heat problem. Engine efficiency improves in every respect if you can duct cool air to the carburettors. While this rule holds for all carburettors, only SUs fed from an airbox offer the opportunity to easily mount the air filters towards the front of the car and duct the filtered air to each side of the air box.

You may be more interested in this concept if I add that for every 5°C increase in intake air temperature, the engine loses 1 per cent of its power and torque. This may not seem much, but most of us have noticed how responsive the car feels once it is warm but before it gets hot – say after the first mile or so of driving as the engine comes off cold but before it reaches its normal working temperature. This is the sort of improvement you can expect from carefully managed intake air temperature.

Furthermore, putting SUs at the back of a V8's engine may have been a masterpiece of BL packaging, but this is the hottest part of the engine bay and therefore the worst place to put fuel-related items. Drawing the elevated temperature air from this area is not brilliant either. Under load there should be enough air and fuel flow to ensure that the fuel doesn't boil in the fuel lines, but when you stop and allow the carburettors and fuel lines to soak in the residual heat, you could expect

restarting difficulties, vapour locks and poor running.

In short you could expect that a carefully designed induction feed to the carbs drawing ambient air could be worth 20 to 25bhp to cars with 'block-hugger' exhaust systems. Such an arrangement should start with a fabricated air box similar in concept to the original MG V8 one, perhaps enlarged to provide about the same capacity as the engine (eg 3500cc or 4000cc as appropriate) with the inlet on one side, as seen earlier in picture 11-1-6. However, rather than fit the air-filter in the engine bay, connect the air box to a remote filter mounted under a front wing opposite the steering. A plastic wheelarch liner should protect the filter.

The task becomes more difficult and probably less essential when RV8 style exhaust manifolds/headers are in use. The induction must be extended forward to the front of the car, perhaps behind the front lights, if you are to avoid counterproductively heating the intake air with your exhaust manifold!

AFB INDUCTION

The vast majority of converters will instinctively think of fitting an aluminium four barrel (AFB) carburettor atop their engine – and provided you choose the

correct size of carburettor for your engine capacity, one or other of these products will serve you very well indeed regardless of your engine manufacturer. There are other makes of AFB carburettor available (Demon, seen at 11-1-9-1 and 11-1-9-2, being one such) but since Holley and Weber (also marketed as Carter and Edelbrock) have largely made this a two-horse race, space dictates I focus on these leading brands. Let us explore the differences and some advantages of each in a moment but first a few details need to be cleared up –

● The original Buick/Olds/Pontiac 215/3500 engines mostly came fitted with AFB carburettors – Rochesters, an example of which is seen at 11-1-10 (previous).

● I have already mentioned Weber carburettors and some readers may have the DCOE horizontal carburettor in mind. With a Weber AFB carburettor we are talking about the same company but a different range of carburettors entirely.

● Weber, Carter and Edelbrock four-barrel carburettors are all manufactured using the same Weber base casting. An example can be seen at 11-1-11 (previous).

● Holley carburettors are, however, quite different – and also very highly regarded and shown in 11-1-12 (previous).

The Holley

Originally developed in the USA for the 215

most V8 engines. Holley makes a range of carburettors – so you must get the right model or 'flow-rate' for your particular engine capacity. All the expert speed shops and aftermarket suppliers will be able to advise you on the options most suited to your particular engine, tune and capacity. There are 'double-pumpers' available – these are fitted with two accelerator pumps and, to my mind, are not the best option for road-going cars. The version you need has a secondary vacuum facility and secondary metering plate and jets pre-fitted.

For the 215/3500cc engines at the modest end of our power bands, the 8007 390cfm series shown in photo 11-1-13 (previous) works well – after being set-up on a rolling road. More on that in a minute, but check that 'list 8007' is stamped on the top where the air filter mounts before unboxing the unit.

As supplied, the Holley has an electric automatic choke and, if you retain this method of choke actuation, will need only

11-1-16 The Holley as delivered has only the front (left) metering plate in place. The right side float chamber was supplied but was useless until a longer fuel transfer tube and rear barrel metering plate were fitted. (The new plate is situated by the throttle cable mounting screw.)

11-1-17 With the choke flap fully shut, the three additional hole modification carried out by Oselli when upgrading the Holley carburettor can be clearly seen. The car starts first 'twist', summer or winter.

11-1-14 It is important to feed and blank off the Holley apertures as appropriate. From left to right of this photo are: outlet under accelerator pump – blank off; outlet to left of choke – blank off; angled outlet above choke – connect to rocker box; angled outlet under front float chamber – blank off; mid-height outlet from front plate – connect to distributor.

GM Buick and Oldsmobile V8 engines, this USA carburettor is a frequent and favourite method of improving the performance of

11-1-15 There is a slight 'click-stop' when the Holley's manual choke is fully off. Do make sure your choke arm is fully forward and the click-stop engaged when the choke is not in use.

a 12V supply wired from the 'on' side of the ignition switch so that, with the ignition switch 'off', there will be no power to your carburettor. Take great care to ensure it is a 12V line you take to the carb and not, say, a 7V supply from your coil. A small earth

lead is also required – all this can be seen in photo 11-1-14.

My own Holley electric choke caused me some irritation when, after about 10,000 miles, it started to stick, giving the car a tick over/idle of about 2500rpm. After checking that the flap was not fouling the air cleaner I purchased a Holley manual choke kit 45-225 and re-used my original 1800cc MGB choke cable. I did have to fabricate a small bracket to provide the 'choke-off' spring return but would recommend the manual choke seen in 11-1-15 from the outset.

11-1-18 A Carter 500cfm carburettor viewed from the front of the car. Note the electrically controlled choke on the left side of the picture (which also gives an excellent view of the heat shield).

11-1-19 Here is another, rather clearer, view of a heat shield intended to reduce fuel percolation. It can clearly be seen front and rear of the Carter 500 carb with another cut-away area, this time for the choke mechanism.

11-1-20 When is a Weber an Edelbrock? Answer, when it's got an Edelbrock nameplate affixed to its front. This photograph gives us the opportunity to double-check the vacuum connections required for the Weber range of carburettors. You will note the large vacuum pipe that exits the body centrally (between the two mixture adjusting screws). This needs blanking off, as does the smaller pipe that can be seen just to the right and slightly lower. Connect the other small outlet (to the left of centre) to your distributor. The constant vac. connection to the brake servo goes to the rear of the carburettor.

The initial Holley 4160 set-up needs some explanation as, at least in my experience, they rarely run 'straight from the box'. Most will at least need jetting for your particular application. Depending upon which of the numerous Holley models you purchase, you may find it essential to -

● Fit a secondary metering plate and jets and thus bringing into use the relevant pair of secondary barrels shown on the right of photo 11-1-16 and the spec to Holley model 4150.

● Modify the choke flap on the primary barrels (to prevent over-choking) by machining three holes in the flap (shown in photo 11-1-17.

● Fit much smaller main (primary barrel) fuel jets to obviate flooding and cylinder washing.

This work necessitated a whole series of adjustments and minor alterations on a rolling road and doubled the initial cost of the carburettor – making it an expensive choice. Consequently there are some rules I suggest you adopt if you are thinking of a Holley. Be sure to buy your inlet manifold and carburettor from one expert source and do the deal based upon an all-inclusive package that includes his initial set-up/jetting the carb so that the engine will initially run and that it is subsequently tuned on a rolling road. Further, Holley carburettors are notorious for blowing power valves; modification ($10-$15) kits are available to prevent this and should be included in your package deal. If your intended supplier of Holley and inlet manifold cannot offer this service, find another source.

11-1-21 The Edelbrock control rods are rather like SU needles. I was putting these into my new carburettor to go atop my 3500cc Rover engine. RPI can definitely pre-jet this range of carbs for your engine for a small additional fee, or advise on, and supply, the most appropriate jets for your engine, leaving you to carry out the simple fitting task.

The Weber range

In 1957, Carter (now Weber) came out with a new generation of four-barrel carburettors called AFB (Aluminium Four Barrel). The compact design, light weight, simplicity of operation and flow capacities quickly made the AFB a

11-1-22 This picture also shows the front of the carburettor (note the pipe connections) but is included to show the Edelbrock foam air cleaner. This particular example had to be lowered by a couple of inches to allow this MGB bonnet/hood to close.

favourite and it is currently offered as Carter's 9000 series incorporating electric chokes, simple linkage connections, and Positive Crankcase Ventilation (PCV) valve activation. All have dual pattern drilling on the base plate to marry to both 5.125 x 5.625in and 4.25 x 5.625in intake manifold bolt patterns.

The best Weber carburettors for the 215/3500cc and 3900cc V8s are either the 400 (model 9400) or 500cfm (model 9500) models. The 300in³/4600cc engines will need the 9500 model shown in photographs 11-1-18, to 11-1-20 (previous). The 400cfm model has the ideal capacity for the 215 or 3500cc engine but, unfortunately, it is no longer available new and second-hand ones tend to be expensive. The 500cfm is theoretically a little too large for these displacements but works well on 215/3500 engines (something that I can confirm). Perhaps this is a tribute to their flexibility

Weber 500cfm carburettors are readily available from speed equipment stores and mail order outlets in the USA at around $200. These have the added attraction in that they reputedly work straight from the box and any tuning that is required is easily accomplished. You will get some idea as to the ease of the task from picture 11-1-21. The same ranges of carburettors are available in the UK from RPI Engineering for about £200.

Edelbrock models are, as I mentioned earlier, virtually the same as Weber/Carter but, to avoid confusion, I should emphasize that each use a different part number. The Edelbrock 1404 (shown in photograph 11-1-22) is very similar to a Weber 500cfm (model 9500) with a manual choke.

Holley/Weber comparisons

Performance is bound to be the first comparison and diagram D11-1 shows the detail. These graphs of power and torque are the result of tests carried out on my own standard SD1 3500cc engine with the original Holley 4150 carburettor substituted by a Weber 9500/Edelbrock 1404. The timing was advanced from the Holley's 3° BTDC to 6° BTDC for the Weber, but that was the only alteration. Fuel was 95 RON unleaded.

Up to 4000rpm the performance of the carburettors is inseparable. The Holley started to run out of fuel above 4000rpm, however, and it became possible to see some daylight between their respective performances. However, remember that most of us use 4000+rpm infrequently so, in truth, the difference in performance is negligible. In comparative fuel consumption tests, using the same engine and identical road conditions (as near as practical), the Holley returned 27, and the Weber 31 miles to the Imperial gallon at average speeds of about 64mph (circa 10 and 11kpl respectively at 102kph).

You may be interested in the differing methods of construction and adjustment. The Holley is assembled from three main components: a main body and two (pannier style) float chambers bolted fore and aft. This construction means there are assembly joints below the level of the fuel and, although gaskets are incorporated into the design, I must report that I found it essential to frequently tighten the eight float chamber retaining bolts if I was to avoid the smell of fuel in the car. The Weber, on the other hand, is built from two main sub-assemblies split horizontally above the fuel level. Both carburettors use two primary and two secondary chokes (venturis) fed via twin float chambers.

The fuel/air ratio of Holley carburettors is adjusted by selecting and fitting primary and secondary fuel transfer jets. A range of jet sizes is available to weaken or enrich both primary and secondary chokes. The fuel metering of a Weber is very similar to that of SU carburettors in that the fuel is fed from low down in the float bowls and drawn up through the fuel channel in the carburettor's body. As it passes into the carburettor it also has to pass through a jet, although two vacuum operated metering needles (rods in Weber's terminology) further govern its flow. Therefore, the combination of jets and needles in the Weber makes jet selection less critical than with the Holley.

Furthermore, it may take an inexperienced mechanic some time to change either of the Holley's primary or secondary jets. The task involves a major stripdown of the carburettor. This can take

a couple of hours if one includes removing all the old gaskets (a good reassembly tip is to smear the new gaskets with grease or Vaseline) and float chamber cross tube. The Weber's needles and jets take 10-15 minutes to change.

Both carburettors have a cold start enrichment facility: the Weber's is manually operated by the conventional Bowden cable, whereas the Holley employs an automatic electric choke.

Both makes employ an accelerator pump to inject extra fuel upon opening the throttles. Both work well, although the Weber has the additional advantage of allowing the stroke to be easily adjusted. The Holley requires the substitution of a new/different pump if adjustments are required.

The respective methods of operation are interesting, particularly the transition from primary to secondary choke(s). The Holley pulls open the primary throttle plates fully as you start to accelerate and the engine starts to move up the rev range. When sufficient load is achieved the resultant vacuum will start to pull open the secondary throttles against a control spring. Naturally, the secondary throttle's

opening point is critical. If too early, it will cause mid-range over-fuelling but, if too late, you will notice a mid-range flat spot due to a weak mixture. The selection of the Holley's secondary jets and vacuum control spring is both tricky and important.

The Holley's reliance on vacuum-actuated secondary chokes can result in some fuel inefficiency. For example, when you are pulling hard uphill, the extra load/vacuum will try to open the Holley's secondary chokes when they are not actually required.

The Weber's primary to secondary transition has two important additional controls not present in the Holley range: a throttle linkage to the secondary chokes, and a further pair of plates that need engine vacuum to open them. Consequently, the Weber's secondary choke will only open when the throttle is at least 70 per cent open and the engine is pulling sufficient vacuum to open the additional plates. This arrangement allows for good fuel economy (bearing in mind the capacity of the engine) and good bottom-end torque because the engine is not being over-fuelled.

AFB inlet manifolds

Both makes of carburettor will fit on any of the wide range of inlet manifold options open to you. Obviously you will be governed by the engine that you are selecting your inlet manifold for – but even so, the subsequent options open to you are numerous and confusing. You do not have to go down the expensive aftermarket route and I will try to outline some budget solutions as well as focusing on some rather more expensive, but probably more effective, options too.

Although we are only looking at three different engine options, and perhaps a total of eight AFB carburettor choices, space prevents us exploring each combination here. Fortuitously there are numerous aftermarket experts who will be able to advise on your particular

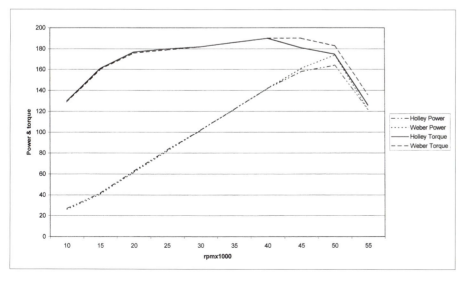

D11-1 Holley & Weber comparisons.

11-1-24 The full range of Edelbrock manifolds is both respected and impressive. This is one example of a 'Performer' fitted to a Rover 3500cc engine.

selecting an inlet manifold, quite apart from its significant effect on the performance of your engine.

For US based Buick/Rover 215 engine enthusiasts, particularly those on tight budgets working towards moderate performance targets, do not pass over the original Buick/Oldsmobile/Pontiac inlet manifold too swiftly. The resulting performance can be very satisfactory and costs can be contained to about $50/$75. In the UK, those seeking modest expenditure and performance can have the 'roof' of a Rover inlet manifold machined flat, a plate affixed and some secondary machining carried out, in a similar manner to the preparation work necessary prior to mounting the 'V'-shaped manifold adapter and their SU carbs.

For those anxious to maximise their engine's potential, the list of inlet manifolds is amazing but personally I would short-list and explore the relevant Offenhauser or Edelbrock manifolds for your engine. Offenhauser is the US company which developed inlet manifolds for, amongst others, the GM (now Rover) V8 engine. Initially it made the single plane model that is still preferred by some experts. This is still available and mounts the carburettor a shade higher (remember, height is critical in your MGB conversion) than the alternative and subsequent dual-plane design.

Edelbrock manifolds generally are well thought of. Two in particular suit MGB V8 applications – part number 2198 and their "Performer" model, p/n 2121. The latter can be seen in picture 11-1-24 and is designed for Ford 289 to 302 engines.

In fact, the options open to US Ford and Chevy enthusiasts appear endless and include some dual-quad intakes but, perhaps best of all, used manifolds are quite common at US autojumbles/swap-meets. In the UK, Offenhauser manifolds are made by John Woolfe Racing and can be obtained from several sources in the UK, including RPI Engineering. We saw an

combination of engine/capacity/tune/ manifold/bonnet-space/budget and intended use. Some general thoughts may be useful, however.

You may not be aware that differing styles of inlet manifold from the same manufacturer can alter the head-room

taken up above the engine; the change is not dramatic and in many other installations the difference is not material. However, in an MGB V8 conversion, ½in (10mm) can be the difference between closing or not closing your bonnet/hood. Height is an important consideration when

example in photograph 11-1-20. In the US, Offy and Edelbrock manifolds are available from numerous aftermarket outlets and speed-shops.

AFB Installations

Possibly less important in the UK, but whatever manifold/carburettor you use, two problems can occur. The first is 'heat-soak' from the inlet manifold and its contents. In fact, when I switched from Holley to Edelbrock carburation (on the same manifold) I had to fit an Edelbrock thermal barrier between carb and manifold, even in the colder UK climate, in order to reduce hot re-starting difficulties caused by heat-soak. Edelbrock retailers can supply a thermal barrier in several thicknesses – mine was 0.375 inches (10mm) thick but thicker and, therefore, more effective ones are available and can be used if you have the under-bonnet space available.

In hotter climates heat percolation of the fuel in the float bowls and/or vapor lock in the fuel-lines adjacent to the carburettor can occur. Obviously hot starting difficulties will result too, and in these circumstances a heat shield and/or a thermal plate between the carburettor and the intake manifold may be required. However, most proprietary heat shields are available made from aluminium but it is my belief that you would get superior performance by using a thin sheet of a non-heat-conducting material, such as paxalin, fibreglass, kevlar or another (preferably fire retarding) laminate. Certainly you will improve the effectiveness of the aluminium shields if you apply a self-adhesive reflective insulant called 'Thermo Shield' – available from Summit in the USA, and via Agriemach Ltd and Demon Tweeks in the UK. However, this will do nothing to stop carb/manifold direct heat transfer through the aluminium and, while you can also fit the thermal barrier I mentioned earlier, you resolve both problems at once with the non-metallic shield solution.

The aluminium shields are available

11-1-25-1 The 'Low Rider' filter assembly sitting on a Rover engine. This uses a paper filter element (Mr Gasket number 1480A). While it works well, a 3500cc engine needs the paper element replacing at least every 5000 miles ...

from several sources. We saw examples of heat shields in photographs 11-1-18 and 11-1-19. To the best of my knowledge no one in the UK supplies pre-made heat shields. Clive Wheatley, who has US contacts, may be able to import one for you, although they are easily made from a piece of 10in (250mm) square material of about 0.125in (3mm) thickness. In the UK's climate, however, the necessity for a heat shield should be minimal, particularly if you follow the RV8-style exhaust manifold recommendations that have sprinkled this book.

Air filters

Rather like the inlet manifold issue discussed above, the actual air filter you fit will very much depend upon the capacity of your engine (and thus the volume of air you expect to pull though the filter) and the head-room available. The options are numerous but I would guess that the most frequently used air filter, particularly amongst moderately-powered conversions, is the 'Low Rider' 14in diameter x 2in high assembly seen in photo 11-1-25-1 and 11-1-25-2. A K&N replacement element will minimise air flow restrictions and the filter element is cleanable/re-usable too.

Watch that the height of the front

11-1-25-2 ... while larger capacity engines like this Ford using this filter may need the element changed even more frequently – in which case find a 2in tall K&N air cleaner that fits the 14in diameter of this case.

edge of the 'Low Rider' air filter does not exceed 95mm above your rocker covers, or bonnet fouling will certainly occur. Drawing D9-8 (chapter 9) will act as a check but if you find picture 11-1-26 replicates your car, then it is possible to have the manifold's carburettor mounting face re-machined such that 0.2in (5mm) is removed from the front edge and nothing from the back. For my part, I'd prefer not to machine the inlet manifold and would look around for an alternative solution, some of which we will explore pictorially in photos 11-1-27-1 and 11-1-27-2 (overleaf). Consequently, when buying your carburettor you are prudent to

11-1-26 Bonnet interference is clearly a problem here, but you will angle the carb and the air cleaner downward at the front and reduce the filter front lip height by about 0.560in (14mm) if you machine the manifold as described in the main text.

11-1-27-1 Compare and contrast this full-height Edelbrock Pro Flo foam filter (part number 1002) ...

11-1-27-2 ... with this lowered version. The base of this filter had to be trimmed to reduce the height of the unit by some 2in (50mm) in order that the MG's bonnet/hood could be closed.

take advice and buy the inlet manifold and filter simultaneously.

Speaking of K&N filters, K&N's complete air filter assembly (part number 60-1280) is suitable for any engine up to 400bhp. It has a 14in diameter and comes from the Xtreme range. However, its net height above the carb flange is 2.75in (gross height is 3.8in) and it sits atop the 5in diameter of a Holley or Weber AFB with a single top stud mounting. Although it retails at about £80 in the UK, it has to be worth exploring – if you are sure there is adequate space available in your MGB engine bay.

Pipercross has recently introduced its PX800 specialist design for Holley carburettor air filtration. This has a

recessed base plate that extends down almost to the base of the carburettor, allowing for much greater filter depth and a high capacity foam filter element while retaining minimum overall height. They are all available from Demon Tweeks in the UK and most speed-shops in the US. Incidentally, the Weber/Carter/Edelbrock 400 and 500 carburettors use the same Low Rider/Mr Gasket 14in diameter air filter as the Holley and, consequently, I presume the Pipercross alternative will also fit the Weber four barrel carburettor.

Further, medium- and high-powered engines will be faced with a real space problem when it comes to finding an air-filter that flows sufficient volume without restriction yet fits under the MGB's bonnet. The Pipercross and Edelbrock foam filters may be very useful in this circumstance, and the pictorial sequence 11-1-28-1 to 11-1-28-4 may provide inspiration.

ELECTRONIC FUEL-INJECTION

Carburettors are a compromise. You have to have venturi/chokes that are small enough to generate the essential vacuum required to draw and atomize the fuel at cranking revs – or the car will not start. However, the size of the venturi

11-1-28-1 I thought this bespoke fabrication and K&N filter serving a 4-litre Rover would go under an MGB bonnet but ...

11-1-28-2 ... these twin 500cfm Edelbrocks with their tall air cleaners would need a significant bulge but look very effective.

11-1-28-3 The 3in (75mm) height of this nice-looking Ford filter might just go under an RV8 bonnet/hood while ...

11-1-28-4 ... this superb conversion will need a hole in the bonnet before it will close. There shouldn't be any air starvation problems then! Note the absolutely first-class headers made by Fast Cars Inc.

may not then be adequate to supply all the volume of mixture the engine needs at high revolutions. If you increase the size of the venturi/chokes, you may well improve top-end performance but are likely to reduce the torque, pick-up and general performance at the bottom end of the engine's rpm. Fuel-injection does not need a venturi vacuum to draw/atomize the fuel into the engine thus the choke size does not need to be a compromise as is illustrated by picture 11-2-1.

11-2-1 Fuel-injection systems will deliver and atomize the fuel in the incoming air-stream regardless of the size of the inlet passages – one reason why fuel-injected engines generally perform better than conventionally inducted engines.

The benefits do not end there, however, for –
● It is 'greener' with probably fewer harmful emissions than carburettors and offers the ability to use a three-way catalytic converter.
● It is more fuel-effective, offering more power for lower fuel consumption (which isn't quite the same as saying it offers lower fuel consumption).

11-2-2 The raised plenum chamber of this Rover EFI-equipped engine makes it hard to imagine that it will fit under an MGB bonnet/hood – but it will! Note the 'extra air valve' that sits just this side of the plenum.

● EFI has the ability to self-adjust to modification and is ideal in its ability to cope with all road-going conditions.
● It is the way engine management is going with more and more cars fitted with EFI in order to comply with ever-tightening emissions regulations.

All the engines focused upon here were fitted with EFI and the simplest solution to EFI induction in your MGB conversion is to acquire your selected engine and EFI system as one unit. Picture 11-2-2 is an example of a Range Rover engine and EFI system acquired as one 'package'. Generally speaking this will present the fewest acquisition and start-up problems, although it is also quite practical to retro-fit an EFI system from say a Ford-302-powered breaker and transpose it to your Ford 302 naturally aspirated engine. I would add the caveat that you would be prudent to buy the complete EFI set in one go. Buying components individually can be expensive. Furthermore, you can

inadvertently create a mismatch and, thereafter, find it difficult to resolve the problem at home.

A complete system, preferably removed from the donor car yourself, is perfectly transposable to your ex-carburettor engine. There may be some merit in changing the camshaft, but there is nothing unique about EFI engines that makes an ex-carburettor version out of the question. Unless I had been fortunate enough to see the system running, I would get the engine control unit (ECU) tested before installing it in the car. However, I would guess this pure electronic component will generally prove less susceptible to problems than some of the electro-mechanical components within the system (e.g. the throttle potentiometer). I will cover how to test the ECU later in this section.

Some may see an EFI system as more difficult to install and operate than a carburettor induction set-up. Certainly each EFI sensor and component is crucial to the system's operation and one failing component, even a dirty connection to a sound component or an air leak anywhere in the system, can generate disproportionately bad performance. In that sense EFI is more complex than any normally aspirated induction method but, surprisingly perhaps, need not be significantly more expensive to install.

So let's explore some of the basics of electronic fuel-injection. There are two fundamental EFI variants – single-point or multi-point injection – and Ford and Chevy have used both types of system at various times while Rover have only used a multi-point injection system. Both types are currently available via aftermarket EFI systems. Single-point injection may sound little better than a carburettor but, while I favour multi-point systems, the single point injection does have the advantages of simplicity and of atomizing the fuel far better than a carburettor at low/mid engine revs and is still definitely preferable to carburation.

Fuel feed details

A feature that applies to whichever electronic fuel-injection system you have or whatever the engine in question, the fuel supply is quite different to any carburettor fuel supply arrangement. It is essential

we explore the principals applicable to an MGB with EFI in conjunction with drawing D11-2. Fuel is pumped at high pressure, normally about 60psi, through fuel pipes and is regulated to, usually, 36psi by the fuel pressure regulator before being fed round fuel 'rails', from which the injectors are fed. The injectors (one per cylinder in multi-point injection system) open on an electronic command from the system's Electronic Control Unit which is programmed (or 'mapped') to hold the injectors open for the right period of time to suit the engine's circumstances. These circumstances vary, and data regarding throttle opening position, air flow, engine rpm, engine coolant temperature and exhaust oxygen (in the case of a catalyst car with a Lambda sensor) all affect the Electronic Control Unit's 'decisions'.

Additionally, the inlet manifold pressure controls the fuel pressure regulator seen in picture 11-2-3 via a diaphragm/vacuum pipe arrangement very similar to the advance/retard mechanism within a distributor. Unused fuel from the fuel rails is fed back down a fuel return pipe which, as the name implies, returns the fuel to the tank.

To the specifics of a MGB EFI installation, there are alternatives but the most suitable fuel tank necessitates

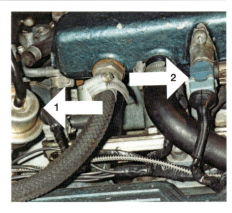

11-2-3 Arrow 1 highlights the fuel pressure regulator while arrow 2 identifies the 'fifth injector' – which increases the volume of injected fuel in AFM systems when the coolant is below normal operating temperature. On the left is the vacuum take-off, while, on the right, the moulded hose connects to the extra air valve.

modification of a new MGB fuel tank to incorporate a fuel return pipe, a swirl pot and a larger diameter pipe to feed fuel to the quite different high pressure fuel pump. Under absolutely no circumstances should you try to modify a used fuel tank or, indeed, any component that has been used with fuel. My MGB's tank after fitting a Ford Granada internal swirl pot and incorporating the essential fuel-feed and return pipes can be seen in photograph 11-2-4.

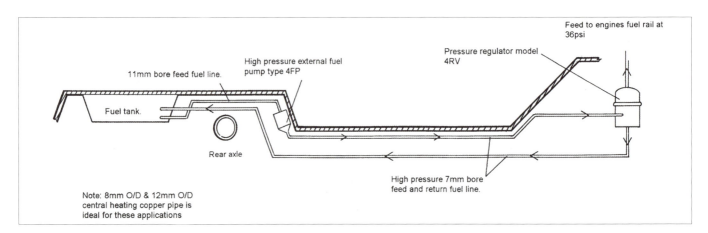

D11-2 Electronic fuel injection fuel supply feed and return for the MGB.

11-2-4 A modified MGB fuel tank for use with either of the EFI systems explained in this book. The 'inclusion' is where the return fuel swirl-pot has been inserted.

Your EFI fuel pump might come from an externally-pumped EFI car such as a Vitesse, Maestro or Montego. The submersible type fitted within the Range Rover's tank is of no use whatsoever. A Lucas model 4FP (or a 12-volt 2.1 bar equivalent) fuel pump is ideal and must be mounted in line with the bottom of your fuel tank (i.e. like the chrome-bumper MGB original SU fuel pump) but perhaps it is better placed in photo 9-2-18 (chapter 9). It must be fed from the tank via 11mm (minimum) bore pipe and I found a 12mm central heating pipe is ideal. These pumps distribute fuel via five rotating metal rollers. They supply fuel at very high pressure and in considerable volume but, conversely, do not draw fuel well and, if strained, make considerable noise. If the pump is noisy, a resistor can be wired in (just like a ballast-resisted coil) to reduce running voltage and pump noise. The Maestro, Montego, Rover, Vitesse and MG RV8 all use pump resistors, although I have not felt the need.

You will also need to pipe into the pressure side of the pump a fuel filter (Lucas part number 6FU or an equivalent). However these older style filters can be

about 3in (75mm) in diameter and hard to locate. There are alternative injection fuel filters (metal-cased for the systems high pressures) but as the size of these reduces so does the service life. The original large Lucas canister types have a normal service life of 4 years or 48,000 miles, which means that in normal European conditions the filter will probably last much longer before being at all restricted. However, the much smaller aftermarket injection filters (often listed for some early Vauxhalls and possibly half the size) make for much easier fitting – but then you halve the service life too.

The filter is best located before the pressure regulator and I found the engine bay to be the ideal location. However, many EFI cars have the fuel filter tucked under the car adjacent to the fuel-pump. Make absolutely sure that the is no way a curb, rough ground or any obstruction can damage the filter, pump or any fuel-lines you site under the car. EFI systems require two pressurized fuel pipes, both of at least 7mm bore size. I used 8mm central heating pipe to constantly circulate fuel from the pump to the engine bay and the engine fuel rails, with excess fuel being returned to the tank. Also take great care to ensure the fuel-filter you fit is a special, canister-looking EFI filter. These are much more expensive that the low-pressure conventional fuel-filters but the EFI ones do last for several years. Today many EFI systems, including the aftermarket systems, also fit a pre-pump filter that I think is a very good idea.

One advantage of EFI in our MGBs is that the engine bay of most V8 conversions suffers from high temperatures, as has been explained elsewhere. In summer, with conventional MGB fuel flow systems, this heat can lead to vapor locks as the temperature of the fuel within the fuel line rises. Elsewhere in this book you will find suggestions to combat the engine bay temperature problem generally, but the fuel vapor lock problem is automatically

eliminated with the EFI re-circulating fuel system since the fuel is never static within the engine bay long enough to warm up. Not a reason in itself to go for EFI – but an added benefit.

Air flow detail
All engines need oxygen to mix with the fuel they get from injectors (in the case of

11-2-5 An overview of the AFM analogue EFI system while ...

11-2-6 ... the later mass-meter/hot-wire digital system does look a little different.

EFI) or from the carburettor(s) in the case of normal induction. Thus the supply of air is important to all engines – but it is also vital to know how much air is entering an EFI engine in order to inject the correct volume of fuel. Consequently an accurate means of measuring the incoming air is essential. This is basically carried out by one of two methods – air flow metering for the earlier air flow systems or air-mass-metering (for the later hot-wire systems) shown

11-2-7 The throttle potentiometer sits here, more or less in the same place whichever EFI system you have.

11-2-8-1 This is the AFM being offered up, in this case on the left side of the engine bay. In fact it can sit either side and ...

respectively in pictures 11-2-5 and 11-2-6.

With either EFI system the actual volume of air is controlled by a throttle-disc that differs little from that seen in the choke of a carburettor. In the case of EFI systems it has the potentiometer seen at 11-2-7 attached to one end to tell the ECU the position of the throttle and whether the driver wants to go faster or slower.

Which method your system uses to actually measure the resulting volume of air will largely depend upon the age of the system. The former system is older (and less efficient) and relies on the air pushing a flap aside in the AFM. The extent to which the flap is displaced tells the ECU how much air is entering the engine. Lucas/Rover air flow meters supplied data to their (analogue) ECU's and the same type of operation will apply to the Ford air flow systems we noted in chapter 3. Pictures 11-2-8-1 and 11-2-8-2 show you what to look for.

Later air-mass-metering systems for both engines used digital computing methods and the hot-wire meter measured

11-2-8-2 ... looks like this in close-up.

the mass of air passing a heated wire within the meter by its reduction in temperature. Since there is no flap to interrupt the air flow, these are more effective, and they are

11-2-9 The mass-meter does look different if only because the 'arc' required by the AFM's flap is missing. Note the excellent K&N air-filter clipped straight onto the front of the mass-meter.

also accepted as being the more accurate method too. A further advantage of the later systems is that they have become progressively more frequent with many parts common across makes of car. In

11-2-10-1 The first thing that greets you are eight upturned trumpets. Glenn Towery tells me that he gets hot-wire EFI under an unaltered MGB bonnet/hood by sitting the Rover engine as low as possible, and shaving 0.75in off the bottom of each of these trumpets and bending the fuel rail down.

11-2-10-2 With the trumpets removed (sometimes more difficult than it sounds; see later photo caption for more information) the lower plenum chamber looks like this.

view of the age of flapper systems and the advantages of the later system, I intend to only detail the digital hot-wire method. An air-mass-meter can be viewed again at 11-2-9.

You may be interested in what is underneath the later system's plenum cover – in which case take a look at shots 11-2-10-1 and 11-2-10-2

The engine control unit

This is a mini computer that receives information from the numerous sensors, including the mass-meter and throttle potentiometer. Other sources of information are engine rpm (from the distributor, or possibly a front pulley sensor), water temperature and, if applicable, unburnt oxygen (from a lambda sensor). The ECU then interprets what is required in terms of injector opening times. When relocating an ECU to an MGB give a great deal of thought as to where the unit should be positioned. Under a seat or behind a trim panel in the cockpit are two good locations, although, as picture 11-2-11 shows, I put mine behind the glove box.

In the Rover world, hot-wire systems were used for a long line of Range Rovers and from 1989 onwards in 3.5, 3.9, 4.2 and 4.6 variants (respectively Discovery, Range Rover and LSE Range Rovers). It is also in use on MG's RV8. However, Ford and Chevy also offered this method of induction on a variety of models. Consequently EFI systems are far more prevalent than they used to be. The problem might be getting the plenum chamber under the MGB's bonnet/hood – but we will get to that a little later. First we need to acquire the correct parts.

The hot-wire parts required

When you buy an EFI system, whether as a separate kit or as part of an engine/EFI package, ensure your system includes:

1) Manifold assembly including the plenum and throttle body and the following components – eight injectors, coolant temperature thermistor, stepper motor, fuel rail, fuel pressure regulator, throttle potentiometer, throttle mechanism and breather pipes.

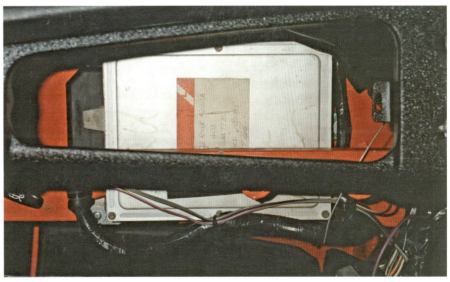

11-2-11 The multi-pin plug is on the left of this shot but the analogue ECU just fitted on the bulkhead/firewall between my wiper wheel-box and the side wall, leaving room to remove the multi-pin plug if need be.

11-2-12 Glenn Towery achieves the same objective with far less effort, but this hot-wire system has been modified as detailed in the 'Reducing the height' section (below) and fits without any bonnet/hood alterations.

11-2-13-1 Making a hot-wire EFI fit! An excellent before (on the right) and after comparison of the lower plenum chamber, or central casting, that required machining top and bottom to aid a reduction in overall system height sufficient to close a standard MGB bonnet. The eight 'trumpets', or rams, will also be given machine-shop attention at a later date, but their top face should first be measured (from the top lip of the casting) and only then removed from the centre casting.

The trumpets are an interference fit, aided by some sealer, and will be stubborn, but any badly damaged ones are replaceable! Ram removal may be aided by drilling a pair of 5mm holes right at the root of each ram to enable you to get some leverage.

From the bottom face of this central casting have 15mm (about 0.6 inches) machined off. On assembly, this will drop the fuel rail down to the point where it may touch the lower casting extensions in one or two spots. You can see the fuel rail in photograph 11-2-10-1 and, should this interference prove the case, just ease a couple of mm off each of the affected protrusions. Another consequence of this machining will be the complete removal of the shoulder onto which the two front and rear rams sit, and a reduction in height of the four central shoulders.

Turning our attention to the top lip of this central casting, you will have to have the two locating dowel holes in the top face redrilled, so it might save some hassle if their depth were increased at this point, before you lose their position! We need to take 3mm off the top lip and then proceed with caution (ensuring prior to each cut that you retain, undamaged, the threaded holes for the vacuum (servo) and two adjacent 'take-offs'). The most you can expect to remove from the top lip is 4mm but, with luck, you will reduce the overall height of this casting by, perhaps, 18.5 – 19.0mm.

2) Air flow meter and connection pipes to throttle and air filter.

3) Air filter – although a K&N filter can be and maybe best purchased separately.

4) Injection wiring harness.

5) Two injection relays.

6) Road speed sensor (although this may have to come from a separate source).

7) ECU; most easily identified by its 40-pin socket.

One advantage of the hot-wire system is the adaptability and flexibility of the current design. It's possible to fit a 3.9 system to a 3.5-litre engine (or vice versa) without modification or re-mapping and achieve excellent results, although the ideal is to use the right system with the appropriate engine in order to achieve optimum performance and fuel economy.

Additionally, you will need at least one fuel filter that is best purchased new and you will need a fuel pump and may also feel this is best purchased new too.

Ford and Chevy systems will be available locally across the USA, and Rover specialists may have EFI systems. Possible additional sources are T and S Imported Automotive, which specialises in parts for and from UK cars and D+D Fabrications, the foremost aluminium engine specialist in the USA. In the UK you can try RPI

Engineering which is the UK's foremost Rover engine specialist and supplies turnkey engines complete with EFI to all corners of the world.

Reducing the height

Written with the Rover system mainly in mind, hopefully some of what follows will help you get your bonnet/hood closed over the Ford and Chevy variants. The first objective is to lose height from the

EFI system, which can be done, as photo 11-2-12 confirms, and, consequently, the car runs very well with a normal bonnet line. However, if you find that you still cannot shut the bonnet/hood then you will have to employ some of the emergency/standby options listed shortly.

The primary objective is explained photographically at 11-2-13-1 to 11-2-13-3. You may find drawing D11-3 (overleaf) helps to clarify my captions,

11-2-13-2 Stage two of the lowering exercise. Here, the un-machined unit is on the left and it is clear to see that we need to remove metal from the bottom of this top plenum chamber. How much? Start with 7mm and then proceed with caution for it is important not to remove so much metal that you break away the sealing edge it 'makes' with the central casting. You will possibly manage 9mm if you are prepared to run several lines of weld (alloy, of course) along the revised seal line and subsequently machine the seal face flat. However, we will presume a height reduction of 8mm in this component making an overall reduction of 26.5mm (18.5 + 8mm). From the photograph it will be noted that this machining process 'breaks into' the lower of the three tapped holes in this casting. The holes provide mountings for the idle speed stepper-valve and, in view of the light weight involved, most EFI conversions dispense with the lowest bolt and achieve a satisfactory seal with the remaining two. It will become obvious, but you will also need to unbolt and discard the water heating adapter from beneath the throttle housing.

11-2-13-3 The third comparison photo in this series shows the original on the left and the 26.5-28mm lower assembly on the right. It will come as no surprise to hear that the numerous fixing bolts are too long and will need to be reduced/replaced to effect this sub-assembly. The eight central casting to manifold bolts will be 15mm over length and the six top plenum bolts will prove 13mm too long.

but the work involves some very special machining of the eight inlet trumpets, the plenum chamber cover and the lower plenum chamber.

The secondary option is to raise the level of the bonnet/hood either by the purchase of an RV8 bonnet from your Rover dealer or to utilize a fibreglass reproduction MGC bonnet. We saw both pictorially in chapter 9. The MGC bonnet/

hood will need a secondary bulge but I think this actually improves the appearance compared to the basic MGC bonnet. However, this is a modification to a very visible part of the car which, consequently, needs to be carried out very professionally. If you do elect to raise the line of any bonnet, do ensure the additional bulge is in the same material as the original, otherwise unsightly cracking round the joint might

result after a period of heating/expanding and cooling/contracting.

Getting it & keeping it going

If you have a running EFI system, some of what follows is inapplicable. However, if you are restoring a non-runner it would be wise to test the main EFI components by substitution on a friends car. Do this one component at a time for the AFM, ECU and EAV (extra air valve – the EFI's choke or enriching method), all seen in picture 11-2-14. It is not practical to change every sensor nor the harness over but you are off to a solid start if you know that the main electronic and electro-mechanical parts operate as intended.

You can get the ECU tested for a modest sum – about £25 in the UK. Photos 11-2-15-1 to 11-2-15-3 (overleaf) give you an idea as to the complexity of these 'simple' on-board computers. I recommend professional testing unless you have been

11-2-14 For identification purposes, left to right, these are an AFM system AFM, ECU and EAV (extra air valve).

able to test it via a friend's functioning system or lucky enough to see your system running before you removed it from the car. In the UK, call ATP on 01543 467466 to locate your nearest bench test facility. You will either get a clean bill of health via a test procedure printout or you will get a fault diagnosis. Of course, the latter will not be welcome, but it is better to be sure the

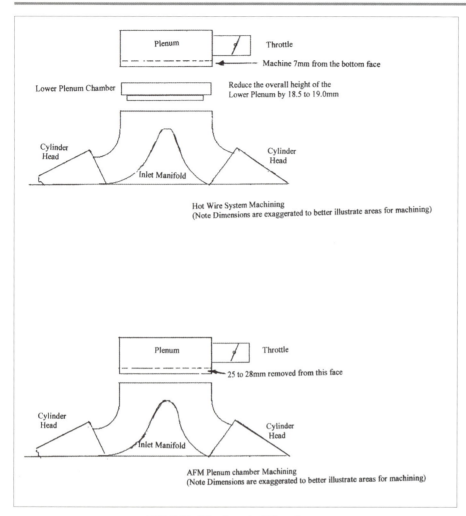

Plenum — Throttle

Machine 7mm from the bottom face

Lower Plenum Chamber

Reduce the overall height of the
Lower Plenum by 18.5 to 19.0mm

Cylinder Head

Cylinder Head

Inlet Manifold

Hot Wire System Machining
(Note Dimensions are exaggerated to better illustrate areas for machining)

Plenum — Throttle

25 to 28mm removed from this face

Cylinder Head

Cylinder Head

Inlet Manifold

AFM Plenum chamber Machining
(Note Dimensions are exaggerated to better illustrate areas for machining)

D11-3 Modifications to EFI systems.

11-2-15-1 A comparison between the ECU for an air flow system (left side) and the more complex but compact hot-wire on the right.

11-2-15-2 The air flow ECU looks complex enough but ...

11-2-15-3 ... in fact the miniaturization of the hot-wire ECU only increases one's respect for these units and, underlines the wisdom of getting yours checked before installation.

ECU, that is at the centre of your system, is in order before fitting it.

That said, it is air leaks and dirty connections that are the most common problems within any EFI set-up. As picture 11-2-16 illustrates, there are lots of opportunities for corroded or dirty plug/socket connections to cause erratic running. Air in the fuel or air leaks in the induction side of the system may not stop the engine from running, but one small leak is enough to stop the car running effectively.

However, if the car will not play at all it is likely that a dirty connection is the cause. There are many sensors, each with plug and socket connections, and it just takes one to stop the system or to cause quite disproportionate bad running. Consequently, it is vital that as you assemble your system you take meticulous care to ensure there are no air leaks and to clean every electrical connection. Fit new air hoses and clamps as a matter of course. Push every plug and socket together, pull them carefully apart and put them together again several times in order to ensure the best possible contact is made. The majority of sensors that feed information to the ECU do so by varying their resistance, so a dirty connection will almost certainly increase the resistance that the ECU 'sees', causing it to take inappropriate action and the car to run poorly if at all.

Most enthusiasts new to EFI expect/assume the majority of problems to emanate from the electronics generally and the ECU in particular. In fact, without

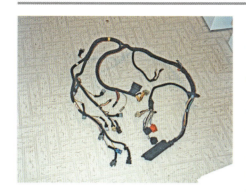

11-2-16 An EFI supplementary harness should be acquired from your donor in one piece – like this. Even if it is undamaged every end on this example connects to a socket that forms part of the injectors, sensors or potentiometers – so there are lots of opportunities for bad connections. Every bad connection will have to be resolved if the system is to give of its full and considerable potential.

moving parts to wear, the ECUs are amazingly reliable considering their age. What can cause ECU problems is water ingress (often the consequence of a damaged case) or dirty/corroded 35-pin plugs and sockets – sometimes brought about by water damage. Both require **gentle** warmth (e.g. the airing-cupboard) to dry them out, followed by some clipping and unclipping of the multi-pin plug to clean the contacts. Frequently that is sufficient to get you going. So, if you have not had yours checked, my suggestion is to presume your ECU is fine and that it is the information that it is receiving that is at fault and creating problems.

To take that theme stages further, if you have a problem, say over-fuelling, push the plugs in turn that fit onto two sensors (the temperature and thermo-time) and/or the extra air-valve. The temperature sensor is easily understood in that it is the automatic choke of an EFI system. Too low a temperature reading (whether real or the result of a faulty sensor or connection) will result in the ECU asking the injectors to stay open a bit longer to provide more fuel. If your pushing the connections tight

together brings about an improvement (it might take a few seconds) it is likely that the temperature sensor plug/connection is faulty. The thermo-time sensor performs a not dissimilar job except that it checks not only the coolant temperature but a time delay too. You will often find the time stamped on the body of the sensor – 15 seconds would be typical. Consequently, the thermo-time sensor's job is to further enrich the mixture for the first 15 seconds of running if the coolant temperature requires it. It should play no part in the proceedings when you are restarting a warm engine. The resistance within the sensors reduces as the temperature of the coolant increases – but a faulty connection increases resistance – hence the over-fuelling.

Nor are the connection problems confined to the simple sensors we have discussed. The air flow meter (AFM) or in later systems the Mass-meter each have a multi-plug that has to handle some tiny voltages, as does the throttle positioning sensor/potentiometer. Both cause untold and apparently unconnected problems. I was asked to look at one system where the fuel pump would not run unless the power feed from the EFI system was bypassed – where upon the system ran beautifully. Must be a fuel pump fault, right? The problem actually turned out to be a dirty connection on the air flow meter plug and socket. If the air flow meter fails to signal the ECU that air is passing through the meter, the ECU declines power to the fuel pump relay, so no fuel pump. Some switch cleaner on the plug and socket at the air flow meter fixed it in a few minutes. WD40 or Duck oil silicone sprays may be even better as they will delay the thin film of corrosion reforming.

Some electro-mechanical (i.e. moving) sensors are prone to dirt, corrosion and wear, thus generating inaccurate readings. The flapper air flow meter and the throttle position potentiometer are cases in point

and are particularly vulnerable to a build-up of corrosion if left unexercised for long periods, as might be the case in a non-running restoration project. I have highlighted them in pictures 11-2-17-1 and 11-2-17-2. They are mechanical in nature and thus the next most likely cause of problems. Use carburettor cleaner sparingly and work the mechanical movement gently in an effort to clean the sliding contacts and try again. If you are unsuccessful, service/exchange replacements are available but you are better to steer clear of main-dealers since replacements of this nature (as well as any replacement sensors you need) are much cheaper elsewhere. However, once you have found the (probable) problem it is vital that you avoid digging around inside the suspect unit – you will likely ruin a possibly

11-2-17-1 Arrow 1 focuses on the electro-mechanical throttle potentiometer and arrow 2 on the meter in this air flow system, while ...

11-2-17-2 ... the same numbering focuses on the same potential trouble spots in this hot-wire system, that, you will note, is actually fitted to an MG RV8.

repairable assembly beyond recall.

Finally, a couple of 'fine-tuning' suggestions applicable once you have your system running. An ultrasonic clean of each injector is highly recommended. Your nearest Lucas agent will carry out a service for about £15 per injector – which sounds a lot when multiplied up by eight but the results will be startling. I have never bothered to have my fifth injector, the cold start one, cleaned, but if you suspect yours is failing to completely close (i.e. it dribbles fuel), have that cleaned too. The air-cleaner for both systems can be improved to an advantage by fitting a K&N air-filter to the front of the air flow meter. It slips onto the front of either air meter as we saw in pictures 11-2-9 and 11-2-17-1 and will not upset the air/fuel balance but allow the air to be drawn into the engine far easier than through the original elements. The K&N filter has a much longer service interval too and never needs changing, just cleaning and re-oiling.

Tuning/power/torque changes in a OE EFI system are usually carried out by re-chipping the original ECU. It is very difficult for the experts never mind the amateurs to alter the pre-programmed ECUs so, with so much of the engine fuelling being left to the ECU, it is almost essential to fit an alternative performance-orientated chip. RPI sells Tornado chips for Rover engines and most aftermarket suppliers will have a similar suitable offering for your engine.

However, because the aftermarket EFI systems incorporate a re-programmable ECU, there is no need to change their chip – they are a truly DIY tuning systems.

EFI help and spares

In the UK there are three important EFI test, repair and spares specialists –
● ATP Electronic Development, Hednesford, Staffs (01543 467466, Fax 467426) is an ECU test and repair specialist.
● Car Electronic Services specialises in

'performance reconditioning' of EC's and has an excellent diagnostic website at www.carelect.demon.co.uk
● Fuel Parts UK, Worcs (01527 835555) specialises in the supply of replacement sensors and I suggest UK owners call for theirr nearest distributor if they need replacement sensors.

AFTERMARKET EFI

If you have an engine but no induction system there is now a real aftermarket EFI alternative to consider. The big advantage of the aftermarket systems are that you have some technical back-up if you strike difficulties. There are several makes available, one of which (an Edelbrock) can be viewed at picture 11-2-18, and each supplier will be able to supply a choice of numerous proven fuel maps, which gets you off to a great start. In fact, if you have a laptop computer and an interest in DIY tuning, the Holley Commander 950 injection system may be your induction of choice. The Edelbrock system is also tunable but it comes with its own stand alone programming unit so you do not even need a laptop.

Holley has prepared three-dimensional fuel-maps for each of the major EFI systems, engines and engine-tunes and you can download several and try each. All downloads are self-extracting ZIP-compressed files. At the time of

11-2-18 This is a multi-point aftermarket EFI system. Several makes are available, this being an Edelbrock on a Ford crate engine. Note the Ford's large diameter dizzy.

writing, thirteen new maps have just become available to cover the small-block Chevrolet engine combinations alone!

These maps are invaluable as a baseline for many engines. The base engine parameters must still be checked before the engine is started, because these may be different than yours (as these maps were generated for specific vehicles). Holley says that it is up to the customer to perform additional tuning for best operation and to ensure safe fuel and ignition timing levels. However, by selecting a map that closely resembles your engine specification you simplify the task of tuning your fuel-injection system.

Holley multi-point EFI systems are primarily intended for carburettor inducted, non-emission, non-computerized Chevrolet and Ford small block V8 engines. Available in kit form, they are engineered to provide all the components and hardware needed and include intake manifold, billet throttle body, billet fuel rails, injectors and related miscellaneous parts are partially pre-assembled and tested prior to packaging. Holley suggests that stock, crate or custom-built engines will benefit from multi-point fuel-injection system.

Throttle bodies are available in several styles and fit small block Chevys' 23° standard port heads (early and late) or Vortec cylinder heads and, as far as I could ascertain, all Ford small block V-8 engines. The sensors included in each kit are for throttle position, MAP, engine and air temperature, exhaust oxygen and idle air control motor and the wiring harness is designed for 'plug-in' installation.

Holley claims impressive torque and horsepower gains over standard carburation. However, this is not without control for it also says that its EFI offers superior idle, warm up and part-throttle driving characteristics along with improved fuel distribution, excellent throttle response and fuel economy.

The heart of any such EFI system is

a programmable ECU. The fact that it can easily be programmed provides the user with a high level of tuning flexibility. The Holley system allows for real-time tuning of all parameters via Windows based software and, I must say, sounds an exciting option for any V8 conversion.

EXHAUST SYSTEMS
Exhaust routes

We have explored the two exit routes of the exhaust manifolds/headers in earlier chapters. You do not need me to repeat the cooling benefits of the RV8-style system (through the inner wing/fender as seen in picture 11-3-1).

I have seen before and after dynamometer figures comparing block hugger and RV8 style systems on an otherwise unchanged 4000cc car. The RV8 'through the wing' exhaust delivered 13bhp more power. I also understand that the MGOC note fewer starter motor problems with the RV8-style exhausts.

You probably do not need me to dwell on the fact that there is usually insufficient space between the engine block and the MGB's frame-rails for adequately sized pipework for today's big capacity engines. Even so, there are some details to watch out for when buying exhaust manifold headers for your MGB conversion – possibly starting with whether you are going to install a single or twin exhaust system.

The exhaust manifold/header finishes, thus the exhaust system starts, after the 'Y'-junction that couples both manifolds together in a single-pipe exhaust system. Consequently, your manifold design is dictated by whether you are going for a single- or twin-pipe system. I prefer the out-of-the-way location (alongside the fuel tank) for a single-pipe system's silencer/muffler. There are actually two single pipe routes the first one emanates from block-hugger manifolds and follows the original V8 exhaust routing in that the right side

11-3-1 This looks like a four-into-two-into-one RV8 system. Note the extra material welded to the inner wing/fender to compensate for the structural strength lost when the inner wing was cut.

pipe is brought across the car to join with the left tail at a 'Y' piece junction adjacent to the gearbox. From there a singular pipe, of perhaps 2.25 or 2.5in diameter, follows the traditional MGB exhaust route down the left side of the car to the outside of the fuel tank and exits close to the left side overrider as shown in photo 11-3-2.

Pictured at 11-3-3, this route changes (to advantage) if you are using a pair of RV8 manifolds/headers yet retaining a single pipe systems because the 'Y' piece now moves further back under the car and thus the pipes present the sump and gearbox with less opportunity to absorb heat from the exhaust.

11-3-3 This single-pipe exhaust has the advantage of RV8 manifolds and allowing the exhaust to utilise the traditional MGB exhaust recess in the main body crossmember. Note the absence of clamps – this system just pushes together.

11-3-2 This might be said to be the traditional MGB V8 exhaust route. Note the undesirable proximity of the right side manifold to the engine sump, and the highly undesirable proximity of the brake pipe (running across the front crossmember) to two exhaust pipes!

However, the twin exhaust pipes seen in picture 11-3-4 allow the use of smaller individual pipes which slightly increases ground clearance, provided you are not obliged to position a pair of silencer/mufflers under the middle of the car. One Australian conversion resolved this problem by moving the fuel tank to the boot/trunk and locating the silencers/mufflers in the resulting void we see at 11-3-5 (overleaf). Generally, the twin pipe system reduces the exhaust system's twists and turns which helps the efficiency of the engine but necessitates centralizing the fuel tank (as

11-3-4 Twin exhausts make a wonderful noise but may need a balance pipe linking each system. However, although the diameter of the pipes is less than a single bore system, the twins do not release additional ground clearance unless they also utilise the recess in the crossmember.

we saw in photo 9-3-4).

The engine's efficiency is also determined by the diameter of the manifold/headers and the exhaust system – hence all the advertisements about free-flowing systems. Much of what the ads say is true but you need to keep two points in mind when buying an exhaust system are the use that you expect of the car and that (too) big is not necessarily beautiful. The use you expect to put the car to will determine the rpm range where you want the most torque most of the time. This dictates the diameter of the manifold tubing as, for your engine displacement and expected rpm, there will be an optimum tube diameter: too large a bore and the speed of the exhaust gases are slowed, the scavenging of the cylinders is impaired and the efficiency of your engine is not optimised. It is true that a smaller set of manifold pipes have a reduced maximum capacity of exhaust gases than large ones, but the exhaust in the smaller pipes moves faster and scavenges better. So, provided the capacity of the manifold is adequate for the gases generated by your expected rpm, small(er) may be better than too large a diameter.

There is no finite formulae I can give you to determine the optimum manifold pipe bore – you will have to rely on the experience of friends, advice from your club or the experience of a exhaust specialist. As a rough rule of thumb I would guess that a powerful road-going V8 will mainly operate between 2000 and 4000rpm and consequently will need 1.5in, possibly 1.6in primary tubes. Much larger and you'll lose the bottom-end torque that I think is such an enjoyable part of an MGB V8 conversion.

Whatever your engine, the more gentle and smoother the bends away from the cylinder heads the more effective the exhaust system. In this context, when looking at exhaust manifolds/headers, be sure there is no evidence of the 'necking'

11-3-5 This twin pipe silencer/muffler exhaust system is practical because the fuel tank now occupies the boot/trunk. Although we are focused upon exhaust systems, I cannot resist mentioning that this Chevy conversion is using a shortened Commodore axle with a 4.1:1 rear diff ratio – making acceleration very interesting! In fact, I understand first gear is never used and wheel-spin easily induced, even in fourth gear.

restrictions that occur when the tube is bent empty or filled with sand. You need exhaust manifold and pipework that has been bent using a mandrel – which reduces the necking to negligible proportions. Adopting the RV8-style exhaust manifolds/headers is particularly helpful as the manifold/headers exit through the inner wings thus minimising the radii and helping the smooth flow of escaping gases.

Acquiring a system

Pre-fabricated and well proven block-hugger and RV8 exhaust manifolds for Buick/Rover engines are available in both stainless and mild steel. If your funds permit, use stainless steel. They are available the UK from all the traditional V8 conversion specialists, Clive Wheatley (whose system is pictured at 11-3-6) and RPI Engineering. In the USA, D+D Fabrications can, amongst others, supply the traditional tubular manifolds/headers, in stainless or mild steel, as well as RV8 systems.

However, Ford and Chevy engines present the converter with a difficult choice. The volume is very low so there

is no prospect of pre-fabricated Chevy headers appearing in the marketplace in the near future. At the time of writing, one supplier is tooling up to make headers for Ford engines and hopefully by the time you read these words you will be able to buy some types of Ford headers from Coyote. A picture can be found at 11-3-7. The alternatives are to consign the car to an exhaust fabrication specialist – which would likely prove expensive – or make the headers yourself.

The Ford engine has a much wider lower block than Rover engines which more or less necessitates RV8-style headers. To get the best from these big capacity engines, long slow bends are really needed in about 1½in (40mm) diameter pipe. Unless very skilfully carried out, there is a danger that home made headers will require major surgery of the inner wing/fenders – which is not a good idea because these are an important structural part of the front of an MGB. Any major holes will therefore require re-enforcing and by more than the relatively minor re-enforcing rings used on Rover/RV8 inner wing/fenders. You inner wings/fenders may need re-enforcing with channel or square tubing.

When it comes to making the headers, you will need to start with some sort of pre-formed tubing, perhaps even a set of Hedman Hedders (Ford part number 88420) block-huggers in 1.5in (about

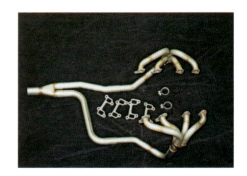

11-3-6 This picture of a Clive Wheatley RV8 manifold system is interesting as the system requires only two clamps.

11-3-7 These are the prototype Coyote Ford RV8-style headers. The production versions will be mandrel bent and, thus, not have the welds you see here.

38/40mm) diameter – which you will need to cut apart. Your priority is to preserve the flanges and find and earmark any tubes (on each side) that can be re-used without alteration. You will likely need more tubular bends sourced from your local fabricator, or using pre-bent aftermarket tubing from Summit (SUM-621002) or Headers by Ed in the US or Demon Tweeks in the UK.

Tacking the assembly together takes care if only because the flange will (almost certainly) warp and will need clamping at frequent intervals to a very heavy plate or bolting to an old cylinder head. Bearing in mind you are forming bespoke header(s) you are best to do the work in the engine bay – in which case use old heads on a plastic block for the initial tack-welds. As you proceed, be sure the spark plugs (and their wrench/socket access) have sufficient room and that there is space for the plug leads without them resting on the header.

One fabrication problem you will likely encounter when attaching new pipes to the stubs above the collector flange is that is not possible to weld completely around the fourth pipe. Larry Shimp tells me he solved this problem by cutting a triangular window in the pipe and welded the area from the inside. After completing the internal weld he welded the triangular section back in place on the outside.

Another tip from Larry is that fitting

and removing any exhaust system is easier if you use special smooth clamps seen in pictures 11-3-8 and 11-3-9. They do not crush the pipes when fitted and are available from Dave Bean Engineering, while SuperTrapp or Walker's Mega-Clamp will be found in Summit Racing's catalogue. Other sizes are available but for MGB V8 conversions. Summit's part numbers are:

WLK33228 – 2in diameter
WLK33229 – 2¼in diameter
WLK33240 – 2½in diameter

Finishing

If you do have to make your own manifold/ headers, they will look much better if nicely finished. There are numerous high-temperature paints available but there is no doubt that, if you can afford the cost, a company named Jet Coating could provide the best solution. Jet Coating apply several coating finishes but its 'Sterling' formula (seen in pictures 11-3-10 and 11-3-11, latter overleaf) can be applied to new or used parts and withstands temperatures up to 1300°F. This high-luster coating comes in silver, matt-black, blue and cast-iron grey and provides a brilliant appearance. Double-coating (inside and out) on manifolds/headers is possible and has obvious longevity advantages on headers.

Installation tips

It may surprise you to learn that not only do fabricated manifold/headers need to be

11-3-8 The larger of these clamps is from Walker while the small one comes from Dave Bean. SuperTrapp's version is more or less identical to Dave Bean's offering.

installed carefully, they also need to be run/ broken-in properly too if they are to enjoy a long warp and leak-free life. In an MGB with a Rover engine, it's a good idea to use cap or allen-headed set-screws for the bottom row of exhaust-manifold-to-head fixings and apply exhaust gasket sealant to **both** sides of each exhaust gasket. Buick/ Rover exhaust gaskets are obtainable from your Land Rover dealer, although Clive Wheatley holds some interesting dual gaskets, seen in picture 11-3-12.

If you decide not to use gaskets (many engines these days do not require gaskets), be sure that the faces of both cylinder head and manifold/header are absolutely clean before fitting the manifold/header for the first time. It helps if you can wire-brush, then Scotch Brite, and then de-grease both faces with thinners.

11-3-9 These work like exhaust clamps, but are stronger and made so that you can butt together the pipes.

11-3-10 These (Ford) headers were made at home but have been jet coated as was ...

11-3-11 ... this Oldsmobile/Rover header. The sump and engine mounting plate are also superbly Jet Coated too.

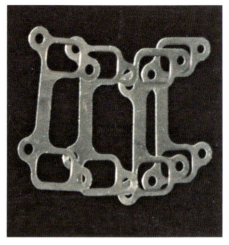

11-3-12 Clive Wheatley's twinned Rover gaskets which considerably quicken gasket orientation.

Even if you are to use bolts to secure the manifold, temporarily fit two appropriate studs at each end of the manifold. Coat round the holes in the flange with Permatex Ultra RTV Gasket Maker – which is good for 700°F but unfortunately not currently available in the UK. UK converters should use Loctite Ultra Copper RTV that is good to 375°C and available at most motor accessory shops.

Offer the manifold to the head and secure it there via the two outside studs. Fit a couple of central bolts, exchange the temporary studs, fit any outstanding fastenings and, from the centre each time, progressively and evenly bring the fastenings up to their final torque.

Start the engine for the first time and run it for just a few minutes before allowing it to cool completely. Re-torque the fastenings. The key to a reliable head/header seal is to get the engine tuned correctly as quickly as you can. Do not run the engine and certainly do not drive the car until you are sure the engine is running as well as it can. Get a mobile tuning with gas-analysing equipment done asap because an out-of-tune engine can run hot and warp/damage your fabricated manifolds/headers before you know it.

Once your are sure the tune is correct, drive the car gently initially for no more than 15 minutes and again allow the engine to completely cool before you re-torque the fastenings. Now you can drive the car a little more vigorously for 30 minutes, again, re-torque the fastenings once the engine is cold.

The final stage is to use the car normally but, once cold, check the manifold/header fastening torque after every run; keep doing this until there is no movement of the fastening each check. If leaks subsequently occur between the head and a manifold flange, it is heat that, directly or indirectly, is the primary cause and you need to search for and remedy any local or general overheating. A bespoke/custom copper gasket will help but involves a lot of work and, in the vast majority of cases, should not be necessary.

FURTHER READING

How to Build & Power Tune Holley Carburettors by Des Hammill (published by Veloce in the SpeedPro series) – Excellent advice on choosing and setting up Holley carburettors for individual applications, and a unique identification system for whole carburettors and individual components.

Holley Carburettor Handbook and *Holley Carburettors and Manifolds* by Mike Urich (published by HP Books) – Gives flow-rate calculations and advice on how to select the best Holley for your application. They are available from Summit in the US or John Woolfe Racing in the UK.

Super Tuning by Alex Walordy – Provides tuning information on Holley fuel-injection systems. Includes a section on Dominator® carburettors, Holley double-pumper and track tuning.

Holley Carburettors, Manifolds and Fuel-injection by Bill Fisher and Mike Urich – Covers election, installation and tuning information for a wide range of Holley carburettors.

Holley Carburettors Manual by Dave Emanuel – A guide to selecting, modifying and rebuilding 2- and 4-barrel Holley carbs.

Chapter 12
Ignition & tuning

All the best induction equipment in the world is useless if you cannot ignite the charge. An effective ignition system within any car is therefore important and I shall highlight some areas where your ignition system may be in need of upgrading.

THE IGNITION SYSTEM

The ignition system is one of the major causes of breakdown and under-performance in any motor car. The basic contact breaker design is now long in the tooth and although later Rover engines adopted the more modern contactless Opus electronic system. Sadly, the Opus system developed a reputation for unreliability and was superseded in SD1s after 1982 with the improved 'Constant Energy' system. Not surprisingly, today's engines are fired quite differently – the most modern run without a distributor and use numerous (not one) ignition coils. If you have the option of a V8 with these facilities, do make sure you grab it as a conventional ignition system is under some stress in a V8.

The inductive discharge system

We will look at a couple of tips as to how to make the Rover systems run a shade more reliably in a moment but you are probably best to upgrade the ignition system simultaneously or, at least, shortly after fitting the V8. It may help you understand the respective benefits of what's on offer if we initially refresh our minds as to the key components within the traditional inductive discharge ignition system and their respective weaknesses. The system works via a primary 12-volt circuit that connects our contact breaker points (seen in picture 12-1-1) and an ignition coil together. Power is fed from the ignition switch to one side of the coil, from the negative/contact-breaker side of the coil (negatively earthed cars) to the points and from the other contact on the points to earth. When the points are closed, current flows through this circuit and a magnetic field is generated within the coil, it is held there momentarily until the distributor's cam opens the points.

12-1-1 The contact breaker points are all-important to an ignition system but are susceptible to neglect, wearing of the heel of the plastic cam follower, and burning (and that's before we start on bounce and other undesirables). They really are best changed for the much more reliable breakerless versions.

The primary (12-volt) circuit is broken and the high-tension voltage within the coil's secondary winding looks for a discharge route-provided by the high tension lead to the distributor cap and via the rotor arm to one plug lead. The appropriate spark plug provides the final route to earth, asking the voltage to jump a small gap and generate a spark within the cylinder.

An elaborate cycle, all the more impressive when one thinks that at 3000rpm this has to occur 200 times per second in an eight cylinder engine. Each opening and closing of the points generates an additional small low-tension spark which in isolation, is of no consequence. However, over 100 hours (6000 miles at 60mph) and at circa 200 times per second, it is understandable that these sparks will eat at our contact breaker points and wear will take place. The erosion of the points is slowed down dramatically by the installation of a condenser (a small capacitor) which will reduce low-tension sparking at the points. This is a bonus as the primary purpose of the condenser is to speed the cut-off of primary current across the coil. Without the condenser, the decay-time would be too protracted, which reduces the secondary voltage discharge and therefore the size of the high-tension spark. Without a condenser the ignition system is unable to induce a spark and your engine will not run.

Put like that it's a wonder it ever works at all! However, as one gets into further detail, there is more to concern those who seek reliable high performance. The coil needs about 15 milliseconds to reach its peak magnetic saturation and, in fact, has insufficient time to reach full saturation above 1000rpm in an eight cylinder engine. This explains the use of multi coil ignition systems in some modern and high performance classic cars.

Optimising the timing

In general terms, whatever your engine and its state of tune, remember that in most cases the fuel you are now using is quite different from that available when the car was first built and the original tuning manuals written. Further, you have probably

modified your engine, carburation and exhaust system – all of which makes the original manual's timing settings redundant. A well-modified engine should burn fuel more efficiently than a standard engine and consequently need a flatter/earlier advance curve. This means that you need less degrees of advance as compared to an unmodified or standard engine as the rpm increases. Consequently, having most likely spent quite large sums of money (anything over £50 is 'quite large' to my mind!) on the engine and its ancillaries, you really are best consigning the final tuning task to someone with expertise, a rolling-road and gas analysing equipment. They will be able to alter the position of the advance curve and use the power/torque information from the rolling road print-outs to confirm that they are on the right track. There is no point, to my mind, in spending cash on new parts, let alone a complete new ignition system, if you have not yet made the best of what you already have. Since few readers will have a rolling road tucked into the corner of their garage, let's look at ways to optimise your existing system at home and without a rolling road. If you are still dissatisfied with your results afterwards and are confident that what you have is giving of its best, then by all means then go out with cheque book in hand.

Most standard ignition advance arrangements are not aggressive enough and, particularly with modified engines, are usually missing an opportunity to get the most from the engine. Clearly you can damage your engine by being too aggressive, but that does not mean we have to be overly conservative. There are two key parts to the ignition advance curve, the 'static' (starting) and the 'all in' (fully advanced) points. Lets start with the static point for any advance curve – the number of degrees the ignition fires btdc (before top dead centre) on tick over/idle. The reference point is always, of course, 'number one' cylinder, and the

first crucial point to note here is that there is no common way by which the various manufacturers number their cylinders or firing order.

The reference books will tell you your engine should fire 4 or 6 or 9° btdc depending upon which book you are reading and the engine in question. Certainly those suggestions will have been written in good faith and on the basis of experience, but, even so, they cannot take all the factors related to your engine into account. Camshafts are very different today too, while, furthermore, yours would not be the first engine to have its front pulley married to the crankshaft with the timing marks out of position. I have heard of the outer part of a front pulley turning slightly on the inner-damping ring which, needless to say, alters the accuracy of the timing marks somewhat. So I suggest you first check the accuracy of the timing marks by using a plastic probe in cylinder number one to note when the piston reaches TDC. An inactive area of about four degrees will usually be seen, when the probe seems not to move. With a little back and forth movement of the crank these two extremities can usually be found and marked on the pulley. The mid-position between these two points is actual TDC and if you find the original timing marks on the pulley are out of position, then you also need to adjust the timing pointer/finger accordingly. Thereafter use the best reference of the lot – your engine – to set the starting point for your timing curve.

With high-powered cars, the initial part of the following suggestion will be difficult due to the wheelspin that will likely result! You may consequently have to focus more on the 40-70mph acceleration tests that follow later. Nevertheless, have fun trying – perhaps on a test track somewhere. Get the engine nice and warm and slacken off the distributor clamp to allow you to turn the body of the dizzy both ways. Start the engine and let it tick over/

idle while you initially retard the ignition to about 3° btdc and then gradually advance the timing 1° at a time for as long as the idle revolutions per minute are increasing and the engine is running sweetly. When you go past the optimum point, the engine will start to sound harsh and the rpm will reduce slightly – at that point retard the timing by a couple of degrees and watch the rpm reduce by about 50/75rpm from its optimum. Re-clamp the distributor, stop the engine and after a couple of minutes, re-start it to ensure that indeed it does start, that it still sounds sweet and that it drives nicely. If you have a stroboscopic timing light you will probably find you have set the static advance at about 10° btdc depending on engine, compression, fuel and camshaft.

With a stopwatch (your wristwatch is not accurate enough) do some acceleration trials by timing 0-30mph, 0-50mph, 0-70mph – all from a standing start with you accelerating as rapidly as possible through the gears to 30/50/70mph as the case may be. Although not of primary interest just now, nevertheless you could also do a couple of 40-70mph acceleration tests solely in top gear and record the times. The purpose/value of the 40-70mph results will become clear during a second round of timed tests designed to establish what suits your engine as far as its ideal 'all in' advance point. However, we still have a little groundwork to do, so using a strobe light, we need to establish at what rpm the mechanical advance ceases and what the that maximum advice point is. You will probably best achieve this with a partner sitting in the car increasing the engine rpm in say 250rpm increments while you watch the timing marks on the crankshaft pulley with the strobe-light. In fact you will probably need to mark the crank pulley with additional spots at about 10° intervals. Your results should show something like a maximum of 20° of further advance (i.e. 30° total) at 3400 rpm.

Moving on to the second set of timed tests – we are going to run a series of 40-70mph timed tests in top gear and progressively advance the static timing a couple of degrees each time. You should see the 40-70mph times gradually diminish as you complete each run. Your static timing will, of course, become progressively over-advanced and, as a consequence, your 0-30/50/70mph times will get worse and the engine will probably tick over/idle a bit on the rough side. Not to worry, that will correct itself as soon as we reset the static timing at the end of our 40-70mph tests. After perhaps four 40-70mph runs, the elapsed time will start to start to increase again (as you pass the optimum point of maximum advance) and you need to revert the distributor to the optimum 'all in' setting, do a check run, find a parking spot and do a few calculations.

Let us say that your ideal static advance was 10° but that you have subsequently advanced that by a net 6° during the 40-70mph tests. We established that the distributor mechanical advance was 20° but we could now check that by removing the cap and base plate and looking at the centripetal advance weights. They should, at least in our example, show 10°, which would confirm our strobe observations since crankshaft advance is always twice dizzy advance. So we can now figure out our ideal 'all in' advance figure, which would be (6° + 20°) 26° beyond the ideal static point – thus 36° btdc. Now you can revert the static figure to its ideal 10° btdc and tighten the dizzy's clamp while we figure out what to do next.

Chances are that, with a standard distributor, your maximum advance is not being fully applied before about 3400/3500 rpm. Fully advanced at 3200rpm would be more acceptable but still rather conservative – at least for a modified engine. Cars with very aggressive cams may be an exception, but most cars' maximum advance should be in place by

the time you are at about 3000rpm. Some might say that the all-in-rpm should be even earlier than that; in any event, you need to buy and fit some weaker springs for your distributor's weights. Weaker springs allow the distributor's weights to swing out earlier – which moves the top of the shaft earlier and introduces the advance curve earlier. Finding the best springs at home is a bit of trial and error fun using your 40-70mph times as your guide/measure. Try the car before and after you change the springs, if no improvement is noted either change back to the original springs or try different springs – until you feel you have optimised the ignition system you already have.

You may find your engine starts to pink/detonate after the full-advance point which would suggest your total advance is too great. This is not very likely with a 10° advance distributor (advancing the crankshaft by 20°) but with a high compression engine (say 10:1) it is possible when the distributor offers more degrees of advance. In such cases you will wish to advance it earlier using softer springs while restricting the amount of total mechanical advance. You can do this in a very simple and (initially) easily reversible way. The pillars, arrowed in picture 12-1-2, to which the springs are attached also act as a stop to prevent the balance weights swinging out further than their 10° (or 13° or whatever) of allotted advance. If you slip a short length of $^3/_{16}$in (4.8mm) i/d tube over the stop-pillar you will, in effect, restrict the movement of the weight by the wall-thickness of the tube you choose. A typical restriction would be $^1/_{16}$in (1.5mm), which requires you use $^5/_{16}$in o/d tube. In the experimental stage plastic tubing will be fine for a few tests until you get it right whereupon you need to adopt a more permanent solution. A piece of steel tube turned up to your needs is fine, but it must then be hardened – whereupon you can forget it, as it will last for years. Most tuners looking to restrict the advance will put a blob of hard mig weld on the weight to restrict its swing. You do need hard mig wire, however, which is rarely found in the home workshop.

Less likely, but conversely, you may feel you are not getting enough total advance. Perhaps you have the curve now coming in early enough but feel your 40-70mph acceleration times would improve with a little more total advance. They are hardened, so you will need a lick with an angle grinder, but a sliver off the face of the balance weight will allow it to move that bit further, thus increasing the total advance. Only take a sliver off each time and, if you go too far, build back some of the face with a blob of hard mig. However, with all that before you, you will perhaps appreciate why I said it is ideally a job for rolling roads.

Some specifics may help you identify what to do if:

● The engine is reluctant to spin over or is simply 'locked'. The timing is (far) too advanced and the piston is, in effect, trying to be pushed backwards.

● The engine regularly hesitates to spin when you turn the key but then fires straight away – it is less extreme, but still probably too far advanced.

12-1-2 There are two pillars, both with small control springs attached. You can accelerate the advance by fitting weaker springs, delay it by fitting stronger springs, and restrict the advance by welding a blob to the edge of the weight or fitting a tubular stop to the pillar.

● You get pinking/pinging when you put your foot to the floor in a high gear (the higher the better the test) you are probably too far advanced.

● The engine performs poorly, probably with an initial 'flat spot', it is probably retarded.

Slightly retarded is safest since you will do no damage to the engine from the timing although over advanced can cause damage.

If you are fitting an electronic advance curve you will need to secure the existing base plate within the distributor with one that does not slide. This is easiest accomplished by fixing the sliding top 'half' to the fixed bottom plate with a very small self-tapping screw. However, it is important that you first find the correct relationship between top and bottom plates such that the spark is triggered just when the front edge of the rotor-arm covers the cap's contact. Drill a hole in an old cap at the front end of a contact and watch and adjust until its right – then secure the top base to the bottom one.

The vacuum advance diaphragm is virtually inoperable during acceleration testing since there is very little manifold vacuum available to move the diaphragm. Consequently, you are well to leave the vac pipe connected. However, it is worth noting that on cruise, manifold vacuum levels do increase and the diaphragm can advance the timing by a further 10°/15°, dependent upon the diaphragm in place in your car, with little performance benefit but perhaps an extra 2-4mpg.

Drawing D12-1 summarises a typical change in advance curves. With a mechanical (i.e. expanding weight) advance system, the advance-curve is, in fact, a straight-line. This is a major disadvantage when compared to modern-day electronic mapping since the mechanical method necessitates that the spark's advance is always a compromise. Electronic systems have no restrictions and the advance-

curves are true curves, with the advance changing three-dimensionally and often quite dramatically to ensure the optimum advance in almost any circumstance. We will look at electronic engine-management in a little more detail shortly but, for the time being, we are confined to mechanical/straight line curves and have advanced it as a result of:

● Moving the static advance from, say, 10° to 14° btdc (moves start of line upward by 4°).

● Fitting weaker springs to allow a faster rate of advance (slightly sharper inclination to the line).

● Adding weld or spacers to limiting the movement of the advance weights (curtails revised curve by 2°).

IMPROVING YOUR EXISTING SYSTEM

Ford distributors come in two diameters. The small diameter (picture 12-2-1-1) is about the same as a normal Rover distributor and will be what you have to fit if you are planning a Low Rider 14in diameter air cleaner. However, the alternative seen at 12-2-1-2 is about 50 per cent larger in diameter.

Situated at the front of the engine as they are, aside from diameter, the height of the Ford distributors can be a problem. A Mallory 'twin-points' distributor can be fitted but offers little benefit in terms of height and, in fact, necessitates moving the MGB bonnet/hood crossmember. The best solution is to fit a shorter distributor and currently Crane make the shortest/lowest distributors. Crane's model 1600 uses a large diameter cap, while model 1601 uses a small cap; both models have the advantage of using electronics to program the advance curve. In fact the torque & power curves we see at drawing D12-2 are from a Ford 302 using a Crane 1601 distributor after a couple of preliminary advance curves were discarded. The electronic ignition programming eliminates

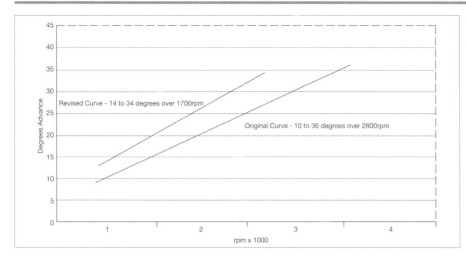

D12-1 Typical examples of original and revised advanced curves.

(graph labels: Revised Curve - 14 to 34 degrees over 1700rpm; Original Curve - 10 to 36 degrees over 2600rpm; y-axis: Degrees Advance; x-axis: rpm x 1000)

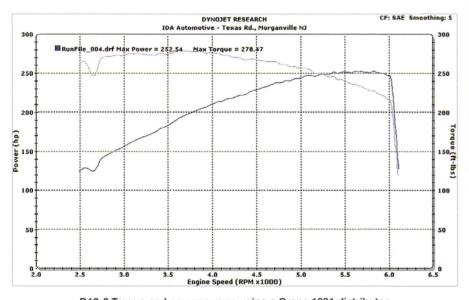

D12-2 Torque and power curves using a Crane 1601 distributor.

(graph: DYNOJET RESEARCH — IDA Automotive - Texas Rd., Morganville NJ — CF: SAE Smoothing: 5 — RunFile_004.drf Max Power = 252.54 Max Torque = 278.47 — Power (hp) / Torque (ft-lbs) vs Engine Speed (RPM x1000))

12-2-1-1 The smaller of the two Ford dizzies is necessary if you plan a large air cleaner ...

12-2-1-2 ... while the larger is much the better option from a performance point of view, particularly if you are using one of the high-performance ignitions systems discussed later in this chapter.

the centrifugal advance mechanism and allows for a significantly lower distributor. With such a distributor you will also need to fit a modern ignition system (possibly a capacitive-discharge, discussed shortly).

Whatever distributor you use on your Ford engine, be sure that the cam gear is correct for the cam used. The roller cams generally need steel gears, with bronze for the other designs. Gears are available separately from the distributor manufacturer if, for example, you buy a used distributor with the wrong gear.

Buick/Rover engines are not without their distributor problems – although I have never heard of a properly installed Rover engine having problems getting the bonnet/hood closed over the distributor. However, the eight cam lobes can cause the original contact breaker points to bounce and we will explore ways to eliminate this problem very shortly. The vacuum advance diaphragm also seems particularly prone to failure. It seems hard to believe that

it is not completely impervious to fuel vapour but Rover, and I understand other manufacturers too, now fit a trap in the vacuum line. Having had several vacuum diaphragms fail, I recommend you fit one.

Rover distributors are easily identified by their code numbers, 35 being the prefix for all V8 distributors and originally meant 3500cc. D is always the next letter but it is the subsequent letters that provide the detailed identification. E related to Opus systems, M signifies early constant energy systems with separate remote amplifier. LM signifies the later constant energy system with the module on the distributor body.

12-2-2 The latest Constant Energy ignition systems mounts the amplifier on the side of the Rover distributor (arrowed here). However, there is also nothing to stop you replacing the Opus system with a modern electronic ignition trigger – discussed shortly.

Lastly all distributor numbers end with an 8, signifying 8 cylinders. So the listing shows ...

35D8 = points distributor

35DE8 = Opus distributor

35DM8 = Constant Energy – remote amplifier

35DLM8 = Constant Energy – distributor mounted module (including Land Rover remote conversions referred to on the next page)

The Lucas electronics system fitted to the SD1 and subsequent Rover engines was certainly better than the contact breaker points system it succeeded but has a reputation for being less than 100 per cent reliable. It still uses a vacuum advance diaphragm but an electronic (Hall-effect) trigger replaces the contact breaker. Perhaps because of its reliability questions there are various versions (I think, four) of Opus & Constant Energy ignition systems. This means that if you are to use the system, you need to get everything from one donor vehicle. Ironically, the latest

system, which you would think the best option, had a small black plastic amplifier mounted on the side of the distributor body. An example can be seen at 12-2-2. These proved unreliable in heat – which is unfortunate in an MGB V8 conversion because under-bonnet temperatures are definitely elevated. However, Land Rover recognised the problem and issued a modification kit (still available, I believe) which you should fit if you have one of these distributors because it allows you to move the amplifier to a cooler location, as seen in picture 12-2-3.

We all realise that the contact breaker points within the distributor wear or burn over the course of 5000/6000 miles and need replacing. From my earlier paragraph, we now, I hope, understand why this wear takes place and why the contact breaker gap (which was so frustrating to get right

12-2-3 This is a late Lucas Constant Energy system with the separate AB17 amplifier acting as a saddle for the coil. Both amp and coil are mounted away from the engine heat with the mounting plate also acting as a heat sink. In contrast to the earliest Lucas electronic systems, this is an effective and very reliable system with operating principles that are exactly the same as those used on modern engine management systems.

in the first place) opens with use. An additional disadvantage of contact breaker points is that they bounce at modest revs with a V8 largely due to the eight lobes they need to negotiate every revolution. It's the 'heel' of the points that follow the distributor's cam that bounce causing misfiring and lost performance. Most of us fit 'sports' coils with a slightly lower primary coil resistance (in the region of 2.9 to 3.0ohms). These improve our sparks and help starting and road-going performance, but how many realise this step reduces the life of our distributor's 'points' – albeit slightly. The normal coil has a primary resistance of 3.1 to 3.5ohms so the current through the coil (and also across the points) is slightly increased. Consequently there is a lot to be said for replacing the points and condenser with a retro-fitted breakerless system, and, with numerous systems to chose from, we had better explore some options.

RETRO-FITTING BREAKERLESS SYSTEMS

For eight cylinder cars, the argument for electronic ignition is strong. The more lobes on the distributor cam, the more difficult it is to control the points and, in particular, stop them from bouncing at medium and high revs. The modern electronic ignition systems offer advantages in that bounce is eliminated and maintenance reduced. Many owners will see the latter as a significant benefit since the points and their associated condenser are prone to unreliability.

The main body/spindle assemblies of Rover distributors are becoming very scarce and, regardless of the spindle bearing wear, need to be kept safe. In fact, most bearings in the body of the distributor are worn resulting in some side-play in the shaft. With a normal contact-breaker ignition this generates inaccuracies in timing. The systems we are exploring

12-2-4 A typical external amplifier module, in this case a Newtronic one, which marries to the ...

12-2-5 ... Newtronic chopper disc fitted to the cam that once opened and closed the contact breaker points. Incidentally, this is my TR6 six-cylinder set-up.

12-2-6 A (four-cylinder) Lumenition system as you might receive it. An outline as to ease of fitting is included in the main text.

12-2-7 Currently the most compact of the breakerless ignition systems available is the Alden 'Igniter' we see here. Alden systems are known as 'Pertronix' in the USA.

all render shaft-play inconsequential, regardless of the make of distributor, and thus rejuvenate all but the most worn distributors.

There are two types of system – magnetic and optical. Both systems use an amplifier (a typical one is at 12-2-4) to turn a minuscule initial pulse into something that is sufficiently powerful to switch the coil on and off in the same way as the contact breaker has done for years. However, it is the way that initial pulse is generated that separates the two systems. The magnetically activated systems have eight tubular equi-spaced magnets fitted inside a circular disc. The disc is fitted over the cam that once opened the points. A sensing module fitted to the distributor's base-plate produces a tiny electrical pulse every time a magnet passes. The optical systems use a chopper-disc, again mounted over the same cam, but these discs have eight slots to 'chop' an infrared beam passing between a light-emitting diode and a silicon phototransistor – and you can see a shot of my Newtronic disc in picture 12-2-5. In this system it is the transistor mounted on

the base-plate that generates the initial electrical pulse.

The latest breakerless types of aftermarket system that are available are also changing with amazing speed. Cambridge Motor Sport, like all our contributors, can offer systems from Aldon, Lumenition (picture 12-2-6), Newtronic (seen at 12-2-4 and 12-2-5) or Petronix but currently favours Alden's Igniter system because, as you'll see from picture 12-2-7, it fits within the distributor body/cap without the need for external amplifiers. The Igniter system looks a little like a mini-cassette and, like all these systems, is very easy to fit. It is magnetically activated (my preference too) and completely replaces the points and condenser arrangement. These latest ignition systems require nothing further than a couple of wires connected to the coil. Costs vary dependent upon manufacturer and the type of system but think in terms of £50 to £150.

A couple of installation tips may help you when fitting electronic ignition, although you will need to read and follow the installation instructions applicable to your particular system carefully. They are mostly, to the best of my knowledge, only suited for negative-earth/ground cars. If your (early) MGB is positive ground you can still explore some of Aldon's equipment but you may be best postponing this

improvement until the car is negatively earthed.

The vast majority of electronic systems can be fitted with the distributor in situ, but there is much less reaching down into the engine (and less chance of dropping a screw) if the distributor is first removed to your workbench. You will need to align a cut-out on the new system's disc with the cam on the distributor shaft. Obviously it is important to connect the new system's wires precisely according to the manufacturer's instructions – but it is also essential that the actual electrical terminations are meticulously connected to their respective wires. Crimp all those that you are required to do yourself very tightly, solder them well and make sure they are all professionally insulated with a proper 'Boot'. A wrap of insulation tape is ok for a test-run, but it will unravel as soon as it gets hot and could leave you stranded.

HIGH-TENSION IGNITION COMPONENTS

If you want the best performance from your car, it is very important to use top-grade, high-tension ignition components. The distributor cap, plugs, high-tension leads and coil are all equally and vitally important to both the short term good performance of the car and its ongoing reliability. We will look progressively through these components but for the majority of readers the distributor will be in place at the end of the exercise and therefore the distributor cap retains its vital place in our high-tension chain. Reactions and experiences are mixed as far as distributor caps are concerned. Most have had no problems with any make of cap while others are convinced there is trouble around the corner if you use anything other than a genuine OE cap. I always pay the extra and use genuine Lucas on my Rover engines and have never had a problem.

Spark plugs

The spark plugs and ignition leads can have quite an influence on a car's performance and both warrant our close attention. We mostly take spark plugs for granted but the standard design can affect the issue via their temperature and many may not appreciate that the concept has been improved via Multi-Earth Electrodes – which we will look at shortly. First, let's spend a few moments brushing-up on one or two of the subtleties of the traditional single electrode spark plug since there is little point in improving the engine and then fitting the wrong plugs. Such a step may nullify your best efforts and result in expensive damage.

There are numerous modifications that will not affect the spark plug selected. If you plan no more than a change of air-filter, inlet manifold, exhaust manifold/ header silencer/muffler or distributor then it is unlikely you will need to consider a change of spark plug. However, if you increase your engine's compression ratio, change the cylinder head configuration, introduce a gas-flowed head or change the pistons, then a change of spark plug may be helpful. Modifications that increase the compression ratio are likely to generate more power and with more power comes more heat which may necessitate the spark plug removing more heat than was the case in the engine's original configuration. Thus it is usual to fit a 'colder' plug as an engine's level of tune is increased. We will need to check symptoms but in this circumstance you might be well advised not only to fit colder plugs but also to adjust the plug gaps to take account of the denser mixture that is the consequence of increasing the compression ratio.

So what are the symptoms that signal a change to a colder plug should be considered? Pre-ignition is the simple answer, for this **might** be the consequence of the spark plug tip getting too hot and acting as a hot/pre-ignition source. Assuming you have raised your compression, that there are no other causes of your pre-ignition and that you are not experiencing plug fouling, then a plug that conducts more heat away from the tip is worth trying, and the next 'colder' plug should reduce tip temperatures by 75/80°C. In any event, it is better to run with too cold a plug than too hot a one. The worst that can happen with too cold a plug selection is that your plugs will foul-up. On the other hand, too hot a plug will result in pre-ignition which can cause serious engine damage, so study your plugs closely for signs of silver or black specs, melting or breakage at the tip, any of which signal pre-ignition problems.

If you are experiencing plug fouling problems following engine modifications do study the plugs closely and do not be too quick to fit a hotter plug. True a hotter plug will conduct less heat away from the tip, and will therefore run at a higher temperature thus burning off more of these deposits but you first need to assure yourself that there are no alternative problems requiring your attention before hotter plugs are fitted, particularly if you have already raised the combustion temperatures by increasing your compression ratio. The type of deposit/fouling can vary and needs to be reviewed: heavy, dry, black deposits can suggest an overly rich mixture and potential carbonation problems, retarded timing, or simply too wide a plug gap; wet, black, oily deposits can indicate a leaking head gasket or piston ring/valve-stem problems. The latter may not necessarily be serious if you have just rebuilt the engine, for some gentle running/breaking in (with the correct oil) may improve the situation. There are lots of alternatives to consider before you resort to a hotter plug. Incidentally, it is very difficult to thoroughly clean the insulator within a fouled spark plug and so the plug is unlikely to be fully recoverable and is best replaced.

The spark plug gap warrants further discussion. Bear in mind that a spark plug is made for many applications and so the gap set at the factory during manufacture may well be a very popular setting, but may, in fact, not be correct for even your standard engine nevermind your uprated one. So start with the OE recommended gap, remembering that insufficient gap can cause pre-ignition while too wide a gap can generate misfires, loss of power and poor economy, as well as the problems mentioned in the previous paragraph. If you have raised the compression from OE spec you could reduce the gap by about 0.002/0.003in or if you have fitted a high-powered ignition system you can open the gap by about the same amount. In other words, if you have both raised your compression and fitted a high-powered ignition system you should stick to the recommended OE gap setting. If in doubt, always use a slightly wider gap in preference to a slightly smaller one, thereby reducing the risk of pre-ignition.

A final detail for those switching to EFI or engine management systems – i.e. systems controlled by an on-board computer – particularly if you experience erratic idling, misfire at high rpm, engine run-on or abnormal combustion. Stray voltages from your ignition system may confuse your electronics and the fitting of resistor spark plugs can improve that situation. A resistor plug has a resistor built into the core, and is also used to reduce radio interference, making little or no difference to your engine's performance.

Now all you need to know is how to select hotter or colder plugs. I wish I could report a standard system for plug grading, but since there is no uniformity between manufacturers we will look at two contrasting examples and leave you to establish the specifics for your preferred brand. The concept is simple, one group of manufacturers uses a higher number to denote a colder plug. The popular NGK brand uses this system and as, an example, its BP6 plugs are the next colder plug to their BP5. On the other hand, Bosch uses a lower number to denote a colder plug.

Finally, we must look at the newest design of spark plug available, the multiple-earth electrode plug, and its benefits. The design is not in fact that new as VW was using a triple electrode plug on production cars from the early 1980s but the multi-earth plugs are now widely available and are introduced to benefit users of standard ignition systems in two ways. We will explore these in a moment, but first what is a multiple earth electrode spark plug? A photograph probably best illustrates them

and picture 12-3-1 compares the traditional single electrode plug with a 4-electrode replacement. The first benefit offered by such plugs is one of performance. You will appreciate the traditional design slightly shrouds each plug's spark from the incoming air/fuel mixture but the multi earth design does not. Did I notice a difference? In truth, I have not noticed a major leap in engine performance. I have only used the new plugs for a short period as yet and suspect that the performance benefit may be in the latter part of a traditional plug's life. The multi-electrodes are supposed to remove more heat from the plug, to keep the electrodes cooler and to fire more effectively in difficult combustion conditions. The second benefit is longer life for the newer spark plugs possibly with less drop-off in performance. The multi-electrodes allow the electrical spark to choose its route to earth. It will always select the nearest earth electrode ... until that electrode wears where upon the spark will select an alternative route to earth. This clearly extends the life of the plug. Whether it will be a four times longer life remains to be seen but I hope so as the newer design costs over twice the cost of a traditional spark plug. Most major manufacturers make this design now and, depending on the manufacturer, they are available with two, three or four earth electrodes.

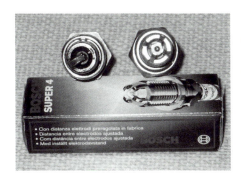

12-3-1 The improvement made to even the common spark plug is evident here, with the newer four earth version on the right.

These plugs may not be suited to capacitive discharge (i.e. very high voltage) ignition systems and you should **check with the respective manufacturers** of both your intended ignition system and spark plug before marring the two together.

However there are even more advanced high performance plugs now available with Platinum or Iridium electrodes. These are designed for better heat conduction but offer huge advances in longevity – albeit at much higher individual cost. Some platinum plugs have a 60,000 mile life and whilst they will last perfectly well for this and longer distances, there are performance/cold and damp starting/fuel economy advantages in replacing them at half that. Nevertheless, 30,000 miles is still quite some distance. However, that pales into insignificance when compared to the modern Ford V8 engine fitted to the MG ZT 260 where the platinum plugs fitted as standard have a 90,000 mile change point!

Like any chain, the overall strength is only as good as the weakest link, so we cannot overlook that which ties our super ignition system together – the possibly not-so-super ignition leads.

The plug leads

Like the spark plug, the plug lead has changed dramatically in the last few years. The sillicone based lead has completely taken over from the now obsoloete copper and carbon cored leads, but for any form of ultra fast road or competitive use an induction wound core is recommended. There are several grades and, for that matter, several manufacturers. For conventional coil ignition systems 7mm high-tension leads are probably satisfactory, although the 8mm size is better still. For those with some of the more sophisticated ignition systems we have yet to discuss in fast road use you are advised to use 8mm leads while 8.5mm leads are probably best for ultra fast road and competitive applications. You will appreciate that the larger the lead, the greater the conductivity and the better the resultant sparks.

Magnecor is one of several manufacturers that make ignition cables suited to any ignition system that has been upgraded. In fact, V8s with the standard ignition systems may benefit from their superior grade 7mm and 8mm cables/leads. These leads are specifically designed and constructed to conduct the maximum output generated by the ignition system to the spark plugs and to provide suppression for radio frequency and electro-magnetic interference. The 7mm and 8mm cables incorporate a ferrimagnetic core for radio suppression, a 2mm chrome-nickel 120 turns per inch winding designed to provide magnetic suppression, and a capacitive reserve to help ignition coils regenerate at high engine revolutions. Insulation is via an EPDM insulator with fibreglass reinforcement all covered by a high strength, high-temperature-resistant silicone rubber jacket. The 7mm cable jacket is designed to withstand 400°F (190°C) and the 8mm cable jacket some 450°F (210°C). This manufacturer claims that when used on older, worn engines or engines operating in extreme cold or hot ambient temperatures, easier starting and improved running under load will be noted. Further, the 8mm leads will resolve many of the problems usually exacerbated by the installation of many high-energy aftermarket ignition systems. Magnecor suggest that some engine modifications subject the standard ignition leads to extra heat that can destroy non-silicone insulated cables.

There are 8.5mm and even 10mm leads available for the competitors. Magnecor's KV85 Competition (8.5mm) and R-100 Racing (10mm) Ignition Cables are designed for racing applications and/or where ignition cables are required with a heat resistance in excess of 450°F.

All Magnecor components, including cable, speciality terminals, boots and crimping tools are available separately should you want to make your own ignition leads up.

Charging the ignition coil

The standard ignition coil is quite suitable for standard cars enjoying no more than spirited road use, although you would be wise to at least upgrade to a Lucas Gold, Bosch Red, Bosch Blue or Aldon Flame Thrower coil for fast road use. Of these, the Bosch Blue is probably the most potent, generating some 47,000 volts and consequently necessitates a breakerless ignition trigger. However, the coil's recharge constraints explored earlier remain a weakness, at least for the ultra fast road and competitive cars, even with all the above high-tension improvements in place. You will recall that with an 8-cylinder engine, the coil had insufficient time to fully re-energise itself once the engine exceeded 1000rpm – barely above tick over/idle.

Today we have improvement opportunities if not for the ignition coil itself at least in the way its magnetic field is regenerated for each spark. Called a capacitive discharge system, this achieves its objective by incorporating capacitors within a (new) ignition module. These capacitors are charged up to about 350-volts, which is of course, much higher than the car's 12-volts. The high voltage is discharged across the coil's primary circuit thereby dramatically shortening the coil's regeneration time.

Before we look in outline as to what systems are on offer, some of you may be interested in how that swifter coil charge is utilised to best effect in these advanced ignition systems. Increasing the spark plug gap and getting a nice fat spark across the gap is of course the simple answer to getting the most out of all high performance ignition system. Surprisingly

the amount of energy needed to sustain a spark across a wide gap is not significantly different to that required to sustain a spark across a small gap. However, it is what happens before the spark strikes that is different and increases with the size of the gap. Preceding the spark, an ignition system, even a conventional one, must create a plasma between the electrodes to provide a path for the spark to follow. A swirling dense air/fuel mixture makes it hard enough, but the higher the compression the more difficult the pre-spark plasma finds it to form. It therefore makes sense that the higher the voltage (i.e. the pressure of the coil discharge) the better the chances of bridging the gap and doing so quickly (we are looking for instantly).

A conventional ignition system, particularly one used with a high-compression engine turning high rpm, can and does miss. This is not (usually) the fault of the ignition system failing to present some sort of spark to the plug, but more likely that the spark was insufficiently strong or sustained to ignite the cylinder charge. A higher voltage would certainly have helped, but a very much higher voltage sparking across a bigger gap would help enormously. Obviously the surface area of spark presented to the mixture increases proportionally with the gap, and thus we can be talking about 25 to 50 per cent increases. However, a much higher voltage sparking across a bigger gap several times is likely to ignite the charge, every bit of it, every time. Hence the value of capacitive and multiple discharge systems.

Jacobs makes such a system (called Energy Pak Computer Ignition) and can provide the essential compatible coil. It is a combination of capacitive discharge and multi-spark ignition. This automatically fires multiple sparks per cylinder spanning 20° of the crankshaft rotation up to about 3000rpm. With the naked eye there appears a series of four discharges to the plugs at each firing. Obviously you only need one to fire the cylinder's charge in most circumstances, but this steam of sparks virtually guarantees that the plug will fire under the most adverse conditions, including very high compression ratios. Above 3000rpm there is insufficient time to fire each plug more than once. You get a glimpse of the primary Jacobs components in photos 12-3-2-1 and 12-3-2-2.

Alternatively, you can consider an even more sophisticated capacitive discharge system. The Automatic Controls Corporation in the USA makes a multiple spark discharge (MSD) unit. The primary capacitive discharge voltage of the MSD system is 470-volts – nearly 40 times the car's original 12-volts. The MSD 6AL unit is probably best for our 8-pots and you may find one refinement interesting, fun and useful. The MSD system allows you to adjust the ignition timing by +/- up to 7° from the driver's seat. You may find photographs 12-3-3-1 and 12-3-3-2 helpful but be sure to hear one in use as I understand they can be noisy, particularly when sited in the passenger compartment. An MSD power capacitor is available to fit in the power supply line that will reduce the buzzing noise.

Instead of buying individual units, a complete MSD ignition kit may interest you comprising the 8579 Distributor, a 6AL Ignition unit with rev-limiter and a Blaster coil. MSD equipment is available from Summit in the USA and Real Steel in the UK.

Crane Performance offers the Fireball HI-6 multiple-spark capacitive discharge electronic ignition. This bears exploring as it is less expensive than some and, further, it has a built-in programmable rev-limiter and can be run with Crane's PS91 coil. Ford engine converters may find the Crane equipment particularly interesting in view of the reduced height of Crane's

12-3-2-1 Phil Vella took this great shot of a Jacobs 'Ultra-Coil' for me. It forms part of an MSD kit and can only be used in conjunction with its ...

12-3-2-2 ... multi-spark discharge 'Black box'.

electronic distributors (as mentioned a few paragraphs back).

When buying an electronic ignition system, it may be worth ensuring that a rev limiter is included. Without this safety device some well-modified V8's can easily reach 7500 or 8000 rpm

Earlier I stressed the wisdom of a breakerless trigger for the ignition system and you may, therefore, be surprised to hear that these capacitive discharge products can be used, if required, with standard contact breaker points or one of the retro-fitted breakerless systems described earlier. Certainly if you retain a contact breaker, changing points is

12-3-3-1 An MSD unit nicely tucked away on the heater platform in this Ford conversion, and, if you want a closer look ...

12-3-3-2 ... Dick Taylor kindly contrived this shot to illustrate not only the model 6-BTM MSD unit, but also, just to the left, the (normally) remote ignition adjustment control. The rheostat would be located on the dashboard/fascia, allowing the driver to alter the amount of ignition advance at will.

eliminated and the only maintenance required is an occasional check to be sure some gap is present since the heel of the points eventually wears, even with a well-lubricated cam. However, remember that some cam bounce is inevitable at high rpm and consequently, I would strongly recommend a breakerless trigger in spite of the point-retention option (apparently) returning when you use capacitive discharge.

Users of capacitive discharge ignition systems assure me that spark plugs do not foul with these units, even if you run a colder plug, which reduce the likelihood of

…ression engines, …g gaps. One friend …t is two grades colder … a 0.050in (1.25mm) gap. Furthe… and cold starting was always dih… with his carburettor set-up, which tended to run rich at lower engine revs. The problem went away once he fitted a big fat capacitive discharge spark. You can apparently occasionally detect that the large-gapped plugs are fouling under slow running, but they clear within seconds of putting your foot down.

I will close with the comment that current prices for capacitive discharge systems in the USA make the option very attractive indeed, so shop around. Don't forget to cost the new matched coil and the breakerless trigger – not to mention a really good set of plug leads.

ENGINE MANAGEMENT IMPROVEMENTS

We have spent some time examining how to get a bigger more consistent spark fired across an ever-widening sparkplug gap. All good stuff but we have not improved upon the point at which that spark ignites the mixture. The systems have all retained the original concept of an ignition advance curve that is controlled, to put it in basic terms, by mechanical weights and springs. In other words, we now have the ability to generate a bigger bang but not, as yet, the refinement to control the subtle delivery of that bang. The problem is that subsequent engine development has shown that the optimum point at which the spark needs to be delivered varies and certainly does not follow the sort of simple curve that centrifugal force with or without vacuum control generates. At some points in the rpm range the ignition needs to be slightly retarded while the increase in rpm of only perhaps 500rpm necessitates an amazing amount of ignition advance. A job routinely carried out by electronics in today's engines via engine management systems.

Engine management is controlled by two halves – fuel management, usually called electronic fuel-injection (EFI) and ignition management. The beauty of electronic ignition management is that it can do just what I was referring to in the previous paragraph, it can read the engine's various parameters (eg rpm, throttle position, temperature etc) and has the computing power to convert its ignition map into the optimum ignition point. How does it know the correct ignition map? You, or a suitably experienced professional, experimented until the ignition map or curve or standard was set for your engine with its induction, compression, plugs etc optimised. A laptop computer loaded this to the system's CPU (central processing unit). If you subsequently note a flat spot or some other detail you would like to smooth out, it is just a matter of a slight tweak to the ignition or, if you also have EFI, the fuel map(s) via a laptop.

Superchips fully-mapped ignition conversions using the Luminition Optronic distributor trigger are well proven. The conversion requires the distributor base plate be tack-welded so no movement is possible, after which the Lumenation trigger is simply connected to a solid extension of the camshaft and therefore engine rotation. A remote ECU is pre-programmed by Superchips but is easily altered by use of a dedicated hand-help programmer that can be hired or bought separately. These systems are 'only' 2 dimensional but the mapping is still far better than any mechanical system can ever achieve. Consequently more torque, a smoother engine, more power and better fuel efficiency are quite normal improvements

It's now time to touch on the other half of Holley's control systems – ignition management via the Commander 950 system. Offered in kit form with online mapping, these Holley kits are intended to upgrade any existing ignition system or to

provide a state-of-the-art electronic control module, if none is currently available. Holley claims that the Commander 950 is the most powerful and capable ECU available on the market today in spite of its size (5.5in x 4.75in x 2.0in). These Holley engine management system kits contain an ECU, wiring harness and sensors with laptop communication cable and software also available. A series of individual GM, Ford and Chevy orientated kits are available but there is also a universal controller kit for customized applications. These systems are designed only for fuel and spark management so cruise control, transmission control, AC, ABS, etc. cannot be installed or controlled by the Holley system.

The stand-alone systems contain all components necessary for installation, including a detailed installation guide. Commander 950 ECU control functions are fully programmable with a personal laptop computer with Windows 3.1, 95, 98 or NT. Real-time tuning of all parameters is simple to use for the beginner yet has all the features necessary for experienced tuners.

Adjustable timing is available with any of the following distributors – 1980-1/2-1990 GM 7-pin (coil-in-cap), 1984-96 GM (external coil), 1984-later Ford 7-wire TFI. Consequently, Holley retains the dizzy to direct the sparks, full timing for start-up and warm-up fuel enrichment, acceleration fuel enrichment based on MAP and TPS sensors and a programmable RPM scale. The timing control function can be achieved through the use of small-cap computer-controlled GM HEI (stock GM or Holley PN 890-160), large-cap computer-controlled GM HEI, Ford TFI distributor, magnetic crank trigger or hall effect crank trigger. Thus a crank sensor is required either on the flywheel or on the front pulley to initiate the spark.

Last but not least there are facilities to control the electric cooling fan, an integrated rev limiter and data-logging.

Chapter 13
Electrics

Any problem will seem less daunting if you break it down into smaller parts – and a car's electrical system is no exception. When upgrading or rewiring (or troubleshooting) consider the car's electrical circuits as eight smaller systems:

1 – Charging and battery capacity

2 – Distribution and fuses

3 – Starter

4 – Ignition

5 – Lights, emergency flashers, courtesy-lights

6 – Auxiliaries/accessories working only when the ignition is part-way 'on' – radio, horns

7 – Auxiliaries working only when the ignition is fully 'on/run' – instruments, wipers, heater, brake lights, reverse lights, electric cooling fans, direction indicators, heater rear window (GT only)

8 – Earth/grounds

We will explore the consequential changes appropriate to a V8 conversion under these categories too.

CHARGING
Alternators

Wherever you are, or whatever the capacity or tune of your engine, it is essential to properly supply the electrical system and recharge the car's battery. A 55 amp rated alternator is the minimum recommended. When EFI is in use add another ten amps capacity, and a further five when a heated rear screen is in use on GT variants. In the UK, therefore, we could be looking at a 55-65 amp alternator shown in picture 13-1-1. For US cars a 65 amp alternator is required but with air-conditioning, to cover the additional load of the compressor; 80 amps may be prudent, particularly when hot ambient conditions dictate the frequent use of perhaps three electric fans. All these capacities exceed even the largest alternator fitted to an MGB, thus an upgrade is required.

Space is a major problem, particularly for those squeezing a Chevy engine in. In fact, you may have to resort to fitting the alternator elsewhere (as picture 3-5-5 showed us).

For Buick/Rover and Ford conversions you should get the alternator up front – although some thought may be required as to location and mounting method. Fortunately alternators these days are getting much more efficient,

13-1-1 This is a new 65 amp alternator complete, in this case, with an aluminium drive pulley. It is about 5in (125mm) in diameter and may be difficult to squeeze into some engine bays so ...

13-1-2 ... consider this much smaller, lightweight unit with its internal fan.

so the output capability for any given size of alternator is increasing. Picture 13-1-2 endorses this point. This is aided by the trend of incorporating the cooling fan inside the alternator, and this can be seen in photograph 13-1-3. Size for size, therefore, with the output of the alternator about double what is was five to ten years ago, the necessity for a larger amperage alternator need not generate a space problem, even inside the most crowded engine compartment.

In the UK, Clive Wheatley (picture 13-1-4) and/or Cambridge Motor Sport (picture 13-1-5) have these and other

13-1-4 The traditional 45 amp MGB GT V8 alternator and excellent reproduction V8 mounting bracket available from Clive Wheatley,

options available. However, you may care to visit your local breaker's yard and look for small alternators. They are common on modern Japanese cars and I'm sure you will find one that is small enough. However, you also need to ensure that the direction of rotation, wiring arrangements and output potential are suitable for your intended application.

In the US, converters need hardly go further than their nearest speed shop as General Motors' (Delco) internally regulated alternators, called type S1, are the units of choice for most MG V8 conversions. The GM alternators come in a couple of sizes/

amperage ratings – 10SI and 12SI, and are relatively inexpensive. These are some of the most common alternators in the US and are, consequently, available everywhere. However, a look at www.madelectrical. com/electricaltech/delcoremy.shtm will give more information. The exact model chosen will depend on the amperage required and the clearance available in the alternator's proposed mounting position. D+D Fabrications has Delco 80 amp, three-wire units available.

Incidentally, I think you are best avoiding single-wire alternators. They cost more than the equivalent three-wire, have no advantage in an MGB and don't work until the engine revolutions become elevated. A standard three-wire will generate usable amounts of current at idle. The idea of a one-wire alternator is to simplify installation and, while this may work on many cars, the MGB (depending upon its year) has either three or five wires connected to the Lucas alternator or two connecting wires if it is still fitted with an early dynamo. In short, it's actually easier (in an MGB) to use the more usual three-wire alternator. Furthermore, you'll lose the use of your ignition warning light if you use a one-wire generator.

13-1-3 A modern high amperage alternator with internal fan. Note the different fan/ drive belt (no more 'V' belts) which gives food for thought insofar as water pump and crankshaft pulley shapes are concerned.

13-1-5 A neat Cambridge Motor Sport 45 amp alternator conversion kit. Also in shot is the large aluminium pulley that you will need to drop alternator (any alternator) rpm down to something more practical when the engine is running at the high rpm expected in competition. Note the special single mounting pivot supplied with the kit.

13-1-6 A traditionally cooled 45 amp alternator located in the usual place, if only to accommodate a substantial compressor for an air-conditioning unit. Note the high efficiency radiator fixed in this D+D Fabrications demonstration rig.

The conventional V8 alternator location for the Rover engine is in front of the right-side rocker cover as we see in photos 13-1-6 and 13-1-7. However, a left-sided installation will be better for Ford conversions or if a large alternator is selected. An alternative location and adjustment method is shown in picture 13-1-8 and holds good for Ford and Buick/Rover engines.

You will certainly need to upgrade the power carrying cable from the alternator to the starter solenoid. The solenoid terminal acts as a primary distribution point, being connected directly to the battery by a much larger cable. The cable size to carry 55 to 80 amps is quite thick and frankly I find it difficult to terminate and route – thus you may find fitting two parallel cables easier – assuming your alternator has two (large) power spade connections in its rear. If you

13-1-7 MGOC Managing Director Richard Monk's pristine factory MGB GTV8 with its 100 amp internal fan, serpentine belt-driven alternator fitting comfortably under the bonnet line. The power connection for alternators with more than 65 amp capacity and almost all internal fan alternators (at least on European cars) is a heavy-duty bolt-on connection. The three-wire/spade connections of the European 3 pin DIN spec plug common to most MGs (two large spades together and a single small spade) is simply not an option because of the power generating capacity of these alternators.

are upgrading to say a 55 amp alternator, bearing in mind your MGB probably had something like a 32 amp alternator and cable, it will be necessary to fit a second cable that is capable of carrying the extra output (23 amps in this example). The length of wire run is an important parameter for power-handling capacity as well as cross-sectional size. For short distances, smaller wire will carry as much current safely as a larger wire for longer distances. For this reason, power cables should always be routed to be as short as possible.

In the UK, a 44/03 sized cable carries 25 amps. However, if you are moving up to an 80 amp alternator, I think you are best throwing out the original cable and fitting a pair of new cables each capable of 40 amps – namely 84/03. In US gauges, a 10ga wire will safely carry 40-60 amps, an 8ga will carry 60-80, and 80-100 amps

can be carried by a 6ga. Most of the kits listed below only supply 10ga wire for the main alternator feed to battery feed, and this has been proven to be adequate. Advance Auto Wire supplies 8ga for this function.

If you have fitted the alternator in front of the rocker cover, the terminations are likely to be a problem in that there is no room for the conventional plug between the rear of the alternator and the rocker box cover. On a GM SI alternator, the location of the two smaller wire terminals can be located at 3, 6, 9 or 12 o'clock by slightly opening the case, and rotating it to one of these four positions and re-closing. Inside a Lucas alternator's plug you will find two or three 'flag' (right-angled) terminals. When fitted in front of an obstruction (e.g. a rocker-cover) there may not be sufficient room for the proper three-pin plug – in this event you will have to insulate each terminal with a proper insulating boot. Do not use tape – it gets hot and oily and comes undone with disastrous results. If you can find some PTFE adhesive tape, stick this to the rocker box as an insurance

13-1-8 The alternator mounting hole was opened to allow the alternator to be fixed to the lower outer bolt hole on the head. A 1/4in aluminium bracket was fabricated to stabilise the outer end of this bolt and attaches to two of the water pump retaining bolts. The top adjusting arm is made by bending a standard/stock piece to the opposite 'S' shape from its original configuration. Note the serpentine tensioner in the top right corner.

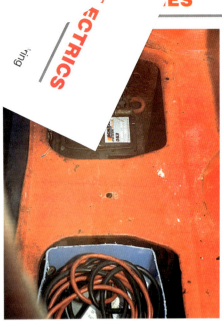

13-1-9 One UK '063' size fits beautifully into the chrome-bumper car's battery tray and is 7in tall, 8.25in wide and 6.75in front to back (178 x 210 x 172mm). One may be adequate but two provide for trouble-free V8 motoring – though they are subsequently difficult to remove so a pre-fitted, nylon four-sided 'harness' might be welcome if/when you need to remove them.

against vibration bringing your booted terminals into contact with the rocker cover.

Battery issues

The ease by which your battery capacity is increased depends upon whether you have a chrome- or rubber-bumper car. With a rubber-bumper car you have just one battery location and thus need to choose the highest capacity ampere-hours (AH) battery that fits the space available. With chrome-bumper cars you have an advantage in that you can fit two 12 volt batteries – one in each battery-box – and wire them in parallel (i.e. positive terminal to positive terminal and negative terminal to negative terminal).

I have long since used 12 volt Ford Escort acid batteries in my chrome-bumper cars but UK readers can fit a couple of

13-1-10 An Optima gel battery with traditional MGB posts is also available with US GM-style side terminals. It is truly maintenance-free and has an amp rating of 720 at 0°F, and 910 at 32°F.

Type 063 batteries. One can be seen in picture 13-1-9 but since each would have 44AH capacity, they will enjoy capacity of 88AH – enough to keep you going in the longest of traffic jams! A 0.5in piece of exterior ply may need to go in first to provide a flat base.

More than one owner has transposed their battery to the boot/trunk of the car but I am not convinced this is either necessary or a good idea. If you relocate the battery to the boot/trunk you take two retrograde steps – you reduce the available luggage space and take the considerable weight of the battery(s) from low-down inside the wheel-base to a much less desirable high(er) location outside the wheel-base.

That said, you would do something to redress a front-end heavy Ford or Chevy conversion if you were to put the battery in the boot/trunk and vent the battery and its mounting via a small pipe out though the floor. Do not forget that the voltage drop increases with the length of the battery to starter cable, so you need to counter that problem by increasing the size (try welding cable) of the cable.

If you are a rubber-bumper owner seeking greater battery capacity, and think it more sensible to modify the rear shelf to chrome-style battery fittings, the cradles are available new and require minimal welding, furthermore, they increase the rigidity of the back-end of the bodyshell.

Used chrome-bumper battery covers are easily procured.

It is true that the original MGB battery location makes maintenance access very difficult – but there are solutions that obviate the necessity of relocating the batteries. There are, of course, the so-called 'maintenance-free' acid batteries but Larry Shimp draws my attention to his truly maintenance-free gel Optima battery. These are offered with various terminal arrangements but the best choice is model 75-35. Dimensions are 9.4in long, 6.8in wide with a height of 7.6in. This model has standard top terminals (the same as any standard battery as we see from picture 13-1-10.

These batteries contain a gel electrolyte, are sealed and are therefore completely maintenance-free. Larry suggests a thick plywood base is required cut to fit in the original battery tray. This brings the bottom of the tray up to the level of its 'L' section surround and is necessary because the new battery has a bigger base than MG originally intended. He restrained his battery with a simple but effective arrangement using the original MGB clamp over the top/centre of the battery.

Battery/electrical isolators

The MGB's rear battery position lends itself

13-1-11 This isolator switch makes/breaks the main cable leading from the battery to the rest of the car, and provides both a safety feature and, with the key removed, some added security from casual theft.

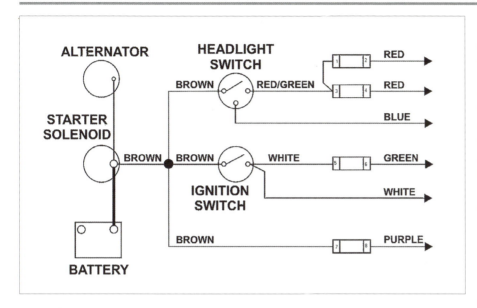

D13-1 Schematic outline of a typical MGB general wiring and the four-fuse arrangement.

to your fitting an isolator switch on the type seen in photo 13-1-11 behind the drivers seat on the heel-board.

DISTRIBUTION AND FUSE CIRCUITS

The MGB is a forty-year-old design. Certainly by today's standards, with the ever-growing emphasis on electrical equipment and ancillaries, the MGB's distribution and fuse system is inadequate. On later models, from about 1977 on, MG added an ignition relay to help the distribution of power and avoid overloading the ignition switch. In this case, the white wire from the ignition switch operates a relay, and power is then sent from the relay to the fuse box via white/brown wires.

The fuse facilities were also upgraded from the initial two to four fuses around 1969 and, subsequently, several line-fuses were also added – but by the time the car went out of production it was under-fused by contemporary standards. Thus, when you are upgrading the car, do incorporate additional fuses by one means or another. We will discuss some options shortly but first it may help to outline the

four-fuse system and colour-codes so you can picture which fuse serves which circuit. You may find diagram D13-1 helpful too.

● The brown wiring circuit feeds straight from the battery's positive terminal and is consequently unfused and always live as long as the main cable is connected to the battery. Amongst other tasks, the brown circuit feeds the ignition switch and also the fuse that connects terminals 7-8 on the fuse-block. Terminal 8 of the fuse-block provides the purple circuit with an unswitched, fused power source. The normal fuse rating is 17 amp which should be adequate for interior/courtesy lights although a slightly higher rated fuse is often fitted if a cigarette lighter is in frequent use. The MGB's fuses are, incidently, glass tubes with a slip of paper inside showing the fuses 'rating'. A 17 amp fuse is rated to take 17 amps constantly and should blow at about twice the continuous rating – say around 34 amps. This fuse will also protect the horn circuit.

● The white circuit is that part of the loom that becomes live when the ignition switch is 'on' but, being an extension of the brown circuit, remains unfused. One part of the

white circuit feeds terminals 5-6 on the fuse-block. Terminal 6 of the fuse-block provides the green circuit with an ignition-switch-controlled, and now fused, power source. The official fuse rating is 17 amp, but many cars, particularly GTs with heated rear windows, run with a slightly high-rated fuse. This is probably the fuse that feeds the most used electrical features including brake/stop lights, direction indicators, reverse lights and the electrical instruments feed from the voltage stabiliser.

● The brown circuit also feeds the light switch with an unfused power supply. The light switch has two unfused outlets – a red/green cable that leads to terminals 1 and 3 of the fuse-block and a blue cable that provides the headlamp dip control switch with its supply when the light switch so directs.

● The red/green sidelight circuit deserves further explanation. You may have noticed that I mentioned that the one red/green cable from the light switch feeds two fuse positions (numbers 1-2 and 3-4) in the fuse-block. A link or bridge at the back of the four-fuse fuse-block loops between terminals 1 and 3 to achieve this. Many home enthusiasts fail to notice this link and re-fit the fuse-block upside-down. They then become very puzzled by the consequential anomalies that their electrical system will display as they have erroneously connected the supposed ignition switch controlled green circuit with the always-live purple circuit. A TR6 fuse-block, and maybe others, looks identical to the MGB box, but does not have the link on the back. Thus, when using four-way fuse-blocks of unknown origin, check this detail before fitting the block or risk subsequent confusion. Properly installed, the red cables that actually run to the left and right sidelights or parking lights are therefore fed by terminals 2 and 4 and are consequently fused using 17-amp-rated fuses.

So an MGB fuse box is just not adequate because the current passing

13-2-1 One of several MGB orientated products from Advance Auto Wire. This one is an auxiliary four-way fuse block with relay. It comes prewired for MGB use and can be used to supplement the existing, but inadequate, MGB fuse arrangement.

13-2-2 This is an example of the fuse/relay 'heart' of one of the numerous excellent Hot Rod preassembled wiring kits available in the USA. This is a 12-circuit system supplied by Painless Wiring.

13-2-3 Advance Auto Wire's powerblock wiring kit. In addition to the wiring and panel shown here, these kits include all the wiring, connectors, terminals, etc. needed to completely replace the original wiring. With eight fuses, two flashers, and seven relays, Lucas woes will be a thing of the past.

through each fuse is too great. It is also worth considering that almost everything going through the ignition switch also goes through the fuse-box. There are several ways you can approach the upgrade, but first lets look at the purpose of fuses.

Contrary to what many believe, the only purpose of a fuse is to protect the car's wiring from damage when some sort of problem occurs elsewhere. Intrinsic within that protection is the car itself. A simple short in a fused circuit will blow the fuse while the same problem in an unfused circuit will overheat the wiring, melt the insulation and ultimately result in a fire. Obviously, if you have eight electrical components being supplied by eight wires all fed from one fuse you have a higher probability of blowing the fuse than if each component and feed wire is fused individually. Bear in mind that eight individual components and their feed wires

are eight times more likely to short than one component/wire. Furthermore, if each of our eight components is taking 5 amps, and they are all simultaneously in use, then that fuse and its associated wires have to be capable of carrying 40 amps (and will probably get hot and oxidize). However, eight individual fuses will only need to carry 5 amps each and are most unlikely to get hot. If a problem should occur in one component or the wire feeding it, then only that component will stop operating when the fuse blows, not the other seven as well.

Another benefit that separate fuses bring is that each individual fuse's rating can be tailored to suit the feed-wire's capacity. Our eight components are unlikely to each warrant 5 amp fuses although some components (say the radio) will be fed with very light-gauge wire and warrant a 5 amp fuse. However, a feed wire to electric fans may pull 20 amps and need a 30 amp fuse. Headlamps, if you fuse them as a pair (not what I recommend), require a 25 amp fuse each for the low and high-beam circuits. Even the wiper and heater motors each need a 15 amp fuse. So the fuse requirements vary and it is time to look at our options:

1 – Your first option is to replace the current fuse-block with a modern multi-

fuse box, with at least eight, possibly twelve fuse positions. This enables you to retain most of the original wiring harness but to fuse more cables individually. Naturally, your selection of fuse rating must be compatible with the current associated with each circuit. I recommend that you aim to fit the modern blade-type fuse, available in a very wide range of capacities, from 1 to 40 amps. Careful labeling on the lid of the fuse holder should guide you to any problem fuse quickly enough. Such fuse-blocks are readily available from Summit in the US and Demon Tweeks in the UK.

2 – One alternative method may be less daunting to the less electrically-orientated reader. You can buy preassembled individual circuits from a variety of sources. Advance Auto Wire supplies auxiliary fuse-blocks with four fused circuits, two on/hot all the time, and two on/hot only when the ignition key is on. The latter circuit is relay operated to avoid adding any load to an already overworked ignition switch and can be viewed in picture 13-2-1. Two circuits are fused at 15 amps and two at 7.5 amps and they come prewired with 8ft of cable. You could, therefore, use a preassembled kit each time you felt a need to upgrade a circuit or fuse. For example, you could install a supplementary assembly for the electric fan(s) and perhaps one for the headlights (if you were upgrading them). The load removed from the current four-fuse-block would possibly enable you to postpone its full replacement, particularly if you also fitted the ignition relay advocated a little later in this chapter.

3 – The most drastic but best long-term solution involves replacing all the MGB's front harness assembly with a complete harness/fused wiring kit. Numerous companies in the US can supply prewired harnesses to a wide range of specifications. One example can be seen at 13-2-2 and while these are excellent products, they are not designed with the MGB in mind. In fact they are primarily aimed at American street rods using General Motors-style steering columns with built-in direction and hazard flashers, headlight and ignition switches. The installation of these kits is aided by numerous excellent pictorial representations, but these lose much of their value when you are installing the kit in a different car with different circuits, switches and connectors. However, Advance Auto Wire can supply a Powerblock kit (pictured at 13-2-3) designed to upgrade the entire harness/loom and made specifically for an MGB. Thus, not only are the various MGB circuits and switches catered for, but Advance Auto Wire has also used its experience of the quirks that come with 25-40 year old MGB electrical components. Consequently, the Powerblock system is designed to take account of the voltage dropping resistances that occur in old switches. Not only does this resistance drop the voltage to loads such as the headlights, making them quite dim in many cases, the resistance also creates a lot of heat within the switch, which often results in switch failure and can result in a fire. Using numerous relays eliminates this problem. Most relays will operate with as little as 6

volts, so voltage drop is no problem. With the extremely low current draw of relays, heat is not a problem either. Replacing a switch will cost about £40/$50, and can take up a whole weekend to replace. A relay costs around £5/$5, and take all of 30 seconds to replace.

Advance Auto Wire's system is also colour-coded to comply with the original MGB codes, giving continuity compatablity. All connectors are supplied, including the bullet/sleeve connectors originally used in an MGB, together with the required multi-block connectors (detailed shortly). Further, each kit includes three copies of a complete wiring diagram along with a comprehensive instruction manual. Internal wiring of all switches is shown, along with the colours of the wires to/from each switch. Thus you have the option of wiring from the diagrams or simply connecting the correct colours. Finally, but most importantly for many, technical support is just a phonecall or e-mail away.

4 – For those with neither the time nor inclination to carry out any of these suggestions – I have one further thought. Select a new MGB V8 front loom that matches the dashboard you expect to use (i.e. chrome- or rubber-bumper) and use that as a starting point. It would have most of the attributes you need (e.g. distributor, fans) in the correct place and have the reliability of a new harness. There may be upgrades you need for your particular conversion, but these could be easily accomplished using one (or more if necessary) of Advance Auto Wire's compact individual circuits. In the UK, Auto Sparks and/or Moss would be pleased to help with the new main loom. I would not try to merge the two looms but cover any supplementary loom you fitted with black tape and secure it alongside the new main loom covering.

I would suggest you use coloured wires for ease of identification and continuity and once it is installed, remove

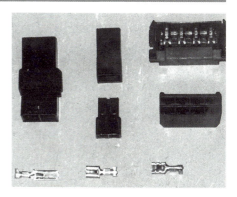

13-2-4 Some examples of modern multi-plug block connectors and their male and female spade terminals. The terminals are held secure within the multi-block by small 'tangs' which, in this picture, are best illustrated by the left side male where the tang can be seen clearly.

and bind it in a non-adhesive black insulating tape. Moss does adhesive for the ends (part number MQC1001) and non-adhesive for most of the long lengths (part number GAC9906X) loom tape. Wrap it with a 50 per cent overlap. Another excellent option is to use corrugated split loom. This has an added advantage in that you can open it up to work on your wiring and then close it back with no problems, yet offering full protection.

Whichever kit you use, even in the confined space of an MGB, you should have no difficulty in fitting the fuses, relays etc in. Although many fuse holders will come with a cover to help keep dirt and the weather at bay, you will help the reliability of your fuses if you site them inside the car. The bulkhead behind the glove pocket would be fine for fuses and relays, although it might necessitate removing the glove pocket one dark, wet night in the middle of nowhere. My recommendation, therefore, would be to place fuses and relays high-up on either side of the passenger footwell. You could make up a hardboard ceiling to the passenger footwell and site it just under the glove compartment. This would provide an excellent internal base on which to mount all your updated electrics. To really

13-3-1 The dual gearing arrangement provides these relatively small aftermarket high-torque starters with a tremendous increase in torque over a conventional starter. These units are also much lighter than a conventional starter and draw less current. The starter solenoids are positioned above the starter body and are angled slightly away from the engine, assisting clearance with the MG frame rail.

13-3-2 Weber gear reduction starter motor on the left compared to the standard Buick/Oldsmobile aluminium-nosed starter. Buick/Olds also used a cast-iron-nosed starter motor which can be identified by its 0.5in (12.5mm) larger diameter.

do the job properly you could even hinge the front edge of your hardboard panel and have it drop down to allow easy access to all the fuses, relays and terminal blocks in the event of trouble.

Connectors

Wherever you site your main electrical units, there will be inter-harness connections to make as part of your distribution system. You can use securely mounted terminal blocks but the modern two, four and eight way multi-block wiring connections shown in photograph 13-2-4 (previous) are much the better way. They offer 1/4in (6mm) male-to-female spade terminals housed in a nylon moulding and carry more current than the original MGB inter-cable connectors. Obviously if you

buy a new MGB front harness it will come with new connectors. Indeed, this will be one of the significant advantages of this solution. Use them by all means but I advise any new or supplementary wiring be fitted with modern terminations. I would also use a very light film of petroleum jelly when pushing all the connectors together in an effort to ensure the highest possible conductivity and longevity.

Final point on fuses – **always** carry sufficient spare fuses of the correct size.

STARTER CIRCUIT

The position of the starter, relay and some of the wiring and cable may alter but the electrical circuit that is required to crank the engine is going to remain largely unaltered and should not present too many problems.

In general the original starter motor for your engine will be the most cost-effective route to actually turning your engine over. However, there could be occasions when the expansion capacity of the engine and/or a high level of engine tune overtaxes the standard starter. You may wish to reduce the weight of the front end of your car and/or to reduce the current drawn from the battery by the starter-motor. However, the most likely problem is a lack of space between engine and MGB side-rail, particularly if your original starter has its solenoid on the side of the starter motor.

Ford does a 4.5in diameter starter motor as standard for some of its engines so, if you have a 302 and need to find an extra 1/2in clearance one of these may work. Ford Motorsport also markets a permanent magnet mini starter which is about 3 1/2 in diameter (part number M1100-A50), but whatever your engine there is almost certainly an aftermarket gear reduction small starter motor upgrade that will solve several problems in one go.

The design features a small gearbox in the nose of the unit (seen in picture 13-3-1) so that the starter motor drives a small gear encased in the starter housing. In the UK, Cambridge Motorsport will be able to supply you, while in the US a gear

13-3-3 Now 15 years old, my steel starter motor heat shield needed electrical and thermal insulation now provided by ...

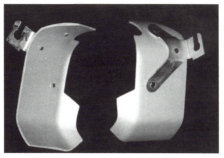

13-3-4 ... the superior material used in Clive Wheatley's modern equivalent.

IGNITION CIRCUIT

The primary ignition circuit will probably change for three reasons:

● the different position of the alternator, coil etc.

● your upgrading the ignition trigger to a modern breakerless system

● fitting a relay into the ignition circuit to provide for the power supply for the auxiliaries listed in section 6.

13-4-1 I had to move/position my coil away from the inner wing/fender in order to make space for the bonnet/hood stay. It is a very good idea to protect the coil from any ingress of water; plastic covers are available and recommended.

reduction starter for the all the engines we are focused upon will be available at about £200/$350 from Tilton Engineering Inc. (part number 54-100022). For Buick/Rover engines the cheaper alternative seen at photograph 13-3-2 is available from Weber via D+D Fabrications.

Chevrolet altered the bellhousing material, the original starter motor design, its mounting and flywheel in 1962. Because of the vast numbers of Chevy engines built since the change, I only intend to explore the post-1962 components. The bellhousing should be made from aluminium. Your block should have three starter fixing bolt holes in the block although only two are required when mounting the starter. You are best acquiring the engine, starter motor and flywheel simultaneously because, not surprisingly, the starter motor's end castings will vary with flywheel diameter. Furthermore there were two types of flywheel – 153 and 168 toothed units and the starter's spigot mounting and casting bolts varied accordingly.

Provided you have adopted the RV8-style of exhaust system, you should be able to dispense with a starter motor heat shield. My fabrication can be seen at 13-3-3 but Clive Wheatley now stocks an improved moulded plastic heat shield, shown in photograph 13-3-4, which gives added insurance if you already have, or plan to fit, the block-hugger style.

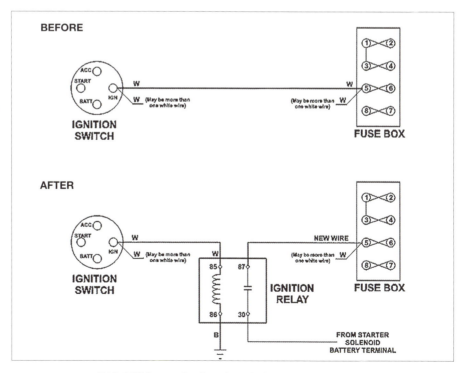

D13-2 Wiring a relay into the existing ignition circuit.

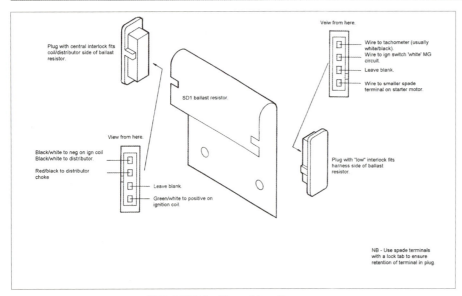

Plug with central interlock fits coil/distributor side of ballast resistor.

View from here.

SD1 ballast resistor.

Veiw from here.

Wire to tachometer (usually white/black).
Wire to ign switch 'white' MG circuit.
Leave blank.
Wire to smaller spade terminal on starter motor.

Black/white to neg on ign coil
Black/white to distributor.
Red/black to distributor choke

Leave blank.
Green/white to positive on ignition coil.

Plug with "low" interlock fits harness side of ballast resistor.

NB - Use spade terminals with a lock tab to ensure retention of terminal in plug.

D13-3 SD1 ignition wiring diagram.

Ensure the coil is low enough and packed out far enough not to interfere with the bonnet's telescopic stay in the manner seen in picture 13-4-1.

The ignition switch is already heavily stressed with electrical load and is best relieved of any additional loads imposed by electric fans, electronic fuel-injection or supplementary driving lights. Thus the ignition relay shown in drawing D13-2 is a really good idea. I have shown it wired between the ignition switch and the fuse-block in order that all the existing green circuit loads become carried by the relay. However, the relay would be even more effective if the new wire running to terminal 5 on the fuse-block were routed to a supplementary fuse-block. Naturally any additional loads (i.e. fans, lights) should be wired through the additional fuse capacity.

I would, however, feed the EFI direct from terminal 87 (the secondary output) of the relay and **not** through the existing/additional fuse-block. This will still avoid imposing the electrical demands of the EFI system on the ignition switch – which is the primary object of the exercise.

Ballast resistors

Many early MGB's do not incorporate a ballast resistor in their ignition circuit while many V8 transplants, if you take the engine's ignition circuit and components over to the MG, were equipped with a ballast resistor. Post-1975 MGB's do indeed have the facility built into the front harness in the form of a pink wire – which may not be what you were expecting but, nevertheless, if your donor's ignition circuits expect one, this will be fine.

The ballast resistor and a 7-volt coil are fitted to help the car start. The coil is normally fed from the ignition circuit via the ballast resistor but, when cranking, an additional lead connects to the coil carrying as near to 12 volts as the car can manage while cranking the engine. It will probably provide about 9, possibly 10 volts and thus generates a healthy spark from a 7-volt coil. For those transplanting an SD1 engine, ignition circuits included, you need to be aware that SD1 electronic distributors require this 12-volt feed from the smallest spade terminal on the starter motor to the aluminium-cased ballast resistor. Thus the resistor wire built into MGB wiring harnesses is obsolete.

Drawing D13-3 shows the SD1 electronic wiring arrangements for the ballast resistor and the related SD1 ignition circuit. Other distributors/systems demand different wiring arrangements, particularly aftermarket ignition systems such as Mallory, MSD, Accel, etc. Follow the manufacturer's recommendations as to whether or not a ballast resistor is needed. The question of needing a ballast resistor or not can be one of the most confusing aspects of an engine swap.

The voltage shown on your coil and/or its internal resistance determines whether a ballast resistor is required. A coil marked 6 or 7 volts and/or with an internal resistance of 1.5 ohms will require a ballast resistor.

On the other hand, a coil with external markings of '12 volts' or an internal resistance of 3 ohms or more does not need a ballast resistor.

Generally I would advise using an ignition circuit with a ballast resistor in the 'run' supply line and a 6- or 7-volt coil. However, if you want to use a non-ballast coil but your existing (post-1975) MGB wiring incorporates a ballast resistor, just run a wire from terminal 5 of the fuse box to the plus ('+') terminal on the coil. You can identify terminal 5 from drawing D13-1 but, with the bonnet open, it will either have one or more white wires or one or more brown/white wires already connected to it. You may leave the existing wiring on the plus terminal of the coil or remove it – the ignition circuit will work perfectly either way.

A 12-volt coil without a ballast will draw roughly the same current as a ballast coil with a ballast, so the rest of the circuit doesn't see any difference. This remains the case whether you are using either a contact breaker points system or one of the more modern electronic ignition systems.

If the coil you buy comes with a resistor and you are about to fit it to a '75 or later MGB (with its pink wire resistor built into the front harness), do **not** wire the supplied ballast into the existing wiring. You will have two ballast resistors in the circuit and performance will suffer as a consequence. It's preferable to use the existing (pink wire) resistor, or bypass it as described above before installing the new ballast resistor.

SD1 Opus distributors

If you are using a second-hand, pre-1982 SD1 distributor (which isn't a good idea but, given the cost of a new one, is understandable), do acquire and carry a spare at the first opportunity. The superflex wires from the pick-up to amplifier are very reliable for thousands of miles but do eventually expire. The pick-up and amplifier are connected by a trio of superflex cables, and if any one of these cables or the amplifier goes, you are not only in for a tow but a very expensive shock. A service exchange distributor usually needs to be ordered by a motor factor and cost £150-200! I would suggest you use the SD1 dizzy body/cap etc but change the trigger mechanism to a modern electronic/breakerless unit such as the Newtronic unit.

Incidentally, the SD1 distributor changed several times. Up to about 1982 the amplifier was inside the distributor and a loose, black 'flash-cover' was used. After that date a clear, fixed flash-cover was employed and improvements made to the distributor. Pre-1982 SD1 systems with the Opus ignition require a ballast resistor, post-1982 cars with the clear flash-cover were of the Constant Energy type and require a clean 12V non-ballasted supply. Incidentally, the coil for these post-1982 systems are the low primary resistance type so you need to match the coil and its power-feed with both the dizzy and the amplifier – the colour and mounting of the dizzy's flash-cover being your starting point!

13-4-2 A fuel pressure regulator. It's adjustable and you might just be able to see the figures (arrowed) around the edge of the case. These usually go in the engine bay and allow you to adjust the setting while watching the effect on engine and carburettor.

The electric fuel pump

At first sight you may not regard the fuel pump as part of the ignition circuit, but since the white ignition circuit activates it I felt this was the most appropriate location for some information on fuel pumps. In theory, a normally aspirated moderately powered V8 should be adequately supplied with fuel by the MGB's standard SU fuel pump. However, it will be stretched and consequently does need to be in absolutely tip-top order. If in any doubt, or your car is to have a medium or high-powered engine, my advice is to fit a new pump – and if you are in need of a new pump, fit an uprated one.

My reasons for suggesting both a new and uprated pump start with the fact that the SU pump has developed a questionable reputation for reliability. Secondly, the higher output V8 engine, say, above 150bhp, does inevitably gulp fuel at a faster rate than the original MGB GT V8 ever did, which works the SU pump harder than originally anticipated, particularly during motorway/freeway driving. Thirdly, the SU uses out-dated technology and,

13-4-3 A Facet Red Top fuel pump installed in the boot/trunk of my GT. Note that the fuel lines MUST be high-specification impermeable to fuel vapour if you are mounting a fuel pump in an enclosed space: outside the car is preferable.

while not foolproof, electronics immersed in an inert gas do seem to my mind to stand a better chance of reliable continuous operation. Finally, while there is a wide variety of pumps to choose from, a gear type pump probably offers longevity over a diaphragm type pump because modern fuel compositions contain some strange chemicals that may attack all but the most modern diaphragm pumps.

Any pump you buy must present less that 7psi to the carburettor. The maximum fuel pressure presented to any SU is particularly important, as 4psi is all an SU will cope with before the fuel will force the float valves off their seats and alter the fuel height in the float chamber/main jet. This may not initially show up as a leak, but rather as difficulty in adjusting the SUs and getting the mixture correct – particularly at idle/tick-over. The EFI fuel supply requires 60psi and is a totally different problem covered elsewhere. The geared carburettor pump and an EFI pump do, however, have one thing in common – they generally have the pump motor submerged in the fuel being pumped. This helps cool the motor and avoids the need for internal seals. The only drawback is that the (carburettor) pump has to be mounted vertically. Failure to follow these installation instructions results in the motor not being fully submerged in fuel with consequential overheating and failure.

You can buy a 7-10psi pump and reduce the pressure at the carburettor by fitting the pressure regulator shown in picture 13-4-2 (previousf) in the fuel line. However, a regulator increases the cost of the pump insulation and, with the choice of pumps available, should not normally be necessary.

The fuel pump's location is important and I think the best location is low down on the rear of the heel-board, just in front of the rear axle. Generally you need to mount fuel pumps in line with the bottom of the fuel tank. If you have a vacant battery box, this keeps the pump out of the way of the propshaft and clear of water splashed up from the rear wheel. It also provides enough space to orientate any pump correctly. A pre-pump filter will be needed for most geared pumps to ensure dirt is prevented from damaging the pump's precision gears, and this too can be fitted in this location. I have fitted pumps in the boot/trunk as shown in photograph 13-4-3 (previous), which certainly keeps the pump away from the dirt and rubbish the poor old SU pumps were subjected to but the safest solution is to fit the pump and/or filter in a less confined space.

Examples of suitable low pressure pumps (7psi or less) are: Facet Red Top pump, number 480532K; Carter P4070 (vane type pump, no seals, submerged

motor); Holly 12-801, dry motor; Mallory 4070, gear-rotor, dry motor; Accel 74701; or the Edelbrock 1791, dry motor. The Carter pump has a reputation for being a little noisy, particularly if fitted without mounting kit 18-140. The Holly pump can be heard but is the quieter of the two. The other pumps are excellent but cost more than the Carter and Holly pumps. Dan Masters sent me a couple of pump-installation photos you will find helpful at 13-4-4 and 13-4-5.

I would fuse an EFI fuel-pump but have not fused my Red-Top – but that is a personal choice. An additional safety device to fusing is a cut-off switch. Cut-off switches come in two versions – those that disconnect the pump in the event of an impact and those that cut the fuel off when the engine oil pressure drops. The contemporary inertia type of protection developed a reputation for unreliability. The grey-cased switches had a ball inside them, which could corrode. The result was a lack of conductivity and no fuel but, worse still, the resistance could also generate so much heat within the switch that the switch case melted. The problem could be minimized by dismantling the switch periodically and cleaning the ball and its contacts, but frankly you are better to buy a later (in the UK a Jaguar) inertia switch because a fuel pump failure is best avoided.

Both Holley (part number 12-810) and Carter (part number A68301) make oil pressure fuel pump cut-off switches that stops power reaching the fuel pump when the engine's oil pressure drops. These can save an engine as well as act as a safety cut-off in the event of an accident that stops the engine. This type of switch requires a connection to the starter circuit to allow the pump to run during starting. This oil pressure-controlled switching can be achieved using a switching (normally 5-pin) relay connected in series with a standard electric oil pressure switch.

13-4-4 This is a Holley 'Red' (120-801-1) fuel pump rated at 71-97 GPH @ 4-7psi. Holley also makes a 'Blue' pump (12-802-1 rated at 88-112 GPH @ 9-14psi) and a 'Black' one (12-815-01 rated at 120-140 GPH @ 9-14psi). Mount your fuel pump to a sheet-metal plate pre-cut to ...

13-4-5 ... fit to the front of your battery tray. This allows easy access to the pump if necessary and uses otherwise wasted space in front of the battery. Note the rubber mounting bushes in this and both preceding pictures, used to reduce pump noise. Rather than drill holes in the battery tray try 4 (or 6) bridge clamps instead.

LIGHTS & EMERGENCY FLASHERS
Lights

The headlamps on an MGB are inadequate for today's driving conditions and their effectiveness reduces as the performance of the car increases. Thus, you are strongly advised to upgrade the headlamps by fitting quadoptic bulb-carrying reflectors and halogen high intensity bulbs. The problem with this upgrade is that the switches and wiring within the original car will not handle the current consumed. Consequently, I recommend a supplementary harness from Advance Auto Wire (seen at 13-5-1). Full instructions come with this upgrade and consequently require no further amplification here although I have added a circuit diagram (D13-4) to enable you to evaluate this upgrade in more detail.

Further, the headlights will still be the minimum necessary for serious night driving and a pair of supplementary driving lights are advisable. You can wire these so that they come on when the headlamps are on full-beam, in which case a further harness is unnecessary. For this type of operation you still need a driving light switch and a relay but wired into the headlight circuit so that this switch must be 'on' and the headlights must be in the high-beam position for the driving lights to work. This way, when you dip your beams when meeting an oncoming car, you don't have to remember to turn off your driving lights as well – they automatically go off. Obviously this method allows you to just have the headlights on without the driving lights by simply switching the driving lights off. Instructions for this arrangement are included with the supplementary harness.

You will need to resolve one personal preference – do you fuse the headlamps or not? Opinions are divided. For my part, provided I had a sufficiently large fuse-block, I would use four positions to fuse each side of the car on each circuit individually. However, I would not put both dipped lights through one fuse and both full-beam through a second fuse. I think it safer not to fuse the headlights at all. Whether you choose to fuse or not to fuse the headlamps, the wiring to these units needs to be particularly well installed, insulated and supported – and you need

to be sure to check your headlights and the wires leading to them on a regular basis. Remember – when you need your headlamps you really need them.

Emergency flashers

If you car does not already have hazard warning flashers fitted, in today's traffic conditions you should fit them and the attached circuit diagram D13-5 will assist.

Original style MGB hazard switches seen at 13-5-2-1 (overleaf) are still available and are probably the easiest route to finding the double pole/double throw (DPDT) switch you need to simultaneously disconnect the flasher circuit as you engage the hazard lights. If you are modifying your dash and don't want to use an MGB switch, any double pole/ double throw switch that you like will work provided it is rated for 10 amps or better. There are 'pull' versions available too,

13-5-1 These twin Advance Auto Wire units contain relays for the dipped circuit and one for full-beam function to take the majority of the current away from the headlamp switches. A set of substantial wires is included to carry the current to the lamps without any voltage drop.

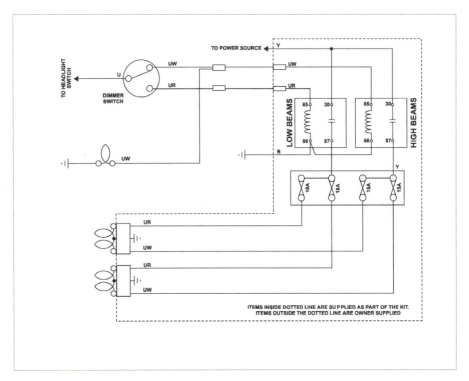

D13-4 Using a kit to add fuses and relays to the MGB's headlight circuit.

seen at 13-5-2-2. If the switch you want to use doesn't match your dash décor, it can always be located under the dash – just as long as it is still easily accessible. Take care with the positioning though as UK annual MoT tests require that the hazard lights must operate if fitted and my guess is that the switch consequently needs to seen.

AUXILIARY CIRCUITS (1)

These circuits become live at the first turn of the ignition key and, apart from viewing them as a self-contained system, I do not think there is much I can say of value about the radio, horn etc. The radio should have its own line fuse and the horn its own fuse in your uprated fuse-block. Some cars have

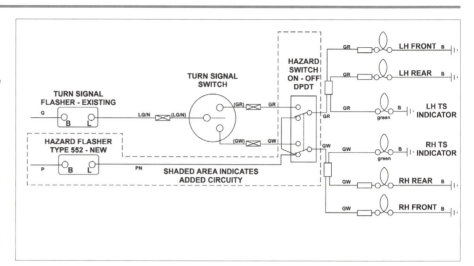

D13-5 Circuit and switch wiring for additional hazard lights.

13-5-2-1 The original MGB emergency/ hazard flasher switch can be seen on the left end of my radio console, but you may be interested in ...

13-5-2-2 ... its rear terminations that require 5mm spade terminals (a shade smaller than you might expect). The 'pull' switch shown here comes preassembled from, I believe, a TR6 catalogue, and may be an acceptable alternative if you do not want to use the original MGB version.

their screen-wipers (and washers) on this circuit – which I quite like because it takes some load from the auxiliary circuits and fuses.

AUXILIARY CIRCUITS (2)

The ignition switch should automatically control all these facilities. Thus this is unquestionably the most complex and heavily loaded of the circuits and consequently where you should focus most of your additional fuse capacity. I would suggest that you loop a power feed cable from the ignition relay to one side of each of the 5 or 6 fuses earmarked for these circuits. The other side of each fuse can then be coupled into its respective circuit.

I would, however, not recommend you fuse the actual ignition circuit itself – let that remain unchanged. Nevertheless taking these numerous auxiliary circuits off the ignition switch's load will improve its longevity, so lets look at some of the circuits involved in a little more detail.

Electric cooling fans

Since many MGBs have at least one electric cooling fan you may think that there is little to discuss. However, the cooling fan(s) you need to fit to a V8 should be rather more powerful than anything

MG fitted originally. We looked at the fans themselves in chapter 5 but modern fans draw more power and need wiring correctly if they are to operate at maximum efficiency. Thus here we will look at heftier feed/earth wires, electrical circuits, fuses, switches and relays.

The first order of business is the power supply for the fan(s) and you need to fit a separate (possibly a line) fuse to the power supply circuit and take the fan power feed from somewhere that has adequate capacity. Definitely not the ignition switch! Consequently, the first recommendation is that you fit a 30amp-rated relay(shown at 13-6-1) for the fan(s) and that it's primary (control) circuit is fed from the ignition (white) circuit. Mind you, I think it even more advantageous if you fit an ignition circuit relay too, in which case the fan relay's primary/control circuit should be fed by the secondary terminal of the ignition relay!

The size of the wires on the primary (control) side of the fan relay is not too important although the circuitry may exercise your mind. We will look into these options very shortly, but it is vital that you feed the power to and from the second half of the relay with correctly rated wires. If you are considering using much less than

13-6-1 If you do elect to fit a relay in the fan circuit, one of these beauties is what you are likely to buy with plenty of electrical capacity for two fans, if relevant.

44/0.3 cable size (which carries 25 amps) for both wires you either have insufficiently powerful fan(s) or inadequate cables feeding them. I would also use this size cable to earth/ground the fan(s).

The primary (control) wiring arrangements for cooling fans is very much a matter of personal choice – only here you are spoilt for choice. The easiest and quite satisfactory arrangement is to wire both electric fans (assuming you have two) to operate in parallel or simultaneously and only when the engine is running (i.e. the ignition is switched on). This is the method that most closely emulates the original V8 arrangement and the circuit can be viewed in the top half of D13-6. One interesting alternative twin-cooling fan switching arrangement is shown in the lower half of D13-6. This method is recommended by Kenlowe and allows one fan to switch on/off entirely automatically by thermostat while the second fan is wired to a manual control switch on the dashboard. Kenlowe points out that several exotic cars use this arrangement. They think this saves the cost and (slight) wiring complexity of a relay, but I still think a relay prudent for some of the bigger fans! In any event the warning light

does need to be sited in an eye-catching place and wired to the automatic fan.

However, you can supply the fan's thermostatically controlled switch from an always-live circuit. The argument for this arrangement is that the temperature often rises sharply when the car stops and the hot water in the system rises. In due course the whole system cools down but on the occasions when your stop is short the car can be hard to re-start. By allowing the fan(s) to operate with the engine off, you may keep the top coolant temperature from rising high enough to cause a re-start problem. The downside of the 'always live' feed is that you drain the battery of power – although you may remember that in chapter 5 I strongly recommended fitting substantial battery capacity to alleviate frequent and prolonged use of electric fans and that we explored some battery-capacity options earlier in this chapter.

If this option appeals, you need to study D13-7 and buy a relay and a three

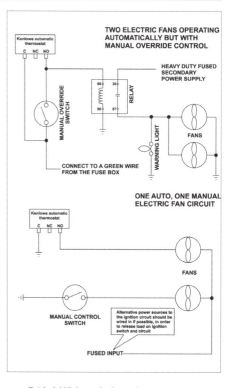

D13-6 Wiring choices for twin fans.

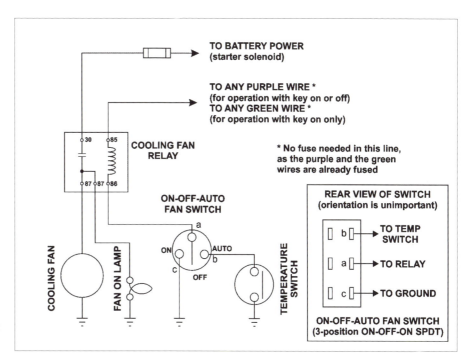

D13-7 Alternative fan wiring arrangements.

position SPDT switch providing for 'on', 'off' (useful when working on the car) and 'auto'. In fact Dan Masters drew out this circuit at my request in such a manner that you can choose (even change) the power feed. You can take the feed to the relay from the purple circuit (thus allowing the fan to work at any time even with the ignition switch off) or change the feed to the green circuit restricting the fan(s) to operate only when the ignition is on. The three-position control switch operates in the same way regardless of where the power is drawn from. If you prefer not to have the off position, buy a two position SPDT switch and wire it as shown for the three position switch.

However, there is another series of options depending upon where and the type of thermostatic switches you fit. Most use an adjustable thermostatic switch mounted adjacent to the top radiator hose but I mentioned the non-adjustable alternative in chapter 5. These are mounted low down in the coolant circuit and picture 13-6-2 should remind you of this type of switch.

Finally, there is one electric fan oddity that can be initially puzzling, but need cause no concern whatsoever. Sometimes the 'on' or warning lamp can glow faintly when you thought the fan was off. This is brought about by the car's forward movement and the resultant air flow through the fan causing it to spin. In this circumstance the fan's motor acts like a generator causing the warning lamp to glow faintly.

EARTH/GROUND

The earth/ground wire must carry just as much current as the feed wires connected to each of your electrical fittings. Generally speaking, earth wires throughout the car are inadequately thin, poorly terminated and connected to the battery. The heaviest current within the electrical system is that used to drive the starter motor. There must,

13-6-2 These thermostat switches are non-adjustable but have been adopted by the majority of modern cars. A switch positioned in the bottom hose and coupled to an always-live feed may activate momentarily when you turn the engine off but should not run the fan(s) extensively as the hot water will rise beyond them. However, you will not then be cooling the engine in order to ease any hot-starting problems you may have!

therefore, be a superb route by which the return current can get back to the battery, not just back to the chassis of the car. Thus it is vital that the battery's earth/ground terminal (usually the negative terminal) is perfectly earthed to the chassis and that the engine/gearbox is perfectly connected to the chassis and that both connections are made with substantial (braided if you like) straps. One of numerous examples is at 13-7-1. If you don't provide a good earth/ground, the electrical system will find one for you. Many times, the absence of a good ground has caused a meltdown of choke cables, throttle cables, etc., as they are forced to substitute for a resistance-free route to earth/ground.

Incidentally, if your car is an early MGB and is still positive-earthed/grounded, this is the time to change it to negative earth/ground and you are best to take this step before any other electrical work or purchases take place.

13-7-1. A typical braided earth/ground strap – not to be confused with the engine steady-bar we see in close proximity. Thoroughly clean all the mating faces and apply petroleum jelly and new large washers before tightening each connection. If in any doubt, fix a second engine earth/ground lead elsewhere – you can't over-earth/ground a car!

As important as the starter is, the earth/ground connections of every electrical component within the car are just as important to its reliable and consistent performance. Current from the battery must flow through each component and to do so requires not only a good feed but also an unimpeded earth/ground return. If you are using the chassis of the car as the way of returning the current to the negative battery terminal (and have provided the substantial battery to chassis strap) then all you need to do is ensure that each earth return wire is capable of handing the current required of it. It also **must** be connected to the chassis without the impedance of rust, paint, dirt and/or loose connections. A substantial soldered 'ring' terminal with a film of petroleum jelly securely fastened to the chassis will usually do the trick and last for years.

However, if you have any fibreglass panels you will have to make additional earth/ground arrangements because fibreglass is an insulator. Thus, a small supplementary earth/ground harness will be required to collect all the electrical returns and carry them back preferably to the battery earth/ground strap or to the nearest metal chassis point. In fact, there is absolutely nothing to stop you running earth returns back to the chassis connection of the battery even if you do not have fibreglass panels on the car. The supplementary harness will need to use appropriate wire sizes for the return currents involved if it is to be effective.

OTHER ELECTRICAL/ DASHBOARD MATTERS
Wiring routes
Consider routing the main rear electrical harness through the inside of the bodyshell, as per the RV8 seen in 13-8-1, in preference to the normal underbody routing. There are very few connections/ plugs affected by this change since most have to be outside the car anyway (e.g. harness to fuel tank, harness to fuel pump).

The rear harness carries wires to the boot/trunk light, tail-lights, brake lights, fuel gauge, reverse lights, etc., from under the dashboard through a (Roadster's) rear panel and across the boot floor. Obviously the occasional wire, such as those feeding the fuel gauge and pump, needs to be routed through small and suitably grommeted holes to the required locations. If the main rear harness is tucked into the corner formed by the right inner sill and the right side floor-pan, it stays clean and undamaged. It is also protected by any sound proofing you install as well as the car's carpets. However, you do have three things to remember:

● Do not forget to insert a plastic closing plug into any original cable routing holes you do not use.

13-8-1 The retaining clips welded down the right side of the prop-tunnel of this RV8 permit internal routing of the rear harness. My main reason for suggesting this is that it is far easier to reinstall your harness inside the car than under it. The second benefit is, of course, the fact that corrosion/dirt no longer attacks the harness.

● Take care when installing your right side seat that you don't trap any part of the harness under a seat runner. I would run two inch wide adhesive tape down the length of the harness to hold it securely in place in its corner.

● Do ensure your main-front-harness-to-main-rear-harness connection (the subject of picture 13-8-2, and located at the rear right side of the engine compartment, just behind the fuse-box) is not compromised or bodged. You may find that you need to extend one or two of the rear wires to reach the mating wires incorporated in the front harness. However, several of the main harness cables come from within the car's cockpit, and these can be teased out of the rear harness and the front/rear harness connections made under the dashboard. This is an advantage in that it enhances the long term reliability of these connections since they are moved away from the inevitable corrosion that engine heat and weather generate.

Cable capacities
When upgrading any electrical component consider the extra load such changes

13-8-2 The meeting point of the various electrical subharnesses is an important checking/test point on an MGB.

impose, not only on the wires themselves, of course, but also on the switches, the inter wiring connections and the fuses. For example, a pair of 100-watt halogen headlamps will consume 17 amps, whereas the original 65-watt bulbs (and the switches, wires and connections) were only designed for 11 amps. The wiring kits supplied by Advance Auto Wire are capable of handling 120 watt lamps. Even if you have fitted a larger alternator to supply the additional amperage for this and any other upgrades, you have only looked after the first and last links in the electrical supply chain. Sooner or later your car's reliability will suffer.

An EFI fuel pump will similarly require much more electrical power and a much heavier-duty supply cable.

Diagram D13-8 immediately overleaf may help you select the most appropriate cable sizes:

Amps	European cable size	Amps	USA cable size/gauge
5	9/0.3	5	18
8	14/0.3	10	16
17	28/0.3	15	14
25	44/0.3	20	12
35	65/0.3	30	10
42	84/0.3	60	8

D13-8 US/UK cable sizes

Cable splicing

It is much better for the long-term safety and reliability of the car to fit a new, unbroken, insulated cable if a cable proves to be too short. However, while not a recommended practice, it is almost inevitable that some cable-lengthening will be required during a V8 conversion and I felt it better to recognise the practicality of the situation and to give you the best advice I could on extending car-cables satisfactorily.

I have seen some absolutely unbelievable practices – unsupported wires twisted together with a turn of adhesive tape being the most common. Frankly you are endangering your car, your life and even the lives of others by such negligent workmanship. Certainly doing the job properly takes a bit longer but the safety and reliability benefits surely make it essential to do a proper job.

How do you do a proper job? There are two solutions. First and preferably use a proper compatible (e.g. bullet or spade) connector. However, these must be fitted well and it is important that you properly crimp and then solder the electrical connections. Most professional connections (e.g. bullets) will not subsequently require insulation. Some

spade terminations require that a pre-moulded insulating boot be fitted – in which case fit the boot but if you haven't got them you could use some good quality heat-shrink insulation. My preferred method of making connections is to use uninsulated connectors and to crimp and solder the cable-ends to the connector. Then cover the joint with heat-shrink sleeving, but **not** insulating tape. The heat-shrink sleeve needs to have been slipped over one of the cables before you joined them.

There are different grades of heat-shrink sleeve – but for the extra cost involved, and bearing in mind the job the sleeve does, you are better to buy the best quality. Standard sleeving shrinks down to about ½ the original diameter and has no sealant. The best quality sleeves are more expensive but shrink to ⅓ diameter and have a sealing compound that prevents the ingress of water and any subsequent corrosion of the joint. Note that heat-shrink tubing needs storing carefully as it is very sensitive to temperature. Store in a cool place out of direct sunlight, ideally in the dark.

Dashboards and switches

No matter which MGB dashboard you use you will meet one small problem in respect of the two tiny rivets above each heater control knob. Original replacements are no longer available, so use two stainless steel rivets (part number AHA9999) from Moss. I held mine in position with a small blob of Epoxy two-pack, applied from the back of the dash, before I fitted the dash to the car.

The choke hole/position in the dash may not be required if you retain the electric choke with Holley carburation or use EFI. The Holley comes with an electric choke and EFI thinks for itself, which means you could use this dashboard hole for some other purpose in preference to a blanking grommet. A manual fan override switch and light is a necessity – and this

13-8-3 More differences exist between very early chrome-bumper dashboards, shown at the top of this picture, and their later rubber-bumper counterparts than you might think. The steering-column actually fastens to all chrome dashboards – a detail that changed in 1976 with the rubber-bumper models when a much bigger cowl was provided for. The main dials were also reduced in size for the rubber-bumper cars, and the dash (at least in Europe) was covered with a larger plastic moulding. You may also notice that the switch holes changed from round to square, but this alteration actually occurred about 1969 during the chrome-bumper production run.

might be a good, eye-catching spot for the warning light, even if you have to locate the switch elsewhere. However, Holley users may ultimately need to retro-fit a manual choke so maybe a blanking grommet is best. Whatever its intended use, I suggest the half flat hole be modified to the correct size/shape before painting the dashboard.

The air control adjuster and knob will fit in the way intended. However, the control that operates the heater valve may have to be fitted 180° from its intended position (this detail is covered in chapter 5).

Use of the rubber-bumper car column and column switches means that you'll have a more comprehensive switch set than that on chrome-bumper cars, and the wiper and washer controls are also much closer to hand.

For chrome-bumper converters who have retained the original steering column (hopefully, introducing a secondary shaft in order to avoid the V8's right side exhaust manifold), there is a bonus. You don't need to change dashboards since the switches and instruments are suited to the V8, although the speedo and tachometer will require modification to adjust them to your V8's gearing and cylinders. Picture 13-8-3 shows you the differences between the early and late dashboards.

Instruments

There is no need to retain the original MGB instruments and certainly those seeking to modernise the cockpit may feel a modern dashboard and fittings are essential. Times and styles have certainly changed and maybe one compromise is to buy reconditioned MGB instruments with magnolia faces in place of the original black faced dials. My choice is to try to hide the changes I have made by ensuring that the car's exterior and interior are as original as I can make them. I get a great deal of satisfaction from surprising some unsuspecting BMW owner!

If you have fitted my suggested 1974-76 dashboard, the switches suited to these dashboards are the square variety, while the speedo and tachometer are 3 1/8in (80mm) in diameter. This is about 10mm smaller than the main instruments of a chrome-bumper car (seen at 13-8-4). The original fuel gauge (picture 13-8-5) and temperature/oil gauge are, however, universal and can be used on all MGB dashboards.

You have a choice of two basic routes to the car's instrumentation – use original MGB dials appropriate to the year of your dashboard or select a set of instruments from the many aftermarket offerings.

If going down the traditional/original route you will need to convert your speedo and tachometer. This can be done in the UK for about £75 the pair by Speedy Cables in Wales or, if in the USA, ask Classic Instruments. The tacho needs changing from 4-cylinder to 8-cylinder operation and this can be carried out at

home if you are curious www.zaks.com/mgb/leonsmgb/Better_tach.htm gives you information on how one converter carried out the change to his original MGB tacho.

A change of tyre size and/or a different rear axle ratio will necessitate re-calibration of the speedo. At the same time you could address the question of a suitable speedo cable. I touched upon speedo cables in chapter 4 but ACI Engineering (in the USA) can supply

13-8-4 A pair of reproduction main dials for a chrome-bumper MGB V8 – note the 140mph speedo calibration!

13-8-5 This is typical of the smaller MGB gauges which, although the dial face changed, are a universal size right through the production run.

a range of bespoke speedo cables and, perhaps more importantly, a ratio adapter which corrects your existing speedometer after rear axle or wheel-size changes.

Note that the cable connection seen in photograph 13-8-6 on the smaller diameter speedo (80mm) differs from the larger earlier speedo, so a change of size of speedo necessitates a new speedo cable. When re-calibrating your speedo, you will need to advise the specialist of:

● the radius from wheel centre to ground.
● the number of speedo cable revolutions required for six full turns of your road wheels (both road wheels at once – best achieved by rolling the whole car forward by six revolutions of the rear road wheels).

Converters changing steering column switches should note the different MGB harness layout and plug/socket arrangements. The simplest solution is to fit steering column switches and front harness from the same MGB source. Consequently it is a good idea to obtain your steering column at the same time as these switches and the harness.

Most aftermarket suppliers (e.g. Summit in the US and Demon Tweeks in the UK) have ranges of instruments to

13-8-6 The central screw fixing for the speedo cable differs from one size of speedo to the other. Thus, if you change speedo sizes, you will need to change speedo cables, too.

choose. US converters could do worse than purchase a copy of the magazine *Street Rodder* to see all the gauge vendors available, including Autometer (pictured at 13-8-7 and 13-8-8), VDO (pictured at 13-8-9), Classic, Dolphin and Dakota. Most ranges include 2$\frac{1}{16}$in (i.e. the 52mm fuel, temperature, oil etc.) gauges that fit all the MGB dashboards but you will need to ensure that your short-listed suppliers can supply the larger dials (i.e. speedo and tachometer) appropriate to your dashboard. Remember that these dials come in two sizes and you need matching aftermarket replacements that at least fill the holes in your dashboard. Another selection criteria is that you should only use instruments with $\frac{1}{4}$in spade terminals for all connections, including illuminating lamps. This ensures your harness connections can be made swiftly but perhaps more importantly without a lot of connections to the 'pigtails' that most use.

The aftermarket route has attractions. You are spared the alterations mentioned above and can use electrical senders and wiring instead of the original mechanical interfaces. Just make sure that your range of aftermarket gauges can marry to senders that fit the engine (water temp and oil pressure) and gearbox (speedo) and that there ways to calibrate yours. If you use aftermarket gauges, do **not** use the original MGB voltage stabiliser attached to the rear of the main dials. Aftermarket gauges don't need a stabiliser, as they operate with a dual-coil arrangement, and sense the difference between the supply voltage and the sender voltage. The voltage difference

13-8-7 and 13-8-8 Examples of the very attractive-looking modern Autometer gauges.

will depend only on the sender, and not the supply voltage. If you have an MGB with aftermarket gauges but they swing wildly, then chances are the original voltage stabiliser is still in situ.

A late Ford T-5 gearbox/transmission uses electrical sensors rather than cables to drive the speedometer. A cable adapter is available from Hanlon Motorsports or, alternatively, I'm sure electronic internal workings can be fitted within the tradition MGB speedo-head but a late gearbox may signal the use of an electronic speedometer. VDO certainly makes a model that runs directly off the Ford sensor and is one of the few suppliers making 4 inch electric speedometers for late model dashboards. There are many more choices for the smaller 3$\frac{1}{8}$in (80mm) gauges used in later cars. The VDO fuel gauge ideally requires a Stewart-Warner sender (240-33 ohms) but works with the MGB fuel sender unit.

Another solution (possibly the ideal compromise) is to have your original instruments fitted with modern electronic

13-8-9 VDO gauges normally come with black bezels/rims, but here the bezels have been replaced with chrome rims from old MGB gauges. I think this gives the gauges a more authentic appearance.

internal workings. Both Speedy Cables in the UK and Classic Instruments in the US can completely replace the 'guts' of an old gauge with new movements. Thus your tacho will go from 4- to 8-cylinder operation and the speedo will utilize the electronic pulses from a late gearbox – yet both will appear original.

Chapter 14
Conclusion

Whatever engine and power category you are aiming for, several rules apply. First and foremost, please ensure that all parts of your conversion, including the structural issues discussed, are compatible with the power you are planning.

Secondly, remember you can get a great deal of fun, satisfaction and performance for a modest cost from a 3500cc/215in^3 powered MGB. If that doesn't sound sexy enough, consider the 4000cc/246in^3 which I believe is the ideal power plant for the MGB, although I could easily be persuaded to use a 4200cc/258in^3 Rover engine.

Thirdly, you do not need to carry out all your proposed changes simultaneously. If you carry out the upgrades in the correct order, there is no reason why you cannot spread the cost of the whole conversion over a number of months, even years, and get enjoyment from the car while your wallet rests. To succeed with this method, the order that you tackle the changes requires your careful consideration, and I trust this book has helped in this respect. Remember – safety related modifications need to take priority over speed and power.

Fourthly, do buy all related parts from one supplier simultaneously. Buy the parts you need to upgrade the car in kits, for want of a better phrase, and buy each kit from the same supplier. Parts for brake improvements are a good example – **do not buy the calipers from one source, the discs from another, the lines from somewhere else and other components from a fourth vendor.** Buy the lot in one go from one reliable retailer. This may cost you a small amount extra but this policy will be worthwhile before your conversion is complete. You do not have to use the same specialist every time, indeed there are good reasons for selecting someone who you think is the most advanced technically and/or competitively when it comes to brakes but another retailer when it comes to engine parts. Go to one source for all flywheel, clutch and clutch release components. Get pricing information from more than one supplier with each set of related parts you are contemplating purchasing.

Suspension packages are an exception; I consider it important that you fit the same manufacturer's equipment to the back as to the front even if these upgrades are 12 months apart (always carry out the front improvements first). There are other areas where this 'one supplier' situation becomes less straightforward too. The engine is a case in point; in an ideal world, one supplier for all your engine bits is the prudent approach. However, you could find the cost or technical solution not to your liking and find it preferable to split the engine into top and bottom. However, I would not split it down further than that and strongly recommend that you buy all your camshaft, followers, valves, valve-springs, cylinder-head, rocker assembly etc. from one supplier in one go. This method makes it most unlikely that you will suffer problems but, if you subsequently find the valve springs are binding, there is one source that will accept responsibility and take the requisite corrective action. If you have bought the parts separately and/or from different suppliers you will be without recourse.

Enjoy your MGB V8 both in your garage and on the road. Above all, remember the MG motto – 'Safety fast'!

Appendix
UK rebuilt vehicle requirements

FOREWARNED

In the UK it is a legal requirement to notify the DVLA of changes made to any vehicle's details. There are pages of UK regulations regarding what is acceptable and what requires consequential action; for example, undergoing a subsequent SVA (Single Vehicle Approval) test before the car can be registered and used on the road. The SVA test can be a major hurdle in itself and is undoubtedly best avoided if possible, therefore you need to start your conversion in the knowledge that since 1996 there are restrictions as to what you can and cannot do.

Then there is the question of the registration mark. Put another way, you are best building the car in such a way as to minimise the likelihood of a 'Q' plate being issued. The knock-on consequence of a 'Q' plate is difficulty in selling the converted car, thus a significant devaluation of it. Were you to start your conversion using an MGB GT with its attendant registration documentation, but during restoration or conversion change the engine size/type, gearbox, front suspension, rear axle and fit these

in a Roadster's bodyshell (all of which is technically possible) then you are likely to have difficulties when notifying the DVLA. Basically you will end up with a 'Q' plate, and will just draw attention to your case if you request a change in vehicle type (from GT to Roadster) and/or a change in chassis prefix (from GHD to GHN) – in which case you could, were the rules followed to the letter, lose both the VIN AND the registration number and be saddled with a 'Q' plate – always assuming the car passed its SVA test!

So, if you start with a GT (and its attendant GHD prefix) you will likely have to live with that chassis prefix even if the vehicle rolls out of your workshop as a Roadster. Some potential buyers will be comfortable with that situation if/when it comes time to sell the car, other may not be happy about paying Roadster prices for a GT chassis prefix.

As I said, there are pages of regulations but with the help of the MGOC, I have selected a few of the most pertinent clauses to consider:

(15) A rebuilt vehicle may keep its identity provided it retains enough of the original

components, including the unmodified or new chassis/monocoque bodyshell. It must also contain at least two major components from the original vehicle. The major components are currently considered to be the suspension (front and back), axles (both), transmission, steering assembly and engine. If a second-hand or modified chassis/monocoque body-shell is used, a 'Q' registration mark will be issued and the vehicle will be subject to type approval.

(27) A 'radically altered' vehicle is a vehicle that has been radically altered from its original specification. If there are sufficient components from a donor vehicle, including the unmodified chassis/ body shell/ frame, the vehicle will retain its original registration mark. If a second-hand or modified chassis/monocoque bodyshell/ frame is used, a 'Q' registration mark will be issued and the vehicle will be subject to type approval.

(54) The Reconstructed Classics category was introduced by the DVLA following the 1996 review of the rebuilt, radically altered and kit vehicle procedures (INF 26) and was intended to support the restoration of classic vehicles.

(55) There are instances when a vehicle will have been built as a faithful reproduction of a classic vehicle, using parts sourced from more than one vehicle. In this instance, if there is sufficient documentary evidence to confirm that the completed vehicle comprises all genuine period components, of the same specification all over 25 years old, the vehicle will be allocated a non-transferable age-related registration mark. The age-related registration mark will be based on the date of manufacture of the youngest vehicle component.

One SVA test detail

If you face an SVA test, you will of course need to get hold of a copy of the (very) comprehensive requirements. They include all manner of detail, much more than I have space to even summarise here. The requirement list goes on and on and on, but there is one point that is particularly relevant to V8 conversions. Documentary proof of the date of manufacture of the engine will be required. Alternatively there is a real possibility of an up-to-date emission requirement being applied. This would necessitate engine management and a 3-way catalyst exhaust system thus duplicating effort and extending the cost of the conversion. On top of this, the test fee is a minimum of £150 and can increase to £225 depending on individual circumstances. Best avoided if possible!

Some 'Q' plate detail

Whether the original registration/number or an alternative is issued is decided by an allocation of points by the DVLA assessors. This can be a sensitive detail and in many respects the less said by owners to the DVLA the better. Problems usually arise when owners ask for a new identity because the original GHD prefix refers to a GT and they want a Roadster's GHN prefix. Today the DVLA is in no way flexible and regards a vehicle's identity as fixed in stone. Possibly the one exception is

when the original number is compromised through a rebuild, when it issues a specific DVLA VIN. This may not be a disaster if the rest of the vehicle can be attributed to the same original car. However if there is any doubt, perhaps a non-original V8 engine has been fitted(!), the inspectors always err on that safe side, mark the car as being of 'indeterminate age' and issue a 'Q' plate.

Allocating the points

The points scheme just mentioned involves the inspectors allocating points for individual parts of the vehicle. Four points are awarded for an original chassis/body, one for the engine, one for transmission, one for front axle, one for rear axle, one for front suspension, one for rear, one for steering etc. The most sensitive part of any vehicle as far as the DVLA is concerned is the original body as this has the VIN attached, and everything else is bolted to it. In essence, you can replace everything attached to the original body over a period of time due to fair wear and tear, because the identity of the car remains the same. However, touch the body and big questions will arise, and the same happens when a host of changes are carried out simultaneously. Whilst older MGs have separate chassis/VIN plates and many do not have any numbers stamped into the vehicle's structure, modern cars do, and the rules were drafted more with these in mind than our MGs.

So the registration authorities regard the car's original body as sacrosanct – unless it is replaced by a brand new one. In their eyes a new bodyshell has not been allocated with a vehicle identity number as it is initially nothing more than a spare part, although a rather large one! New Heritage bodyshells are stamped with a new body number, just as all original BMC and BL-made MGB bodies had body numbers but these have no bearing whatsoever on the cars official identity. Only the VIN, or car or chassis number as it was before

October 1979 is the vehicle's identity, and this is allocated by the vehicle's original manufacturer usually at the start of the final assembly process ... and, as I have stated, is sacrosanct.

Identification numbers

You may be wondering why the MGB has a chassis (or in the case of later cars, a VIN) number, a body number and a commission number plate. Basically the body and commission numbers are internal accounting conveniences. In the case of MGB's we need to remember that the painted (and fully trimmed) bodies were made by Pressed Steel Fisher and the body number was the initial means of identifying/checking them. The body number actually was used during much of the MGB production life, but officially when PSF delivered the trimmed bodies onto the Abingdon assembly lines, the commission number was used for tracking the painted and trimmed bodies. Only when the mechanics had been fitted and final assembly had been completed at Abingdon was the vehicle identity issued in the form of a chassis/VIN number.

The normal procedure

When fitting an existing car with a replacement bodyshell, the normal procedure would be for your original chassis/VIN number to be allocated to a new Heritage body with you retaining the original registration number. In these circumstances Heritage is viewed as the original manufacturer – although technically it is not the original supplier but a component supplier. Sadly, production has now stopped, but much the same approach was applied to Stadco, the makers of new MG TF bodyshells for MG Rover! However, provided the rest of the vehicle is viewed as being mainly that of the original vehicle, your individual attitude and approach to the inspector can influence the process more than most owners think. At least some of the evidence the inspectors rely on is what you supply as the vehicle owner. The inspectors confidence (or otherwise) in you is carried over to the documentation and can, in the wrong atmosphere, increase the likelihood of a 'Q' plate.

The likelihood of a 'Q' plate also increases with the number of components changed. For the most part, the engine aside, the sub-components of the car do not have individual and recorded identity numbers. Some had no original manufacturers marks on them in the first place – which is why there are suggestions from the DVLA that it would be best for all modified cars to undergo SVA testing, which most would not pass!

Consequently the MGOC suggest owners doing V8 conversions declare the changes of vehicle details – description, colour, engine capacity and engine number – in the normal way by simply submitting the V5C (Registration Certificate, formerly the V5 Registration Document) with the changes noted in the relevant sections. Where appropriate a simple covering letter may be helpful.

Owners are probably best following the KISS (keep it simple stupid) approach. Try not to complicate issues by volunteering that you got the suspension from here and the brakes from there and the axles from two other cars, but maybe regard them as rebuilt components. The above clauses/extracts show how such honest but misguided comments will raise questions that the DVLA officers have no leeway with and can only then invoke the inspection procedures – which is where many conflicts stem from and classic heritages and values are destroyed.

GT to Roadster conversions

Where the conversion also includes a change from a GT to a Roadster the situation becomes (very) difficult. Only when a brand new body has been used and a clear receipt exists is the process likely to be relatively simple. In these circumstances the owner should not apply for any change in the chassis/VIN, but accept that this is always going to be a GHD prefix that tells the knowledgeable enthusiast about the vehicle's heritage.

However, given this fact, perhaps it would be an idea to make a virtue out of a necessity by asking the DVLA to modify the vehicles description to MGBGT Cabriolet Conversion. This is adding to the description rather than a substantive change, may be less of a problem to the DVLA's rule-driven mindset, yet is also 100 per cent honest given that the car is clearly a Roadster which has been created from an original MGBGT. Most importantly it complies with the requirement to notify changes to the vehicle.

This may be a very brief summary of some relevant issues, but it demonstrates the importance of bearing the re-registration aspects of any conversion in mind from the start of the project. Arrangements may change with time, but I doubt they will relax! Re-registration could be, but need not be, a minefield unless you are thinking of a simultaneous GT to Roadster conversion. The technical challenge of building a Roadster from a GT is nothing compared to the subsequent legal complexity and frankly such changes are best avoided

Index of suppliers

ACI Engineering Inc, 6728 Lover's Lane, Portage, MI 49002, USA. Tel: 269 327 1991 (Speedo cable and converter manufacturer)

Advance Auto-Wire, 210 Windship Lane, Woodstock, GA 30189, USA.
Tel: 770 926 2213 (ordering) or 865 982 9373 (tech support)

www.advanceautowire.com
(MGB wiring improvements)

Agriemach Ltd, Wayfarers, Old Domewood, Copthorne, Crawley, West Sussex RH10 3HD, UK. Tel: 01342 713743
www.agriemach.co.uk/products
(Exhaust tape wrapping & coolant additives)

American Autowire, 150 Heller Place, #17W, Bellmawr, NJ 08031 2555, USA.
Tel: 800 482 9473
www.factoryfit.com
(Electrical harnesses and components)

Auto Sparks, 80-83 Derby Rd, Sandiacre, Nottingham NG10 5HU, UK.

Tel: 0115 9497211
(Electrical cables, harnesses & components)

Autocar Electrical Equipment Co Ltd. 49-51
Tiverton St, London SE1 6NZ, UK.
Tel: 0207 403 4334
www.lumenition.com
(Lumenition ignition equipment)

Automotive Racing Ltd, Wheler Road,
Seven Stars Industrial Estate, Coventry
CV34LB, UK. Tel: 024 7663 9595
www.apracing.com
(Frictional racing products)

Automotive Racing Products, 1863
Eastman Avenue, Ventura, CA 93003, USA.
www.arp-bolts.com
(High-tensile engine studs)

Autoworks International, 462 Vernon Way,
El Cajon, California 92020, USA. Tel: 619
401 6900
www.autoworks.cc
(External slave cylinders for T5 gearboxes)

Avo UK, Caswell Rd, Brackmills Ind Est,
Northampton NN4 7PL, UK. Tel: 01604
708101
www.avouk.com
(Performance suspension systems)

Avon Tyres Racing, Bath Road, Melksham,
Wiltshire SN12 8AA, UK. Tel: 01225 703101
www.avonracing.com
(Cooper Avon tyres)

British Motor Heritage Limited, Range
Road, Cotswold Business Park, Witney
OX29 0YB, UK. Tel: 01993 707200
www.bmh-ltd.co.uk/mgb.htm (New MGB
Heritage bodyshells and components)

British Wiring Inc., 20449 Ithica Road,
Olympia Fields, Il 60461, USA. Tel/fax: 708
481 9050
(Electrical wire, connectors, terminals for
UK cars)

Brown & Gammons Limited, 18 High Street,
Baldock, Herts SG7 6AS, England. tel
01462 490049
email: sales@ukmgparts.com (RV8 spares)

British V8 Newsletter, 2403 Homestead
Drive, Silver Springs, MD 20902, USA.
www.britishv8.org
Email: BritV8News@speakeasy.net
(Technical and practical advice on
squeezing big engines in British sports cars)

Peter Burgess Automotive Performance
Engineering, Unit 1, Amber Buildings,
Meadow Lane, Alfreton, Derbyshire DE5
7EZ, UK. Tel: 01773 520021
Email: peter@burgesstuning.free-online.
co.uk
(Cylinder head gas-flowing and tuning)

Camberley Auto Factors Ltd, Unit
1, Hawley Ind. Estate Hawley Lane,
Farnborough, Hants GU14 8EH, UK. Tel:
01252 517272
www.koni.com
(UK distributor for Koni suspension
systems)

Cambridge Motorsport Ltd, Caxton Road,
Great Gransden, Nr Sandy, Beds SG19
3AH, UK. Tel: 01767 677969
www.cambridgemotorsport.com
(Performance products and tuning)

Canton Racing Products, 232 Branford Rd,
N. Branford, CT 06471, USA. Tel: 203 481
9460
www.cantonracingproducts.com
(Sumps and numerous racing orientated
engine products)

Classic Conversions, Unit 7 Treeton
Enterprise Centre, Front St, Treeton,
Sheffield S60 5QP, UK. Tel: 0114 288 9556
www.classicconversions.co.uk (Importer of
Dellow bellhousings and Toyota gearboxes)

Classic Instruments PO Box 411 1299

M-75, South Boyne City, MI 49712, USA.
Tel: 231 582 0461
Fax: 231 582 3114
Email: info@classicinstruments.com
(Instrument supplier and conversion
specialist)

Clive Wheatley V8 Conversions, High
Grosvenor, Worfield, Bridgnorth, Shropshire
WV15 5PN, UK. Tel: 01746 710810
Fax: 01746 710999
(MGB V8 spares and conversion parts)

CNC Inc. 1221 West Morena Blvd, San
Diego, CA 92110, USA. Tel: 619 257 1663
Fax: 619 275 0729
www.cnebrakes.com
(Hydraulic slave cylinders)

Components Automotive 73 Ltd., 4/6
Wulfrun Industrial Estate, Stafford Road,
Wolverhampton WV10 6HG, UK.
Tel: 01902 311499
www.comp.co.uk
(Compomotive alloy wheels)

Concours West (CWI), 159 Anchor Rd,
Castle Rock, WA 98611 USA.
Tel: 360274 3373
www.geocities.com/~concourswest.htm

Coyote Conversions, LLC, 11475 Ridge
Point Drive, Middleville, MI 49333 USA.
Tel: 269 795 1148
Email: Mgbv8@iserv.net
(Ford 302 headers)

Crane Cams, Inc., 530 Fentress Blvd.,
Daytona Beach, FL 32114, USA. Tel: 386
252 1151
www.cranecams.com
(Performance equipment, including
camshafts, distributors and ignition
systems)

Crower Engineering and Sales,
3333 T-Main, St Chula Vista, CA 91911
5899, USA. Tel: 619 422 1191

www.crower.com
(Camshaft specialist)

Currie Enterprises, 1480, N Tustin Ave, Anaheim, CA 92807, USA.
Tel: 714 528 6957
Email : info@currieenterprises.com
(Rear axle specialist)

Dave Bean Engineering, 636 E. Saint Charles St. SR#3, San Andreas, CA 95249, USA. Tel: 209 754 5802 (special exhaust clamps)

D+D Fabrications, 8005 Tiffany Drive, Almont, MI 48003 USA. Tel: 810 798 2491
www.aluminumv8.com
(Premier US Buick/Rover engine and component specialist)

Dellow Automotive Pty Ltd, 37 Daisy St, Revesby, NSW 2212, Australia. Tel: 02 9774 4419
www.Dellowauto.com.au
(Gearbox adaptation Kits)

Demon Tweeks, 75 Ash Rd South, Wrexham Ind Estate, Wrexham LL13 9UG, UK. Tel: 01978 664466
www.demon-tweeks.co.uk (Performance equipment factors)

EBC, EBC Buildings, Countess Road, Northampton NN5 7EA, UK. Tel: 01604 583344
www.ebcbrakesuk.com/automotive (Brake components including 'Greenstuff' pads)

EBC, 806 Buchanan Blvd, Unit 115 256, Boulder City, Las Vegas NV89005, USA.
(Brake Components including "Greenstuff" pads)

Edelbrock Corporation Headquarters, 2700 California Street, Torrance, CA 90503, USA.
Tel: 310 781 2222
www.edelbrock.com/automotive/index
(Performance carburettors, manifolds,

cylinder-heads and EFI)

Fast Cars, Inc, 845 East Superior, Wayland, MI 49348, USA. Tel/fax: 269 792 6632
fastcars@chartermi.net
(MGB Front suspension and Brake upgrades)

Flex-a-Lite, PO box 580, Milton, WA 98354, USA. Tel: 253 922 2700
www.flex-a-lite.com
(Radiator cooling fans)

FlowKooler, 289 Prado Road, San Luis Obispo, CA 93401 USA. Tel: 805 544 8841
Fax: 805 544 5615
www.flowkooler.com
(High flow water pumps and cooling equipment)

Ford Racing Performance Parts, 44050 N. Groesbeck Highway, Clinton Township, MI 48036 1108, USA. Tel: 586 468 1356
www.fordracing.com/performanceparts
(Crate engines and Ford performance equipment)

Frontline Costello, 239, London Rd East, Batheaston, Bath, BA1 7RL
Tel 01225 852777
www.mgcars.org.uk/frontline

GKN Driveline, Kingsbury Road, Minworth, Sutton Coldfield B76 9DL, UK.
Tel: 0121 313 1616, Fax: 0121 313 2074
http://www.gknservice.com/gkn-ids/jsp/location/uk.jsp (Propshaft and u/j specialists)

Griffin Thermal Products, 100 Hurricane Creek Road, Piedmont, SC 29673, USA.
Tel: 864 845 5000
www.griffinrad.com Email sales@griffinrad.com (aluminium coolant radiators)

Hanlon Motorsports, 3621 St. Peters Road, St. Peters, PA 19470, USA. Tel: 610 469 2695

(Speedometer cable adapters)

Heads by Ed Inc, P.O. Box 7494-WX, Minneapolis, MN 55407 Tel: 612 729 2802
www.headersbyed.com
(Header/manifold components)

Hi Spec Motorsport, Unit 5 Parker Ind Centre, Watling St, Dartford Kent DA2 6EP, UK. Tel: 01322 286850
www.hispecmotorsport.co.uk

Holley Performance Products, 1801 Russellville Rd, PO box 10360, Bowling Green, KY 42102 7360, USA.
www.holley.com
(Performance carburettors, fuel-injection, fuel-pumps and ignition equipment)

Hoyle Engineering Ltd., 52 Reigate Road, Epsom, Surrey KT17 1PX, UK. Tel/fax: 0208 393 2555
www.hoyle-engineering.co.uk
(Front and rear suspension upgrades)

Jacobs Electronics Technical Service, Mr. Gasket Performance Group, 550 Mallory Way, Carson City, NV 89701, USA.
www.jacobselectronics.com

J-E Engineering, Sisken Drive, Coventry, CV3 4FJ, UK. Tel: 0247 630 5018
www.jeengineering.co.uk
(Specialists in Rover V8 component machining and uprated engines)

John Hills MG Centre, 18 Arden Business Centre, Arden Road, Alcester, Warks B49 6HW, UK. Tel: 01789 400449, Fax: 01789 400708.
(MGB spares, refurbished MGB bodyshells and RV8 fibreglass panels)
John Woolfe Racing, Woolfe House, Hammond Road, Bedford MK41 0RQ, UK.
Tel: 01234 220700
www.woolfe.com

K&N Engineering, Inc., PO box 1329, 1455

Citrus St, Riverside, California 92502, USA.
Tel: 951 826 4000
Email: tech@knfilters.com
(Performance air filters)

K&N Filters (Europe) Ltd. John Street,
Warrington, Cheshire WA2 7UB, UK. Tel:
01925 636950
Email: uk.sales@knfilters.com (Performance
air filters)

Kenne-Bell Performance Products, 10743
Bell Court, Rancho, Cucamonga, CA91730,
USA. Tel: 909 941 0985
(Engine performance products)

Kenlowe Ltd, Burchetts Green,
Maidenhead, Berkshire SL6 6QU, UK.
Tel: 01628 823303
www.kenlowe.com
(Electric radiator fans)

Lokar, 10924 Murdock Dr, Knoxville,
TN 37932, USA. Tel: 865 966 2269
www.lokar.com
(Ancillary equipment including speedo
cables and Ford flexible dipsticks)

March Performance, 6020 Hix Rd,
Westland, MI 48185, USA.
Tel: 734 729 9070
www.marchperf.com
(Fan and drive belt pulleys)

Magnecor, 24581 Crestview Court,
Farmington Hills, MI 48335, USA.
Tel: 248 471 9505
Email: mag @ magnecor.com

MAW Solutions Ltd, PO box 177, Stamford,
Lincs PE9 2WF, UK. Tel: 01780 765140
www.mawsolutions.com
(Davies-Craig electric water pumps and
thermostatic cooling fans)

Mcleod Industries, 1125 North Amando,
Anaheim, CA 92806, USA.
Tel: 714 630 2764

(Annular clutch release cylinders and
bearings)

MG Car Club Ltd, PO box 251, Abingdon,
Oxon OX14 1FF Tel: 01235 555552
www.mgcars.org.uk/carclub/index

MG Owners Club, Octagon House, Station
Rd, Swavesey, Cambs CB4 5QZ, UK.
Tel: 01954 231125
www.mgownersclub.co.uk

MGOC Spares Ltd, Swavesey, Cambs,
CB4 5QZ, UK. Tel: 01954 230928
www.mgocspares.co.uk
(One of largest stockists of MG spares,
Rover-V8 conversion parts & V8 engines.)

Moss-Europe, Hampton Farm Ind Estate,
Hanworth, Middx TW13 6DB, UK. Tel: 020
8867 2020
www.moss-europe.co.uk
(Europe's largest stockist of MGB spares)

Moss Motors, PO box 847, 440 Rutherford
Street, Goleta, CA 93116, USA. Tel: 800
667 7872
www.mossmotors.com
(US stockist of MGB spares)

Motor Sports Association (UK), Motor Sport
House, Riverside Park, Colnbrook SL3
0HG, UK. Tel: 01753 765000
www.msauk.org
(Competition Year Book provides stress
dissipating information)

MSD Ignition, 1490 Henry Brennan Dr,
El Paso, TX 79936, USA. Tel: 915 857 5200
www.msdignition.com
(Performance ignition systems)

North American MGB Register,
P.O. Box 3203, Kent, OH 44240, USA.
Tel: 800-NAMGBR-1
www.namgbr.org

Newtronic Systems, Unit 3 BTMC,

Challenge Way, Blackburn, Lancs BB1
5QB, UK.
www.newtronic.co.uk
(Electronic ignition systems)

P-AYR Products, 719 Delaware Street,
Levenworth, Kansas 66048, USA.
Tel: 800 322-3285
(Makers of temporary lightweight plastic
Ford engine blocks)

Pertronix Performance Products,
Tel: 800 827 3758
www.pertronix.com
(Performance ignition systems)

Powermaster, 7501 strawberry Plains Pike,
Knoxville, TN 37924, USA.
Tel: 800 862 7223
www.powermastermotorsports.com (High
output alternators)

Rally Design, Units 9-10, Upper Brent
Estate, Faversham, Kent ME13 7DZ, UK.
Tel: 01795 531871
www.raldes.co.uk
(Damper and Wilwood brake stockist)

Robsport International, North House,
Dunsbridge Turnpike, Shepreth,
Nr Royston, Herts SG8 6RA, UK.
Tel: 01763 848673
www.robsport.co.uk
(New and used Triumph TR7 and 8 spares)

The Roadster Factory, PO box 332, Killen
Road, Armagh, PA 15920, USA.
Tel: 800678 8764
www.the-roadster-factory.com

RPI Engineering, Wayside Garage, Holt Rd,
Horsford, Norwich NR10 3EE, UK.
Tel: 01603 891209
www.v8engines.com
(Specialists for standard and uprated V8
engines, transmissions and associated
equipment)

S+S Preparations, Glen Mill Classic Car Centre, Newchurch Rd, Stacksteads, Bacup, Lancs, OL13 0NH UK.
www.ss-preparations.co.uk
(TR 8 spares stockists and tuners)

Speedy Cables, c/o Caerbont Auto Instruments, Caerbont Enterprise Park, Abercrave, Swansea SA9 1SH, UK.
Tel: 01639 732213
www.speedycables.co.uk
(Instrument suppliers and conversion specialists)

Summit Racing Equipment, PO box 909, Akron, OH 44309, USA. Tel: 800 230 3030
www.summitracing.com
(Aftermarket factors)

Superchips Ltd, Buckingham Industrial Park, Buckingham, MK18 1XJ, UK.
Tel 01280 816781
Email: sales@superchips.co.uk

Superflex Ltd, Hornsmead, Knowle Lane, Wookey, Wells, Somerset BA5 1LD, UK.
Tel: 01749 671404
www.superflex.co.uk
(Polyurethane suspension bushes)

Superpro Europe Ltd, home Farm, Middlezoy, Somerset TA7 0PD, UK.
Tel: 01823 698437
Email: neil@superpro.eu.com
(Polyurethane suspension bushes)

Tilton Engineering, 25 Easy Street, Box 1787, Buelton, CA 93427, USA.

Tel: 805 688-2353
www.pegasusautoracing.com (Clutch annular slave and master-cylinders)
Towery Foreign Cars, PO box 354, Cheswold, DE 19936, USA.
Tel: 302 734 1243
Email: mgv8glen@bellatlantic.net (MGB V8 conversions and parts)

Transdapt Performance Accessories, 16410 Manning Way, Cerritos, CA90703, USA. Tel: 310 921 0404
(Oil filter housings, mountings and lines)

Transmission Technologies Corp, 23382 Commerce Drive, Farmington Hills, ML 48335, USA.
Tel: 248 471 3200
www.tremec.com
(Tremac transmission/gearboxes)

TS Imported Automotive, 404 Bessinger Rd, Pandora, OH 45877, USA.
Tel: 419 384 3022
Email: tedtsimx@ql.net
(New, used and rebuilt Rover parts)

US Radiator Corporation, 4423 District Blvd., Vernon, California 90058, USA.
Tel: 323 826 0965, Fax: 323 826 0970

V8 Conversion Company, 123 High St, Farnborough, Kent BR6 7AZ, UK.
Tel: 01689 858716
(V8 conversion parts)

Victoria British Ltd., Box 14991, Lenexa, KS 66285 4991, USA.

Tel: 800255 0088
www.longmotor.com
(US spares stockists)

Ward Engineering, 23 Spencer Walk, Tilbury, Essex, RM18 8XH, UK.
Tel: 01375 846986
www.ward-engineering.co.uk
(Reconditioning and narrowing of Jaguar axles)

Weber Performance Products, 2985, East Blue Star, Anaheim, CA92806 USA.
Tel: 714 630 2171
www.weberperformance.com (Annular clutch release cylinders and other performance products)

Weiand Performance Products, 1801 Russellville Road, PO box 10360, Bowling Green, KY 42102 7360, USA.
www.holley.com/weiand
(Weiand electric and mechanical water pumps)

Wildcat Engineering, Old Creamery, Rhydymain Dolgellan, Gwynedd LL40 2AV, UK.
Tel: 01341 450200 www.roverv8engine.co.uk
(Rover engine performance equipment, including high-flow cylinder heads)

XJS Breakers, Unit 7, The Potteries, Southend Lane, Waltham Abbey, Essex, UK.
Tel: 01992 768007 and 0780 1140454
(Used parts for XJS, XJ6 and XJ40.)

J.E. Developments
(John Eales)
The Rover V8 engine builder

Cubic Capacity (cc) of available engine sizes

	Bore/mm				
	88.9	**90.0**	**94.0**	**94.5**	**96.0**
63.0			3497.7		
71.1	3531.6	3619.6	3948.5	3990.6	4118.3
77.0			4274.9	4320.5	
80.0			4441.5	4488.8	
79.4					4597.7
82.0			4552.5	4601.1	4748.3
86.3			4794.6	4845.7	5000.8
91.5			5079.9	5134.1	5298.4

(left axis label: **Stroke/mm**)

- Large stock of Rover V8 parts
- Dry sump systems
- Downdraught and side inlet manifolds
- Sump baffles
- Small diameter flywheel and starter motor
- Forged steel adjustable rocker assemblies
- Hewland adaptor plate/bell housing
- Bell housing for T5, Getrag, etc
- Balancing
- Forged steel conrods
- Forged pistons for most capacities at 89.4mm, 90mm, 94mm, 94.5mm, and 96mm
- New cross bolted 3.5 and 3.9 blocks available
- Cross drilled crankshafts at 63mm, 71.12mm, 77mm, 80mm, 82mm, 86.36mm, 90mm and 91.5mm

Claybrooke Mill
Frolesworth Lane
Claybrooke Magna
Nr. Lutterworth
Leicestershire
LE17 5DB

Tel: 01455 202909
email: john@ealesxx.fsnet.co.uk
web: www.rover-v8.com

Index

Specializing in the MG / 302 Headers

STEVEN CARRICK

(616) 889-9707
MGBV8@iserv.net

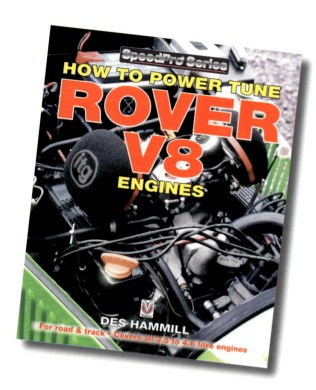
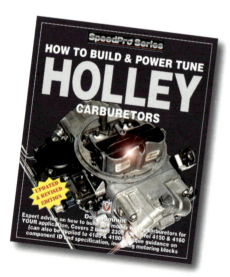
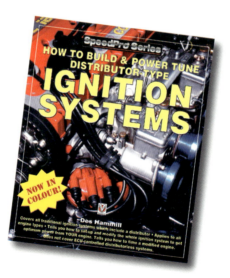
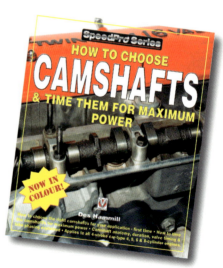